Postcolonial Opera

Postcolonial Opera

*William Kentridge and
the Unbounded Work of Art*

Juliana M. Pistorius

OXFORD
UNIVERSITY PRESS

Oxford University Press is a department of the University of Oxford.
It furthers the University's objective of excellence in research, scholarship,
and education by publishing worldwide. Oxford is a registered trade mark of
Oxford University Press in the UK and certain other countries.

Published in the United States of America by Oxford University Press
198 Madison Avenue, New York, NY 10016, United States of America.

© Oxford University Press 2025

All rights reserved. No part of this publication may be reproduced, stored in a retrieval system, transmitted, used for text and data mining, or used for training artificial intelligence, in any form or by any means, without the prior permission in writing of Oxford University Press, or as expressly permitted by law, by license or under terms agreed with the appropriate reprographics rights organization. Inquiries concerning reproduction outside the scope of the above should be sent to the Rights Department, Oxford University Press, at the address above.

You must not circulate this work in any other form
and you must impose this same condition on any acquirer.

Library of Congress Cataloging-in-Publication Data
Names: Pistorius, Juliana Maryna, 1988– author.
Title: Postcolonial opera : William Kentridge and the unbounded work of art / Juliana M. Pistorius.
Description: [1.] | New York : Oxford University Press, 2025. |
Includes bibliographical references and index. |
Identifiers: LCCN 2025004496 (print) | LCCN 2025004497 (ebook) |
ISBN 9780197749210 (paperback) | ISBN 9780197749203 (hardback) |
ISBN 9780197749241 | ISBN 9780197749234 (epub)
Subjects: LCSH: Opera—Political aspects—South Africa—History—20th century. |
Opera—Political aspects—South Africa—History—21st century. |
Opera—Social aspects—South Africa—History—20th century. |
Opera—Social aspects—South Africa—Hisory—21st century. |
Kentridge, William, 1955– Criticism and interpretation. |
Postcolonialism and music—South Africa. | Puppet theater—South Africa. |
Opera—Production and direction—South Africa—History—20th century. |
Opera—Production and direction—South Africa—History—21st century. |
Handspring Puppet Company.
Classification: LCC ML3917.S62 P57 2025 (print) | LCC ML3917.S62 (ebook) |
DDC 782.109687—dc23/eng/20250206
LC record available at https://lccn.loc.gov/2025004496
LC ebook record available at https://lccn.loc.gov/2025004497

DOI: 10.1093/oso/9780197749203.001.0001

Paperback printed by Marquis Book Printing, Canada
Hardback printed by Bridgeport National Bindery, Inc., United States of America

The manufacturer's authorized representative in the EU for product safety is
Oxford University Press España S.A., Parque Empresarial San Fernando de Henares,
Avenida de Castilla, 2 – 28830 Madrid (www.oup.es/en).

For Daniëlle,
fellow traveler

Contents

List of Figures	ix
Acknowledgments	xi
About the Companion Website	xiii
Introduction	1
1. **Return**	25
2. **Confession**	53
3. **Mourning**	92
4. **Time**	130
5. **Place**	159
6. **Totality**	202
Conclusion: Future	240
Bibliography	255
Index	269

Figures

1.1 The stage setting for Kentridge's production of *Il Ritorno d'Ulisse in Patria*	34
1.2 Puppet Penelope and the two puppet Ulisses, each accompanied by their puppeteer-singer teams	35
2.1 A schematic representation of the stage setting for *Confessions of Zeno*	64
3.1 Black Box contraption	97
3.2 A selection of drawings based on archival documentation, displayed alongside the *Black Box* installation	102
3.3 The series of images projected onto the backdrop during "Fairground"	114
3.4 Shadow figures beating each other to death in *Black Box/Chambre Noire*	118
3.5 "Totenliste," from *Black Box/Chambre Noire*	122
4.1 A partial view of *Refuse the Hour*'s stage	139
5.1 Frieze figures showing the contrast between dark organic matter and the washed embankment wall	164
5.2 Figures 36, 37, and 39 from *Triumphs and Laments*	166
5.3 "Quello che non ricordo," number 34 of the *Triumphs and Laments* frieze	186
6.1 Mncedisi Shabangu in *The Head & the Load*	208
6.2 Hamilton Dlamini in *The Head & the Load*	209
6.3 Nhlanhla Mahlangu, Hamilton Dlamini, and Luc De Wit in *The Head & the Load*	210
6.4 Nhlanhla Mahlangu in *The Head & the Load*	211
6.5 Joanna Dudley in *The Head & the Load*	211
6.6 "Ursonate," with Dlamini, De Wit, and Mahlangu in the foreground and the map of Africa projected onto the background	227

Acknowledgments

The research for *Postcolonial Opera: William Kentridge and the Unbounded Work of Art* was funded by a Leverhulme Early Career Research Fellowship (ECF-2018-706). I am grateful to the Leverhulme Trust for its generous financial and material support. The University of Huddersfield provided me with a friendly and well-resourced institutional environment; my thanks to every colleague who welcomed me and my research into the community.

This project would not have been possible without the support of Kentridge Studio. I am grateful to William Kentridge, who answered my questions with characteristic eloquence and allowed me a privileged glimpse into his creative processes and workshop dynamics. Anne McIlleron and Natalie Dembo are the formidable forces that keep the studio cogs turning. They fielded my requests for information, material, and advice with generosity, patience, and enthusiasm. None of this book could have happened without them. Philip Miller was equally generous in interviews and material assistance: our conversations during the early days of the COVID-19 pandemic helped me keep faith in the project and provided crucial insights into the workings of the pieces I discuss here.

I enjoyed opportunities to discuss the preliminary findings of my research with colleagues at several conferences and colloquia. My thanks to the organizers of the "Opera in Post-Apartheid South Africa," "Contested Frequencies," "Opera and Popular Culture," and "Vicarious Vocalities" conferences, as well as the convenors of colloquium series at the University of Bristol, University of Huddersfield, University of Aberdeen, Rhodes University, King's College London, and Royal Birmingham Conservatoire. The exchange of ideas at these events proved of immeasurable value to the development of my arguments.

Postcolonial Opera benefited from conversations with a number of valued colleagues and friends. I am grateful to Genevieve Arkle, Timothy Coombes, Jane Forner, Tereza Havelková, Sarah Hibberd, Jonathan Hicks, Megan Steigerwald Ille, Yvonne Liao, Emily MacGregor, Takalani Mulaudzi, Neo Muyanga, Colleen Renihan, Inja Stanovic, and Tiffany Stern for sharing their wisdom with me. Stephanus Muller first encouraged me to develop my thoughts around Kentridge into a larger project; I remain indebted to his generosity of thought and engagement. The working group of the Black

xii Acknowledgments

Opera Research Network has been a support structure and sounding board throughout this project. I am thankful to Naomi André, Joy Calico, Michael Mohammed, Wayne Muller, Hilde Roos, Allison Smith, Donato Somma, and Lena Van der Hoven for their friendship, collegiality, and encouragement. Robert Adlington and Igor Contreras-Zubillaga were reading group buddies, listeners, cheerleaders, mentors, and friends during my time at Huddersfield and beyond. They, along with Daniel Grimley, William Fourie, and Carina Venter, read and commented on parts of the manuscript. I am hugely indebted to their wise and thoughtful counsel. Any remaining errors, omissions, and misarticulations are my own.

As always, my family provided me with a firm and cherished foundation from beginning to end. I first discovered Kentridge's works in the company of my sister, Daniëlle. It remains one small part of a treasured and lasting bond. My parents, Gustav and Ronél, offered love and support across continents and, for ten months of lockdown, in extremely close proximity. Theo and Lisa helped me believe that anything is possible. Daniëlle, Wynand, and in the closing weeks of writing, little Mia, reminded me to retain my sense of wonder. Finally, heartfelt thanks to Yves T'Sjoen for encouragement, enthusiasm, and boundless patience. Altijd en overal.

About the Companion Website

www.oup.com/us/PostcolonialOpera

Oxford has created a website to accompany *Postcolonial Opera: William Kentridge and the Unbounded Work of Art*. Material that cannot be made available in a book, namely, video clips that illustrate key arguments from individual chapters, is provided here. The reader is encouraged to consult this resource in conjunction with the chapters. Examples available online are indicated in the text with Oxford's symbol ▶

Introduction

The relationship between opera and coloniality is complex. As Edward Said famously declared, opera "belongs equally to the history of culture and the historical experience of overseas domination."[1] The art form, Said suggests, functions as a tool for colonial expansion. But in recent decades, the genre has also increasingly been used to narrate histories of colonial trauma, struggle, and recovery.[2] In former colonies and imperial metropoles alike, opera makers have been using the form to examine critically the past practices and enduring legacies of colonialism. The irony is glaring: an art form implicated in colonial violence and oppression is being recuperated to participate in postcolonial remediation.

In *Postcolonial Opera: William Kentridge and the Unbounded Work of Art*, I ask what it means for a colonial form to represent the experiences of those it used to exclude and undermine. I examine whose interests the art form serves and whose stories it prioritizes. Stopping short of developing a model for what opera should look and sound like in the postcolony, I nonetheless ask how the genre needs to adapt in order to meet the challenges of ethical representation and reparation. Along the way, my investigation distills matters of historical narration, cultural and racial representation, class politics, ownership, and hybridity. In short, the art form emerges as a proving ground for the issues played out in the postcolony at large.

My examination of the social and political role of opera in the postcolony takes as a starting point the multimedia operatic experiments of South Africa's most celebrated contemporary visual artist, William Kentridge (born Johannesburg, 1955). Using Kentridge's creations as case studies, I probe contemporary opera's potential to process the troubled histories that haunt the postcolonial present.

Kentridge articulates an explicit critique of colonialism and apartheid throughout his oeuvre. Infusing his art with piercing references to the colonial violence and exploitation that shaped his home country, he confronts

---

[1] Edward Said, 1994 [1993], *Culture and Imperialism*, New York: Knopf, 137.

[2] In the 2022–2023 season alone, for instance, three different stagings of Scott Joplin's *Treemonisha* (1911), by Opera Theatre of St. Louis, Volcano Opera, and Isango Ensemble, have examined histories of colonialism and slavery from American, Canadian, and South African perspectives, respectively.

Postcolonial Opera. Juliana M. Pistorius, Oxford University Press. © Oxford University Press 2025.
DOI: 10.1093/oso/9780197749203.003.0001

2 Postcolonial Opera

the West with its most egregious historical excesses. The artist's work hence lends itself to postcolonial critical reading. Simultaneously, Kentridge's international standing inscribes his performance pieces into systems of global circulation and patronage. The artist has held large-scale exhibitions at venues such as New York's Metropolitan Museum of Art (2004) and Museum of Modern Art (2010), the National Museum of Modern and Contemporary Art, Seoul (2016), and the Royal Academy in London (2022). He has won major international awards including the Carnegie Prize (1999), the Kyoto Prize (2010), and the Dan David Prize (2012), and his works are often sponsored or commissioned by large international organizations, displayed in important galleries, or acquired by well-funded international museums. Kentridge's creations travel to international metropoles from New York to Beijing, addressing audiences both directly touched by and largely unfamiliar with the actualities of Western coloniality and postcolonial critique. In other words, the artist's works may be from and about the postcolony, but they are not always *for* the postcolony. This raises not only the thorny issue of representation but also prompts interesting questions around operatic circulation, the institutions and audiences to which the art form speaks, and the routes it follows as it travels to and from different cultural and political spheres. Kentridge and his operas embody a certain geographic multiplicity, straddling the local and the global in an ambitious and often bewildering play of historical signification.

Subject

Kentridge's art is shaped by a particular embeddedness in both Europe and South Africa. The same is true of my examination of his work. Like Kentridge, I am a white South African who has had the opportunity to pursue some education abroad. Our experiences of the postcolonial present differ in many ways from those of the Black and Indigenous citizens with whom we share a country. In the context of this book, both Kentridge and I may be described as "postcolonizing subjects." I use the term "postcolonizing subject" to refer to those individuals who find themselves in the postcolony as descendants of colonizers and other settlers, rather than the colonized. In the context of South Africa, postcolonizing citizens are by and large white and middle class. My use of the term "postcolonizing" seeks to acknowledge that such persons are themselves also postcolonial (in the sense of being situated in a society coming to terms with the legacy of colonialism), but that their subject position differs from that of the formerly colonized person, to whom I refer as the postcolonial subject but who might perhaps more accurately be described as postcolonized.

The distinction between the postcolonized and the postcolonizing subject is essentially the difference between subjection and subjectivity. In Leela Gandhi's description, subjectivity describes "the condition through which people are recognised as free and equal—or 'full'—individuals within civil society." The colonial project, Gandhi observes, awarded colonizers "the privileges of citizenship and subjectivity." Colonized persons, on the contrary, were no more than objects, "suspended in a state of subjection."[3] Whereas the postcolonizing subject has always enjoyed subjectivity, the postcolonized person has faced a struggle to transform from subjection to recognition as a political subject. In the postcolonial present, the unequal distribution of colonial subjectivity endures not only as a memory but also as a lasting inheritance of inequality.

In many ways, the position of the postcolonizing subject is equivalent to that of whiteness. I am wary, however, of treating the two positions interchangeably. This would reinforce a binary described by Alfred J. López as "a race-based meta-opposition" that views "white as colonizing [and] colonial/nonwhite as colonized, postcolonial."[4] Such a configuration neglects the fact that white persons in former colonies also occupy a postcolonial position, even if this position is different from that of racialized subjects. As López writes, "There remains in the early twenty-first century a postcolonial whiteness struggling to come into being, or rather a number of post-empire, post-mastery whitenesses attempting to examine themselves in relation to histories of oppression and hegemony of their other."[5] In other words, just like their racially marked counterparts, white postcolonial subjects have to come to terms with a political and historical present shaped by the legacy of colonialism.

The postcolonizing subject need not necessarily be white. Not all those who worked in the service of the colonial project were white, nor did colonial projects oppress only those who were not white. In other words, whiteness and colonial power constructs do not always repeat each other straightforwardly. To homogenize the postcolonial and postcolonized subject positions along racial lines would be to deny the variability of colonial experience, even within racial groupings. It neglects, for instance, the subordinate forms of whiteness that attached to Irish and Italian subjects in the British and American spheres,

---

[3] Leela Gandhi, 1998, *Postcolonial Theory: A Critical Introduction*, Edinburgh: Edinburgh University Press, 169.

[4] Alfred J. López, 2005, "Introduction: Whiteness after Empire," in *Postcolonial Whiteness: A Critical Reader on Race and Empire*, New York: State University of New York Press, 1–30, 6.

[5] López, "Whiteness," 6.

4   Postcolonial Opera

respectively, where they were regarded as non-white, not because of their skin color but because of a perceived lack of civilization.[6] While whiteness cannot be separated from "the institutionalization of European colonialism," I think of the postcolonizing subject as one whose subject position is not determined so much by racial identity as by a presumed cultural and ancestral connection with an idealized and authoritative "motherland."[7] The postcolonizing subject is one who always has one eye on Europe, both as a place of origin and as a site of aspiration.

In South Africa, constructions of whiteness are conditioned not only by colonialism, of course, but also by apartheid. Here, the white subject is inscribed into a system of settlement but also into a more recent regime of systematized and legislated racial oppression. Melissa Steyn describes post-apartheid whiteness as "diasporic," since this apparently contradictory racial identity brings together the dominant or normative position enjoyed by the white subject with the marginalized status of those "dislocated from their own centers of identification."[8] For Steyn, the post-apartheid white subject's experience of surrendering political dominance generates a situation of perceived ostracism, which renders the site of erstwhile power inhospitable. Consequently, diasporic whiteness locates its home outside the borders of the former colony, in an idealized "elsewhere," where whiteness retains its authority. This aspect of diasporic whiteness resembles the dual orientation of the postcolonizing subject, who reaches for Europe as she grapples with the complexities of her place and role in the postcolonial present.

From a post-apartheid point of view, Kentridge's subject position is not directly equivalent to oppressive whiteness. The artist's personal history incorporates a legacy of anti-apartheid activism. Both his parents worked in opposition to the regime, and Kentridge himself played a central role in the anti-apartheid performances of Johannesburg's Junction Avenue Theatre Company in the 1970s. The artist hence operates from a framework of anti-apartheid whiteness, which renders him somehow "less complicit" in the oppressive heritage of his race. Here, it is important also to recognize that Kentridge himself is of Jewish descent. Unlike dominant histories of colonial settlement and expropriation, the artist's presence in South Africa hence reflects a more complex narrative of displacement and resettlement. Without dismissing the powerful consequences of those legacies of subjugation that have shaped Jewish routes and relocations, however, my reading of Kentridge's

[6] López, "Whiteness," 18.

[7] López, "Whiteness," 19.

[8] Melissa Steyn, 2005, "'White Talk': White South Africans and the Management of Diasporic Whiteness," in *Postcolonial Whiteness*, 119–135, 124.

subject position in postcolonial South Africa centers around more local histories of political and economic privilege, and of affinity with a European heritage. In Samuel Agbamu's description, Kentridge is "an artist of the periphery, an African of European descent, [who] uses his liminal perspective" to explore the question of what happens when Europe is confronted with the legacy of colonialism.[9]

The artist himself acknowledges his link with Europe throughout his oeuvre, where the imperial continent appears not only nostalgically but also alienated and absurd. In Kentridge's work, white characters face the devastation wreaked by apartheid and capitalist modernity while enjoying the cultural accoutrements of Europe. For Carolyn Christov-Bakargiev, the ambiguous presence of Europe in Kentridge's South African settings captures something of the dilemma the artist faces as a postcolonizing subject. "[Kentridge] cannot make modernist paintings—that is, he cannot pursue the fiction of making South Africa look 'white'—yet he cannot speak for the 'black,' nor provide a platform or voice for the 'other,'" Christov-Bakargiev writes. In response, the artist explores "a zone of uncertainty and shifting meanings."[10] Here, Christov-Bakargiev equates the aesthetic project of modernism to the construction of normative whiteness. This position excludes Black subjects from the codes and cultures of early twentieth-century Europe. More important, it acknowledges the unequal racial dynamics built into artistic movements centered in the metropolises of the West. Rather than embracing these practices unequivocally, Kentridge incorporates them into his works with a distinct measure of ambivalence. The artistic forms of Empire enter his oeuvre as "memory, citation, and pointed bricolage"; they represent a European heritage at once beautiful and bleak.[11]

Opera may be considered a musical counterpart to the postcolonizing subject position. Arriving as part of the colonial project, the art form keeps an eye firmly on Europe, even as it circulates in new formations throughout the postcolony. Facing the shifting cultural, economic, and political dynamics of the postcolonial present, opera, like the postcolonizing subject, must adapt to altered frames of reference, new normativities, and fluctuating priorities. Though I push back against simple historical constructions of opera as colonial import in Chapter 1, the art form undeniably remains inscribed in a European cultural heritage, which complicates its position in the postcolony.

---

[9] Samuel Agbamu, 2022, "Smash the Thing: William Kentridge, Classical Antiquity, and His Refusal of Time in O Sentimental Machine," *Classical Receptions Journal* 14(2), 264–287, 282.

[10] Carolyn Christov-Bakargiev, 1998, *William Kentridge*, Exhibition catalogue: Palais des Beaux-Arts de Bruxelles, 81.

[11] Andreas Huyssen, 2018, "Memories of Europe in the Art from Elsewhere," *Stedelijk Studies* 6, 1–10, 8.

6 Postcolonial Opera

From this perspective, Kentridge's operatic projects may be read as a response not only to the *artist*'s place in the postcolony, but also to the place of the *art form*.

Genre

I investigate Kentridge's engagement with operatic postcoloniality through six of the artist's performance pieces. Kentridge has established himself as an opera director of renown, with productions of canonical works at theatres including the Metropolitan Opera House in New York, La Scala in Milan, La Monnaie in Brussels, Covent Garden in London, and the Opéra Bastille in Paris. Alongside these productions, he has developed a number of experimental works that play disruptively with the conventions of opera-as-genre. Some of these creations derive from the artist's repertoire productions; others are new compositions conceived for a variety of settings and intermedial configurations. It is from this collection of experimental works that *Postcolonial Opera* draws its case studies. They include a puppet production of Monteverdi's *Il Ritorno d'Ulisse in Patria* (1998), a chamber opera titled *Confessions of Zeno* (2001–2002), an automated installation called *Black Box/ Chambre Noire* (2005), the lecture opera, *Refuse the Hour* (2012), the processional opera, *Triumphs and Laments* (2016), and a First World War commemoration piece titled *The Head & the Load* (2018). With the exception of *Ulisse*, each of these works is an original creation that straddles different media and performance traditions. The works are intermedial, interdisciplinary, and difficult to classify. Performed in contexts ranging from museums to theaters, from warehouses to a river bank, they exceed the traditional boundaries of the opera house.

Calling these works operas may not always seem obvious. Indeed, the matter of labels is particularly vexed where Kentridge's performance pieces are concerned. The works I discuss here can be described as many things. They may be termed art installations or performance art, experimental music theater or digital multimedia. With their intermedial composition and generic indeterminacy, the pieces lend themselves to critical appraisal from a range of disciplinary perspectives. Some commentators may hence understandably resist my decision to classify my chosen case studies as "opera." But just as each of the generic descriptors mentioned above summons a specific academic discourse, my invocation of the category, "opera," is intended to activate a particular set of theories and methodologies, one focused especially on matters of sound and embodied performance.

The works under discussion here all possess hereditary links with opera. They are often saturated with operatic quotations or derive directly from operatic Ur-texts. In some cases, the singing style invokes opera, and in other cases the work's framing points to the genre. Aspects of the productions hence lend themselves to operatic appraisal, as much as they invite comparison with other theater and art disciplines. My reading of these pieces foregrounds their sonic properties, including their references to other operatic works and the ways in which their soundtracks comment on or complicate their visual components.

Kentridge himself appears relatively nonchalant about the matter of nomenclature. In an interview, I asked the artist whether generic labels mattered. His response was noncommittal:

> Do generic classifications matter? Not rea- . . . I'm not sure what we call *The Head & the Load*. It's certainly operatic, so in some sense I'm happy for it to be a new thinking about what an opera can be. The *Sibyl* also, which is six voices and no orchestra—it's also a kind of opera, or a . . . no, it's not an oratorio . . . maybe it's an oratorio. I don't think the opera has to be limited by necessarily narrative shape, or narrative structure. Uhm [long pause] . . . it's a hard one. No, I'm not stuck to . . . types of classifications like that.[12]

Undecided, personally, about the genres to which his performance pieces belong, Kentridge confirms that he is comfortable for classifications such as opera to attach to his works. Importantly, the artist specifies that a piece such as *The Head & the Load* (the subject of Chapter 6) does not qualify as opera *tout court*, but rather that it represents "a new thinking about what an opera can be." It is this "new thinking" that I am particularly interested in exploring, specifically from a postcolonial perspective.

Taking account of the "new thinking" that characterizes the operatic projects under discussion here, one possible disciplinary approach would be to interpret Kentridge's projects as examples of postopera—a category that invokes the operatic but exceeds it. Jelena Novak's conception of postopera foregrounds what the author calls "the voice-body" in new opera.[13] For Novak, postopera focuses not so much on narrative and verisimilitude but on the material framing of the spectacle of the singing body. Responding to operatic quests for immediacy or realism, postopera stretches the limits of the form to explore shifting technologies of narration and sonic embodiment.

---

[12] Kentridge, interview with the author, February 15, 2021.
[13] Jelena Novak, 2016, *Postopera: Reinventing the Voice-Body*, Abingdon: Routledge.

8 Postcolonial Opera

Like Novak, I am interested in thinking about compositions that exceed the boundaries of opera writ large. My perspective, however, is rooted not in Western avant-garde experimentalism (though aspects of this tradition exert an undeniable influence on Kentridge's work), but in a postcolonial context where the genre continues to remake itself. Rather than describing Kentridge's works as a negation conditioned by the terms of the original, I wish to assess them as positive instantiations of an operatic imaginary adapted for a new context. Not non-operas, anti-operas, or opera-after-opera, but innovative takes on opera-as-is, Kentridge's works, in my reading, reveal something about the assumptions and expectations that attach to the genre, both within and outside the postcolony.

When speaking of opera, I incorporate notions of form and genre interchangeably. Though I acknowledge that (neo)structuralist approaches distinguish between genre (a historically specific and interpretive grouping of texts) and form (a pattern that "organize[s] materials in distinct and iterable ways"), my interpretations of Kentridge's works take account of these two categories without strictly delimiting where form ends and genre begins.[14] Like the symphony and the song cycle, opera may be both form and genre. What matters is that the practice conjures a set of conventions that generates expectations among performers, creators, audiences, and non-audiences alike.

Formally, opera may be expected to include acts of narrative signification, a combination of different visual and sonic media, and singing voices, often sounding with a particular timbre. Generically, and keeping in mind Eric Drott's description of genre as "a dynamic ensemble of correlations, linking together a variety of material, institutional, social, and symbolic resources," opera may be expected to refer to an event presented in a theater of some sort, performed by persons with musical training, and attended by a public schooled in a particular set of behaviors and listening competencies.[15] But as scholars' perennial return to the topic of opera-as-genre (or form) demonstrates, these simplistic descriptions are far from conclusive.[16]

---

[14] The definitions are adapted from Caroline Levine, 2015, *Forms: Whole, Rhythm, Hierarchy, Network*, Princeton, NJ: Princeton University Press, 13.

[15] Eric Drott, 2013, "The End(s) of Genre," *Journal of Music Theory* 57(1), 1–45, 10.

[16] On the genre of opera, see Herbert Lindenberger, 2010, *Situating Opera: Period, Genre, Reception*, Cambridge: Cambridge University Press; Bianca Michaels, 2013, "Is This Still Opera?: Media Opera as Productive Provocations," in *The Legacy of Opera: Reading Music Theatre as Experience and Performance*, ed. Dominic Symonds and Pamela Karantonis, Boston: Brill, 25–38; Colleen L. Renihan, 2016, "The Politics of Genre: Exposing Historical Tensions in Harry Somers's *Louis Riel*, in *Opera Indigene: Re/Presenting First Nations and Indigenous Cultures*, ed. Dylan Robinson and Pamela Karantonis, Abingdon: Routledge, 259–276; Joy H. Calico, 2018, "Genre Designation as Ambiguating Force: Olga Neuwirth's *Lost Highway* as Opera," in *Ambiguity in Contemporary Art and Theory*, ed. Frauke Berndt and Lutz Koepnick, Hamburg: Felix Meiner Verlag, 151–164.

Indeed, what constitutes opera, both as form and as genre, shifts along with time, place, and circumstance, yielding a musical practice that is at once open to reinterpretation and bound to a vague, but often forcefully policed, set of conventions.

In *Postcolonial Opera*, I take account of the conventions that attach to opera by treating the art form first and foremost as an institution. Caroline Levine writes that "institutions are as much or more constituted by patterns as they are by bounded spaces, as much organized by rules and practices that need to be repeatedly re-enacted as they are by containing walls."[17] In other words, institutions bring together genre and form in a play of socially and politically constructed reiteration. They rely on adherence to a set of mutually agreed or externally imposed limits. Simultaneously, however, they are open to adaptation as circumstances require. Most important, institutions are structured by expectation: both those on the inside and those on the outside harbor a set of anticipations regarding the working of the institution, its contents, purposes, and methods, and the behaviors appropriate to its functioning.

The same applies to opera. Organized around a set of sonic, media, and behavioral conventions, the art form fills its audience (and those who do not count themselves as part of that audience) with expectations, which in turn guide their attendance at and reception of performances. When a production does not comply with expectations, its unusual characteristics are remarked upon and assessed as exceptions to the genre's unspoken rules. As audiences are taught to expect new practices or experiments, their perception of the conventions that make the form also change. Thus, opera-as-genre transforms along with the expectations that attach to it.

Kentridge's view of opera reveals that the artist himself similarly conceives of the form as an accumulation of expectations and conventions. Asked what he understands the genre to be, he answered as follows:

What I understand the form to be; where the limits of opera lie to me: well, in the one sense, the limits of opera are what an opera house will allow us to put on their stage with the resources it has, which is to say, a canvas seventeen metres wide, ten metres high, twenty metres deep; a top-class orchestra of a hundred musicians; choir of sixty or seventy; a shop that can build the sets, that can make the costumes; all of those resources coming towards it—so it's a chance of making a four-dimensional drawing on a scale that otherwise is not possible. But in the other

---

[17] Levine, *Forms*, 57–58.

10 Postcolonial Opera

> sense, the limits of opera would be, "what is the emotional directness you can have in which you use music as a central engine of something happening on stage." So whether it's a chamber opera, or whether it's an opera not fit in an opera house, but uses the fact of the human voice in this way. I'm not sure whether it's . . . lack of amplification is an important part of it; a live audience certainly feels an important part, even if it's only a virtual live audience. But it's also the combination—the "muchness" is what makes an opera. The fact that it's an overload—something you read, or listen to the words of, something you hear in terms of the music, something you look at in terms of what is on stage. So it's always about a kind of sensory excess. And one has to enjoy and work with the, with the overload, with the overdetermination of what the form is in its heart.[18]

Kentridge's description of opera incorporates some conventions characteristic of what may be called "traditional" or canonical Western opera, including the use of a sizable orchestra, the staging capabilities of a fully equipped house, and the cooperation of an all-powerful managerial body. Additionally, the artist's emphasis on liveness, on the unamplified voice, and on the excess or "overload" of the performance, all invoke an operatic tradition most readily associated with the grand productions of repertoire works seen at theaters such as the Metropolitan Opera House, La Scala, or Covent Garden. Alongside these features, however, Kentridge emphasizes "emotional directness," which is activated by music and fulfilled by the actions on stage. Here, the artist shifts away from standard features of operatic production, to a more nebulous and personal interpretation of opera-as-genre. For Kentridge, operas must move their audiences. The way they do so is by articulating their content through the medium of voice. When the human voice no longer succeeds in moving its audience, opera reaches its limits.

The Kentridge works under discussion here disrupt some of the expectations associated with traditional Western opera. They do not always adhere to the specifications Kentridge outlines above. But they do all incorporate human voices in various configurations, whether in digitally manipulated form, as recordings, or as live, embodied song. Thinking of these works and their vocal register *as opera*, I believe, may reveal much about the expectations that usually attach to the form. Moreover, such a critical perspective opens opportunities for rethinking the limits and possibilities of opera and vocal performance in the postcolony.

---

[18] Kentridge, interview with the author, February 15, 2021.

Unboundedness

Despite his apparent indifference toward the matter of generic classification, there is one operatic descriptor Kentridge resists. Critics often refer to the artist's productions (both of canonical operas and of original works) as *Gesamtkunstwerk*.[19] In the tradition of *Gesamtkunstwerk*, or "total work of art," however, Kentridge identifies a radical openness of form, which to him is better captured by notions of unboundedness than totality. He therefore responds to the *Gesamtkunstwerk* label with an alternative classification, that of "unbounded work of art":

> [*Gesamtkunstwerk* is] the idea of an artwork that doesn't have boundaries. And in a way the artwork that doesn't have boundaries has more to do with Dada than with Wagner, I think. And so my indebtedness is more to what the Dadaists did a hundred years ago . . . hundred and five years ago now . . . which was to blast open the category of what a visual artist could do. So even though when I was a student growing up the sense to be a visual artist was to paint with oil paint on canvas, looking at the Dadaists, and following them, I understood that was a very small part of what it was to be an artist, and the Dadaists had shown that it was possible for a sound to be an artwork, or a spoken poem, or a performance, or a found object. And I think all of contemporary art today is indebted to what the "wilder" of the Dadaists dared to do in that period. So that makes a . . . if not a total work of art, certainly an unbounded work of art . . . exist. And so whether I'm working on a drawing, or an opera, or a piece of sculpture, or a piece of theatre, or an essay, they don't feel utterly different activities. Obviously the form, the medium that you're working with, is different.[20]

For Kentridge, the work of art may comprise any configuration of media and forms. Creating an opera, in other words, functions more as an extension of the artist's visual practice than as a completely new generic activity. This generates a sense of inconclusiveness in his work. Michael Godby writes that "all Kentridge's work . . . is provisional in the sense of being both open and incomplete."[21] Always-becoming, the pieces resist permanence, generating

---

[19] See, for instance, Peter Frank, 2023, "William Kentridge: In Praise of Shadows at the Broad Museum, Los Angeles," *White Hot Magazine*, https://whitehotmagazine.com/articles/at-broad-museum-los-angeles/5705, accessed June 2, 2023; Michael Parry, 2019, "William Kentridge: That Which We Do Not Remember," *Medium*, https://medium.com/@vaguelym/william-kentridge-that-which-we-do-not-remember-347f02e367b5, accessed June 2, 2023. I return to the matter of totality in Chapter 6.

[20] Kentridge, interview with the author, February 15, 2021.

[21] Michael Godby, 2019, "Unwritten History: William Kentridge's *Triumphs and Laments*, Piazza Tevere, Rome, 2016," in *What Was History Painting and What Is It Now?*, ed. Mark Salber Phillips and Jordan Bear, Montreal: McGill-Queen's University Press, 215–233, at 219.

12 Postcolonial Opera

instead a nomadic artistic form that "cannot and should not be something everlasting, concluded, universal, and unitary, and hence always the same."[22]

At face value, such radical openness suggests merely that Kentridge believes "anything can be part of the work of art"—a kind of theatrical "free for all." But in the context of histories and networks of operatic exchange, the idea of unboundedness imagines an operatic practice that retains meaning and coherence beyond aesthetic or formal constraints. Navigating between different conceptions of the form, Kentridge's operatic experiments cross the border between Europe and Africa, but somehow manage to remain tethered to both cultural and political territories. This is not formlessness, which is too quickly evocative of colonial imaginaries of primitivism and chaos, desperately awaiting the organizing influence of Western modernity. Rather, it suggests a reconfiguration of what form might mean.

Unboundedness refers to the loosening of restrictions around genre, history, and ownership, to listen not only for exchange but also for transnational parallels that may predate colonial contact. These are archives of cultural memory that exceed paper trails and documentary collections. Indeed, the form itself becomes a performative archive of encounter, exchange, and coexistence; a microcosm of collisions and agreements that emerge when different cultural or political traditions cohere around shared concepts. The unboundedness of postcolonial opera thus establishes an epistemological framework within which to problematize established narratives of colonial encounter and cultural circulation.

Postcolony

Postcolonial Opera takes as a basic premise what Walter Mignolo calls the "modernity/coloniality bind"—an acknowledgment that "coloniality is . . . constitutive of modernity—there is no modernity without coloniality."[23] The modernity/coloniality bind derives from a simple recognition that the technological, intellectual, and cultural modernization of Europe (and, subsequently, the rest of the world) was enabled by coloniality. In William Fourie's words, "Modernity, with its civilizing mission of betterment, is a product (financially, but also epistemologically) of coloniality, as much as coloniality is a product of a modernizing Western society." As a result, "The song of

---

[22] Gabriele Guercio, 2017, "A Paradoxical Monumentality," in *William Kentridge: Triumphs and Laments*, ed. Carlos Basualdo, 129–143, at 138.
[23] Walter D. Mignolo, *The Darker Side of Western Modernity: Global Futures, Decolonial Options*, Durham, NC: Duke University Press, 3.

Western modernity will also always be sung in time with the song of Western coloniality."[24] Opera, I shall emphasize repeatedly throughout this book, is inescapably intertwined with the dynamics of modernity and coloniality. Recent studies including Rogério Budasz's *Opera in the Tropics: Music and Theater in Early Modern Brazil* and Charlotte Bentley's *New Orleans and the Creation of Transatlantic Opera, 1819–1859*, have highlighted the fact that the art form served as a marker of cultural modernity as it traveled around the world to colonial spheres.[25] To these observations may be added that the technologies that enabled operatic innovation, discussed in Gundula Kreuzer's *Curtain Gong Steam: Wagnerian Technologies of Nineteenth-Century Opera*, relied on colonial extraction for their development.[26] Thinking of opera hence necessarily involves thinking of colonialism.

Beyond its implication in regimes of colonial settlement and exploitation, opera also offers possibilities for the recovery of colonial histories. Dominant accounts of colonial pasts, especially as they relate to Black and Indigenous citizens, are notoriously unreliable. As Achille Mbembe writes, "The historical experiences of Blacks did not necessarily leave traces, and where they were produced, they were not always preserved."[27] Colonial authorities' documentary neglect of colonized persons' experiences creates an epistemological problem in the postcolonial present: "How could one write history in the absence of the kinds of traces that serve as sources for historiographical fact?" Mbembe asks. He continues: "The history of Blacks [can] be written only from fragments brought together to give an account of an experience that itself was fragmented, that of a pointillist people struggling to define itself not as a disparate composite but as a community whose blood stains the entire surface of modernity."[28] Black and Indigenous histories of colonialism require alternative forms of narration for their recovery. Given the incomplete and provisional nature of the information that marks both the existence of these histories and their loss, contemporary reconstructions of such derelict pasts must proceed in a manner that exceeds orthodox codes of historical reconstruction.

---

[24] William Fourie, 2020, "Musicology and Decolonial Analysis in the Age of Brexit," *Twentieth-Century Music* 17(2), 197–211, at 207 and 209.

[25] Rogério Budasz, 2019, *Opera in the Tropics: Music and Theater in Early Modern Brazil*, Oxford: Oxford University Press; Charlotte Bentley, 2022, *New Orleans and the Creation of Transatlantic Opera, 1819–1859*, Chicago, IL: University of Chicago Press.

[26] Gundula Kreuzer, 2018, *Curtain Gong Steam: Wagnerian Technologies of Nineteenth-Century Opera*, Berkeley: University of California Press.

[27] Achille Mbembe, 2017 [2013], *Critique of Black Reason*, trans. Laurent Dubois, Durham, NC: Duke University Press, 28.

[28] Mbembe, *Critique*, 29.

14 Postcolonial Opera

Opera, Naomi André argues in *Black Opera: History, Power, Engagement*, offers one option for ethical engagement with the fractured histories of colonialism and racial oppression.[29] André reveals how the "shadow cultures" of Black operatic activity echo the historical neglect of Black experiences in general. As the art form comes to terms with its own historical exclusions, she argues, opera may offer one vehicle by which to approach a corrective engagement with history. The genre itself enacts an atypical form of narration, structured around the subjectivity of the singing voice, distributed across media, and conditioned by unstable temporalities. Moreover, the operatic event, which is itself transitory, may also function as a metaphor for Black (and colonized) historical ephemerality. In Kentridge's operas, this quality is underscored by the drawings that make up the productions' animated backdrops. Kentridge's visual practice references the idea of the trace: rubbing out and redrawing through a series of infinitesimal adjustments, the artist leaves an archive of almost invisible marks across his animations. These lines, remainders of what had come before, haunt his backdrops; they too become ghosts of history, like the people whose stories they seek to tell. Incorporating processes of erasing and redrawing, Kentridge's drawings animate the disavowals, sedimentations, and residues that condition Black historical reconstruction in the postcolony. Thus, the artist's operatic works imagine new ways of thinking colonial and postcolonial history.

Up to this point, I have spoken of "the postcolony" as a kind of generalizable historical and geographical everywhere—a single place whose sole distinguishing feature is the fact that it had been colonized. However, this critical-theoretical sleight of hand should not be allowed to obscure the heterogeneity of diverse colonies and postcolonies, nor the fact that my study is firmly situated in and shaped by a particular place and past.

Were I to be asked, "where is the postcolony?" for this book, I would have to answer, "South Africa." *Postcolonial Opera* emerges specifically from the South African context, and from a set of questions formulated in response to the position of opera in that country. In recent years, South African opera has become a productive field of scholarly inquiry. As Christopher Ballantine shows, the art form appears to have experienced something of a post-apartheid renaissance, with new singers, companies, and productions enjoying unexpected support and success.[30] This state of affairs marks a reversal from apartheid-era operatic activity, which was conditioned by racialized restrictions and white

---

[29] Naomi André, 2018, *Black Opera: History, Power, Engagement*, Champaign: University of Illinois Press.
[30] Christopher Ballantine, 2019, "Opera and the South African Political," in *The Oxford Handbook of Sound and Imagination*, ed. Mark Grimshaw-Aagaard, Mads Walther-Hansen, and Martin Knakkergaard, Oxford: Oxford University Press, 291–311.

cultural exceptionalism.[31] When apartheid ended in 1994, training and performance institutions were desegregated and official infrastructures began to accommodate the operatic "shadow cultures" that had always existed at the margins of civic performance.[32] Since then, the art form has become an integral part of Black South African cultural citizenship. In contemporary South Africa, academic engagement with opera is especially interested in the racialized politics of the form.[33] Much work has been done to examine the genre's role in contemporary social and political formations.[34] This includes opera's potential for advancing reconciliation, and attempts to inscribe the genre with "Indigenous" signification.

These studies form part of a larger engagement with the racial and colonial politics of the operatic form. Recent work on opera, race, and tensions between Indigeneity and settlement, especially by scholars based in the United States, Canada, and Australia, engages with opera's capacity to reflect matters of colonial encounter and Indigenous recovery, and imagines new futures for the form.[35] As I seek to connect my work to these discourses, I heed Leela Gandhi's warning that "the postcolonial deference to the homogenising and all-inclusive category 'colonialism' . . . fails to account for differences [between] the culturally and historically variegated forms of both colonisation and anti-colonial struggles."[36] Gandhi is especially wary of critical practices that conflate settler colonialism and exploitation colonialism. "Such claims," she writes, "entirely neutralise, in the name of subject formation, the widely divergent logics of settlement and struggles for independence. Equally, they confer a seamless and undiscriminating postcoloniality on both white settler cultures and on those indigenous peoples displaced through their encounter with these cultures."[37] I have already explained my critical approach to the

[31] See especially Hilde Roos, 2018, *The La Traviata Affair: Opera in the Age of Apartheid*, Berkeley: University of California Press.

[32] See Roos, *La Traviata*.

[33] Naomi André, Donato Somma, and Innocentia J. Mhlambi, 2016, "*Winnie, The Opera* and Embodying South African Opera," *African Studies* 75(1), 1–9; Melissa Gerber, 2020, "Postcards from the Platteland: Avant-garde Aesthetics and Nostalgia in *Poskantoor*'s (2014) Paratexts," *SAMUS: South African Music Studies* 40, 239–268.

[34] Lena Van der Hoven, 2020, "'We Can't Let Politics Define the Arts': Interviews with South African Opera Singers," in *African Theatre 19: Opera and Music Theatre*, ed. Christine Matzke, Lena Van der Hoven, Christopher Odhiambo, Hilde Roos, Woodbridge: James Currey, 77–89; Andrew Olsen, 2012, "Mozart's African Jacket: *Die Zauberflöte* and its Localisation in *The Magic Flute (Impempe Yomlingo)*," *Journal of the Musical Arts in Africa* 9(1), 67–80; Sheila Boniface Davies and J. Q. Davies, 2012, "'So Take This Magic Flute and Blow. It Will Protect Us as We Go': *Impempe Yomlingo* (2011) and South Africa's Ongoing Transition," *Opera Quarterly* 28(1–2), 54–71; Juliana M. Pistorius, 2023, "A Modern-Day Florestan: *Fidelio on Robben Island* and South Africa's Early Democratic Project," *Twentieth-Century Music* 20(1), 107–125.

[35] Mary I. Ingraham, Joseph K. So, and Roy Moodley, eds., 2016, *Opera in a Multicultural World: Coloniality, Culture, Performance*, Abingdon: Routledge; Pamela Karantonis and Dylan Robinson, eds., 2011, *Opera Indigene: Re/presenting First Nations and Indigenous Cultures*, Farnham: Ashgate.

[36] Gandhi, *Postcolonial Theory*, 168.

[37] Gandhi, *Postcolonial Theory*, 168–169.

distinction between the divergent postcolonial subject positions of the white settler and the Indigenous (or colonized) person. To this, I may add that *Postcolonial Opera* structures its analyses especially around the conditions of settler colonialism in South Africa.

Though the geographical provenance of my case studies and critical framework is specific, certain aspects of the discussion may be generalized across spheres shaped by settler colonialism. Kentridge's works enact a series of cross-continental significations amplified by the artist's position as a global figure. In some ways, these works suggest that the postcolonial is everywhere. With their explicit uncovering of the modernity/coloniality bind, they reveal that the globe in its entirety has been touched by coloniality. By extension, the globe in its entirety may be regarded as postcolonial. From this point of view, the postcolony may refer to the so-called "global South"; it may refer to the African continent; and it may refer to all countries that have endured colonial domination. It may also, however, refer to those regions that executed and benefited from the colonial project.

Building on this premise, I am interested not only in thinking in and for the postcolony but also in using the frameworks developed in this book to think back to Europe. Rosi Braidotti, in an assessment of the importance of turning the scholarly lens from the postcolony onto the former metropole, writes as follows: "If it is the case that a sociocultural mutation is taking place in the direction of a multiethnic, multimedia society, then the transformation cannot affect only the pole of 'the others.' It must equally dislocate the position and the prerogative of 'the same,' the former center."[38] What Braidotti advocates is a critical project that addresses not only the usual subjects of theory but also the normative figures against which these subjects are measured and differentiated. As long as the "former center," or the imperial metropole, continues to function as theory's norm, aesthetic, political, and racial configurations from the postcolony will only ever be described as derivative or disobedient.[39]

In opera, the former imperial center still determines the codes and conditions of the genre. Assessing postcolonial opera as its own norm—as a mode of performance that plays with the conventions of the form, not for the sake of protest but simply to meet the expressive demands of the postcolony— hence allows for a renewed engagement with the genre's social, cultural, and political promise, both at home (wherever home may be) and abroad.

[38] Rosi Braidotti, 2011, *Nomadic Subjects*, New York: Columbia University Press, 8.
[39] I develop this argument at greater length in Chapter 1.

Method

Postcolonial Opera combines a multivalent analytical methodology with a systematic critical approach. Each chapter considers one concept from postcolonial critical theory along with one of Kentridge's works, which functions as a case study to demonstrate how opera relates to the theme under discussion. Chapter 1, "Return," starts at the beginning, with an examination of operatic genealogy. Taking as its case study Kentridge's first operatic project, a puppet production of Monteverdi's *Il Ritorno d'Ulisse in Patria* (1998), the chapter discusses divergent constructions of opera's history in colonial spheres, with a focus on the African continent. It argues for a more nuanced engagement with histories of arrival and return, and emphasizes the transformations and estrangements the art form undergoes as it journeys between spheres.

In Chapter 2, "Confession," Kentridge's first original operatic project, *Confessions of Zeno* (2002), serves as a lens through which to approach operatic performances of confession from a postcolonial perspective. Drawing on Foucault's work on confession in the West, and Fanon's theorization of confessional impossibility in the colony, the chapter asks how opera might undermine or enable confessional performance in the postcolony. Chapter 3, "Mourning," proceeds from guilt to loss. Engaging with the concept of postcolonial mourning through the lens of Kentridge's operatic installation, *Black Box/Chambre Noire* (2005), the chapter asks if an operatic form committed to practices of subversive memorialization and formal deconstruction can be trusted with the work of mourning in the postcolonial sphere.

In Chapter 4, "Time," the question of operatic time in the postcolony serves as a basis from which to explore new modes of theatrical meter and measurement. Kentridge's chamber opera, *Refuse the Hour* (2012), serves as a case study through which to examine the potential of the operatic form to refuse the constraints of colonial temporal regimes on the postcolonial stage. Chapters 5 and 6, "Place" and "Totality," draw on two processional operas created by Kentridge in 2016 and 2018, respectively. *Triumphs and Laments*, the subject of Chapter 5, offers an opportunity to discuss opera's participation in colonial and postcolonial practices of place-making and to imagine curative forms of inhabiting for the itinerant postcolonial subject. In turn, *The Head & the Load*, which was developed as a First World War commemoration piece, serves as a frame through which to analyze the issue of operatic totality from a postcolonial perspective. I conclude my study with a very brief reflection on *Sibyl* (2019). This discussion does not develop further critical perspectives, but serves to synthesize the interpretations presented in the rest of the book.

18 Postcolonial Opera

My investigation approaches each Kentridge work as a text upon which postcolonial theoretical models may be tested. Even where I reflect on the intermedial effects these pieces achieve in performance, my analyses are hence hermeneutic rather than phenomenological. Kentridge's works present unusually dense conglomerations of intertextual references and intertwined significations. Consequently, when viewing these works in live performance, meaning emerges as an unstable or even inaccessible value. Though a phenomenological account of the interpretations and experiences that accumulate during a Kentridge performance would itself be a fascinating undertaking, I prefer to center the discussions in this book around a more systematic engagement with the form and content of each work. I base my analyses on a range of primary materials, including scores, libretti, photographs, interviews, recordings, and where possible, attendance at productions.

Kentridge himself has spoken and written extensively about his own work. On the one hand, the artist's voluminous publications and interviews are essential resources when considering the provenance or critical intention of each piece. On the other, it is difficult not to fall into simple repetition of the artist's own assessments of his creations. I incorporate Kentridge's discussions of his work where such material is pertinent to the postcolonial theme under consideration. For the most part, however, I seek to foster a more distanced critical engagement with the artist's projects. This, in turn, allows the project to expand from a book "about Kentridge" to a book about opera, in which Kentridge's oeuvre features as a central case study.

None of the operas under discussion here is a solo endeavor. For each project, Kentridge works with a set of collaborators, which, apart from occasional additions and variations, remains largely the same. (Kim Gunning, Kentridge's regular video orchestrator, refers to this core group as the "Kentourage.")[40] On the musical front, a key figure is Philip Miller, with whom the artist has worked since 1993. Most of the music discussed in *Postcolonial Opera* was developed by Miller in collaboration with Kentridge, whose musical tastes and interests shape Miller's work throughout. Recently, Thuthuka Sibisi joined the compositional team. Together with Miller, he collaborated on *Triumphs and Laments* and *The Head & the Load*. For *Sibyl*, Kentridge approached another of his regular collaborators, Nhlanhla Mahlangu, who created the opera's score alongside celebrated jazz pianist, Kyle Shepherd.

Miller describes Kentridge's collaborative process in culinary terms: at the beginning of each project, the artist, composers, choreographer, and designers

---

[40] Kim Gunning, interview with the author, September 27, 2023.

Introduction **19**

gather to receive a brief, to which they respond by developing ideas separately. Subsequently, they meet for workshops to share their progress and test initial concepts. The products of these discrete endeavors function as "ingredients," from which Kentridge, "like a chef," assembles the final product.[41] Miller concedes that each production remains very explicitly under the control of Kentridge and carries his imprint more than any other. In Kentridge's own words, collaboration is vital:

> So almost all the performers in the first iteration—whether it's the *Sibyl* or this— are the people who've actually helped construct it, developed the music with the composers, developed the characters in relation to me as the director. And this collaboration is essential. Collaboration properly, in the sense that the invention, the possibilities, are developed by all the people working on it, rather than them simply carrying out instructions from me. Obviously with music as a . . . I'm not a musician, but also with the editing, how it can be constructed visually, how it can be staged, how it should be designed by the costume and set designer. And so long as everybody keeps their sense of certainty at bay, and is open to everyone's doubts, it can function. At a certain point of course one has to make decisions. . . . So at a certain point I do have to say, "yes, for now we're going with these scenes; this is the way we have to make the decisions." But that happens very very late—sometimes just before the dress rehearsal—that final decisions are made.[42]

Despite the distributed nature of each project's creative input, Kentridge evidently remains something of an auteur figure. The artist serves as the initiator of each work, and he retains artistic control over the final shape of the production, even if this control is conditioned by an extended, and deeply democratic, developmental phase.

The case studies in this book all originated in Kentridge's Johannesburg studio, where the artist convenes his creative team at the start of each project. Developed, sometimes over the course of several months or even years, in a socio-political and environmental context that continues to intrigue and inspire, the operas I discuss here form part of an artistic language that is indivisibly embedded in the politics of the artist's home country. Both local and international, the works offer a view on the competing logics of territorial specificity and transnational legibility that adhere to Kentridge's practice.

[41] Philip Miller, interview with the author, April 7, 2020.
[42] Kentridge, interview with the author, February 15, 2021.

20 Postcolonial Opera

Fellow Travelers

Though he only came to opera in 1998, Kentridge's career in theater stretches back to the 1970s, when he was a member of Junction Avenue Theatre Company. Kentridge co-founded Junction Avenue with a group of friends in 1976. The company staged agitprop plays, workshopped by the racially integrated cast and performed for Black audiences to encourage political mobilization and self-determination. Kentridge participated in these productions as actor, scenographer, publicity artist, and occasionally as director.[43] After Junction Avenue, Kentridge staged a number of plays with Handspring Puppet Company. These include *Woyzeck on the Highveld* (1992), *Faustus in Africa* (1995), and *Ubu and the Truth Commission* (1995). It was with Handspring that Kentridge finally made his first opera, a production of Monteverdi's *Il Ritorno d'Ulisse in Patria*. Since then, the artist has staged Mozart's *Die Zauberflöte* (commissioned by Théâtre de la Monnaie, Brussels, 2005), *The Nose* by Shostakovich (commissioned by the Metropolitan Opera in New York, 2010), Alban Berg's *Lulu* (co-commissioned by the Dutch National Opera, Amsterdam; Metropolitan Opera, New York; and English National Opera, London, 2015), and Berg's *Wozzeck* (co-commissioned by the Salzburg Festival; Metropolitan Opera, New York; and Sydney Opera House, 2017).[44]

As he develops large productions such as the ones listed here, Kentridge creates companion pieces that incorporate the visual and sonic material of the main operas. These projects serve a variety of purposes: some are intended to test the scale and relationality of props; others experiment with choreography; yet others serve as models or templates for the animated drawings that ultimately become part of the backdrop. Sometimes, such co-creations emerge after the completion of the main production, as vehicles through which to develop themes only hinted at in the opera.

---

[43] See Dan Cameron, Carolyn Christov-Bakargiev, and J. M. Coetzee, 1999, *William Kentridge*, London: Phaidon; Leora Maltz-Leca, 2018, *William Kentridge: Process as Metaphor and Other Doubtful Enterprises*, Oakland: University of California Press, esp. 105–113.

[44] For more on Kentridge's early operas, see Rachel Fensham, 2008, "Operating Theatres: Body-Bits and a Post-Apartheid Aesthetics," in *Anatomy Live: Performance and the Operating Theatre*, ed. Maaike Bleeker, Amsterdam: Amsterdam University Press, 251–261; Bronwyn Law-Viljoen, ed., 2007, *William Kentridge: Flute*, Johannesburg: David Krut; Serena Guarracino, 2010, "The Dance of the Dead Rhino: William Kentridge's Magic Flute," *Altre Modernità: Rivista di studi letterari e culturali* 4, 268–278; and Maria Gough, 2010, "Kentridge's Nose," *October* 134, 3–27. Little has been written on the Berg operas other than a few reviews such as these: Anna Katsnelson, 2015, "A Real 'Lulu' of a Tale," *Forward*, November 27, 28–29; Anthony Tommasini, 2015, "Review: Finding Beauty in a Wrenching 'Lulu' at the Met," *New York Times*, November 5, https://www.nytimes.com/2015/11/07/arts/music/metropolitan-opera-lulu-review.html; and Shirley Apthorp, 2017, "Wozzeck at Salzburg—a Breathtaking Reassessment," *Financial Times*, August 9, https://www.ft.com/content/9b8814c2-7c63-11e7-ab01-a13271d1ee9c.

Kentridge's assistant, Anne McIlleron, refers to these operatic offshoots as "fellow travelers."[45] They accompany the artist on his journey toward operatic completion, and serve as records of his processes and priorities. Kentridge's fellow travelers are neither derivative nor preliminary—they function as companions that allow the artist to work out themes suggested by the operas, to experiment with options, or to bring a different coherence to the constitutive parts of the original productions. Of the works under discussion in *Postcolonial Opera*, two are fellow travelers: *Black Box/Chambre Noire* accompanies the artist's production of *Die Zauberflöte*, and *Refuse the Hour* travels with the large-scale video installation, *The Refusal of Time* (2012). The other pieces I discuss are not offshoots of larger projects. Rather, they constitute the large projects themselves, which in turn yield their own collections of fellow travelers.

A striking feature of Kentridge's traveling constellations is the fact that they share a vast array of family resemblances. Across his oeuvre, the artist repeats themes and replicates materials. In *Postcolonial Opera*, such inter-compositional reiteration allows for larger refrains and critical concerns to emerge across the artist's operatic experiments. In certain cases, analytical approaches to one work may equally be applied to another. The result is an extraordinarily coherent critical project, in which works with divergent topics end up reaching the same conclusions. While the repetitions and reiterations of Kentridge's operatic concerns emerge throughout the book, some of the most salient premises bear highlighting here.

The first leitmotiv that characterizes Kentridge's operatic compositions is an intertextual incorporation of key texts from Euro-American modernism. Leora Maltz-Leca writes compellingly about the artist's dialogues with Western avant-gardes. She observes that the work of figures such as Dziga Vertov, Georges Méliès, Samuel Beckett, and Bertolt Brecht acquires "an unexpected afterlife in South Africa" thanks to their guest appearances in Kentridge's creations. At the same time, these artists' works change during their southward journeys, "assuming distorted refractions or gaining immoderate weight."[46] These intertextual references reveal Kentridge himself as a person with a vast and sophisticated cultural vocabulary. They also appear to construct a particular type of ideal audience—one with an extensive knowledge of the practices and masterworks of Western high art. More important, however, such quotations inscribe Kentridge the artist into a European heritage, even as they acknowledge his South African roots. For Maltz-Leca, the

---

[45] Anne McIlleron, personal communication, February 9, 2021.
[46] Maltz-Leca, *William Kentridge*, 16.

22 Postcolonial Opera

apparent fragmentation suggested by Kentridge's bi-directional artistic practice compels her to ask "how to account for a practice so steeped in Euro-American modernism—albeit a particular, southern-inflected version—yet equally defined by the histories of racism and colonialism, and the ongoing economic and social injustices of the South African postcolony?"[47] In a way, this question captures the ambivalent, and at times contradictory, disposition of the postcolonizing subject. It returns throughout this book as a focal point around which to assess not only the work of Kentridge but also the work of opera in the postcolony.

A second leitmotiv in Kentridge's operatic experiments, and one that extends from the first, is the theme of uncertainty. The ambiguous subject position articulated in Kentridge's (and opera's) relationship with Europe generates a practice marked by coincidence, mistranslation, ignorance, and doubt. Kentridge emphasizes that the meanings of his works are neither determined nor preconceived; rather, like his drawings, they emerge though a process guided especially by accident and fate—a mode of making he calls "fortuna."[48] The artist often states his faith in uncertainty, productive procrastination, miscommunication, and chance.[49] These qualities, he argues, complicate Enlightenment ideals of rationality and measurability. In their place, they generate a mode of knowledge-making that exchanges predictability and control for surprise, enchantment, and skepticism.

Kentridge's commitment to uncertainty derives from a similar unification of modernity and coloniality as that articulated by Mignolo. For Kentridge, colonialism and the Enlightenment are mutually generative: "The one is built into the other," he writes. "By bringing Enlightenment to the "dark continent" you have the disasters of colonialism."[50] The artist demonstrates his argument by referring to Plato's parable of the cave. Plato describes a group of people tied up in a dark chamber, who are forced to look at the silhouettes of moving objects projected onto the cave wall. When one of the prisoners is forced outside, he realizes, gradually, that the images he saw inside the cave were no more than shadows, and that they possessed no substance in and of themselves. Objective reality, he learns, exists in the light; it is material, measurable, and concrete. This man, empowered by his newfound knowledge, returns

[47] Maltz-Leca, *William Kentridge*, 16.
[48] Lillian Tome, ed., 2013, *William Kentridge: Fortuna*, London: Thames and Hudson.
[49] See, for instance, William Kentridge, 2014, *Six Drawing Lessons*, Cambridge, MA: Harvard University Press.
[50] William Kentridge, 2010, *William Kentridge: Anything Is Possible* [film], Art 21/PBS 2010, https://art21.org/watch/william-kentridge-anything-is-possible/full-program-william-kentridge-anything-is-possible/.

to the cave to free his fellow prisoners and to lead them toward the light of truth.[51]

Kentridge identifies in Plato's cave parable a form of epistemological tyranny. The knowledge bearer who descends back into the cave forces those he came to "rescue" to abandon one form of knowing in favor of another:

> For Plato the journey was always one towards enlightenment. Each new layer would explain the previous darker less direct region. And although the philosopher king, who had seen the sun and understood the truth was duty bound to return to the underworld, this was as a missionary, bringing the truth and the knowledge of the light with him. There was never a question of anything being learned from the shadows, of the world above. He had the monopoly of truth. My interest in Plato is twofold. For his prescient description of our world of cinema—his description of a world of people bound to reality as mediated through a screen feels very contemporary—but more particularly, in defence of shadows, and what they can teach us about enlightenment.[52]

The artist resists Plato's argument that truth necessarily attaches to light; rather, he argues, much can be learned from shadows. In Agbamu's assessment, Kentridge thus rejects "an imposed authoritarian enlightenment, of the sort which justified the violence of colonialism."[53] In its place, he suggests an approach to knowledge that embraces contradiction, ambivalence, and the magic of personal experience.

Kentridge's work unmasks the processes behind apparent certainties to show that all truths are made and maintained. The artist applies the same approach to the media he uses to realize his projects. Even as he relies on impressive feats of design and mechanization, the artist always exposes these technologies of deception. In the chapters that follow, I return more than once to Kentridge's preference for revealing the processes and mechanisms behind his theatrical feats. My interpretations of these moments of processual honesty and mechanical exposure are informed by critical postcolonial perspectives on modernity, performance, and labor. In Kentridge's operatic experiments, I argue, the work of opera emerges as the work of modernity and, by extension, the work of colonialism. These productions stress the complex interplay

---

[51] For a summary of the parable as well as commentary and analysis, see Martin Heidegger, 2002 [1930], *The Essence of Truth: On Plato's Parable of the Cave Allegory and Theaetetus*, trans. Ted Sadler, London: Continuum.

[52] Kentridge, 2001, "In Praise of Shadows," https://www.kentridge.studio/in-praise-of-shadows/, accessed July 28, 2021. See also Kentridge, *Six Drawing Lessons*.

[53] Agbamu, "Smash the Thing," 283–284.

24 Postcolonial Opera

between representation and exploitation, aspiration and coercion, dissemination and dispossession.

Rather than investigating what separates opera from other forms of music theater in the postcolony, *Postcolonial Opera* asks what the stakes might be of calling something opera in this context. The critical framework I develop here to account for opera's political and ethical place in the postcolony is not the last word on the art form and its imperial afterlives. Nor is it a blueprint for postcolonial operatic practice. Instead, this book offers an exploration of operatic possibilities shaped by and for the challenges of the postcolonial present.

1
Return

At first, I could not decide whether to call this chapter "Arrival" or "Return." My dilemma was genealogic as much as linguistic. If arrival refers to "the action or an instance of something being brought or conveyed to a place," and return to "an act of coming or going back to or from a place," then the history of opera in the postcolony may be constructed to reflect either or a bit of both.[1] One may think of opera as a form that arrives in non-Western cultural spheres alongside colonialism, or one may think of it as a practice that exists prior to colonialism, and which returns to, or recovers, its extra-colonial ancestry after the decolonial mo(ve)ment.[2] The tension between these two approaches, both of which are concerned with movement, place, and perspective, forms the basis of this chapter.

The questions I consider here center around issues of ownership. They are about who gets to claim the history of opera and to call the art form theirs. This, in turn, has an impact upon whose interests the genre represents, whose politics it performs, and who may see themselves represented in the work. It touches on issues of appropriation, on who controls (or should control) the narrative, and on who gets to decide what is or is not appropriate for the form. Rather than answering these questions, however, I use them as a starting point to think about the relationship between opera and the afterlives of coloniality. In other words, I do not set out to decide who owns opera. I do not seek to establish definitively how opera came to be practiced in places far from Europe's centers, nor do I attempt to lay down rules for the art form's execution. Instead, I use the various constructions of opera's history in colonial and postcolonial spheres to examine the diverse values that attach to the form. I ask what it means to think of opera as a genre that arrives with colonial expansion, or, conversely, as an art form that reinvigorates pre- and extra-colonial performance traditions. Finally, I reflect on the transformations opera undergoes

---

[1] "arrival, n," *OED* Online, March 2023, https://www.oxfordlearnersdictionaries.com/definition/english/arrival?q=arrival, https://www-oed-com.libproxy.ucl.ac.uk/view/Entry/11044?redirectedFrom=arrival, accessed April 24, 2023; "return, n," 2010, *OED* Online, March 2023, https://www-oed-com.libproxy.ucl.ac.uk/view/Entry/164595?rskey=rRQGVj&result=1&isAdvanced=false, accessed April 24, 2023.

[2] I use extra-colonial as a descriptor for practices and traditions that have existed or continue to exist in colonized spheres independently of colonialism. They may be precolonial, in other words, but they may also exist concurrently with colonization.

Postcolonial Opera. Juliana M. Pistorius, Oxford University Press. © Oxford University Press 2025.
DOI: 10.1093/oso/9780197749203.003.0002

as it journeys between dominions, and analyze the possibilities for post- and anticolonial commentary enabled by the art form's ambiguous genealogy.

I settled on calling the chapter "Return" for several reasons. First, opera itself is always in some sense a return, born out of a desire to recuperate the magical ancient marriage of word, music, and drama.[3] Second, the word "return" captures something of the reemergent passion—literally, a "return to enthusiasm"—for opera in postcolonial territories such as Australia, South Africa, and Canada. Return also implies a reevaluation or a rediscovery: a renewed engagement with a practice that had been neglected or suppressed, in this case extra-colonial performance. Additionally, return refers to "bringing back," to the act of returning opera from the former colony to the metropole; a reverse journey, with interest. In this sense, the term invokes what John Thieme calls the "postcolonial con-text": a work created in the postcolony, which appropriates colonial originals in an act of "writing back" to Empire.[4] The idea of opera as "postcolonial con-text" reinforces the colonial history of the form, but it also provides a useful critical frame through which to interpret the dialogue between the art form's manifestations in former colony and metropole.

Finally, "return" forms part of the title of Kentridge's first opera, a 1998 production of Monteverdi's *Il Ritorno d'Ulisse in Patria* (1640) with Cape Town–based Handspring Puppet Company.[5] From a chronological perspective, it makes sense to start a study of the artist's operatic experiments with his first production. Coincidentally, *Ulisse* is also an opera about return, recognition, and transformation. In its dramatization of the protagonist's homecoming after an extended and wandering absence, Monteverdi's composition symbolically enacts early opera's attempts to realize the recovery of an apparently lost Greek theatrical ideal. The subject matter, in other words, is appropriate to a discussion of operatic genealogy. Kentridge's *Ulisse* serves as the pivot around which I develop the chapter's questions and arguments regarding arrival, return, and renewal. As in the rest of this book, my aim is not simply to provide an analysis of the case study but rather to use the Kentridge production under

---

[3] As I argue in Chapter 3, this also makes opera a melancholy form. See Blair Hoxby, 2005, "The Doleful Airs of Euripides: The Origins of Opera and the Spirit of Tragedy Reconsidered," *Cambridge Opera Journal* 17(3), 253–269; Carolyn Abbate and Roger Parker, 2012, *A History of Opera: The Last Four Hundred Years*, London: Penguin, esp. 59–61. My thanks to Daniel Grimley for his guidance in formulating this point.

[4] John Thieme, 2001, *Postcolonial Con-Texts: Writing Back to the Canon*, London: Continuum; see also Bill Ashcroft, Gareth Griffiths, and Helen Tiffin, 2002 [1989], *The Empire Writes Back: Theory and Practice in Post-Colonial Literatures*, London: Routledge.

[5] Though it is Kentridge's first opera production, *Il Ritorno d'Ulisse in Patria* is neither the artist's first work in theater nor his first collaboration with Handspring Puppet Company. For more on Kentridge's earlier work in theater, see the Introduction. Kentridge reflects on his decision to stage an opera with Handspring after having done three theater pieces with the company, in Jane Taylor and William Kentridge, 2009, "In Dialogue: William Kentridge with Jane Taylor," in *Handspring Puppet Company*, ed. Jane Taylor, Johannesburg: David Krut Publishing, 176–209, at 193.

discussion as a focus point for questions about contemporary opera production in and from the postcolony.

Opera as Colonial Arrival

"Wherever European colonialism has travelled so too has the opera house," writes Ruth Bereson in *The Operatic State: Cultural Policy and the Opera House*.[6] Bereson's statement neatly summarizes prevalent conceptions of the relationship between coloniality and operatic circulation. It characterizes operatic practices and institutions in colonial spheres as "European implantations."[7] Put differently, Bereson's remark reflects a view that opera's arrival and circulation in former colonies is inseparable from the colonial project.[8] This attitude represents an established line of operatic historiography inspired especially by Edward Said, who regarded opera as an essential component of the colonial agenda.[9] The colonial account of operatic distribution regards the art form's global prevalence as a consequence of colonial circulation. Arriving with colonial forces, opera spread along a geographic trajectory determined by the discovery and extraction of natural resources.[10] As settlers moved farther into colonized territories, searching for fertile land, minerals, supplies, and adventure, they took their songs and entertainments with them. Where the discovery of local riches prompted the establishment of settlements, newly built theaters, schools, and churches formalized and sustained the practice of these cultures. Visiting artists energized local efforts and brought new trends to colonial outposts, while educational projects initiated local and Indigenous people into the wonders of these foreign arts.

In this account, operatic dissemination was closely intertwined with territorial expansion. Here, the cultural repercussions of what Walter Mignolo

---

[6] Ruth Bereson, 2002, *The Operatic State: Cultural Policy and the Opera House*, New York: Routledge, 175.

[7] Melissa Gerber, 2021, "(De)coding Contemporary South African Opera: Multimodality and the Creation of Meaning, 2010–2018," PhD diss., University of the Free State, 13.

[8] See also Rogério Budasz, 2019, *Opera in the Tropics: Music and Theater in Early Modern Brazil*, New York: Oxford University Press; Charlotte Bentley, 2022, *New Orleans and the Creation of Transatlantic Opera, 1819–1859*, Chicago, IL: University of Chicago Press; Nicholas Till, 2011, "Orpheus Conquistador," in *Opera Indigene: Re/Presenting First Nations and Indigenous Cultures*, ed. Pamela Karantonis and Dylan Robinson, Farnham: Ashgate, 14–29. *Opera in a Multicultural World: Coloniality, Culture, Performance*, 2016, ed. Mary I. Ingraham, Roy Moodley and Joseph So, New York: Routledge, also treats opera as a colonial export product.

[9] Edward Said, 1993, *Culture and Imperialism*, New York: Knopf. See also Till, "Orpheus Conquistador."

[10] See, for instance, Dorothy Wickman's brief article, "Opera on the Goldfields" (n.d.), https://ballarath eritage.com.au/article/opera-on-the-goldfields/, accessed June 28, 2023, for a description of opera's circulation along routes of extraction in Australia. In my view, the relationship between opera's colonial circulation and the extraction of natural resources in newly settled territories is a topic that warrants far greater systematic investigation.

calls the "modernity/coloniality bind" become clear: colonial expansion and displacement enabled the extraction of resources, which in turn accelerated the European modernizing project. Simultaneously, the expansionist project served to transmit a musical form—itself a representative of European cultural modernity—across an ever-growing colonial terrain.

As a colonial form, opera fulfilled several purposes. Geographically and temporally isolated from the imperial center, settlers across colonial realms relied on the circulation of new operas to keep pace with developments in the metropole and to sustain a cultural identity that tied them to Europe and differentiated them from the Indigenous population. In this sense, opera became a means of being in two places at once: though physically at the colonial margins, listeners and practitioners could imagine themselves culturally and socially in the metropole.[11] This is true not only for colonial spheres but also for newly independent countries where ruling elites retained close connections with Europe. Benjamin Walton, for instance, describes opera's popularization in South American countries after independence as a marker of civilization and association with Europe.[12] In the context of Mexico, Nancy Vogeley and Leonora Saavedra both show that the art form served as a cultural link between former colony and metropole.[13] And Ronald Dolkart argues that opera was introduced and supported in post-independence Argentina to nurture an image of a modern society shaped by "European bourgeois culture."[14] Likewise in apartheid South Africa, the minority government appropriated opera to serve as a sign of modernity and white exceptionalism. Investing heavily in opera companies, symphony orchestras, and ballet troupes, the regime constructed an image of cultural excellence to claim that South Africa was a bastion of Western civilization at the southern tip of the African continent.[15]

But the ostensible benefits of colonial opera did not only extend to the colonizers. Colonial agents also wielded the art form as a tool with which to control local populations. Rogério Budasz identifies in the colonial circulation of Western opera a "threefold goal of instructing, entertaining, and distracting

[11] The same applies to operatic practice in Europe's provincial regions, as Katharine Ellis (2021) demonstrates in *French Musical Life: Local Dynamics in the Century to World War II*, New York: Oxford University Press, , especially chapter 6.

[12] Benjamin Walton, 2012, "Italian Operatic Fantasies in Latin America," *Journal of Modern Italian Studies* 17(4), 460–471.

[13] Nancy Vogeley, 1996, "Italian Opera in Early National Mexico," *Modern Language Quarterly* 57(2), 279–288; Leonora Saavedra, 2008, "Staging the Nation: Race, Religion, and History in Mexican Opera of the 1940s," *Opera Quarterly* 23(1), 1–21.

[14] Ronald Dolkart, 1983, "Elitelore at the Opera: The Teatro Colón of Buenos Aires," *Journal of Latin American Lore* 9(2), 231–250, at 233.

[15] See Juliana M. Pistorius and Hilde Roos, 2021, "Burgerskap onder konstruksie: *Rigoletto* en *Aida* by die Suid-Afrikaanse Republiekfeesvieringe, 1971," *Litnet Akademies* 18(2), 102–131.

the [Indigenous] population . . . at the hands of missionaries, intellectuals, bureaucrats, political leaders, and cultural producers."[16] Colonizers used education as a means to initiate colonized people into the customs and cultures of the imperial metropole. They framed this instructional project, in which music, along with literacy and religion, played an essential part, as a civilizing mission designed to lift Indigenous people from apparent barbarism toward the rationality and refinement of the West.

In colonial South Africa, the didactic benefits of music education were brandished especially by missionaries, who implemented a vast, formalized program of choral music education in schools and churches established among Indigenous communities. Through careful training in choral singing, colonial instructors enacted a regime of discipline and control on the bodies and minds of Black subjects. According to most accounts of South African opera, it is from this choral tradition that Black operatic practice in the country evolved.[17] As a colonial form, in other words, opera represents the legacy of the subjection of Black bodies to Western ideals of civility and control.[18] Little wonder, then, that South African composer neo muyanga observes that "the genre continues to be viewed . . . as an interloper on the African continent . . . a western imposition or colonial hangover to be eschewed and denied funding in the interests of elevating more local and 'traditional' modes of music and story-telling."[19] Given its colonial heritage, its alienation of local tradition, and its role in the domination of Black subjects, opera raises suspicion among those committed to undoing the enduring effects of imperial control.

"Arrival," then, frames opera as something foreign to precolonial societies. It is an art form imposed from above and outside, with the purpose of inscribing the cultures and traditions of the metropole onto colonized territories. By extension, operatic practice in postcolonial spheres suggests a continuation or adoption of colonial culture—an appropriation of the music of the powerful elite by those whose histories are shaped by exploitation or oppression.

---

[16] Budasz, *Opera in the Tropics*, at 2.

[17] See Naomi André, Donato Somma, and Innocentia J. Mhlambi, 2016, "*Winnie: The Opera* and Embodying South African Opera," *African Studies* 75(1), 1–9, at 4; neo muyanga, 2020, "A Revolt in (more than just) Four Parts," in *African Theatre 19: Opera and Music Theatre*, ed. Christine Matzke, Lena van der Hoven, Christopher Odhiambo, and Hilde Roos, Woodbridge: James Currey, 17–28, at 19; Thembela Vokwana, 2006/7, "Opera in Africa: Music of the People, for the People, by the People," *New Music SA Bulletin* 5–6, 12–16.

[18] Grant Olwage, 2002, "Scriptions of the Choral: The Historiography of Black South African Choralism," *SAMUS: South African Journal of Musicology* 22, 29–45.

[19] muyanga 2015, quoted in Christopher Ballantine, 2019, "Opera and the South African Political," in *The Oxford Handbook of Sound and Imagination*, ed. Mark Grimshaw-Aagaard, Mads Walther-Hansen, and Martin Knakkergaard, Oxford: Oxford University Press, 291–311, at 294.

30 Postcolonial Opera

Opera as Indigenous Form

In opposition to the description of opera as colonial form, a growing number of scholars and practitioners have begun to claim for the genre an Indigenous heritage. Both in South Africa and further afield on the African continent, commentators have traced an operatic history that predates the art form's supposed arrival from Europe. These genealogies, which focus especially on the musicalization of narrative that constitutes the core of the form, present opera as an Indigenous African cultural practice—one that is at home on, rather than alien to, the African continent.[20] Drawing on positions held across the African continental sphere, several scholars and practitioners argue that the art form is itself indigenous to Africa, and that its practice precedes colonial arrival and circulation. These commentators point out that storytelling through music is a basic feature of cultural-historical practices among numerous ethnic groupings on the continent; as a result, they claim, opera—which, at its core, is a form of musicalized narrative—is by definition an "African" form.[21]

South African composer Bongani Ndodana-Breen argues that "opera is essentially storytelling, through song and acting, and that has existed in Xhosa culture and all African cultures."[22] Conductor Mandisi Dyantyis, co-music director of South Africa's enormously successful Isango Ensemble, concurs, describing opera as "a story told through singing, dancing and movement. . . . It's to say that this is not a European art form per se, it is an art form for Africa as well. . . . And actually, it comes more natural [*sic*] to tell stories this way for us."[23]

---

[20] Vokwana, "Opera in Africa"; Kofi Agawu, 2001, "Chaka: An Opera in Two Chants," *Research in African Literatures* 32(2), 196–198; Bode Omojola, 2020, "Towards an African Operatic Voice: Composition, Dramaturgy, and Identity Strategies in New Yorùbá Opera," in *African Theatre 19: Opera and Music Theatre*, 107–135; Wole Soyinka, 1999, "African Traditions at Home in the Opera House," *New York Times*, April 25, www.nytimes.com/1999/04/25/arts/african-traditions-at-home-in-the-opera-house.html?searchResultP osition=1; Samuel Kasule, 2020, "'I Smoked Them Out'; Perspectives on the Emergence of Folk Opera or 'Musical Plays' in Uganda," in *African Theatre 19: Opera and Music Theatre*, 183–193; Tobias Robert Klein, 2020, "The Phantom of the West African Opera: A *tour d'horizon*," in *African Theatre 19: Opera and Music Theatre*, 136–158; Sarah Hegenbart, 2020, "Decolonising Opera: Interrogating the Genre of Opera in the Sahel and Other Regions in the Global South." In *"Gefühle sind von Hausa us Rebellen" Musiktheater als Katalysator und Reflexionsagentur für gesellschaftliche Entwicklungsprozesse*, ed. Dominik Frank, Ulrike Hartung, and Kornelius Paede. Würzburg: Königshausen & Neumann, 169–196. x

[21] Mandisi Dyantyis, quoted in Lena Van der Hoven and Liani Maasdorp, 2020, "'Opera Is an Art Form for Everyone': Black Empowerment in the South African Opera Adaptations," *Unogumbe* (2013) and *Breathe—Umphefumlo* (2015), in *African Theatre 19: Opera and Music Theatre*, 52–76; Vokwana, "Opera in Africa"; Agawu, "Chaka"; Omojola, "Towards an African Operatic Voice."

[22] Bongani Ndodana-Breen, quoted in Geoffrey York, 2011, "*Winnie: The Opera*—On Home Turf and Ready for Her Close-Up," *Globe and Mail*, April 22, https://www.theglobeandmail.com/arts/music/win nie-the-opera---on-home-turf-and-ready-for-her-close-up/article597725/. See also Mareli Stolp, 2016, "Van opera tot 'politopera'? Nuwe st?rominge in Suid-Afrikaanse operakomposisie en—resepsie," *LitNet Akademies* 13(1), 138–160.

[23] Dyantyis in Van der Hoven and Maasdorp, "Art Form for Everyone," 56.

Dyantyis and Ndodana-Breen's comments expand a position articulated by Nigerian author Wole Soyinka in 1999, when he maintained that "nothing is more 'natural' than the expression of the adventures of the deities in a medium of music, elliptical dialogue, movement and spectacle, elements central to the Western opera. This alliance of presentation idioms has always been present in traditional African theater, and the contemporary artist merely takes them along the path of stylistic refinements, in some cases borrowing boldly from the artistic idioms of a totally different culture."[24] Soyinka's argument, published in the *New York Times* as a response to the US premiere of Souleymane Koly's composition, *Waramba*, is partly framed as a polemic on the so-called modernization of traditional African cultural forms. But it also draws attention to the similarities between these practices and Western opera. In effect, Soyinka shows that opera should not be considered an interloper on the African continent. Rather, it is an African cultural form, one that may productively be read through Indigenous epistemologies of performative and musicalized oral narration.

These approaches to operatic performance are governed by ideals of organicism, totality, communalism, and the breakdown of traditional distinctions between genre, medium, and form. In an interview with Hilde Roos, celebrated South African author Zakes Mda describes this operatic conception of performance as "Common Festival."[25] Common Festival, Mda argues, does not distinguish between different art forms, but regards them as an integrated and communal expressive register. Mda's comments echo those of Zimbabwean theater historian Praise Zenenga, whose theorization of "African Total Theatre" traces a long tradition of intermedial performance on the continent.[26] Zenenga contrasts the integrative and grassroots nature of such performances with Wagner's more curated imaginary, and again makes a case for a historical approach that foregrounds indigeneity above colonial arrival.[27]

For the time being, the perception of opera as an Indigenous, extra-colonial tradition has especially gained traction among African scholars and practitioners. Scholarship from and about former colonial spheres in the Americas, Asia, or Australia, still appears mainly to favor the colonial genealogy of operatic practice, although Beverly Diamond has made a case for the

[24] Soyinka, "African Traditions."
[25] Hilde Roos, n.d., "In Conversation with Zakes Mda: 'The Full Story Must Be Told,'" *herri* 7, https://herri.org.za/7/hilde-roos/.
[26] Praise Zenenga, 2015, "The Total Theater Aesthetic Paradigm in African Theater," in *The Oxford Handbook of Dance and Theater*, ed. Nadine George-Graves, New York: Oxford University Press, 236–251.
[27] For a comprehensive consideration of the issue of totality, see Chapter 6.

32   Postcolonial Opera

Indigenous potentialities afforded by Australian opera.[28] Diamond describes opera as "a natural outgrowth of storytelling in aboriginal culture," and argues that the art form may therefore be regarded as an appropriate vehicle for the dissemination of aboriginal values and histories.[29] What Diamond's argument and those of the African scholars and practitioners mentioned above have in common is a historical view that privileges the function of opera—constructing a narration with the use of music and visual media—over the Western conventions that attach to the form. In this reading, opera is neither foreign nor oppressive; instead, it is representative of Indigenous cultural practices and identities that predate and have survived beyond colonial rule.

Striking in these comments is the frequency with which the speakers describe Indigenous operatic practice as "natural." Telling stories using music comes naturally to South Africans, says Dyantyis. There is nothing more natural than using a combination of art forms to narrate myths, writes Soyinka. And opera is a natural extension of Indigenous narrative practices, argues Diamond. Operatic practice, they all suggest, is an organic realization of Indigenous people's conceptions of community, gathering, history, and narration. Unlike Western descriptions, which tend to emphasize the genre's artifice, these accounts view opera as an innate cultural behavior.

On the one hand, it is difficult not to detect hints of ethnic essentialism in such descriptions, especially as they seem to align with Eurocentric stereotypes of Indigenous primitivism, irrationality, and artlessness. Indigenous people participate in operatic performance, they suggest, not because they are sophisticated cultural beings, but because their instinct tells them to do so. On the other hand, however, such an interpretation of the authors' statements may itself be regarded as a crude form of exaggeration. It ignores the most important aspect of the alternative history they construct, namely, that Europeans did not invent musical storytelling. Opera's "naturalism" in Indigenous contexts could be interpreted as a reference to the fact that the practice aligns with extra-colonial principles of cultural expression and aesthetic practice. The introduction of what Westerners call "opera" to colonial spheres merely presented another type of musical narration to cultural groupings that were already deeply familiar with the concept. Operatic practice in postcolonial societies may hence be regarded as a reengagement with, or an attempt to recover and reanimate, a performance tradition that predates colonial arrival.

---

[28] Beverly Diamond, 2011, "Decentering Opera: Early Twenty First Century Indigenous Production," in *Opera Indigene: Re/presenting First Nations and Indigenous Cultures*, ed. Pamela Karantonis and Dylan Robinson, Farnham: Ashgate, 31–56.

[29] Diamond, "Decentering Opera," 54.

This interpretation is regularly advanced by composers, singers, and the-ater practitioners hoping to justify the newfound engagement with and cel-ebration of operatic culture among Indigenous communities in postcolonial contexts such as South Africa.[30] They explain that opera is popular among Indigenous people because it slots almost seamlessly into established cultural traditions. As a result, the art form offers valuable opportunities for the nar-ration of Indigenous histories and for encouraging cultural and political self-actualization. In other words, opera returns in the postcolony not as colonial artefact but as Indigenous recovery.

As acknowledged in the Introduction to this volume, however, opera as sig-nifier still invokes conventions and expectations associated specifically with Western European practice. Post- and decolonial scholars including Achille Mbembe and Mark Rifkin are clear on the fact that it is not possible to re-turn to a world untouched by coloniality and modernity.[31] Likewise, it is not possible to return to an imagined precolonial purity of Indigenous musical narration. Postcolonial opera may signify a return to an older performance tradition, but the form remains inflected by the residues of Western opera and its colonial afterlives. If opera is to return, in other words, it cannot but return differently, as the art form has already been changed by colonial encounter. Arrival and return hence collide in a performance genre whose mercurial na-ture is both symptom and cause of its ambiguous place in colonial and anti-colonial histories. In Kentridge's production of *Il Ritorno d'Ulisse in Patria*, this tension manifests as an interplay between estrangement and arrival, natu-ralism and artifice, and history and the present.

Kentridge's *Ulisse*

Kentridge stages *Ulisse* as a dense historical encounter between different periods, places, and cultures. The artist constructs a bilateral view that takes in both Europe and South Africa, both antiquity and the present, thereby cap-turing not only the travels of the opera's subject but also the itinerant nature of contemporary opera performance. The production was first staged at Kunsten Festival des Artes, Brussels, and has since toured in Europe, the United States,

[30] See Ballantine, "South African Political"; Van der Hoven and Maasdorp, "Art Form for Everyone."
[31] Achille Mbembe, 2001, *On the Postcolony*, trans. Laurent Dubois, Los Angeles: University of California Press; Mark Rifkin, 2017, *Beyond Settler Time: Temporal Sovereignty and Indigenous Self-Determination*, Durham, NC: Duke University Press, 6–7. This observation is integral to the discussion in Chapter 4, where I consider it at greater length.

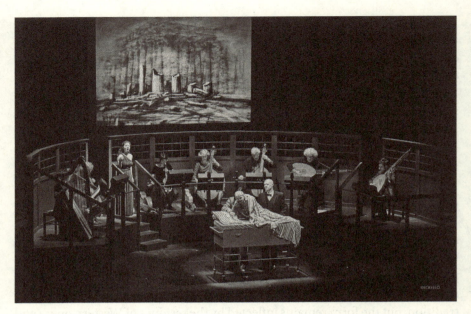

Figure 1.1 The stage setting for Kentridge's production of *Il Ritorno d'Ulisse in Patria*. Photograph: Handspring Puppet Company. Courtesy of William Kentridge Studio.

Asia, Australia, and South Africa. It enjoys regular revivals, most recently at the Hong Kong Arts Festival in March 2023.[32]

In a shrewd convergence between the musical and the medical, Kentridge sets Monteverdi's opera in a seventeenth-century operating theater of the type where public demonstrations on human anatomy were held. The stage comprises a scale replica of such a theater, complete with a mortuary table and raked seating (see Figure 1.1). The seats are occupied by the orchestra, who, facing the audience, simultaneously fulfill the role of spectators. Thus, a kind of theater-in-the-round is constructed, edging the opera even closer to the anatomical display.

Each character is played by three actors: a puppet, a puppeteer, and a singer, all of whom are visible to the audience (see Figure 1.2). Puppet Ulisse lies semi-conscious on the mortuary table. He is not yet dead, but his end is near. The audience witnesses his return to Ithaca as a memory or an illusion, played out in his fading mind. A reduced cast of characters, which includes a second, younger Ulisse but omits Penelope's nurse, Ericlea, and the good-for-nothing Iro, reenact the events surrounding the hero's return. Like Ulisse, these

---

[32] Information on the Hong Kong production is available at https://issuu.com/hkartsfestival/docs/23_ulysses_online_single.

Figure 1.2 Puppet Penelope and the two puppet Ulisses, each accompanied by their puppeteer-singer teams. Photograph: Handspring Puppet Company. Courtesy of William Kentridge Studio.

characters are portrayed by Handspring Puppet Company's characteristic figures, beautifully carved from wood and slightly smaller than life-size. The puppeteers and singers responsible for bringing these wooden performers to life never look at the audience. Instead, each puppeteer-singer team focuses exclusively on their puppet, channeling their own agency through the inanimate object on display.

Behind the puppets, a screen bears Kentridge's signature black and white projections. The video backdrop scrolls through anatomical drawings, reconstructed medical scans, burned-out buildings, and the scorched landscape of post-apartheid Johannesburg. A section of the material is recognizable from Kentridge's animated film, *History of the Main Complaint* (1996), which forms part of the artist's *Drawings for Projection* series.[33] The film depicts Soho Eckstein, an affluent, white South African whose wealth derives from the exploitation of Black workers under apartheid. In the fragment reproduced in *Ulisse*, Soho is in the hospital with a group of doctors and specialists gathered around his

---

[33] On *Drawings for Projection*, see Rosalind Krauss, 2000, "'The Rock': William Kentridge's *Drawings for Projection*," *October* 92, 3–35; Beschara Karam, 2014, "William Kentridge's Animated *Drawings for Projection* as Postmemorial Aesthetic," *De arte* 49(90), 4–23.

36 Postcolonial Opera

bed. Through a visualization of the comatose Soho's dreams or hallucinations, the audience relives a series of events the protagonist experiences while driving. Soho sees a Black man violently beaten in the road. A moment later, another Black man runs in front of his car and is killed. The film switches between the scenes on the street and images of Soho's insides, including his lungs, heart, and brain. As Soho stares into his rearview mirror, the guilt and terror of his accident appear to consume him, until he wakes with a start.[34]

Given the correspondence between Soho's incapacitated state and that of Ulisse, it is not unreasonable to infer that Kentridge here implies a conflation of the two figures. Soho's dreams or recollections also belong to Ulisse. Thus, Monteverdi's character becomes an ancient, operatic pre-incarnation of Kentridge's white South African subject. As if visited one last time by the ghosts of his past, the ailing Ulisse imagines Penelope's suffering at his prolonged absence; he recalls his return to Ithaca and his transformation into an old beggar; his reappearance at Penelope's court; his defeat of the buffoonish suitors vying for his wife's hand; and his and Penelope's eventual, joyful reunion. But he also recalls the horrors of apartheid and his complicity in Black suffering. He is both the hero of Homer's epic and the privileged white protagonist of a history of racialized oppression.

Rachel Fensham interprets Ulisse's journey in Kentridge's production as "a kind of postoperative delirium of the modern white subject."[35] The post-apartheid Ulisse, dying as he comes to terms with his own complicity in the terrors of the past, emerges as a version of the postcolonizing subject I describe in the Introduction. Tethered to Europe even as he dwells in the former colony, the postcolonizing subject feels the lasting effects of the colonial project, not as victim but as beneficiary. Ulisse's hallucinatory subjectivity is split between the imperial center to which his race and his heritage bind him and the postcolonial sphere in which he has sought to make his home.

Kentridge himself recalls that he wished the audience to remain aware of the opera's different layers of historical and geographical signification. He describes his production as "a seventeenth-century Venetian text based on a story from Greece, from three thousand years ago, performed, say, in a European city, by manipulators from South Africa in the twenty-first century, with singers from other parts of the world who don't look necessarily like

---

[34] See Jessica Dubow and Ruth Rosengarten, 2004, "History as the Main Complaint: William Kentridge and the Making of Post-Apartheid South Africa," *Art History* 27(4), 671–690, for a detailed discussion of *History of the Main Complaint*. Rachel Fensham, 2008, "Operating Theatres: Body-Bits and a Post-Apartheid Aesthetics," in *Anatomy Live: Performance and the Operating Theatre*, ed. Maaike Bleeker, Amsterdam: Amsterdam University Press, 251–261, describes the correspondence between *History of the Main Complaint* and *Ulisse*'s video backdrop.

[35] Fensham, "Operating Theatres," 255.

the puppets at all."[36] The juxtaposition between these divergent historical and geographical contexts is negotiated on the backdrop, where images of Soho/Ulisse's post-apartheid South Africa are interspersed with references to ancient Greece. City streets alternate with ruined temples; the infrastructures of South African industry yield to drawings of Hellenic columns. The bilateral gaze constructed in this juxtaposition of time and place sets up a dialogue between the opera's European roots and its South African realization. Each sphere comes more clearly into view by being contrasted with its opposite, reminding audience and performer alike that the operatic moment inhabits a multitude of physical and symbolic territories. In *Ulisse*, then, the interplay of historical, geographical, and cultural signifiers serves especially to process the association between Europe and South Africa, or between imperial metropole and former colony.

Postcolonial Con-text

Kentridge's fusion of a European canonical work with South African actualities is not new. Before *Ulisse*, the artist collaborated with Handspring on several theater pieces based on European texts. These include *Woyzeck on the Highveld* (1992), based on Georg Büchner's unfinished play, *Woyzeck* (1837), *Faustus in Africa!* based on Goethe's *Faust* (1829), and *Ubu and the Truth Commission* (1997), which incorporates the character of Ubu from Alfred Jarry's *Ubu Roi* (1896). Kentridge again turns to a European text with his 2001–2002 opera, *Confessions of Zeno*, based on Italo Svevo's 1923 novel of the same name.[37] More recent stage works such as *Refuse the Hour* (2012), *Triumphs & Laments* (2016), and *The Head & the Load* (2018) are not based explicitly on existing works, but they incorporate a wide range of sonic and visual references to European material, some more recognizable than others. Often treated in fragmentary or subversive ways, these pieces generate webs of meaning that are at once bewildering and revealing. Kentridge's intertexts represent not only the artist's vast and sophisticated cultural vocabulary but also the multifarious affordances of apparently simple references. They complicate the relationships between different contexts, content, and media.

Local adaptations of European cultural products are popular among South African theater and opera practitioners. Kentridge's collaborations with Handspring form part of a distinct trend in South African performance to

---

[36] Taylor and Kentridge, "In Dialogue," 198.
[37] I discuss *Confessions of Zeno* in Chapter 2.

38 Postcolonial Opera

fuse Western canonical works with local contexts and traditions. In opera alone, several productions staged in the last thirty years have sought to dress European works in what Andrew Olsen calls an "African jacket."[38] Since 1994, works such as Puccini's *La Bohème* (Cape Performing Arts Board [CAPAB]), 1998; Isango Ensemble, 2008, Verdi's *Macbeth* (Cape Town Opera [CTO]), 2001), Purcell's *Dido and Aeneas* (CTO, 2002), Bizet's *Carmen* (Isango Ensemble, 2005), Mozart's *Die Zauberflöte* (Isango Ensemble, 2007), and Britten's *Noye's Fludde* (Isango Ensemble, 2013) have all undergone localizing makeovers, with various degrees of success. Localizing techniques have run the gamut from relocating the action to South African settings to recomposing the score for Indigenous instruments. In some cases, performers and producers translated the libretto into local languages, while in others they created entirely new scripts. The nature and extent of these changes were in part determined by the productions' intended audiences. Some of these works were produced specifically for local spectators in a bid to make opera "more familiar" to a South African audience. Others, however, appear to have been produced specifically with an eye on international circulation, with opera companies touring their transformed productions to festivals and theaters in the United States and Europe.[39]

Kentridge's *Ulisse* falls somewhere between the straightforward reproduction of a Western work and its complete adaptation or localization. The score is edited to reduce the length of the production, but it is not adapted for South African instruments or ears. The storyline remains the same, with the omission of Iro's secondary plot having little impact on the main narrative. Only the setting—specifically the video backdrop—incorporates references to South Africa. These visual gestures appear as commentary rather than signifying the opera's relocation to an Indigenous context. In other words, apart from cosmetic changes, Kentridge's production of *Ulisse* remains faithful to Monteverdi's original. Nonetheless, I do regard the project as a form of adaptation: with its incorporation of diverse historical and political subject positions, Kentridge's version of the work generates new meanings, not only in relation to the narrative but also pertaining to the structure and function of the opera itself. It develops a critical perspective on the role of Greek myth, of Homer, of opera, and of Monteverdi in South Africa. Thus, Kentridge's *Ulisse* becomes a version of what Thieme calls the postcolonial con-text.

---

[38] Andrew Olsen, 2012, "Mozart's African Jacket: *Die Zauberflöte* and Its Localisation in *The Magic Flute (Impempe Yomlingo)*," *Journal of the Musical Arts in Africa* 9(1), 67–80.

[39] Hilde Roos's PhD dissertation, "Opera Production in the Western Cape: Strategies in Search of Indigenisation," Stellenbosch University, 2010, offers the most incisive account to date of South African operatic adaptation.

Thieme bases his idea of the postcolonial con-text on the notion of "writing back," first theorized by Bill Ashcroft, Gareth Griffiths, and Helen Tiffin.[40] Postcolonial con-texts, Thieme writes, are "postcolonial texts that engage in direct, if ambivalent, dialogue with the canon by virtue of responding to a classic English text."[41] While Thieme focuses on texts that react to the English canon specifically, the concept of the con-text may usefully be extended to include postcolonial responses to other cultural and linguistic canons as well. Other terms for the same phenomenon may be writing back, counter-discourse, or oppositional literature.[42] Postcolonial con-texts are, in other words, literary (or other) products that originate from pre-existing, Western canonical works or genres but adapt these originals to new times, places, or perspectives. The resulting products are turned back onto their origins as distorted mirror images. Postcolonial con-texts thus generate an exchange between the canon and its outsides, between Europe and its others, and between convention and its subversion.

Con-texts are, significantly, not only intended for consumption in the postcolony; they are also meant for export (or return) to the former metropole. Postcolonial con-texts do not therefore circulate as part of a project of local edification or introduction to the "classics of the West." On the contrary, they serve to complicate notions of "the classic," and of where such classics can or should hail from, whose voices they should sound, and which histories they should tell. Postcolonial con-texts often appropriate existing narratives or forms and refigure them, either to reveal the neglected perspective of the colonial subaltern or to undermine the authority of the canon. Sending these narratives back into the metropole, authors of postcolonial con-texts promote a confrontation between the accepted truths of the original and the mutinous counterclaims of the spinoff. Con-texts hence enter the colonial center as estranged versions of what used to be familiar. As the prefix "con" suggests, they enact a mode of subterfuge that undercuts the stability of canonical certainties. Just as Ulisse arrives back in Ithaca in a new guise, the works signified by the postcolonial con-text return disguised, barely recognizable beneath the changes they underwent during their travels.

If the postcolonial con-text enables a destabilizing response to the hegemony of Western canonical perspective, however, it also runs the risk of reinforcing such hegemony. Written in opposition to the codes of Empire, the con-text's structures, meanings, and practices end up being determined by the

---

[40] Ashcroft, Griffiths, and Tiffin, *Empire Writes Back*.
[41] Thieme, *Postcolonial Con-texts*, 4.
[42] Thieme, *Postcolonial Con-Texts*, 1.

40 Postcolonial Opera

original. As a result, the response may end up replicating the very terms it seeks to resist.[43] Put differently, in the act of negation, the postcolonial context threatens to reinforce the binary structure of "European" and "other," "oppression" and "resistance," "norm" and "not-norm."

To avoid this unproductive tension between hegemony and counter-hegemony, it is helpful to approach con-texts not as oppositional works, but as alternatives, reimaginings, and transformations. In Kentridge's practice, such an attitude emerges clearly from the artist's ambivalent engagement with European citation.[44] Kentridge does not present Western cultural signifiers as the malevolent antithesis of local practices. Instead, the artist's works often summon a very real sense of the beauty of these intertexts. But it is a contingent beauty, situated in and complicated by the shadow of exclusionary histories. From this perspective, Kentridge's *Ulisse* functions not as the antithesis of Homer and Monteverdi, but as a way of thinking the narrative, or its constitutive traditions, differently. It is a transformation constituted by simultaneous embrace and refusal.

The transformations visited upon Kentridge's postcolonial con-texts have a defamiliarizing effect. Once subjected to conversion and reimagination, the texts no longer exist as European signifiers belonging to Europe; nor are they, however, altered in a way that renders them completely at home in the postcolony. Consequently, they become estranged from both. In *Ulisse*, the juxtaposition of South African scenes with ancient Roman material generates a fractured formal and narrative frame, which always seems to include something that does not belong, or which is about to be lost. Neither here nor there, the piece appears as a stranger to both the European and the South African context.

For Liviu Dospinescu, however, Kentridge's approach to Western cultural products embeds them in, rather than estranges them from, both the South African and the European context. Dospinescu argues that the original text undergoes such profound alterations in Kentridge's hands that "it engenders a mutation that places it almost 'naturally' in this south African territory. . . . The original text is transited, crossed by content which is foreign to it and which is 'grafted' onto the old ones without undergoing 'rejection.'"[45] Again, the relationship between the work and the South African context is framed in organic terms. Kentridge's transformations of European canonical texts

---

[43] Thieme, *Postcolonial Con-Texts*, 31.

[44] See Dan Cameron, 1999, "A Procession of the Dispossessed," in *William Kentridge*, ed. Dan Cameron, Carolyn Christov-Bakargiev, and J.M. Coetzee, London: Phaidon Press, 36–81.

[45] Liviu Dospinescu, 2006, "Vers un nouveau théâtre politique: William Kentridge et les discours transculturels." *ANADISS* 2(2), 95–116, at 114. Translation my own.

are successful, Dospinescu appears to argue, because they forge a "natural" link between the works and their new context. The result is a new original, a reconfigured point of reference or something approaching a "mythical structure"—one that belongs both in Europe and in South Africa.[46] Dospinescu reads in Kentridge's fusion of South African subjectivity with the Eurocentric operatic object a "theatrical syncretism" that, following Christopher Balme, neither denies nor idealizes the European originary. In Dospinescu's interpretation, the transcultural impulse of Kentridge's *Ulisse* enacts a theatrical politics that naturalizes Monteverdi's opera as local form, even as it acknowledges the foreign inheritance of the work.

Dospinescu's assessment that Kentridge's mutations place European works "naturally" in the South African territory appears to dismiss the obvious signs of these creations' displacement. If anything, the signifiers of European settlement and cultural-industrial self-assertion appear uncomfortable or incongruent in Kentridge's South African scenery. Communication technologies such as screens, cables, and transmission devices (the gramophone and the megaphone are favorites) dot the artist's depictions of a local landscape decimated by modernity. The idealized artifacts of Western cultural sophistication enter Kentridge's animations as fragments or strays: a Mozart aria rings out during a rhinoceros hunt; a ballet dancer crosses a rocky plain; a trio of suited men balance atop a staircase in a rugged field.[47] These signifiers become part of the South African context, but in a peculiar way. They nod to a foreign historical and geographical sphere, recognizable particularly to those familiar with Western artistic traditions. Put differently, these signifiers are "natural" specifically to South Africans with a knowledge of and embeddedness in European culture. From an Indigenous perspective, in contrast, Kentridge's European signifiers are artificial implantations, no more natural than the piles of mining waste that distort the contours of the South African highveld. Consequently, Kentridge's European signifiers capture something of the position of the postcolonizing subject, who attaches various cultural histories and identities to herself and seeks to maintain them in a kind of balance that does not result in rejection from either sphere.[48]

The transformations Kentridge visits upon his European originals are ambiguous. They gesture to "naturalization" or "localization," but they never fulfill this promise. Enacting both an arrival and a return, Kentridge's intertextual adaptations enter Western canonical works into the South African

---

[46] Dospinescu, "Nouveau théâtre," 114.

[47] The art works I reference here are *Black Box/Chambre Noire* (2005); *Notes Towards a Model Opera* (2015); and *The Embarkation Triptych* (1987).

[48] I discuss the implications of such a split gaze for the postcolonizing subject in Chapter 2.

sphere before turning these signifiers back onto Europe, albeit in altered form. Thus, the artist's creations become postcolonial con-texts, drawing on and responding to the cultural artifacts of empire.

In *Ulisse*, Kentridge fashions his con-text by means of estrangement and artifice. First, the artist effects an estrangement of subject matter: juxtaposing references to Europe, ancient Greece, and South Africa, Kentridge turns Ulisse into a stranger to each of these places—a portrayal consistent with Homer's own characterization of his drifting protagonist. Second, the production relies on the scenographic evocation of the operating theater to achieve an estrangement of form: Monteverdi's opera is rendered neither as Indigenous African performance nor in the conventional codes of Western opera. Rather, it is presented as a form of medical examination or autopsy—an excavation of biological essence effected by song. Thus, the opera crosses the boundary from art to science. Finally, Kentridge achieves an estrangement of embodied performance through his use of puppets. Delivered by a human singer but always mediated through the blank façade of a roughly hewn wooden figure, the opera's songs become artificial enactments of a form perched between the familiar and the strange.

Estranged Bodies

Puppets are no stranger to opera. When Kentridge stages his *Ulisse* for inanimate, human-like figures, he draws on an established Western operatic practice stretching back to early seventeenth-century Venice.[49] But puppet performance also invokes longer traditions of ritual theater and puppetry external to the West. Handspring's practice is inspired especially by the Japanese Bunraku tradition, where puppeteers are visible and ordered according to strict, hierarchical conventions.[50] Whereas Bunraku insists on a highly stylized performance practice, however, the South African company nourishes a more lifelike approach to puppets' gestures, steered especially by a unique focus on breath.[51] Handspring's puppets also connect to histories

[49] Martin Nedbal, 2012, "Live Marionettes and Divas on the Strings: *Die Zauberflöte*'s Interactions with Puppet Theater," *Opera Quarterly* 28(1–2), 20–36, at 22. See also Hayley Fenn, 2021, "Puppets that Sing or Scenery that Breathes: Phelim McDermott's Satyagraha," in *Experiencing Music and Visual Cultures: Threshold, Intermediality, Synchresis*, London: Routledge, 64–78.

[50] Yvette Hutchison, 2010, "The 'Dark Continent' Goes North: An Exploration of Intercultural Theatre Practice through Handspring and Sogolon Puppet Companies' Production of *Tall Horse*," *Theatre Journal* 62(1), 57–73, at 62.

[51] For Bunraku, see Haruka Okui, 2020, "Deformation of the Human Body: Bunraku Puppetry Technique and the Collaborative Body Schema," *Chiasmi International* 22, 351–366; for Handspring's approach to puppets and breath, see Basil Jones, 2014, "Puppetry, Authorship and the Ur-Narrative," in *The*

of African puppetry, especially from Western and Central African countries, where the form remains part of the same traditions of communal performance that give rise to operatic modes of musical storytelling. These include the *kwagh-hir* tradition of Nigeria's Tiv people, Bamana *sogo bò* in Mali, and the *Gelede* tradition of the Yoruba of Nigeria, Benin and Togo.[52]

Despite its prevalence across the African continent, puppetry is not indigenous to South Africa. In fact, puppets, like Western opera, came to South Africa on colonial ships.

Marie Kruger points out that documented evidence of puppetry in South Africa first appears around the same time that European opera arrives in the country.[53] Rather than participating in histories of African communal performance, in other words, South African puppet theater signifies a continuation of colonial practices. Its presence in postcolonial South Africa most immediately evokes the legacy of cultural colonialism. But it also points to encounters between Western European and non-Western theater traditions. Along with other workshop-style theater practices, puppetry has become part of a new repertoire of local cultural traditions. At present, the genre is especially popular in grassroots contexts, where it contributes to adult education initiatives, communal performance projects, and youth empowerment schemes. Puppet theater integrates different forms of creative expression, including acting, voice art, and handicraft. Its multidisciplinary structure interacts readily with the African narrative performance traditions described above. Capable of embodying local theatrical epistemologies, the art form thus integrates the conventions of Western puppet opera with Indigenous performance.[54]

Simultaneously, puppet opera brings into dialogue a range of distinct philosophical orientations. Some of these philosophies are characteristic of Western thinking; others invoke Indigenous worldviews. From a Southern African perspective, the interdependence between puppet, puppeteer, and singer in Kentridge's *Ulisse* appears to represent the humanist philosophy of *Ubuntu*. Derived from the expression, *Umuntu umuntu ngabantu* (a person is a person

---

Routledge Companion to Puppetry and Material Performance, ed. Dassia N. Posner, Claudia Orenstein, and John Bell, London and New York: Routledge, 61–68.

[52] Marie Kruger, 2010, "Social Dynamics in African Puppetry," *Contemporary Theatre Review* 20(3), 316–328; Kruger, 2009, "The Relationship between Theatre and Ritual in the *Sogo bò* of the Bamana from Mali," *New Theatre Quarterly* 25(3), 233–240; Frances Harding, 1998, "'To Present the Self in a Special Way': Disguise and Display in Tiv *Kwagh-hir* Performance," *African Arts* 31(1), 56–67.

[53] Marie Kruger, 2011, "Puppets and Adult Entertainment in South Africa: A Tale of a Tentative Start, Evolving Prejudices, New and Lost Opportunities, and a Fresh Momentum," *South African Theatre Journal* 25(1), 13–34; also Kruger, "Social Dynamics"; Mineke Schipper, 1982, *Theatre and Society in Africa*, trans. Ampie Coetzee, Johannesburg: Ravan Press.

[54] For more on contemporary South African puppetry and its adoption by different social groupings, see Kruger, "Puppets and Adult Entertainment."

44 Postcolonial Opera

because of/through other people), the term "emphasizes that our true human potential can only be realized in partnership with others."[55] Widely rehearsed during the Truth and Reconciliation hearings of 1996–1998, *Ubuntu* stressed a "stronger together"-style collectivism that encouraged South Africans to set aside their differences and work together toward national healing and reconciliation after apartheid. In *Ulisse*, the Afrocentric humanism of this orientation is aesthetically realized. Inseparable from one another, the triumvirate of puppet, puppeteer, and singer articulates a political agency that emerges only from the dissolution of the individual. The distributed subjectivity of the puppet-actors hence undermines Enlightenment constructions of individuality, independence, and self-determination: each participant is no more than a constituent part of a larger whole, represented, if not determined, by a wooden face and limbs.

For Kenneth Gross, the same interaction between puppet and puppeteer may also be understood in Western philosophical terms conditioned by debates around free will and determinism. Gross's description of Kentridge's *Ulisse* asserts that the configuration of puppets, puppeteers, and singers "made it so that the opera became an account of how any of us, in truth and dream, moves through the world, vulnerable to, even isolated by, the very forces that move us, that give us life and will, including the forces of fantasy."[56] Responding to Enlightenment constructions of individual self-determination, Gross argues that Kentridge's *Ulisse* constructs a cast of individuals unable to control their destiny. Whereas the *ubuntu* reading exchanges individuality for community, and free will for collectivism, Gross's interpretation emphasizes that humans exist in the singular, but that their fate remains in the hands of the gods. For Gross, Kentridge's use of puppets hence performs a literal enactment of the opera's Prologue, a meditation by the allegorical figures of Time, Fortune, Love, and Human Frailty on the fact that humans exist at the mercy of uncontrollable forces:

Human Frailty
A mortal thing am I, in human form:
everything distresses me, a puff of wind can fell me;
Time who created me also fights against me.

---

[55] Mvuselelo Ngcoya, 2015, "Ubuntu: Toward an Emancipatory Cosmopolitanism?," *International Political Sociology* 9(3), 248–262, at 253. Though *Ubuntu* is similar to communitarianism, Ngcoya argues that the two philosophies are distinct due to the former's focus on what it means to be human, which precedes the latter's primary preoccupation with legal rights (255).

[56] Kenneth Gross, 2012, *Puppet: An Essay on Uncanny Life*, Chicago: University of Chicago Press, 81.

Time
Nothing is safe
from my bite.
It gnaws
and delights in it.
Flee not, mortals,
for though I limp, I have wings.

Human Frailty
A mortal thing am I, in human form:
in vain do I seek a place safe from dangers,
for frail life is a plaything of Fortune.

Fortune
Desires, joys
and sorrows are my life.
I'm blind, I'm deaf,
I see not, I hear not;
riches and greatness
I distribute according to my fancy.

Human Frailty
A mortal thing am I, in human form:
my green and fleeting youth
is enslaved to tyrannical Cupid.

Cupid
The world calls me, Cupid, the god who pierces gods.
A blind, winged, nude marksman,
no defence or shield is of any avail against my arrow.

Human Frailty
Wretched I am indeed, in human form:
to believe the blind and the lame is a vain thing.

Time
Through me frail

Fortune
Through me wretched

Cupid
Through me distressed

Time, Fortune, Cupid
This man will be.[57]

In Monteverdi's prologue, Human Frailty is subject to the caprices of its more formidable companions, Time, Fortune, and Love. Together, the four allegorical forces create an image of humans as puppets, powerless against the unpredictable whims of fate. Handspring's wooden creations, controlled by their puppeteer-singer masters, realize physically the determinism articulated at the opera's outset. Perched at the interface between determinism and agency, the puppet navigates the irresistible external forces that steer its movements—a compelling metaphor for the political, socio-economic, and cultural dynamics that confound ideals of human self-determination. Thus, they highlight not only the tensions between modernity and spirituality in Enlightenment Europe but also the collision between Western individualism and extra-colonial humanist values.[58]

Kentridge's use of puppets also fulfills a metacritical function. According to Hayley Fenn, the synthesis between opera and puppetry may "reframe certain central tenets" of the art form by disrupting conventions of embodied human performance and by drawing attention to artifice, imagination, and spectacle.[59] In other words, puppets challenge those features of opera that are normally taken for granted—the congruence of singer and actor, or voice and body; the ideal of liveness, or at the very least a-liveness; the quest for believability, or at least for a suspension of disbelief. In puppet opera, the constructedness of the operatic scenario is placed front and center, impossible to ignore. There is no way, the puppets appear to say, of mistaking this for reality.

In Handspring's practice, the artifice of the puppet performance is underscored by the fact that the puppeteers appear onstage with the puppets. For Kentridge, the visibility of Handspring's puppeteers is an essential and appealing part of their practice. Responding to Geoffrey Davis and Anne Fuchs's observation that the visibility of the "actual mechanics of the manipulation"

---

[57] Claudio Monteverdi, 2018 [1640], *Il Ritorno d'Ulisse in Patria* [liner note], dir. John Eliot Gardiner, libretto translated by Boston Baroque, London: Monteverdi Productions, 45–46.

[58] See Hayley Fenn, 2019, "Big Marionette, Little Marionette," *The Opera Quarterly* 35(4), 335–349, at 339, for a discussion of puppets as representatives of the tension between free will and determinism.

[59] Fenn, "Puppets that Sing," at 65.

creates an "alienation effect" based on the fact that the "illusion of the puppets" is broken, Kentridge argues that the visibility of the puppeteers in fact enhances the believability of the puppets, by affording greater sympathy for their limitations:

> No, even when you don't see the manipulators, one is very much aware that these are not live people and that these are puppets you are watching. When you actually see the manipulators with them, in a way you are usually able to accommodate their awkwardnesses and the things they can't do. . . . [A]lthough one's very aware, and sees quite clearly the artifice and how it's all done, how the manipulation is done and where the voices are coming from, nonetheless essentially one's attention is on that puppet as the agent of the play.[60]

What Kentridge describes is an act of looking whereby the puppet is infused with a "life force" external to itself.[61] The audience knows that the actions performed by the puppet are initiated by a human manipulator and that the puppet itself is a lifeless object devoid of agency and emotion. Nonetheless, in the act of looking, the audience idealizes the object-puppet as a subject with a will and a sense of self. In the audience's eyes, in other words, the puppet is both object and subject, both thing and being, both dead and alive. Or, as Kenneth Gross writes, the puppet is "a composite or double body, animate and inanimate at once."[62]

Kentridge's interest in the suspension of disbelief required by puppet opera is characteristic of the artist's practice. He regularly professes his fascination with the process whereby people make sense of the world, including how they find meaning in images, and how they allow—or even will—themselves to be deceived. In a favorite anecdote, Kentridge recounts how he watched a magician transform soap bubbles into glass baubles. The performer would blow soap bubbles, then smash them with a hammer, at which point they shattered as if made of glass. Having demonstrated the magical transformation several times, the actor revealed a small bell hidden between his clothes. At each hammer blow, he would ring the bell, thus creating an auditory illusion of breaking glass. Despite knowing how the magic happened, however,

---

[60] Kentridge, in Geoffrey Davis and Anne Fuchs, 1996, "'An Interest in the Making of Things': An Interview with William Kentridge," in *Theatre and Change in South Africa*, ed. sGeoffrey Davis and Anne Fuchs, Amsterdam: Harwood, 140–153, at 148.

[61] I borrow the term from Fenn, who in turn adopts it from Eileen Blumenthal. Fenn, "Puppets that Sing," 67.

[62] Gross, *Puppet*, 55.

48   Postcolonial Opera

Kentridge observes that the audience could not stop the bubbles from turning to glass:

> And the extraordinary thing was that you could see what he was doing. You could see it was a bell and a soap bubble, but you could not stop yourself still believing it was glass. . . . It made me understand the pleasure of self-deception we have where you see how it's done, but the thing being done is stronger than you are.[63]

The interplay between deception and revelation Kentridge describes here captures something of the duality of the performing puppet's presence on stage. Despite the visibility of its mechanics, the puppet convinces the audience to view it as human. And the audience does so, with a willingness that reveals the delight of make-believe.

This twofold apprehension—what Steve Tillis calls "double vision"—suggests a suspension of disbelief not unlike that required in traditional opera, with its trouser roles and sung conversations and belting heroines at death's door. Like the almost-human-but-not-quite puppets, the more-than-human singers of traditional opera challenge the audience to view them as both agents and pawns, both people and players, both emoting subjects and performing objects. Puppetry, in other words, underscores the artifice of the operatic performance and reminds the audience that they are engaged in an act of co-creation; that they are as responsible as the performers for awarding life and veracity to the scene playing out in front of them.

If the visual aspect of puppet opera invites the audience member to project humanity onto an inanimate object, the sonic aspect does something more ambivalent. The genre's reliance on the singing voice complicates the implied subjectivity of the puppet. Forceful and overwhelming, operatic voice seems to exceed the capabilities of the human. It is a product generated by an interplay between technique, training, and the machinery of a physique ideally conditioned for sound production. Despite the fact that it emerges from a human body, the operatic voice sounds like the voice of an automaton. It is strange, superhuman, and refined to a level of mechanical perfection.[64] In other words, operatic voice is itself a kind of non-human human. It seems to represent a kind of mechanized identity, one belonging to a person/thing that

---

[63] Kentridge, 2022, "To What End: A Visual Lecture by William Kentridge," Berkeley Art Museum and Pacific Film Archive, https://www.youtube.com/watch?v=iWy45ahrTtI. The anecdote also appears in Kentridge, 2001, "The Art of William Kentridge," *Transition* 10(4), 85–86; and Dan Cameron, 2001, "An Interview with William Kentridge," in *William Kentridge*, ed. Michel Sittenfeld, Chicago: Museum of Contemporary Art, 67–74.

[64] Lawrence Kramer, 2014, "The Voice of/in Opera," in *On Voice*, ed. Walter Bernhart and Lawrence Kramer, Amsterdam: Rodopi, 43–58, at 45.

resembles a human but is not conditioned by the limitations of human speech. For Steven Connor, puppets materialize the plausible bodies from which operatic voice could emanate.[65] Put differently, operatic voice seems to be the voice of a puppet.

But, as philosophers including Adriana Cavarero and Stanley Cavell observe, voice also represents interiority and subjectivity. A person with a voice is a person with an identity, a sense of self, and a capacity for agency.[66] When the operatic voices of the performers attach to puppets, they therefore construct a ventriloquistic identity for each wooden figure. In Gross's view, the voice projected onto the puppet gives it a kind of interiority and makes it human. Capable of sound, the puppet transitions from thing to being. But, as Fenn argues, this transformation is unstable. Even as it sounds, the puppet never becomes the owner of its voice. "Whilst the voice becomes part of the puppet's identity," Fenn writes, "it remains the possession of the puppeteer, actor or singer and, therefore, fundamentally disembodied."[67] Operatic voice simultaneously endows the puppet with identity and robs her of it. Puppet opera hence problematizes the traditional relationship between body, voice, and identity by constructing a "constant fluctuation between almost otherworldly disembodiment and deep embeddedness within the body."[68]

In the context of Kentridge's *Ulisse* the interiority afforded by voice complicates the relationship between the puppets and their setting. Kentridge places his puppets in an operating theater. The wooden objects, devoid of interiority, find themselves in an environment that is all about the insides of the body. In Fensham's reading, Kentridge's use of puppets and medical imagery stages the "bare life," in Giorgio Agamben's sense, of the postcolonial and post-apartheid subject.[69] Kentridge's operating theater, Fensham argues, revisits colonialism and apartheid's "machinery of dehumanization," which reduced humans to "virtual corpses." Existing only as biology, the opera's puppet performers are the culmination of such bare life. Ulisse gradually collapses into a disposable collection of organs for harvesting and display. Showing, as Fensham writes, that "the interior organs do not . . . discriminate between perpetrators and victims," Ulisse becomes a stand-in for coloniality's

[65] Steven Connor, 2000, *Dumbstruck: A Cultural History of Ventriloquism*, Oxford: Oxford University Press, 35; see also Fenn, "Puppets that Sing," at 68.

[66] Adriana Cavarero, 2005, *For More than One Voice: Toward a Philosophy of Vocal Expression*, Stanford, CA.: Stanford University Press; Stanley Cavell, 1994, *A Pitch of Philosophy: Autobiographical Exercises*, Cambridge: Cambridge University Press.

[67] Fenn, "Puppets that Sing," 68.

[68] Fenn, "Puppets that Sing," 69.

[69] Fensham, "Operating Theatres," 254.

indifference to its subjects.[70] At the moment of death, the hero is no more a person than the thousands of Black bodies subjected to the brutality of the apartheid regime in which he, as white subject, is implicated. Together with the anatomical objects on display, the puppets' disposable bodies estrange the opera from its human origins.

But the operatic voices projected onto the wooden figures complicate their apparent inhumanity. Gross, for instance, maintains that "[in *Ulisse*] you felt each singer's voice as a *gift* of sound, breath, and feeling, passed through the singer into the object."[71] Whereas the opera's staging reduces the puppets to bare life, their voices return them to a state of being that incorporates and exceeds Kentridge's projections of limbs and organs. Gross's reading, then, suggests that song transforms the operatic subjects' existence from "bare life" to "good life."[72] For all their artifice, through voice the puppets appear to recover the humanity of the postcolonial and post-apartheid subject. Exchanging an opera theater for an operating theater, Kentridge's *Ulisse* complicates the various constructions of humanity represented not only by medicine and art but also by coloniality and liberation.

In *Ulisse*, operatic return shifts from cultural movement to political statement. On the one hand, the production's puppets represent the dehumanized victims and the perpetrators of coloniality. On the other, the work's incorporation of voice effects a reanimation of these subjects. Endowed with song, the puppets reenter the realm of culture. Along the way, they invite the spectator to ask how opera bestows humanity upon its subjects, to investigate what kind of humanity this is, and to listen anew to the distributed subjectivities enacted by operatic voice. Handspring's puppets destabilize the Enlightenment individualism associated with European performance and enact, in its place, a dispersed form of self-actualization. The opera's animations, estrangements, and juxtapositions thus distance the genre from its conventional articulations of subjectivity and cultural identity. In place of these conventions, Kentridge constructs a postcolonial con-text that brings colonial theater cultures into direct contact with extra-colonial traditions of communal performance. Kentridge's production of *Ulisse* estranges opera not only from the opera house but also from the assumptions that maintain the form's equivalence with Western culture.

---

[70] Fensham, "Operating Theatres," 257.

[71] Gross, *Puppet*, 81, original emphasis.

[72] Giorgio Agamben, 1998 [1995], *Homo Sacer: Sovereign Power and Bare Life*, trans. Daniel Heller-Roazen, Stanford, CA: Stanford University Press.

Operatic Return

Kentridge's *Ulisse* seems to assert that opera does not "return" comfortably to a changed South Africa. The production performs an ambiguous encounter between precolonial, colonial, and postcolonial practices. Perched at the intersection between Western operatic practice and pre- or extra-colonial conceptions of communal performance, the opera stages an often violent encounter between distinct traditions of humanistic thought and political agency. Its performers, almost human (but not quite), almost alive (but not quite), represent both estrangement and integration, both the bare life of colonial dehumanization and the good life promised by cultural recovery. Belonging, as Gross describes, to "a family of things partial, fragmented, and broken, a family of relics, remnants, and skeletons," the opera's puppets perform an equivocal subjectivity assembled from the residues of colonial exclusion. Simultaneously, however, they gesture toward alternative conceptions of self and other, subject and object, foreigner and friend.

As the production navigates between the European metropole from which *Ulisse* originates, and the South African outpost at which it arrives, it encourages the spectator to ponder the relationship between these two spheres and to reengage with questions of precedence and replication. The aesthetic choices that inform the production may be decoded in different ways to serve distinctive interpretative interests. Puppets, for instance, may be regarded as extensions of Western operatic tradition or as embodiments of Indigenous expressive forms. The South African signifiers on the backdrop may be viewed to represent the home to which the puppet returns, or they may gesture to the faraway locations of his travels. The work may, in other words, submit to competing claims. Crucially, Kentridge does not seek a reconciliation between these interpretations. As with the artist's other reconstructions of European canonical works, *Ulisse* sets up an unresolved encounter between Europe and its other, thereby to draw attention to the unheard voices, the unseen bodies, and the unacknowledged pasts that exist at the margins of these works.

Like its protagonist, Kentridge's *Ulisse* returns in altered form. It is a context, returning Monteverdi's opera to Europe, but with interest. In this sense, the production "writes back" to the imperial metropole with a message that complicates the established histories, solid foundations, and hegemonic departure points of coloniality.[73] It undermines not only the authority of colonial performance but also the supremacy of Ulisse's subjectivity as white

---

[73] Thieme, *Postcolonial Con-Text*, 2.

52 Postcolonial Opera

colonial hero and the idealized construction of Western operatic individualism. Moreover, the production confronts Empire with the results of its destructive ambition, forcing those who consume opera to recognize the form's complicity in colonial subjection.

Beyond these colonial confrontations, the production participates in a second project of return—this one designed to recover musical storytelling's extra-colonial past. Ideals of precolonial performance will, of course, forever remain just that: ideals. In the wake of coloniality, and beset by the remains of post-industrial modernity, cultural purity has become a fantasy. Rather than recovering Indigenous theater practices as exotic, primitivist residues, the return of extra-colonial opera represents a negotiation between past and present, local and global, and nature and artifice. Complicating established ideas around what opera is, where it comes from, and how it circulates in the formerly colonial sphere, operatic return destabilizes Western assumptions about artistic precedence and imitation, or about which is the original, and which the copy.

The tension between operatic arrival and return cannot easily be resolved. It is a matter of perspective, of the conventions that attach to the genre, and of the competing interests served by different interpretations of the past. Looking in both directions at once, opera captures something of the ambiguous position not only of the postcolonizing subject but of all expressive forms touched, somehow, by coloniality. Opera may be Western. It may also be Indigenous. Bringing these accounts into dialogue with each other offers an opportunity to generate compelling perspectives on the notion of an Indigenous operatic tradition that nonetheless participates in the networks and structures of postcolonial modernity. Postcolonial operatic con-texts such as Kentridge's *Ulisse* exceed the constraints of the form and push back against existing narratives of operatic circulation. Engaged, like Penelope with her quilt, in an endless process of restarting and remaking, postcolonial opera allows both history and the present to remain open-ended. As the art form faces new challenges and encounters new stories, it resists the finality of conclusion which, as for Penelope, may entail attaching itself to a single idea(l) against its will. Navigating distinctions between African and European opera, but somehow managing to remain tethered to both, the postcolonial operatic con-text returns, and returns, and returns.

2
Confession

"Western man [*sic*]," writes Michel Foucault in 1976, "has become a confessing animal."[1] Conditioned by religious, judicial, medical, and even social structures that prioritize self-revelation as a device of personal accountability and care, Foucault's Western subject participates in a confessional regime that governs both the private and the public spheres. Confession is everywhere—in politics and entertainment, self-help and social media. In opera, too, it has long been a favored theme. As Olivia Bloechl argues, the art form's theatricalization of individual struggle, combined with its idealization of the singing voice as a symbol of interiority and authenticity, lends it to performances of confession.[2]

For the colonial and postcolonial subject, however, confessional discourse is more complicated. Situated within a historical and geographical context marked by contradictory and often treacherous constructions of veracity, complicity, guilt, and justice, (post)colonial confession, as Frantz Fanon has shown, fulfills a political function closely aligned with practices of imperial power and control.[3] In the postcolony, confession risks reinforcing colonial conventions of social, political, and judicial administration. It may also reiterate easy assumptions about the nature and extent of personal responsibility as well as the colonial and postcolonial subject's capacity for truth and accountability.

In the context of post-apartheid South Africa, confession cannot be separated from the proceedings of the Truth and Reconciliation Commission (TRC), with its monumental admissions of guilt and even greater acts of forgiveness. Like opera, then, confession represents a set of values and meanings in the postcolonial and post-apartheid spheres that differs from (and ultimately expands on) its Western significations. When these discursive regimes come together—as they do in Kentridge's fifth collaboration with Handspring

---

[1] Michel Foucault, 1990 [1976], *The History of Sexuality: Vol. 1, An Introduction*, trans. Robert Hurley, New York: Pantheon Books, 59.

[2] Olivia Bloechl, 2019, *Opera and the Political Imaginary in Old Regime France*, Chicago: University of Chicago Press, esp. Chapter 3.

[3] Frantz Fanon, 2014, "The Conduct of Confession in North Africa," in *Decolonizing Madness: The Psychiatric Writings of Frantz Fanon*, ed. Nigel Gibson, New York: Palgrave Macmillan, 87–89.

Postcolonial Opera. Juliana M. Pistorius, Oxford University Press. © Oxford University Press 2025.
DOI: 10.1093/oso/9780197749203.003.0003

54 Postcolonial Opera

Puppet Company, *Confessions of Zeno* (2001–2002)—several questions arise regarding the meaning of confessional performance in the postcolony and about opera's participation in such performances.[4]

Confessions of Zeno is based on Italian author Italo Svevo's 1923 novel, *La Coscienza di Zeno*, a psychoanalytic examination of the bourgeois European individual at the turn of the twentieth century. Set in the Austrian (soon to become Italian) town of Trieste, the novel narrates a series of autobiographical confessions authored by Zeno Cosini, a Triestine businessman, on the advice of his psychoanalyst. Kentridge's adaptation, with a libretto by Jane Taylor and score by Kevin Volans, transposes portions of *La Coscienza di Zeno* into a multimedia form that incorporates opera, spoken theater, shadow puppetry, live and pre-recorded film projections, and music for string quartet and tape (see ▶ Clip 2.1). Like the novel, *Zeno* explores themes of revelation, accountability, and guilt in a performance that simultaneously underscores and complicates the legitimacy of the confessional regime in the postcolony.

Zeno was the first of Kentridge's original theater pieces in which live music played an important structural role. Though his first three Handspring collaborations incorporated substantial amounts of recorded music, it was only with *Ulisse* that Kentridge began to integrate his animated process with a live score. But whereas *Ulisse* was a ready-composed product, *Zeno* offered an opportunity to experiment with different approaches to music, theater, and genre.

Like most of the pieces under discussion in this book, *Zeno* is formally ambiguous. It incorporates spoken word, tape recordings, operatic singing, dancing, shadow projections, and a string quartet. From a Western musicological perspective, it is certainly not traditional opera—indeed, Volans himself rejects such a classification.[5] As I explain in the Introduction, however, I choose to regard *Zeno*, like Kentridge's other works that rely on music as a key structural signifier, as opera. This approach not only offers useful insights into Kentridge's experiments with musical and theatrical form but also raises important questions about the political and ethical role of opera in the postcolony. In the case of *Zeno*, such questions extend to the shape and meaning of confessional performance in a postcolonial context as well as the ambivalent position of the bourgeois subject who indulges in European cultural forms (such as opera) while immersed in a place still marked by the enduring legacies of colonialism.

---

[4] As discussed in Chapter 1, Kentridge and Handspring had already collaborated on the plays, *Woyzeck on the Highveld* (1992), *Faustus in Africa* (1995), and *Ubu and the Truth Commission* (1996), as well as the opera, *Il Ritorno d'Ulisse in Patria* (1998).

[5] Kevin Volans, personal communication, December 16, 2020.

This chapter considers what confession—*Zeno*'s confession in particular, but ultimately also confession in general—might mean in the immediate aftermath of colonialism and apartheid. Additionally, it asks what it might mean for *opera* to perform confession in the postcolonial context. Placing *Zeno*'s music and staging in dialogue with existing theories of confession, I ask if Kentridge's piece might suggest a new way of reading the personal transgressions of the bourgeois postcolonizing subject.[6] My interpretive approach examines these transgressions within and through the political context in which they take place. I pay particular attention to the work's ambiguous constructions of veracity and its ambivalent inscription in geographical and historical context. *Zeno*'s equivocal engagement with questions of personal confession and responsibility in the postcolony is realized formally, I argue, by means of an integration of apparently discrepant musical and visual strategies. Thus, the work complicates traditional operatic approaches to confessional performance. Finally, I ask what *Zeno* might reveal about opera's capacity to engage ethically with the politics of personal admission in the postcolonial present.

Background

Kentridge and his collaborators created *Confessions of Zeno* over a period of approximately two-and-a-half years, starting with Part One, "Zeno at 4am," which premiered at the Belgian KunstenFESTIVALdesArtes in Brussels in May 2001. "Zeno at 4am" was originally intended to be a free-standing work of forty-five minutes based on the first part of Svevo's novel.[7] Finding that this first experiment had "provided [them] with a performance language for imagining the novel as a whole," the creative team added a second part based on the rest of the source text, thus turning *Zeno* into a ninety-minute piece of theatrical multimedia.[8]

The full *Confessions of Zeno* premiered in May 2002, again at KunstenFESTIVALdesArts in Brussels. From there, the piece toured for eighteen months, to theaters in Hamburg, Berlin, Kassel, and Frankfurt (2002), Zagreb (2002), Rome (2002), Salamanca (2002), Paris, Caen and Angoulême (2002), Grahamstown (2002), Stellenbosch (2003), Singapore (2003), Las Palmas (2003), Lisbon (2003), and Vitoria, Spain (2003).

---

[6] See the Introduction for an explanation of the category of the postcolonizing subject.
[7] Jane Taylor, 2003, "Taking Stock: The Making of a Bourgeois Life—*The Confessions of Zeno*," *South African Theatre Journal* 17(1), 233–244, at 237.
[8] Taylor, "Taking Stock," 239.

56 Postcolonial Opera

Following its early successes, however, *Confessions of Zeno* has not enjoyed a robust performance history. Kentridge has created a number of fellow travelers, including drawings and a video work titled *Zeno Drawing*, based on themes and material from the theater piece.[9] These have been shown in museums around the world. But the production itself has not, at the time of writing, been revived.[10] Of the original performances, only fragmented recordings survive. I base my analysis on these audiovisual records, in combination with Jane Taylor's libretto and Kevin Volans's score.[11]

Kentridge describes Svevo's novel as a strangely familiar piece of fiction. In the program note for the first German performance of *Confessions of Zeno* in 2002, the artist remarks that he was "touched" when he read the novel over twenty years before, "by the description of Trieste as a rather poor provincial town on the edge of the monarchy—away from the centre, from the real world." Svevo's writing, he continues, struck him for having "such a sense of what things were like in Johannesburg in the nineteen eighties."[12] At first glance, the comparison seems spurious: the terminal years of the Austro-Hungarian imperial fantasy could arguably not be further removed from the uncontained violence and successive states of emergency that characterized the final decade of apartheid rule in South Africa. And indeed, Svevo's novel appears, on the face of it, oblivious to the political upheaval of late-apartheid South Africa. Neither the setting nor the central character reveal any connection to the artistic team's political and geographical context.

Nonetheless, within the frame of a surreal psychoanalytic dream, Kentridge and his collaborators excavate a uniting theme between the two works, namely, the figure of the bourgeois imperial subject who, enclosed in a haze of self-satisfaction, remains apparently unaware of the crises threatening his world. The whole piece is a narration of the titular character's numerous

---

[9] *Zeno Drawing* also incorporates some of Volans's music for the theater piece. For a detailed analysis of *Zeno Drawing*, see Leora Maltz-Leca, 2018, *William Kentridge: Process as Metaphor and Other Doubtful Enterprises*, Oakland: University of California Press, 248–258. See the Introduction for fellow travelers.

[10] In a 2008 interview with Jane Taylor, Kentridge admits that *Zeno* is "a production [he] could imagine redoing to change it." In Jane Taylor and William Kentridge, 2008, "In Dialogue: William Kentridge with Jane Taylor," in 2009, *Handspring Puppet Company*, ed. Jane Taylor, Johannesburg: David Krut Publishing, 176–209, at 203.

[11] My thanks to Jane Taylor for generously making the libretto available to me. Volans's score for *Confessions of Zeno* is published by Chester Music (London, 2002) and is available for hire.

[12] Kentridge, William, 2002, "Confessions of Zeno: Regieanmerkungen von William Kentridge," in *Confessions of Zeno* [production program], Programmheft Nr. 21. Frankfurt am Main: schauspielfrankfurt, 8–9, at 8. The original text reads: "Als ich Italo Svevos Roman *Zeno Cosini* vor über zwanzig Jahren zum ersten Mal las, hat mich unter anderem die Beschreibung Triests als einer ziemlich armseligen Provinzstadt am Rande der Monarchie berührt—abseits vom Mittelpunkt, von der wahren Welt. Ich war verblüfft, wie ein in den zwanziger Jahren schreibender Österreichitaliener so einen Sinn dafür haben konnte, wie es in Johannesburg in den Achtzigern war. Das bewog mich, zu diesem Buch zurückzükommen." Unless otherwise indicated, all translations are my own.

moral and commercial failings, his obsession with his own health, and his repeated failed attempts to give up smoking. For Taylor, Zeno is "the representative bourgeois, with relatively small needs but gargantuan neediness."[13] His recollections betray an attitude that treats "matters of historical and psychological weight . . . as meringue; [while] the trivial minutia [sic] of the bourgeois condition become matters of monumental psychic drama and ethical quests."[14] Kentridge's description of Zeno, as "[a] consciousness without consequence," echoes the apparent political impunity of this figure—one who can get away with total inertia. His "absolute impotence, which forces [him] to act, but then again prevents it," is for Kentridge typical of "people stuck on the cutting edge of a historic event that is about to implode, stuck waiting for the eruption to take place."[15] In Zeno's case this historical eruption is the First World War, but Kentridge is evidently also gesturing toward the dramatic events in South Africa of the 1980s and 1990s. Kentridge and Taylor's Zeno, like Svevo's, seems oblivious to these changes. Rather, he remains suspended in a fog of self-interest, apparently untouched by history.

Zeno's existential malaise is perhaps representative of the early twentieth-century European subject's attempts to come to terms with modernity. In the context of late apartheid and early post-apartheid South Africa, however, these failings appear trivial, self-indulgent even. Against the backdrop of the TRC, Zeno's struggle with his personal flaws is laughably inconsequential. Its performance on stage, in operatic format, seems to endow it with an epic character at odds with the innocuousness of the material. *Zeno*'s preoccupation with small individual drama at a time of great social upheaval may hence signal a retreat from the political into the personal. But it can also be understood to raise intractable questions about what Taylor calls "the scale of the political"—about where, and how, the ordinary lives of politically disengaged, bourgeois citizens fit into the larger struggles of the time; and about where, and how, their Eurocentric preoccupations fit into a turbulent postcolonial cultural landscape.[16] In Kentridge, Taylor, and Volans's treatment, Zeno's personal revelations—both inconsequential and politically instructive—form the basis for an exploration of the ambiguous subject positions of those at once removed from and implicated in colonial violence.

[13] Taylor, "Taking Stock," 238.
[14] Taylor, "Taking Stock," 237.
[15] Zeno, der Held in Svevos Roman, hat ein bemerkenswertes Bewußtsein von sich selbst. Ein Bewußtsein, das aber keine Folgen hat. Diese absolute Unfähigkeit, die Zeno zwingt, zu handeln, oder dann wieder hindert, zu handeln, ist etwas, das man kennt. Menschen, die festsitzen auf der Schneide zu einem historischen Ereignis, das im Begriff ist, zu implodieren, festsitzend und wartend, dass sich die Eruption ereignet (Kentridge, Regieanmerkungen, 8).
[16] Taylor, "Taking Stock," 237.

58 Postcolonial Opera

Taylor's libretto for *Zeno* was not her first collaboration with Kentridge and Handspring Puppet Company. In 1996 she wrote the text for Kentridge and Handspring's *Ubu and the Truth Commission*. Based on Alfred Jarry's absurdist play, *Ubu Roi* (1896), *Ubu and the Truth Commission* incorporated source testimony from the TRC archives to engage with personal recollections shared by witnesses (portrayed by puppets) during the TRC hearings. The play examines the reconciliatory process by which amnesty was granted to apartheid-era perpetrators, represented in the piece by Ma Ubu (mother Ubu, played by Busi Zokufa) and Pa Ubu (father Ubu, played by Dawid Minnaar).[17] Themes of guilt and accountability were hence already part of Taylor's work with Kentridge and Handspring before she wrote the libretto for *Zeno*. Indeed, Taylor herself comments that at the time she wrote *Zeno*, she had been interested in "the realms of confession and autobiography" for several years, ever since her work on *Ubu* and as the curator of a series of cultural responses to the TRC, called *Fault Lines*, in 1996.[18] *Zeno* offered Taylor an opportunity to expand on themes she had already begun to explore in earlier works shaped specifically by the South African Truth and Reconciliation hearings. Her work on the libretto was, in her own words, shaped by an interest in "the modernist version of the confessional novel, and more particularly, in the performance of the confession on stage."[19]

Unlike Taylor, Volans had not collaborated with either Kentridge or Handspring before. Based in Ireland since 1986 and an Irish citizen since 1995, Volans was by 2002 regarded as one of the most important composers to emerge from South Africa. He remains especially renowned for his first two string quartets, *White Man Sleeps* (1986) and *Hunting:Gathering* (1987), which received international acclaim after being recorded by the Kronos Quartet (1987 and 1991). Volans's early works drew extensively on Southern African (and "African") sonic signifiers, thereby giving rise to an extended and often impassioned scholarly debate about the politics of appropriation and representation in his music. Timothy D. Taylor, following a series of interviews with the composer, argued in 1995 that Volans's use of African musical quotations could be regarded as a transgression of South Africa's segregationist politics but simultaneously also as an act of appropriation that reinforced the racialized power imbalance between colonizer and colonized.[20]

---

[17] Taylor, *Handspring Puppet Company*, 79–80.

[18] Taylor, "Taking Stock," 234. For more on *Fault Lines*, see Yvette Christiansë's review of an authors' panel titled "At the Fault Line," which formed part of the program. Christiansë, 1996, "At the Fault Line—Writers in the Shadow of Truth and Reconciliation," *New Coin Poetry* 32(2), 70–75.

[19] Taylor, "Taking Stock," 235.

[20] Timothy D. Taylor, 1995, "When We Think about Music and Politics: The Case of Kevin Volans," *Perspectives of New Music* 33(1/2), 504–536. Kofi Agawu, in *The African Imagination in Music*, likewise

In a series of responses published over the course of the following decade, Martin Scherzinger defended Volans from Taylor's accusations of appropriation by tracing in the composer's work a "political imagination" that "puts into urgent question and doubt various racializing commonplaces about African music."[21] Volans himself voiced a desire to enact a musical reconciliation between Black and white South Africans through his early compositions, but by the mid-1990s he had renounced this political sensibility in favor of a turn to abstraction and questions of form.[22] The matter of coloniality and African representation in Volans's music remains a point of dispute and one to which this chapter will gesture, though I shall not engage explicitly with the terms of the debate.[23]

Confessions of Zeno

The novel, *La Coscienza di Zeno* is, like Kentridge's adaptation, an artifact of empire. Its author, Aron Ettore Schmitz (1861–1928), belonged to a Jewish family of German and Italian heritage. Like Zeno, Schmitz was born and raised in the coastal city of Trieste, which was part of the Austro-Hungarian Empire until 1918. Schmitz's pen name, Italo Svevo, which translates directly as "Italian Swabian," gestures toward a conflicted imperial identity, born of competing cultural and linguistic influences.[24] Svevo's early literary ambitions were realized in two novels, *Una Vita* (1892), and *Senilità* (1898). Both works were largely ignored, so Svevo gave up writing and returned to a career as a businessman. However, after receiving English lessons from James Joyce and becoming friends with the Irish author, Svevo was inspired to return

---

identifies an appropriative impulse in Volans's music. See Agawu, 2016, *The African Imagination in Music*, New York: Oxford University Press, 316.

[21] Martin Scherzinger, 2008, "Whose 'White Man Sleeps?' Aesthetics and Politics in the Early Work of Kevin Volans," in *Composing Apartheid: Music for and against Apartheid*, ed. Grant Olwage, Johannesburg: Wits University Press, 209–235. The quotations are from Scherzinger, "Whose White Man," at 219. Other participants in this debate include Jürgen Bräuninger, 1998, "Gumboots to the Rescue," *South African Journal of Musicology: SAMUS* 18, 1–16; and Grant Olwage, 1999–2000, "Who Needs Rescuing? A Reply to 'Gumboots to the Rescue,'" *South African Journal of Musicology: SAMUS* 19, 105–108.

[22] See Taylor, "When We Think about Music and Politics," especially at 523.

[23] For the latest installment in the ongoing dispute about Volans's use of so-called African material in his music, see William Fourie, 2019, "Between the Musical Anti- and Post-Apartheid: Structures of Crisis in Kevin Volans's String Quartet No.5, Dancers on a Plane," *SAMUS: South African Music Studies* 39, 134–174; Kevin Volans, 2020, "Response to 'Between the Musical Anti- and Post-Apartheid: Structures of Crisis in Kevin Volans's String Quartet No. 5, Dancers on a Plane,'" *SAMUS: South African Music Studies* 40, 17–22; and William Fourie, 2020, "On the Fragile Joys of Interpretation: A Response to Kevin Volans," *SAMUS: South African Music Studies* 40, 23–28.

[24] Deborah Amberson, 2016, "Zeno's Dissonant Violin: Italo Svevo, Judaism, and Western Art Music," *Italian Studies* 71(1), 98–114, at 104–105. Swabia is a region in southwestern Germany.

60 Postcolonial Opera

to writing, publishing *La Coscienza di Zeno* in 1923, again to limited public interest. Joyce, who was convinced of his friend's literary gift, championed the novel and helped to establish Svevo's reputation among Parisian literary circles.[25]

Several authors have remarked on the "literary sympathy" that existed between Joyce and Svevo.[26] While Joyce championed his Italian friend's work, Svevo, in turn, schooled the younger man in matters of Jewishness, ultimately becoming the model for Leopold Bloom in Joyce's *Ulysses* (1922).[27] But if their mutual respect served as inspiration for each other's works, the results were markedly dissimilar. Jane Taylor describes the relationship between Svevo's and Joyce's work as "mirror images of one another, but in the way that a mirror images its opposite self—Joyce's writings persistently engaged with the political, religious, and ideological substance of his identity while Svevo's writings assiduously avoided them."[28] Indeed, Svevo's work, though similarly engaged with questions of self-understanding and consciousness, evades what Irina Rasmussen Goloubeva describes as *Ulysses*' "preoccupations with history [and] compulsion to focus on particular details as ways of interpreting the social."[29] Instead, *La Coscienza di Zeno* portrays a protagonist who is simultaneously self-obsessed and apparently oblivious to the socio-political structures that shape his sense of self and place in the world.

La Coscienza di Zeno is, according to Paolo Bertolini, "a book about self-discovery (and/or self-deception), and self-reflexion."[30] Composed in the style of a long monologue, the narration is a writing exercise conducted by Zeno Cosini under order from his psychoanalyst, Dr. S. A short prefatory note indicates that Dr. S. has decided to publish Zeno's autobiographical report as revenge for the patient's decision to discontinue his treatment.[31]

At the start of the narration Zeno is about to undergo psychoanalytic treatment to address his various maladies. These maladies are revealed throughout the novel to be little more than hypochondriac fixations. The protagonist's

---

[25] Taylor, "Taking Stock," 236. See also John Gatt-Rutter, 1988, *Italo Svevo: A Double Life*, Oxford: Clarendon Press, for details on Svevo's early literary ambitions, his friendship with Joyce, and Joyce's advocacy of his work.

[26] Taylor, "Taking Stock," 236.

[27] Neil Davison, 1996, *James Joyce, Ulysses and the Construction of Jewish Identity: Culture, Biography, and "the Jew" in Modernist Europe*, Cambridge: Cambridge University Press, 171. See also Amberson, "Zeno's Dissonant Violin," 105.

[28] Taylor, "Taking Stock," 236.

[29] Irina Rasmussen Goloubeva, 2013, "'That's the Music of the Future': James Joyce's *Ulysses* and the Writing of a Difficult History," *Modernism/Modernity* 20(4), 685–708, at 686.

[30] Paolo Bartolini, 2012, "Zeno's Thingness: On Fetishism and Bodies in Svevo's *La coscienza di Zeno*," *Italianist* 32(3), 399–414, 408.

[31] Italo Svevo, 2018 [1923], *Confessions of Zeno*, trans. Beryl de Zoete. London: riverrun, 3.

main ailment is his continued inability to quit smoking—a failure Zeno regards as one of the root causes for the many other disappointments and inactions that plague him. In a series of long chapters, narrated achronologically, the protagonist recounts his formative experiences, including his first encounters with cigarettes, his numerous abortive attempts to pursue further studies, and his business dabblings, which yield varying levels of success. The most extensive reflections are dedicated to Zeno's ambivalent relationship with his father, which ends in the "unmitigated disaster" of Cosini Senior's death; his pursuit of the hand of a woman named Ada Malfenti, which ultimately leads to his marriage to her sister, Augusta; his affair with a young local singer, Carla Gerco; and his business dealings with his rival and Ada's husband, Guido Speier. By the end of the novel, the protagonists are caught in the horrors of the First World War. The final entry is from March 24, 1916.[32] Zeno has made a fortune by speculating on the stock exchange and believes himself cured. Despite his newfound sense of well-being, however, he remains preoccupied with life's inexorable march toward illness, old age, and death. "Life is a little like disease," he writes, "but unlike other diseases life is always mortal. It admits of no cure."[33]

The two parts of Kentridge's adaptation are centered on three central episodes from the novel, namely, the death of Zeno's father (Act I), and the titular character's marriage to Augusta and affair with Carla (Act II). Within this abridged dramatic arc, a company of figures much reduced from the novel's cast of friends, family, and associates, comment on and enact Zeno's recollections. The piece is scripted for a small troupe comprising Zeno (a spoken role played by a stage actor), his father (bass), Carla (soprano), Augusta (soprano), and a chorus of shadow projections who represent a surreal variation on the traditional operatic chorus-as-public. In Act I the shadow chorus performs an introductory number, a "pseudo-scientific" chorus and a "chorus of trees," while in Act II it represents the four Malfenti sisters, Ada, Augusta, Alberta, and Anna. Toward the end of Act I a nurse enters, "muttering in isiXhosa"—this spoken part is not listed in the role distribution on either the score or the libretto, and is probably portrayed by one of the two sopranos, as they only appear in character in Act II.[34]

Volans set Taylor's libretto as a series of movements incorporating both sung lines and spoken recitations, all of which are accompanied by string quartet

---

[32] Svevo, *Confessions*, 575.

[33] Svevo, *Confessions*, 578.

[34] Jane Taylor, 2001, *Confessions of Zeno* [libretto]. Frankfurt am Main: schauspielfrankfurt; Volans, *Confessions of Zeno Part 1* [score]; the quotation is at p. 38, bar 83.

62   Postcolonial Opera

and electronic tape. The music incorporates stylistic elements typical of Volans's oeuvre, including interlocking patterns, inexact repetition of figures, frequently shifting time signatures and metrical irregularities, and regular use of harmonics and open strings.[35] Rhythmically driving sections performed at fast tempos are interspersed with dreamlike moments of stillness consisting of sustained high pitches and quiet, open harmonics. But even the suspended moments are undercut by dissonances that give the music a tense, somewhat frenetic quality throughout. Overall, the two acts are strongly reminiscent of the minimalism of Philip Glass and Terry Riley, and though Volans himself rejects the label, it would arguably not be wholly inappropriate to describe *Zeno* as a minimalist opera.[36]

In a short program note, the composer himself describes the music as follows:

> The first part of my music for *Confessions* is completely self-contained, while the music of the second part is eclectic. It relates to other types of music that I have written and draws on some original, ethno-cultural sources. In the "Four Sisters Quartet" I wrote a small variation of Muthambe, which was first played by a famous mbira player from the 19th century, Pasipamire, from the Shona people of Zimbabwe, and combined it with material from the Nyungwe music of Mozambique. This was originally played by Makina Chirenje and his Nyanga pan-pipe group, Tete Valley, from Nsava. Andrew Tracy [sic] recorded it and transcribed the music (from which followed an article, "The Nyanga Panpipe Dance" in *African Music*, Vol. 5 No.1 (1971)). Carla's aria later on in the piece is rhythmically based on dance movements of the Indian Baratha Natyam [sic], which were created by the internationally renowned British choreographer Shobona [sic] Jeyasing, which makes it an extremely challenging vocal part.[37]

[35] See Christine Lucia, 2009, "The Landscape Within: Kevin Volans and the String Quartet," *SAMUS: South African Music Studies* 29, 1–30, for a summary of the stylistic elements that, according to Lucia, "create Volans's identity as a composer" (12).

[36] See Taylor, "When We Think about Music and Politics," 525, on Volans's rejection of minimalism. Lucia ("Landscape") uses the term to describe many of the composer's formal and stylistic procedures.

[37] Volans, 2002, "Anmerkungen zur Musik von *Confessions of Zeno*," in *Confessions of Zeno* [production program], Programmheft Nr. 21, Frankfurt am Main: Schauspielfrankfurt, 22. Original text: "Der erste Teil meiner Musik zu *Confessions* ist völlig in sich geschlossen, während die Musik des zweiten Teils eklektisch ist. Sie hat Bezug auf andere Musiken, die ich geschrieben habe und greift auf einge originäre, ethnokulturellen Quellen zurück. Im 'Vier Schwestern Quartett' habe ich eine kleine Variation von Muthambe geschrieben, die erstmals von einem berühmten Mbira-Spieler aus dem 19. Jahrhundert gespielt wurde, Pasipamire, vom Volk der Shona in Zimbabwe, und kombinierte sie mit Musiken der Nyungwe-Musik aus Mosambik. Diese wurde ursprünglich von Makina Chirenje und seiner Nyanga Panflötengruppe, Tete valley, aus Nsava gespielt. Andrew Tracy [sic] zeichnete sie auf und transkribierte die Musik (folgend einem Artikel, 'The Nyanga panpipe dance' in African Music, Vol. 5, No. 1 [1971]). Die Arie der Carla im späteren Teil des Stück basiert rhythmisch auf Tanzbewegungen des indischen Baratha Natyam [sic], die von der international bekannten britischen Choreographin Shobona Jeyasing [sic] geschaffen wurden, was es zu einer extrem schwierigen Gesangspartie macht" (22).

Volans's description makes three things clear: first, the composer regards the first and second acts of *Zeno* as separate, unrelated compositions—a natural consequence, perhaps, of the fact that the two parts were completed at least a year apart. Second, *Zeno*'s score incorporates material from other Volans works, as well as non-Western musical practices. These musical citations draw the piece into the debate about cultural appropriation in Volans's music (indeed, the mbira and nyanga panpipe quotations Volans mentions appear in other string quartets too, and are the main objects of Timothy Taylor's and Martin Scherzinger's scrutiny). Finally, Volans does not construct an explicit link between his music and the opera's narrative or visual content. This suggests that the composition does not necessarily rely on its contiguous theatrical media for meaning or inspiration. I shall return to these issues, especially as they are borne out in the practice of self-quotation and the integration of "original, ethno-cultural sources." Volans's recycled source materials and African paraphrases, I shall show in detailed considerations of individual sections of the score, contribute to a confessional mode that is simultaneously insular and profoundly political.

Like Volans's music, Kentridge's stage setting also refers to earlier works by the artist. Drawing on a principle developed in his 1999 animated film, *Stereoscope*, Kentridge sets up a formal framework conditioned by ideas of splitting and doubling. In *Stereoscope*, the artist divides the screen in two and shows near-identical images on both sides. Through a process of transformation, the doubled images gradually diverge, until they appear radically different from each other. For Kentridge, this visual disjunction offers a metaphor through which to explore "the complex ways in which we try to construct ourselves as solid, coherent subjects."[38] In *Zeno*, Kentridge transposes this approach to live theater. He describes "this form, of a double projection of two images of the world, sometimes synchronous, at other times discrepant," as an ideal practice through which to approach "the book's theatrical implementation and staging."[39]

To realize the double projection on stage, Kentridge divides the performance space in two. Stage right, the actors and singers interact with each other, while stage left a crew of puppeteers performs an assortment of choreographed movements with puppets mounted on long sticks of wood. In front of the puppeteers, the string quartet is seated—visible, but isolated

---

[38] Kentridge, "Regieanmerkungen," 8.
[39] Kentridge, "Regieanmerkungen," 8. "Der Unterschied zwischen den Bildern (anfangs nur geringfügig, dann radikal) war der formale Rahmen des Spielens mit den komplexen Wegen, mit denen wir uns als gefestigte, kohärente Subjekte zu strukturieren versuchen. Diese Form einer doppelten Projektion von zwei Bildern der Welt, zetiweise synchron, zeitweise ungleich zueinander, bot sich als die Form und als ein Weg an, über das Buch, seine Umsetzung in Theater und mit der Bühne an sich zu arbeiten."

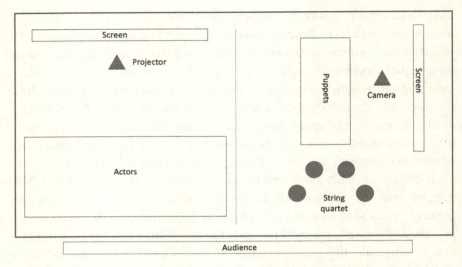

Figure 2.1 A schematic representation of the stage setting for *Confessions of Zeno*.

from the puppeteers behind them. Upstage, two brightly lit screens, placed at right angles to one another, form backdrops to the actors' and puppeteers' movements. Each screen is linked to a projector and playback device containing a video. The projected images are "sometimes simultaneous, sometimes asynchronous, sometimes radically different," thus replicating the interplay between near-simultaneity and incoherence developed in *Stereoscope*.[40] Besides the pre-recorded video projections, a further live film projection is created in performance: in front of the screen stage left, the puppeteers manipulate their puppets to cast shadows on the backdrop. These shadows are filmed in real time, and the image is projected directly onto the screen stage right, thereby functioning as a live counterpoint to the pre-recorded films and the central cast's actions (see Figure 2.1).

Jane Taylor interprets the shadows created by the puppets as "the substance of Zeno's dream world [which] provide[s] us with images from the unconscious."[41] Her description of the distributed forms of vision and labor created by the interplay between pre-recorded drawings, live shadow projections, and embodied performance, is evocative:

On stage the puppeteers are entirely visible, very much a theatrical reality. On the projection screen the presence of the puppeteers is entirely masked and

---

[40] Kentridge, "Regieanmerkungen," 9. "Die projizierten Biler sind manchmal zeitgleich, manchmal asynchron, manchmal radikal unterschiedlich."
[41] Taylor, "Taking Stock," 240.

invisible: we see only the brilliant puppetry event of mystical images playing in magical transformations about the screen. To the side of the stage, we are aware of the elaborate performance that makes that fantasy of effortlessness possible. So in many ways the theatre work *Confessions of Zeno* is about the nature of the illusion. It is as if we witness the raw material of the unconscious (the puppeteers' work) as well as transformed mysteries of dream once the fundamental elements have been transformed into psychological allegory.[42]

Echoing Taylor's description of *Zeno*'s shadows as "the raw material of the unconscious," Leora Maltz-Leca interprets the "disjunction between the actors and the shadows cast on the screen behind them" as a representation of "the bifurcated consciousness or 'double understanding' that [is] the play's subject."[43] This bifurcation, which suggests a subject somehow not unified with himself, is a central preoccupation in Kentridge's own explanation of his use of shadows in the work. In a public talk delivered shortly before the premiere of *Zeno*, the artist offers a long explanation of his shadow practice. He begins by acknowledging that he had used shadow projections in theater productions with Handspring over several years but that these projections had usually been "just an adjunct" to other forms of puppet performance. In *Zeno*, conversely, the shadow play occupies center stage.[44] Kentridge proceeds to recount the "Plato's cave" parable that serves as a leitmotiv in his work, and which I discuss at length in the Introduction to this book.[45] In the context of *Zeno*, Kentridge reads Plato's cave as a comment on matters of essence, type, and the subject's coherence with him/herself. Crucially, he also uses the Plato metaphor to connect *Confessions of Zeno* to Zeno's paradox of motion, even though Svevo's original source text does not appear to refer to the Greek philosopher's work:[46]

There is a paradox here. Shadow is all appearance, immateriality, without substance; but at the same time gives a way of avoiding the seduction of surface—often referred to as appearance as opposed to essence. . . . Understanding that the

[42] Taylor, "Taking Stock," 240–241.

[43] Maltz-Leca, 2018, *William Kentridge*, 256.

[44] Kentridge, 2001, "In Praise of Shadows," https://www.kentridge.studio/in-praise-of-shadows/.

[45] In which Plato compares the pre-Enlightenment subject to a person imprisoned in a cave with only shadows to look at. For Plato, Enlightenment is like being released from the cave and being forced to confront the sun for the first time, leading to a realization that the shadows encountered in the cave were no more than fictions.

[46] Zeno's paradox of motion essentially argues that motion is impossible for various reasons, including that a moving object has to cross an infinitely divisible series of distances before reaching its target, and that all objects are "in place" (static) at any given moment, meaning that they can never be in motion. See Nick Huggett, Nick, "Zeno's Paradoxes," *Stanford Encyclopedia of Philosophy*, https://plato.stanford.edu/entries/paradox-zeno/, accessed September 10, 2021.

66 Postcolonial Opera

blankness of the shadow, the lack of psychological depth, may be an asset—that understanding the world not through individual psychology is often appropriate and stronger. Traditional wisdom has it that the greater the psychological depth of the performance, the closer it gets to the truth of the world. The world of shadows suggests other routes than sincerity or the psychological elements of performance. . . . I make an argument here for something that is neither individual psychology nor a universality, but something I would call a recognised particularity. . . . One's relationship to one's own shadow—which is not the same as oneself, which one does not own, but which is an inescapable attribute and accompaniment, was for me a memorable conundrum. A midpoint between a familiar self and the otherness of the rest of the world. The shadow immediately brings an other into the picture, the other being a source of light—here we are at the start of the shadow paradox. It is both of one and separate from one. . . . Zeno's paradox, as well as I remember it, is that an arrow aimed at a target first has to cover half the distance, and before that half of that distance, and half of that—each distance requiring some time to cross it—so that an infinite number of divisions will yield an infinite amount of time, and the arrow will in fact never leave the bow, never mind reach the target. This held in mind while at the same time understanding that of course the arrow does leave the bow and reach the target . . . is a kind of ongoing ambiguity that was a horror for Plato, and his belief that all such paradoxes would eventually be explained away . . . in a way that makes perfect mathematical sense. But this still does not stop the crossed thumbs being both hands and bird. And what we do when we see is both be connected to a measurable, objective world of optics, surface, light source and physics, and be aware of something utterly beyond that.[47]

The paradox of the shadow lies for Kentridge in the fact that it is both illusion and reality. It both reveals and obscures the subject, awarding her an identity and simultaneously stripping her of her defining features. The shadow represents the individual, but it also reveals her to be no more than a type, recognizable by her correspondence to a predetermined set of outlines.

Kentridge interprets this paradox as a simultaneous doubling and splitting: a mode of identification but simultaneously also a form of disidentification. The subject is revealed to be both essence and projection, both individual and type, both person and system—what Kentridge refers to as "a recognised particularity." Pushing back against the ideal of the coherent subject, *Zeno*'s shadow projections set up a series of political and psychological binaries that are destabilized in the act of performance, thereby revealing the piece to be about much more than just a bourgeois individual talking about himself.

---

[47] Kentridge, "In Praise of Shadows."

Instead, Zeno the shadow figure emerges as a representation of an entire society of "confessing subjects," simultaneously immersed in and detached from the realities of early post-apartheid South Africa.

In *Zeno*, then, puppets function quite differently from how they are employed in *Ulisse*.[48] Whereas in the earlier work, the puppets become avatars for the human performers themselves, usurping their subjectivity in an intriguing interplay between embodiment and estrangement, *Zeno*'s puppets are no more than shadows, participating in the action only obliquely, and revealing, rather than concealing, the subjects' inner lives. As in *Ulisse*, the idea of doubling is structurally important, but it fulfills a different purpose here: whereas in *Ulisse* the performers are doubled, thereby casting doubt on the identity of the political subject, in *Zeno* it is the setting that is doubled, thus creating a backdrop upon which the splitting of the individual—as political subject and as subconscious—can be realized.

Truth, Reconciliation, and Confession

Zeno's creation coincides with the end of the Truth and Reconciliation Process in South Africa. The TRC was set up in terms of the Promotion of National Unity and Reconciliation Act 34 of 1995 to "help deal" with the history and legacy of apartheid.[49] In a series of public hearings, victims and perpetrators of the regime were invited to testify about their experiences before a panel of high-profile commissioners chaired by Archbishop Desmond Tutu. The TRC comprised three committees: the Human Rights Violations (HRV) Committee, which investigated human rights abuses committed under the apartheid regime; the Reparation and Rehabilitation (R&R) Committee, responsible for providing victim support and formulating policy recommendations for social rehabilitation and structural reparation; and the Amnesty Committee (AC), which considered applications for amnesty "for any act, omission or offence associated with a political objective committed between 1 March 1960 to [sic] 6 December 1993."[50] Once a perpetrator had received amnesty from the AC, they were immune against prosecution for that act.

---

[48] See Chapter 1.

[49] TRC, n.d, "Welcome to the Official Truth and Reconciliation Commission Website," https://www.justice.gov.za/trc/. Accessed October 3, 2021.

[50] TRC, n.d., "The Committees of the TRC," https://www.justice.gov.za/trc/trccom.html. Accessed October 3, 2021. Also see Patricia J. Campbell, 2000, "The Truth and Reconciliation Commission (TRC): Human Rights and State Transitions—The South Africa Model," *African Studies Quarterly* 4(3), 41–63.

68 Postcolonial Opera

Following the final public TRC hearings in 1998, the commission compiled a report, the first five volumes of which were presented to President Nelson Mandela on October 29, 1998. Volumes six—comprising the reports of the AC, the R&R, and the HRV—and seven, which contains "the stories of those who came forward to speak of their suffering"—were published in 2003 and 2002, respectively.[51]

At the time of *Zeno*'s development, the TRC was enjoying a significant amount of national and international attention. Its findings, as well as victims' and perpetrators' public testimonies, were subject to extensive critical scrutiny, with weekly television programs such as *Truth Commission Special Report* providing hour-long updates between 1996 and 1998; documentary films such as Bill Moyers's two-part *Facing the Truth* (1999) and Frances Reid's *Long Night's Journey into Day* (2000) bringing the activities of the commission to an international audience; and a series of memoirs by people involved with the TRC, including committee member Alex Boraine (*A Country Unmasked*, 2001), journalist Antjie Krog (*Country of My Skull*, 2000), and chairperson Desmond Tutu (*No Future without Forgiveness*, 2000), offering individual perspectives on the workings of the judicial apparatus.[52]

South African theaters also hosted an assortment of productions engaged with the themes and activities of the TRC. These included Pieter-Dirk Uys's *Truth Omissions* (1996), Khulumani Support Group's workshop play, *The Story I'm about to Tell* (1999), Paul Herzberg's *The Dead Wait* (1997), Walter Chakela's *Isithukuthu* (1997), John Kani's *Nothing but the Truth* (2002), Yaël Farber's *A Woman in Waiting* (1999), *Amajuba: Like Doves We Rise* (2000), *He Left Quietly* (2002), and *Molora* (2003), and of course, Kentridge and Taylor's own Handspring collaboration mentioned above, *Ubu and the Truth Commission* (1996).[53] Ed Charlton observes that the period of 2000–2004 was "a noticeably intense period" of engagement with the TRC by the creative arts, and especially theater.[54] These projects, despite their widely divergent approaches to theatrical process and form, all attempt, in Charlton's

---

[51] It is not clear why Volume 7, which appeared in August 2002, was published before Volume 6, whose publication date is indicated as March 21, 2003. See TRC, 2002, *Truth and Reconciliation Commission of South Africa Report Volume Seven*, Cape Town: Truth and Reconciliation Commission; TRC, 2003, *Truth and Reconciliation Commission of South Africa Volume Six*, Cape Town: Truth and Reconciliation Commission. The quotation is from *Volume Seven*, 1.

[52] See Annelies Verdoolaege, 2005, "Media Representations of the South African Truth and Reconciliation Commission and Their Commitment to Reconciliation," *Journal of African Cultural Studies* 17(2), 181–199.

[53] For more on theatrical responses to the TRC, see Yvette Hutchison's influential 2013 monograph, *South African Performance and Archives of Memory*, Manchester: Manchester University Press, esp. chapter 2, and Ed Charlton's excellent *Improvising Reconciliation: Confession after the Truth Commission*, Liverpool: Liverpool University Press, 2021.

[54] Charlton, *Improvising*, 6.

description, to engage with the TRC as archive, in order to expose not only its failures, but to reimagine "what reconciliation might otherwise constitute."[55]

Throughout the TRC process and in artistic responses to the commission, the concept and practice of confession enjoyed great prominence. With placards bearing messages such as "REVEALING IS HEALING" and "THE TRUTH HURTS BUT SILENCE KILLS" on display at TRC hearings, the commission mobilized, in Charlton's words, "the psychoanalyst's 'talking cure' as a putative means of national recovery."[56] Given the prominence of a psychoanalytically inspired confessional discourse at the time of *Zeno*'s creation, the opera's silence on any aspect of the TRC is nothing if not surprising. Contrary to Kentridge and Taylor's *Ubu*, *Zeno* seems altogether oblivious to the political goings-on of the time during which it was created.

Zeno's admissions are innocuous: he cannot give up smoking; he is a disappointment to his father; he married the wrong woman; he is an inadequate husband; he struggles to leave his mistress; he is plagued by inertia and melodramatic, imagined ailments. His first entry in the opera, an extended monologue that follows a long introductory chorus, exposes his defects: Zeno reflects on his smoking habit ("Today I had my last cigarette. I noted [it] on the fly leaf of the book I was reading, which happened by chance to be a volume called *Positive Philosophy*, which I am having difficulty understanding"); his father's disappointment in him ("The last time I visited him, whenever I looked at him, my father turned his face away. That is supposed to be a sign of insincerity. I now know that it is a sign of pain"); and his regret at not assuaging the latter by giving up the former: "If I had only given up cigarettes, it would have been a great consolation to my father to know that I had at last mastered my appetites. In recent years I have smoked a great many cigarettes and have called each one the last." Zeno's opening monologue ends with a confirmation of the indecision that thwarts his attempts not only to give up smoking but also to embark on any meaningful action in his life: "I am never sure whether by living a simple existence without wine or cigarettes, I am cheating death or life."[57]

Compared to the truths processed in the TRC hearings—and reprocessed in the numerous TRC plays mentioned above—these confessions seem trivial. In fact, they may even be interpreted to make a mockery of the somber interplay of admission and forgiveness crowding South African arts, media, and minds at the time.

---

[55] Charlton, *Improvising*, 18.
[56] Charlton, *Improvising*, 2.
[57] All quotations Charlton, *Improvising*, 10–11.

70 Postcolonial Opera

This foregrounding of a bourgeois, white individual, cloistered in his own small drama against a backdrop of socio-political upheaval, is typical of another of Kentridge's works: the *Drawings for Projection* (1989–2020) series mentioned in Chapter 1.[58] The films in this set, the first of which were created in the final years of the apartheid regime, portray three white central characters (Soho Eckstein; his wife, Mrs. Eckstein; and her lover, Felix Teitelbaum) who, in Dan Cameron's description, "are actively pursuing their inner and outer lives with hardly a glance at the socio-political terrain that surrounds them."[59] In the Soho/Felix films, however, the incongruity of the central figures' preoccupations is visualized clearly through the explicit portrayal of the South African reality within which the characters find themselves. Even if they are not paying attention, Felix's and the Ecksteins' immediate environment is always filled with violence, political unrest, and racial oppression, drawn in Kentridge's signature black and white charcoal style.[60]

The political realities of *Zeno*'s context, on the other hand, are not plainly articulated. Kentridge's projected drawings depict a typical bourgeois world of sculpted gardens, lavish drawing rooms, fountains, and middlebrow entertainments such as visits to the zoo—suggested by the image of a caged panther pacing in its enclosure. References to the First World War, including images of war planes, battleships, and barren landscapes crossed with barbed wire, occasionally intrude upon the gentrified setting but without impressing themselves on the dramatic action, or indeed on the figures' consciousness. Rather than the visceral confrontation between white middle-class narcissism and political abjection depicted in the *Drawings for Projection*, *Zeno* offers a portrayal of bourgeois apathy so all-encompassing and solipsistic it does not even register the turmoil in which it is caught.

Zeno's narrative and visual content appears to undermine the political magnitude of the confessional form in early post-apartheid South Africa. The main protagonist's admissions instead link more clearly to a confessional regime typical of twentieth-century Western psychoanalytical and philosophical discourse, in which the inner world of the individual is the most important truth that can be known. Analyzing Zeno's confessional practice from a range of confessional theories developed in twentieth-century Western Europe

---

[58] The *Drawings for Projection* film series includes the following titles: "Johannesburg, Second Greatest City after Paris" (1989); "Monument" (1990); "Mine" (1990); "Sobriety, Obesity & Growing Old" (1990); "Felix in Exile" (1994); "History of the Main Complaint" (1996); "Weighing . . . and Wanting" (1998); "Stereoscope" (1999); "Tide Table" (2003); "Other Faces" (2011); and "City Deep" (2020). See Chapter 1 for *History of the Main Complaint*.

[59] Dan Cameron, 1999, "A Procession of the Dispossessed," in *William Kentridge*, ed. Dan Cameron, Carolyn Christov-Bakargiev, and JM Coetzee, London: Phaidon Press, 36–81, at 45.

[60] Cameron, "Procession," 45.

reveals something about the assumptions and biases built into ideas around confession. I rehearse these theoretical arguments at length to demonstrate the coherence between Zeno's confessional mode and a form of psychoanalytical self-revelation privileged within and enjoyed by a particular form of twentieth-century European consciousness.

Theories of Confession

Foucault defines confession as "to declare aloud and intelligibly the truth of oneself."[61] He locates within early spiritual and judicial practices a commitment to the notion that (religious and civil) society could function smoothly only if citizens subjected their lives and their thoughts to a relative degree of scrutiny. The confessional mode, Foucault argues, has been wielded successively by the church, the state, the judiciary, and from the middle of the nineteenth century, the medical sciences, to hold the individual to a set of norms against which her thoughts and behaviors are measured. In other words, for Foucault confession is first and foremost a tool of power. It is a form of personal exposure designed to measure an individual's actions according to their adherence or non-adherence to a set of religious, judicial, civic, medical, or social norms. The confessing subject recounts an action or thought, it is weighed for its positive or negative relation to the norm, and then it is judged.

In this sense, confession may be thought of as a form of accounting—a description repeated by Jane Taylor when she describes a key conceptual frame in *Confessions of Zeno* as "the self as a double-entry system, with failings and deceptions weighed against achievement and moral purpose . . . a self considering itself, and assessing its errors, failures and achievements in a great balancing act."[62] Zeno is himself an accountant, though by his own admission not a particularly skilled one. His professional preoccupation with balance sheets, credits, and debits is mirrored in a central concern that shapes his narrative about himself: the question, "Am I good or bad?"[63] The opera hence articulates, as Leora Maltz-Leca argues following Judith Butler, a process of "accounting for oneself."[64] This practice relates closely to the psychoanalytic process of self-narration and autobiography—of giving account of both past and present. But Maltz-Leca continues, "It also begs questions about

---

[61] Michel Foucault, 2007 [1997], *The Politics of Truth*, ed. Sylvère Lotringer, trans. Lysa Hochroth and Catherine Porter, Los Angeles, CA: Semiotext(e), 148.
[62] Taylor, "Taking Stock," 237.
[63] Svevo, *Confessions of Zeno*, 438.
[64] Maltz-Leca, *Process*, 254.

accountability and whether the opacities that cloud our self-narratives have ethical implications in terms of our accountability for our actions or words, deeds and promises."[65] Accounting for oneself, in other words, entails a confrontation with the question of personal responsibility, especially as it relates to a broader nexus of social and political agency. Zeno's dual performance as an accountant and as a subject giving account of himself is visually codified in Kentridge's background projections, which are suffused with drawings of accounting ledgers "filled with columns of credits and debits."[66] These, Maltz-Leca argues, reinforce the confessional performance's depiction as a "complex form of *accounting*."[67]

Before the task of accounting may occur, however, Foucault argues that confession performs a more basic function, namely, to call the self into being. In Christopher Grobe's words, "Confessions make us up—they make us real."[68] Zeno's confessions, in other words, are acts of self-affirmation. Or, as Ed Charlton writes, " 'Speaking guilt' is precisely constitutive of the sovereign self."[69] Confessions therefore confirm the subject as both consciousness and conscience.

In Zeno's case, however, it is not clear who the person is that is called into being by these confessions. Zeno's truths cannot be trusted. Early in the piece, the protagonist expresses his disdain for veracity when he says, "Talking is itself an event—an event that should not be hampered by reality." As he speaks, a phrase is projected onto the backdrop: "What is the point of talking if one only tells the truth?."[70] Zeno undermines a central hypothesis of Foucault's confessional regime, namely, its assumption of truth.[71] If, following Foucault's theorization, the subject is real as long as what she says about herself is true, then Zeno cannot exist as subject. Nonetheless, the figure speaks; he not only speaks, but he participates in a confessional act that continues to function as a form of self-making.

At this moment, Zeno casts doubt not only on his reliability as a narrator but also on the whole confessional project. He reveals the confessional mode to be provisional, as it cannot presume truth. This is supported by the shadow play realized on stage. As Maltz-Leca notes, the stage projection's complex interplay of splits and doublings "index[es] the binary nature of truth: that

[65] Maltz-Leca, *Process*, 254.
[66] Maltz-Leca, *Process*, 254.
[67] Maltz-Leca, *Process*, 254.
[68] Christopher Grobe, 2014, *The Art of Confession: The Performance of Self from Robert Lowell to Reality TV*, New York: New York University Press, xiii.
[69] Charlton, *Improvising Reconciliation*, 30.
[70] Taylor, *Confessions of Zeno* [libretto], 12; Volans, *Confessions of Zeno Part 1* [score], 36 (bb. 56–57).
[71] Michel Foucault, 2014, *Wrong-Doing, Truth-Telling: The Function of Avowal in Justice*, trans. Stephen W. Sawyer, Chicago: University of Chicago Press, 16.

there are invariably at least two, usually contradictory, truths unfolding simultaneously."[72] The very idea of Zeno's self as identical to an essential truth is undermined, thereby throwing into doubt the authenticity of the identity he constructs. Moreover, if he cannot be trusted to tell the truth, his confessed actions cannot reliably be categorized in the double-entry system of confessional accounting and accountability. Thus, the ethical account remains unbalanced, leaving the question "Am I good or bad?" unresolved. In this moment, the very possibility of confession appears to implode.

I find Njabulo Ndebele and J. M. Coetzee's work helpful in thinking about the unreliability of Zeno's confessions and their implication in a broader confessional regime conditioned as much by falsehood as by truth.[73] In Coetzee and Ndebele's interpretations, confessional truth is unstable in that it may represent a fiction that ultimately *becomes* truth: the subject becomes her story in the act of telling. It is not so much the truth of the confession as the act of its telling that reveals the subject *as* subject. Thus, the confession is neither completely true nor completely false; rather, it represents a paradoxical split between who the subject is and who she declares herself to be. Following Ndebele and Coetzee, Zeno's confessions may be described as "self-serving fictions"; they present "the imaginative combination of the facts."[74] Zeno uses his confessions not to *reveal*, but to *create* himself.

I cannot help but wonder why Zeno would resort to fabrication in the process of self-revelation. One possibility, of course, is to soften the truth. Another, perhaps more likely option, is to enhance reality and to infuse the monotony of existence with drama—reflecting, in Coetzee's words, "a desire to be a particular way."[75] In Zeno's case, the character's theatrical preoccupation with small spectacles certainly gestures toward the latter. Zeno wants to be the hero of his own epic.

From a political point of view, the ethics of manufactured confession is dubious. Indeed, it draws into doubt the very purpose of confession. However, for Butler, the falseness or veracity of the confession does not impact the ethics implied by the confessional act.[76] She argues that the communal nature of confession—the fact that "giving an account of oneself" always presumes the presence of another—turns "the scene of address" into "a more primary

---

[72] Maltz-Leca, *Process*, 256.

[73] Njabulo Ndebele, 1998, "Memory, Metaphor, and the Triumphs of Narrative," in *Negotiating the Past: The Making of Memory in South Africa*, ed. Sarah Nuttall and Carli Coetzee, Oxford, Oxford University Press, 19–28; J. M. Coetzee, 1992 [1985], "Confession and Double Thoughts: Tolstoy, Rousseau, Dostoevsky," in *Doubling the Point: Essays and Interviews*, ed. David Attwell, Cambridge, MA: Harvard University Press, 251–293.

[74] Coetzee, "Confession," 280; Ndebele, "Memory," 21.

[75] Coetzee, "Confession," 280.

[76] Judith Butler, 2005, *Giving an Account of Oneself*, New York: Fordham University Press, 21.

ethical relation than a reflexive effort to give account of oneself."[77] So the act of confession, whether to friends or to a psychoanalyst (the examples Butler cites), is always ethical. From this perspective, Zeno's self-indulgent and probably fictional revelations, directed at a vaguely defined audience that might include his psychoanalyst, are ethically and politically significant by virtue merely of their occurrence.

In a critique of Butler's argument, however, Chloë Taylor rightly remarks that "it seems quite gratifying to think that describing one's life to another on a couch or over wine is an ethical responsibility."[78] Taylor invokes Foucault's concept of "speaker's benefit" to describe "the illusion of confessants that they are politically engaged."[79] While Butler's theorization is less explicitly directed at politics and aimed more at the ethical construction of the self, it nonetheless invokes the same dubious conception of engagement. Here, "the speaker's benefit seems equally illusory, but now it is an illusion of ethicality rather than political engagement."[80] What Taylor's argument suggests is that both a political and an ethical reading should consider the possibility that the act of confession may itself function as a form of privilege—a right to subjecthood that presumes the right to speak and to be listened to.

Taylor's critique is particularly compelling when read in the context of the TRC, which formed the backdrop to *Zeno*'s creation and which sought to enact a reparative mode of confessional reciprocity. Furthermore, the politics of confession in the TRC cannot be separated from broader confessional regimes in the colony and the postcolony. The subjectivities constructed and controlled by colonialism and postcolonialism lurk beneath Svevo's Trieste and Kentridge's Johannesburg. Even when not directly acknowledged, they pulse throughout *Zeno* as the "dark underside" of the modernity that enables the confessional subjectivity of the twentieth century. This raises the question of whether the politics and ethics of psychoanalytic confession can seamlessly be transposed to the colonial and postcolonial context.

Postcolonial Confession

If the Western European subject of the twentieth century, embodied by Zeno, may presume the right to confession-as-self affirmation, the same is not true

---

[77] Butler, *Giving an Account*, 21.
[78] Chloë Taylor, 2009, *The Culture of Confession from Augustine to Foucault: A Genealogy of the "Confessing Animal,"* New York: Routledge, 177.
[79] Taylor, *Culture of Confession*, 177.
[80] Taylor, *Culture of Confession*, 177.

for the colonial subject. In a wide-ranging exploration of intersections between Foucault's confessional discourse and anti- and postcolonial theory, Daniele Lorenzini and Martina Tazzioli note that "the injunction for the subject to tell the truth about himself or herself is differently shaped in the space of the colony described by [Frantz] Fanon and in the modern Western societies addressed by Foucault."[81] Confessional exchange in the colony is determined by regimes of power that rely on assumptions about the racialized subject and the discursive authority of the state. These operate dually, to undercut the very possibility of confession and to deprive the confessional act of its political power.

The primary assumption that shapes confessional discourse in the colony is the colonizer's belief that the colonized subject is, as Lorenzini and Tazzioli put it, "incapable of truth."[82] Fanon makes this point repeatedly: in "The Conduct of Confession in North Africa" he acknowledges that the notion that the North African is "a liar" is "widely admitted" by figures of colonial authority such as magistrates, police officers, employers, and doctors, who construct the colonial subject as lazy and mendacious.[83] This is reinforced by the colonized subject's repudiation of her own confessions, which constitute a refusal to enter into a social pact with the colonizer. The withdrawn confession—retracted even in the face of incriminating evidence—casts doubt on the colonized subject's ability to tell the truth, and it undermines the generalization of judicial and civic standards of behavior within colonized societies. Fanon expands this point in *The Wretched of the Earth* where he posits that the colonized subject responds to "the lie of the colonial situation" with a lie.[84] Reacting to the colonizer with reticence and inscrutability, the colonized subject confirms her rejection of communality with the colonizer; simultaneously, she refuses to make herself legible, to turn herself into a truthful subject. In the colonial context, Fanon concludes, "There is no truthful behaviour."[85]

Lorenzini and Tazzioli interpret the mutual non-recognition of colonizer and colonized as a fundamental impediment to the production of "a confessional discourse of truth." The colonized subject's "conducts of confession" are "disqualified from the beginning," they argue, "as 'inconsistent,' 'untruthful,'

---

[81] Daniele Lorenzini and Martina Tazzioli, 2018, "Confessional Subjects and Conducts of Non-Truth: Foucault, Fanon, and the Making of the Subject," *Theory, Culture & Society* 35(1), 71–90, at 72.

[82] Lorenzini and Tazzioli, "Confessional Subjects," 77.

[83] Fanon, "The Conduct of Confession," 88.

[84] Frantz Fanon, 2004 [1961], *The Wretched of the Earth*, trans. Richard Philcox. New York: Grove Press, 14.

[85] Fanon, *Wretched*, 14.

76 Postcolonial Opera

and 'incoherent.' "[86] As a result, "the conditions for the practice of confession are excluded from the very outset."[87]

Throughout his writings, Fanon immediately and automatically inscribes the practice of confession into contexts of criminality (the subject accused of a crime in "The Conduct of Confession"), and psychiatric or physical illness (as in "The "North African Syndrome" and "Aspects of Psychiatric Care in Algeria Today").[88] The absence of a therapeutic confessional regime similar to the psychoanalytic or religious modes described by Foucault is striking. In the colony, it appears, there is no room for self-indulgent and narcissistic ruminations such as those of Zeno.

For Chloë Taylor, Fanon's rejection of a curative psychoanalytic project, which would take confession and the discovery of self-truth as its starting point, is political. "Far from advocating discursive or confessional practices as therapeutic," Taylor writes, "Fanon repeatedly underscores that the Algerians have no use for discussion, for words, for talk of equality and human rights, that all these terms strike them as vacuous while only their own actions will heal the debilitating psychic affects [*sic*] of colonization."[89] Since the colonial project is itself a form of violence visited primarily on the body, it is through embodied action, rather than discussion, that the impact of colonization should be reversed. In Fanon's view, then, the colonized subject will not become free by discovering her "true self" through introspection; rather, the liberated self must be recovered through the embodied refusal of structures of domination, violence, and colonial discipline. Here, the difference between the confessional regime of the bourgeois European subject of modernity and that of the subject of coloniality becomes glaringly clear. Psychiatry and psychoanalysis are functional in the colony only when they are used politically, as Fanon himself does, to aid the process of decolonization by exposing the systematic oppression of the colonized and encouraging political action in response.[90]

As a regime of words rather than actions, confession does little to resist institutionalized colonial power. Moreover, its emphasis on the individual appears at odds with the often communitarian constructions of anti-colonial agency. As Lorenzini and Tazzioli show, the complex dynamics of the colony and the postcolony, where truth is contested, the individual is contingent, and agency is constrained, turn confession into a concept-out-of-place,

---

[86] Lorenzini and Tazzioli, "Confessional Subjects," 77. Citing Fanon, "The Conduct of Confession," 87–88.
[87] Lorenzini and Tazzioli, "Confessional Subjects," 80.
[88] Fanon, *Decolonizing Madness*, 41–50 and 65–72.
[89] Taylor, *Culture of Confession*, 164.
[90] Taylor, *Culture of Confession*, 165.

ill-equipped to respond to the politics of both disempowerment and structural liberation.[91]

In a moving essay on the limited scope of the confessions submitted to the TRC by former apartheid collaborators, Jacob Dlamini questions the value of truths when they are not accompanied by structural change.[92] He describes the case of African National Congress (ANC) youth leader Peter Mokaba, who was exposed as an apartheid collaborator but was nonetheless granted senior positions in Nelson Mandela and Thabo Mbeki's governments.[93] Such apparent indifference to apartheid crimes exposes confession, in Dlamini's view, as an inadequate surrogate for real structural change. This view echoes Fanon's opinion that words and revelations are of limited use when the politics of selfhood and representation are broken at a structural level.

Zeno's confessions complicate Fanon and Dlamini's constructions of confession in post-apartheid South Africa and the postcolony. First, Zeno is neither victim nor perpetrator in the TRC sense. He did not suffer under the colonial or apartheid regime, nor did he participate explicitly in either. As individual, in other words, he has very little to confess. Moreover, Zeno is not a colonized subject. This means he should be capable of truth, though he does not use this ability. Instead, Zeno is apolitical, pursuing his Eurocentric concerns at the southern tip of the African continent, arguably without troubling anyone. As an individual, he is blameless. But as a stand-in for an entire society, he represents the broken structure of which Dlamini and Fanon speak. The question, then, is whether confession as performed by Kentridge's piece can create a link between Zeno, the apparently innocent postcolonial individual, and the enduring colonial structure to which he belongs. If opera sets out to perform confession on the postcolonial stage, the significance of such an endeavor is shaped fundamentally by the relationship between the agency of the sounding subject, her environment, and the context she seeks to evoke with her sounds.

J. M. Coetzee argues, following Charles F. Atkinson, that the confessional impulse which finds "an outlet" in the arts, should inevitably tend to be "unbounded," due to the absence of a confessor.[94] What Coetzee seems to suggest is that the confession not aimed directly at a listening and evaluating confessor becomes somehow ethically and formally unbounded. The conventions of confession need not apply, because the conventional discursive arrangement is disrupted.

---

[91] Lorenzini and Tazzioli, "Confessional Subjects."
[92] Jacob Dlamini, 2016,"Apartheid Confessions," *interventions* 18(6), 772–785.
[93] Dlamini, "Apartheid Confessions," 774.
[94] Coetzee, "Confession and Double Thoughts," 419.

78 Postcolonial Opera

Though not necessarily intended as such, a postcolonial reading of Coetzee's "unbounded confession" may hold useful implications for Zeno's operatic admissions in the context of early post-apartheid South Africa.[95] Coetzee's unboundedness, when understood in relation to Kentridge's own use of the term, suggests a confessional discourse that relies on formal disunity and heterogeneity to facilitate a dialectical exchange between the blinkered individual and the unsettled environment to which she belongs. In this reading, the formally ambiguous operatic confession becomes a vehicle not for the exposure of the colonizing villain or the empowerment of the colonized subject but for the entry of the politically apathetic bourgeois subject into the postcolonial present.

Operatic Confession

Confession has been an operatic preoccupation since the late seventeenth century, especially due to the perceived efficacy of sung revelations.[96] "While confession in any art form was at basis verbal," Olivia Bloechl writes, "its delivery in skilfully crafted theatrical song could enhance its effectiveness by heightening listeners' sense of its subjective truthfulness."[97] Bloechl traces a proliferation of confessional scenes in eighteenth- and nineteenth-century opera, mirroring the Enlightenment and post-Enlightenment era's growing interest in questions of personal freedom, responsibility, and—later—interiority.

In contemporary opera, too, confession remains a popular theme. Recent creations that engage with the topic include Inger Wikström's *The Confession of a Fool* (2002), with a libretto adapted from August Strindberg's novel, *Le Plaidoyer d'un fou* (1893); Susan Hurley's *Anaïs* (2010), on the final hours of the life of Anaïs Nin; *Confession* (2010), by composer Raphaël Lucas and librettists Jacque Trussel and Margaret Vignola; *Dolores Claiborne* (2013) by Tobias Picker and librettist J. D. McCatchy, based on the eponymous novel by Stephen King; and the multisensory opera-in-the-dark, *Confessions* (2016), conceived by Jens Hedman, Rūta Vitkauskaitė, and Åsa Nordgren of the Lithuanian experimental opera company, Operomanija. These works construct the confessional regime as a sonic spectacle mediated through the performance space and the relationship between audience and performer, which is conditioned by ideals of mutual recognition and trust.

---

[95] Coetzee develops his thoughts on confession in relation to the works of Dostoyevsky, Tolstoy, and Rousseau, rather than postcolonial literature.

[96] Bloechl, *Opera and the Political Imaginary*, esp. chapter 3.

[97] Bloechl, *Opera and the Political Imaginary*, 87.

Opera's reliance on the singing voice is an important factor in its appeals for confessional performance. According to Bloechl, it is especially the philosophical link between expressive vocality and personal freedom that reinforces the suitability of opera for performances of self-revelation.[98] Following Stanley Cavell, who argues that the singing voice is a manifestation both of authentic selfhood and of personal and political agency, the singing voice in opera may therefore be understood to represent the interiority of the confessing subject, absolutely truthful because uncoerced.[99]

This interpretation of singing voice as confessional medium builds on Foucault's own early theories of confession, which echoed Jean-Jacques Rousseau in emphasizing the sonorous quality of truthful confession. In his earliest text on confession, an introduction to a new edition of Rousseau's *Dialogues* published in 1962, Foucault argues that voice and hearing are central to the regime of confessional truth.[100] He finds in Rousseau's work an emphasis on multisensuality, from which Foucault extracts a hierarchical structure that places sonority at the top. In Foucault's words, Rousseau privileges vocal expression "because he saw therein—for the music as well as for the language—the most natural of expressions, one in which the speaking subject is entirely present, without reserve or reticence, in each of the forms of what he says."[101] In other words, confession is what Coetzee calls an "auricular discourse."[102]

Lauri Siisiäinen observes that Foucault particularly emphasizes *melodious* vocal expression in this early theorization of the confessional regime. "Inside this confessional regime," Siisiäinen writes, "the explanation or justification given for this privilege of voice (and especially, of its 'chanting,' melodious inflections) is the belief in the 'natural affinity' of the former with the flow of the soul's movements, i.e. emotions, passions, and inclinations."[103] Voice, for Foucault, is the most natural and hence the most representative manifestation of the individual's true self. It is the ideal vehicle for confession.

Foucault later refined his theorization of confession; his work in the 1970s and 1980s takes a multisensory view more closely aligned with Rousseau's

[98] Bloechl, *Opera and the Political Imaginary*, 91.
[99] Stanley Cavell, 1994, *A Pitch of Philosophy: Autobiographical Exercises*, Cambridge: Cambridge University Press.
[100] I base my arguments here on Lauri Siisiäinen, 2012, "Confession, Voice and the Sensualization of Power: The Significance of Michel Foucault's 1962 Encounter with Jean-Jacques Rousseau," *Foucault Studies* 14, 138–153.
[101] Cited in Siisiäinen, "Confession, Voice," 146.
[102] Coetzee, "Confession and Double Thoughts," 419. Foucault's argument in this text can also, as Siisiäinen notes, be read as a precursor to Derrida's notion of "phonocentrism," which was first introduced in 1966, not long after Foucault's introduction. See Siisiäinen, "Confession, Voice," 146.
[103] Siisiäinen, "Confession, Voice," 144.

80 Postcolonial Opera

confessional regime. Nonetheless, the sonic register of confession remains important to Foucault, especially as it relates to the extra-linguistic features of disclosure, such as voice quality, physical movement, and gesture. At this point, however, the philosopher appears to contradict his own earlier construction of confessional vocality, as he indicates that authenticity and truth inhere in "rough, awkward and offensive expressions" rather than refined speech. In Siisiäinen's words, Foucault here stipulates that "confessional expressions are and should be . . . unmediated by decency, neat articulation or eloquence."[104] Instead of melodious finesse, in other words, the confessing voice should embody unrestrained immediacy.

Siisiäinen does not offer an explanation for the apparent reversal in Foucault's theorization, accepting perhaps that it is a natural result of the philosopher's revised approach to confession in general. But in the context of operatic confession, this revision is impactful, as it calls into question the production of confessional truth by the highly trained, constructed voice of the singer. Bloechl resolves this tension by distinguishing between different styles of musical writing, whereby arias composed in a coherent, earnest, and functional style are more successful at performing confession than counterparts presented as "a predominantly sensual experience of lyricism, rhythmic propulsion, or harmonic tension and release."[105] Confession, then, is not merely a matter of voice but also of style: the less rarefied, the more reliable.

In *Confessions of Zeno* these tensions sound out in a complex interplay between sung, spoken, and written text. Given that it is an operatic performance, *Zeno* does seem to reinscribe the auricular paradigm of the confessional regime. But the piece nonetheless complicates the privileging of song as confessional instrument. In Volans's score, the confessing character of Zeno is the only one who does not sing. His father, wife, and mistress address him in elaborate arias and ensembles, but Zeno himself responds using the spoken word throughout. To this split communicative regime is added a series of projected text fragments (also "notated" in the score), which extends, repeats, or completes the vocalized dialogue. In Act I, for instance, the dying father sings, "Do you think . . ." (b.66), and the projected text finishes his question, "that death is the end?." Jane Taylor remarks that the fragments of projected text represent characters' "mental activity." In the case of the father, the words "suggested the aphasia, or the disintegration of the father's speech in a way that might indicate a stroke. Mental activity seems to still be present, but it is at times locked within the thinker, rather than moving freely through the

---

[104] Siisiäinen, "Confession, Voice," 150.
[105] Bloechl, *Opera and the Political Imaginary*, 118.

passage of the voice."[106] Here, the capacity of the voice to reveal the authentic interiority of the subject is undermined by its inability to communicate coherently. Indeed, the projections often appear to hurry along the father's laborious speech, impatiently finishing his sentences for him, as in bb.43–44, where the father sings "what, hm, what, what" while the projection interjects with "what I will say to you tomorrow."[107]

The multiplication of communicative registers—song, speech, and writing—creates what Taylor describes as "a kind of vacuum" between characters.[108] They address each other across temporal and sonic frames, conditioned by their divergent relations to the context of the narration. But it also appears to confirm Foucault's suggestion that true confession cannot be articulated in the polished medium of genteel song. If Zeno is to disclose the truth about himself he must do so in speech. Zeno himself, however, quickly casts doubt on this interpretation, with his admission that he takes little interest in telling the truth. Zeno's spoken words become a performance of deception, which casts doubt on the integrity of the whole confessional project in which the piece claims to engage.

Zeno's lack of musicality in the opera echoes Svevo's source text, where the titular character complains repeatedly about his poor performance on the violin. Despite his enthusiasm, Zeno is plagued by a number of musical shortcomings, including an inability to keep time on his instrument and a lack of proficiency he attributes to ill-health. Indeed, it is one of the earliest sources of tension between him and his rival, Guido, a gifted violinist "who calls himself an amateur only because he has too much money to make a profession of [music]."[109] Zeno is jealous of Guido's skill and finds in the latter's playing an element of artifice, which according to the former, serves only to deceive.[110] His own indifferent performance, on the other hand, should be interpreted as a sign of his honesty—a preposterous suggestion considering Zeno's own admissions of insincerity. But Deborah Amberson follows Sergio Finzi in setting up a dichotomy between Guido's beautiful music, or "musica intonata," and Zeno's "musica stonata"—his out of tune or clashing music—which repeats the two characters' oppositional representations of honesty and dishonesty.[111] Amberson writes that "Guido's music constitutes an unreality for the musician and a deception for the listener while Zeno's musicality, possessing none of these illusory qualities, introduces the unstoppable

[106] Bloechl, *Opera and the Political Imaginary*, 241.
[107] Volans, *Confessions of Zeno Part 1* [score], 34.
[108] Taylor, "Taking Stock," 239.
[109] Svevo, *Confessions*, 150.
[110] Svevo, *Confessions*, 168.
[111] Amberson, "Zeno's Dissonant Violin," 107.

82 Postcolonial Opera

rhythm of reality."[112] Despite Zeno's own admission that he does not always tell the truth, Amberson finds, in an interpretive act that echoes Foucault, an idealized veracity in the unrefined and immediate expression of Zeno's "musica stonata." Zeno, it appears, is both truthful and false: he admits to his own lies, but does not cloak his statements in musical artifice. Thus, the distribution of musical proficiency in both Svevo's novel and in Kentridge and Volans's adaptation highlights the contradictory nature of Zeno as bourgeois individual—a subject whose truth is always conditional on convenience.

Postcoloniality and the Musical Bourgeoisie

Zeno's bourgeois nature is underscored structurally, by Volans's use of a string quartet to accompany the opera. In the socio-historical context both of Svevo's novel and of late apartheid South Africa, it is impossible not to read the string quartet through what Christina Bashford calls "its historical associations with wealth and middle-class consumption."[113] As a favorite participatory entertainment of Europe's aristocratic and upwardly mobile bourgeois classes during the nineteenth century, and as an increasingly cerebral form of classical concert culture in the twentieth, the string quartet represents an artistic horizon associated most closely in colonial and early post-colonial South Africa with the self-serving white, colonial elite of which Zeno would be a part.[114]

The binary between the European and the postcolonial spheres apparently symbolized by the string quartet is reinforced by the divergent material Volans distributes between Zeno's father and the women characters. In his main musical number, an extended, fragmented dialogue with Zeno titled "Death of the Father," the father sings mostly in a syllabic, angular style designed to illustrate his physical and emotional anguish. His rapid, accentuated declamations are characterized by leaps and frequent registral shifts, which strengthen the impression of incoherence created by the splitting of text between voice and projection.

In contrast to the father's music in Act I, Volans's Act II music for the women—the four sisters' ensemble, Augusta's "Honeymoon" aria, Carla's

---

[112] Amberson, "Zeno's Dissonant Violin," 107.

[113] Christina Bashford, 2003, "The String Quartet and Society," in *The Cambridge Companion to the String Quartet*, ed. Robin Stowell and Jonathan Cross, 3–18, at 17.

[114] See Stephanus Muller, 2022, "Michael Blake's String Quartets and the Idea of an African Art Music," *Tempo* 76(300), 6–17, for the apparent incommensurability between the string quartet form and the Southern African cultural-political context.

aria and climax, and the duets between Carla and Augusta—reflects a greater degree of syntactical coherence and rhythmic complexity. Though the sung parts in Act II still resist sustained melodic contours, their angular character is frequently interrupted by long melismas and brief snatches of melancholy stepwise motion, as in the first ensemble of Act II, "Four Sisters," where the first and second soprano—likely representing the eldest of the four Malfenti sisters, Ada and Augusta—echo each other in a floating, melismatic articulation of the word "suspicion." The sisters are singing here of their competing needs and interests, which lead them to doubt their own standing in the family hierarchy:

> In a household of four sisters.
> Four sisters.
> Each with a right to father's knee.
> Each holding a suspicion
> That he waited for the other three.[115]

The melisma on "suspicion" is the first moment of melodic writing in the whole of Act II; the word is hence imbued with a special significance that arguably speaks not only to the sisters' relationships with each other but also to the audience's relationship with Zeno. Again, the unreliability of *Zeno*'s confessional performance is underscored musically.

"Four Sisters" reinforces the difference between the women's music and the father's music not only by means of sustained melodic lines but also through its use of musical quotation. Volans, in the composer's statement quoted above, specifies that he adapted part of this ensemble piece from pre-existing material. In fact, the music for "Four Sisters" exactly replicates material from the second movement of Volans's second string quartet, *Hunting:Gathering*, which is in turn a set of variations on a mbira piece called "Muthambe," "first played by a famous mbira player from the 19th century, Pasipamire, from the Shona people of Zimbabwe."[116] In *Zeno*, Volans transposes the original interlocking string quartet parts of *Hunting:Gathering* for four sopranos and gives the "new" string quartet a simple, sparse accompaniment of sustained

---

[115] Volans, *Confessions of Zeno Part 2* [score], 15.

[116] Volans, "Musik," 22. This is not the only place where *Hunting:Gathering* is invoked. The string quartet's opening material is copied almost exactly in the opening of Act I; a fact that puts paid to Volans's claim that the music for Act I is "completely self-contained" (Volans, "Musik," 22). Volans's (and, indeed, Kentridge's) practice of self-quotation may perhaps be interpreted as what Foucault calls a confessional "pleasure spiral," whereby the pleasure of confession produces guilt, which leads to more confession, etc., in an endless sequence of self-referentiality and reiteration. For more on this, see Chloë Taylor, *The Culture of Confession*, 105.

open fourths and fifths, which eventually transforms into a spirited duplication of the sung parts. Midway through "Four Sisters," Volans incorporates a further quotation from an earlier work, namely, the Nyanga panpipe dance he paraphrases in his first string quartet, *White Man Sleeps*. Like the "Muthambe" material, the sung lines of this section are exact replications of the original string quartet material; in this case, the voices are accompanied by interlocking strings, repeating a series of percussive, staccato quavers in a lilting 24-pulse cycle.

The "Muthambe" and Nyanga panpipe quotations create an explicit link between *Zeno* and the colonial and postcolonial African context. These moments of exact replication—not only of original source material but also of Volans's own earlier compositions—relate the piece to the composer's avowed interest in reconciling Western and African musical styles. Even though Volans claims, by 2002, that he no longer wishes to engage with musical interculturality, this material inscribes *Zeno* into the politics of postcolonial citation represented by *Hunting:Gathering* and *White Man Sleeps*.

Later, in "Carla's Song," a series of rapid, rising scalar passages replicates the driving percussion rhythms that underpin the Indian *Bharatanatyam* dance style—a moment of rhythmic complexity which in Volans's own description repeats patterns from music he composed for the British choreographer Shobana Jeyasingh.[117] Rather than "Africa," broadly conceived, Volans here invokes the Indian subcontinent—another postcolonial sphere marked by contradictory histories of resistance and aspiration. The musical invocations of formerly colonial spaces represented by the quoted material in "Four Sisters" and "Carla's Song" anchor *Zeno* to the postcolony in a manner that contradicts the apparently Eurocentric narrative and visual content of the piece.

In Volans's treatment, the women come to represent a form of musicality that falls outside the canonical Western tradition. Thus, their sonic characterization echoes the typical operatic treatment of the female exotic—foreign, non-normative, and potentially threatening. (Incidentally, Amberson argues that in Svevo's novel, Carla's singing also functions as a form of exoticism since she sounds her best, in Zeno's opinion, when performing Triestine folk songs in a regional style that falls between speech and melody.)[118] The threat, in this instance, is to the construction of Zeno as coherent Western bourgeois subject. Through the women's music, the protagonist and his confessions are

---

[117] The piece Volans refers to here is *Surface Tension*, which was premiered by Jeyasingh's dance company in 2000.

[118] Amberson, "Zeno's Dissonant Violin," 112.

tied to a postcolonial context that presses itself inescapably onto his immediate sonic and social environment. The incorporation of non-Western musical material thereby serves to split Zeno between Europe and the postcolony, locating him simultaneously in both.

If the women's music in Act II reflects an exotic ideal of musical naturalism, the father's musical characterization is more abstract, marked by incoherent refrains and unmelodic exhortations. There is something clinical about Volans's sonic treatment of the father: rather than emerging as a figure with a distinct musical persona, he remains fractured and impersonal. Even the depiction of his emotional and physical anguish in "Death of the Father" appears to lack empathy. Instead, Volans relies on the detached harshness of accented, staccato strokes to describe the character's final thoughts and words.

The father's dying scene is framed by two choruses. The first is a "Chorus of Trees," which performs a solemn, syncopated meditation on the inevitability of Zeno's misdemeanors and of illness and death. It ends quietly, on a series of widely spaced, pianissimo triads. D-flat major (cello and Vl 1) and E minor (viola and Vl 2) are superimposed, creating gentle, suspended dissonances that evoke an ambiguous air of both weariness and suspense. They echo the defeatism of the text:

> The moon will follow the sun;
> The miser will follow his coin
> The mistress will follow her looking glass
> Her lover will follow his groin.
> The echo will follow the shout
> The prize is pursued by the scout
> In the chase
> We forget
> That we all
> Have one fate:
> Whatever moves in the end wears out![119]

From here, the performance segues straight into "Death of the Father," where the chorus's defeatist declaration is confirmed: Zeno's father falls into unconsciousness with a dramatic exclamation: "Be gone with you!" Zeno immediately absolves himself of his father's passing ("It was not my fault"), while the nurse remarks that it is "a pity for the old man to die with all that hair still

---

[119] Taylor, *Confessions of Zeno* [libretto], 12.

86 Postcolonial Opera

on his head."[120] In this moment of tragic absurdity, the roles of the various sounding agents are neatly delineated: Zeno is the agent of self-interest dishonesty while the chorus functions as the harbinger of truth, envisaging the father's demise and the hand of fate in Zeno's and his companions' actions. But the reliability of the chorus's truth is called into question at once: immediately following the nurse's pronouncement, the string quartet launches into a series of rapid, fortissimo triplets, which initiates a "Pseudo-scientific Chorus" apparently aimed at reviving Zeno's father:

> Give him a cordial!
> Peristaltic action
> Gives rise to acid.
> The body has its own physical laws.
> Nicotine is not the cause.
> He may become part conscious
> But will surely lose his reason.
> Chronic bronchitis
> Spittoon bears the witness.
> Acute necrosis
> The old man is witless.
> He may become part conscious
> But will surely lose his reason.
> Give him a cordial
> He may become part conscious
> But will surely lose his reason.
> Chronic bronchitis
> Give him a cordial.
> Insomnia is cured by electric impulses
> But the body convulses.
> Electric shock causes sleeplessness.
> But the body convulses.
> He will lose his reason.[121]

The chorus delivers its message with militant precision, articulating its scientifically questionable instructions in vigorous, syllabic strokes. But the methodical rationality suggested by angular, rhythmic forward progressions is repeatedly undermined by the intrusion of syncopated beats, metrical

---

120 Volans, *Confessions of Zeno Part 1* [score], 44.
121 Taylor, *Confessions of Zeno* [libretto], 14, original punctuation.

misalignments, and unexpected dissonances. These features appear in quick succession, as the chorus shifts from a 9/8 march that repeatedly trips over the extra eighth note at the end of each bar, into a series of sung intervals that seem to transgress onto different pitches as if by accident. Even when the metrical pace halves, it keeps getting interrupted by rhythmic syncopations that disrupt the natural meter of the text. The text is itself irregular, thus rendering the realization of a rhythmically regular setting nearly impossible. However, instead of accommodating or smoothing over the metrical instabilities of Taylor's poetry, Volans appears to underline them with an equally irregular musical realization. Together, these stylistic techniques cast doubt on the integrity of the chorus's scientific commands. Rather than structurally sound rationality, the music descends time and again into comedic absurdism. Thus, yet another apparent "agent of truth" is exposed as little more than a buffoon.

Throughout the "Pseudo-scientific chorus," rhythmic and melodic material strongly reminiscent of and occasionally identical to the opening chorus seems to draw the first act full circle. But just as stasis descends over the last 16 bars, alternating between sustained pianissimo fifths and full-bar rests, a new sonic world intrudes. The score announces the entry of "bugler and street criers SINGING AND PLAYING" (b.139), but does not provide further information. Four bars later, Act I's music breaks off without a double bar line. The rest of the page is filled with a single direction: "4: Mayhem." Surviving footage shows a group of performers—likely the puppet manipulators—surrounding Zeno's father's bed, waving various objects, marching, dancing, singing and ululating joyfully. After the almost mechanistic restraint of the preceding music, the exuberance of this moment is startling. The transition from the "Pseudo-scientific Chorus" to "Mayhem" at the end of Act I echoes the relationship between the father's music and that of the women in the opera: it emphasizes the juxtaposition of a contrived European musical realm with an arguably more spontaneous postcolonial sphere represented by non-Western sonic signifiers like ululations and what Volans calls "ethno-cultural sources" (see ▶ Clip 2.2).

The non-teleological design of Volans's music resists the resolution or closure afforded by the confessional impulse. Dissolving into "mayhem" at the end of Act I, and floating away on quiet open fifths at the end of Act II, the score appears to peter out without achieving anything. Respite, here, is not a prolongation of a tonal point of arrival but a deferral of the crime—an impotent "shrugging of the shoulders," rather than a call to action.[122] What *Zeno*'s music confesses, then, is a version of the splitting performed by Kentridge's

---

[122] My thanks to William Fourie for guiding me toward this observation.

88   Postcolonial Opera

double staging: it confesses the position of the bourgeois postcolonizing subject who feels out of place in the former colony and who mitigates his imperial yearning by recreating a "shadow of Europe" in the postcolony. This is the confession of a person who is not directly guilty of anything but whose persistent disassociation from the abject realities of his immediate environment renders him complicit in an entire structure of criminality and oppression.

The Scale of the Political

For Jane Taylor, Zeno's confessional performance ultimately comes down to a matter of scale. She writes that "the relations of scale of the personal and political are profoundly dissimilar [for Zeno] to those with which we are familiar in South Africa; and part of what we have done with the play is to attempt to interpret this alternative view of national and personal priorities."[123] In TRC-era South Africa, as in other reconciliation contexts, confession is loaded with enormous political stakes. Against this backdrop, Zeno embodies the bourgeois spirit whose affinities, actions, and moral judgments are adapted to a shifting permutation of personal values and external circumstances. Situated alongside the momentous struggles and revelations of those testifying about their lives under apartheid, Zeno's admissions are insignificant—they are the small transgressions of a small life. But for Taylor, that does not negate their political weight. Rather, as this chapter shows, it is the very fact that the bourgeois postcolonizing subject, of which Zeno is the ultimate representative, is able to conduct a life of apparent triviality amid unfathomable suffering and upheaval, that imbues his revelations with profound political consequence.

The political, in Zeno's telling, does not reside in moments of racialized oppression of colonial disenfranchisement—whether as perpetrator or as victim. Rather, it is to be found in every experience he is able to recount *without* having to remark on such events; it is to be found in the things he does not mention because he does not need to; in the worries he does not have because they do not affect him. In other words, the political, in Zeno's world, is constituted as a series of silences and omissions. It is both too small to notice and too large to remain within view; both profoundly personal and entirely public. These are the contradictions that characterize the subject position of the bourgeois postcolonizing individual, whose main crime is privilege.

Zeno actualizes Taylor's question of scale as an organizing principle through which to read the piece's structure. Volans's juxtaposition of Western

---

[123] Taylor, "Taking Stock," 237.

and non-Western musical styles plays with sonic scale as a measurement of cultural proximity and differentiation. Scale, here, is of course suggestive of tonality and the hierarchical organization of individual pitch classes, but it also gestures to the literal and symbolic distances between different cultural and political formations.[124] The scale of the Southern African and Indian quotations' intrusion on the opera's Western musical world might be minimal, but it nonetheless has a profound impact on the piece's various significations. Without these musical incursions, Zeno's split subjectivity—perched between Europe and South Africa—would be no more than a visual conceit, easily lost amid the array of references and suggestions that populate the piece. By quoting his own paraphrases of "Muthambe," the Nyanga panpipe dance, and the *Bharatanatyam* dance, Volans ties *Zeno* explicitly to a contested terrain of struggle around cultural belonging. As much as Zeno—the person and the piece—has its eye on Europe, it cannot escape its own complicated position in the postcolony. Volans's musical gestures anchor the bourgeois postcolonizing subject to two different places at once.

A more evocative reading, however, may be one that interprets scale as a measure of magnitude, rather than distance. This is perhaps most obvious in the use of voice as a measure of scale. Zeno's speaking voice is dwarfed by the operatic exhortations of his companions and especially by the choral sections that represent the public from which he seems so detached. His spoken confessions sound innocuous when heard alongside the complex, monumental sung forms that populate the rest of the piece. The use of spoken word thus reinforces the apparent insignificance of his revelations. They are trifling, both in style and in substance. Scale, in this reading, becomes a measure of texture and register. If the spoken word sounds out the inconsequential self-regard of the bourgeois postcolonizing subject, the sung form represents the scale of the social and the political.

Kentridge's video projections likewise play with scale: using the device of film as a means to manipulate perspective, the artist manages to create the illusion of a public far larger than the actual cast they could afford to employ.[125] Moreover, as Kentridge notes, the projection creates a visual field in which the "small scale jointed paper figures and full sized costumed / disguised performers could be equalised on the screen."[126] Scale hence functions not

---

[124] On scale, tonality, and hierarchy, see Katherine Bergeron, 1992, "Prologue: Disciplining Music," in *Disciplining Music: Musicology and Its Canons*, ed. Katherine Bergeron and Philip V. Bohlman, Chicago: University of Chicago Press, 1–9.

[125] Taylor, "Taking Stock," 243.

[126] Kentridge, 2001, "Zeno at 4 am: Director's Note." https://www.kentridge.studio/confessions-of-zeno-directors-note/. Accessed September 20, 2021.

only as a measure of difference but also as a leveling device—one that can erase the perceived hierarchy between the self-important bourgeois subject and his distressed environment. It also complicates the individual's construal of his own uniqueness. Kentridge's use of shadows becomes a way of "scaling" Zeno—of turning him from individual into type. Thus, Fanon's and Dlamini's concern with a confessional form that works at the level of political structures, rather than individuals, takes form through the play of shadows: whereas Zeno the character might represent confession at the individual level, the piece's shadow projections become themselves the authors of a series of shadow confessions inextricable from the individual, but nonetheless representative of the structure. Simultaneously, however, these shadow projections contradict and complicate Zeno's articulations. Functioning in counterpoint to Zeno's words, the projections, like Volans's music, embody an additional communicative register that occasionally extends, and at other times negates, the main character's statements. Rather than constructing a coherent confessional regime, in other words, the projections and the music appear to underscore the incoherence and unreliability of the bourgeois postcolonizing subject's self-representation.

Zeno's projection as both an independent agent and a representation of structural processes infuses his actions and confessions with a political consequence not immediately apparent in their content. The confessions themselves become a series of shadows, approaching the political but never quite reaching it—much in the style of Zeno the philosopher's paradox of motion—to reveal the bourgeois postcolonizing individual's self-absorption as a deeply politicized response to the enduring structures of coloniality and apartheid. The white bourgeois subject in the postcolony is himself a representative of splitting and doubling: a doubling of Europe in the postcolony and simultaneously a representative of the discontinuities and misalignments between the two settings. Zeno becomes, as it were, the shadow of Europe in Africa.

Opera, in this configuration, is not merely a neutral medium through which to communicate these complex observations. Rather, the art form's inscription in histories and cultures of imperial expansion and racialized oppression plays an important role in articulating the split subjectivity of the bourgeois postcolonizing subject. Like the protagonist, opera is itself both complicit and innocent—a privileged participant in colonial culture, but rarely an active agent of the embodied violence Fanon mentions when he describes the colonial project.

The form itself, then, may be seen as a metaphor for the subjectivity it seeks to critique. But opera's manifold media also make it an ideal vehicle through which to play with, or even deconstruct, this subjectivity. Its centralization of

Confession   91

voice offers a means to explore various constructions of candor and authenticity, thereby offering a chance to consider carefully what confession might mean—and, indeed, who it might be for—in the present context. Likewise, opera's ability to accommodate musical forms and techniques from different cultural spheres and its incorporation of distinct communicative registers (including the visual, the sonic, and the embodied) allows it to sound out the contradictions that inhere in the subject's self-serving revelations. Performing a mode of narrative and generic self-interrogation that unmasks the insular nature of the bourgeois postcolonizing subject, operatic confession offers a way to mediate between the specific and the general, the familiar and the strange, the consequential and the insignificant. Complicating questions of agency and identity in the postcolony, opera itself becomes a tool for scaling the political.

3
Mourning

Opera may be regarded as a melancholy form. Its very existence is steeped in loss. Emerging in the late sixteenth century, as I mention in Chapter 1, out of the yearning for a vanished Grecian theatrical ideal, the genre remains entangled in the efforts, first exerted by the Florentine Camerata, to revive the practices of antique tragedy.[1] Even as contemporary practitioners experiment with techniques and technologies developed over a century of industrial innovation, the art form's retrospective orientation—one focused on recovery, as much as invention—ties it to a past built on absence, rather than presence. Perpetually in search of an imagined origin story, opera is perched on the brink of the very loss it seeks to remedy. If not quite dead, as Mladen Dolar and Slavoj Žižek argue, the genre does appear to be preoccupied with extinction.[2] In Dolar's words, opera is "a persistent revival of a lost past, a reflection of the lost aura."[3] Its never-ending quest to recover what came before shrouds the art form in melancholy.

But beyond opera's antique hankerings, another melancholy mode haunts the form. Throughout Western opera, the racialized Other is incorporated as what Anne Anlin Cheng calls the "melancholic object."[4] Furiously imagined and voraciously consumed, Black and Indigenous bodies (and, indeed, voices) have served as opera's negative double. These melancholic objects— the "nature" to opera's "culture"—have historically ensured the art form's authority as a measure of (white) cultural civility. For every barbarically Black Monostatos, an audience full of racially refined agents of progress has agonistically been called into being. Opera's craving for the absent present of the racialized Other is, again to adopt a term coined by Cheng, a form of "racial melancholy,"[5] which combines with the genre's yearning for the past to create an artistic practice obsessed with what it cannot have.

---

[1] For opera's sixteenth-century origins, which combined existing theatrical forms with attempts to revive Greek drama, see Blair Hoxby, 2005, "The Doleful Airs of Euripides: The Origins of Opera and the Spirit of Tragedy Reconsidered," *Cambridge Opera Journal* 17(3), 253–269; Carolyn Abbate and Roger Parker, 2012, *A History of Opera: The Last Four Hundred Years*, London: Penguin, esp. 59–61.

[2] Slavoj Žižek and Mladen Dolar, 2002, *Opera's Second Death*, London: Routledge, viii.

[3] Dolar, in *Opera's Second Death*, 3.

[4] Anne Anlin Cheng, 2001, *The Melancholy of Race: Psychoanalysis, Assimilation, and Hidden Grief*, Oxford: Oxford University Press, xi.

[5] Cheng, *Melancholy*, xi.

Postcolonial Opera. Juliana M. Pistorius, Oxford University Press. © Oxford University Press 2025.
DOI: 10.1093/oso/9780197749203.003.0004

Opera's melancholy figures—antique tragedies and pre-civil Others—are inescapable. The art form cannot shed or relinquish its melancholic objects, because without them it will cease to exist. As a result, opera persists in a state of irresolution, always grappling with new strategies to resolve its formal and racial voids and exclusions. The art form's melancholy derives from its subjection to a mourning that remains forever incomplete.[6]

In *Black Box/Chambre Noire*, a 2005 installation commissioned by Deutsche Bank and the now-defunct Deutsche Guggenheim in Berlin, opera's unresolved mourning takes on a critical function. Created in the same year Kentridge premiered his production of Mozart's *Magic Flute* at Théâtre Royal de la Monnaie in Brussels, the piece enacts a collision between Western opera and German colonial history. Through one central character—a tiny animated megaphone—the piece invokes Sigmund Freud's concept of *Trauerarbeit* (which I choose to translate as the work of mourning), to signal a purposeful engagement with colonial and operatic grief.

The work's title—*Black Box/Chambre Noire*—refers implicitly to the binary between the enchanted melancholies of Mozart's *Magic Flute*, and the gloomier losses confronted in Kentridge's adaptation of the opera. An equivocal play between light and dark, truth and untruth, history and memory underpins each of the title's various significations: first, *Black Box* refers to the "black box" of the theater—a space of experimental performance and fantasy, but also of brutal truth. Second, it refers to the inner chamber of a camera, the *chambre noire*, where light is captured and inverted to suspend a single image in time. "The stages become camera, the images shown or played out like a record of photographs of the world outside the camera (or theater)," Kentridge writes.[7] Finally, the title also refers to the "black box" of an airplane; the final witness to disaster.[8] Like an airplane's black box, Kentridge's piece bears witness to catastrophe: the catastrophe of coloniality, and more specifically, Germany's catastrophic massacre of the Herero and Nama people of present-day Namibia.

Between 1904 and 1907, Kaiser Wilhelm II's Imperial Army waged an unjust war against the Herero and Nama people of what was then the colony of German South-West Africa. The war's brutal tactics and official policy of all-out extermination resulted in the near-total destruction of the country's

---

[6] I adapt this point, to which I return below, from Sigmund Freud's "Mourning and Melancholia." See Sigmund Freud, 1963, "Mourning and Melancholia," trans. Joan Riviere, in *General Psychological Theory: Papers on Metapsychology*, ed. Philip Rieff, New York: Macmillan, 161–178.

[7] William Kentridge, 2009, "Magic Flute and Black Box: Sarastro and the Master's Voice," https://www.kentridge.studio/magic-flute-and-black-box-sarastro-and-the-masters-voice/, accessed March 22, 2021.

[8] Kentridge, "Sarastro."

94 Postcolonial Opera

Indigenous populations.[9] Today, historians recognize the extermination of the Herero and Nama as a direct precursor to the Holocaust.[10] In 1985, the United Nations officially classified the episode as a genocide, thus marking it as the first official genocide of the twentieth century.[11] *Black Box* animates the neglected history of the German Imperial Army's massacre of the Indigenous Herero and Nama populations of Namibia. Thus, Kentridge commandeers opera to mourn not only its own losses but also the losses inflicted by colonial violence.

Kentridge's choice to use an operatic installation as a vehicle for the work of mourning suggests a measure of faith in the art form's restorative capacity. Such a gesture appears oddly effacing of the genre's inability to resolve its own lacks and voids. Moreover, opera's complicity in the cultural, political, and even physical violence inflicted by the imperial project poses questions about the form's capacity to mourn colonial suffering. After all, if its own melancholy is built on the fetishization of the racialized Other, can opera offer a recuperative or restorative form of mourning to the victims of coloniality?

In this chapter I consider *Black Box/Chambre Noire*'s injunction to mourn. I draw on a growing body of scholarship on the work of mourning in the postcolony, to ask how Kentridge's piece participates in a restitutive agenda caught between the conflicting priorities of remembrance and forgetting. Approaching the work from an operatic, rather than art-historical perspective, I am interested in asking both *how* the piece enacts mourning, and what its formal approaches to mourning might mean—not only for the Herero whose suffering it memorializes, but for postcolonial opera in general, where the struggle to reconcile colonial complicity with post- and decolonial representation remains unresolved.

My analysis offers an overview of the piece, its historical and narrative content, and the circumstances of its creation, before turning to Philip Miller's soundtrack to the installation. As *Black Box* is a "fellow traveler" alongside *The Magic Flute*,[12] I attend extensively to the sonic and scopic relationship between the two works. I pay particular attention to the various transformations visited upon the operatic form (as represented by *The Magic Flute*) in the creators' quest to commemorate colonial violence. My examination takes

---

[9] Dominik J. Schaller, 2013 [1997], "The Genocide of the Herero and Nama in German South-West Africa, 1904–1907," in *Centuries of Genocide: Essays and Eyewitness Accounts*, ed. Samuel Totten and William S. Parsons, New York: Routledge, 89–116.

[10] See, for instance, Benjamin Madley, 2005, "From Africa to Auschwitz: How German South West Africa Incubated Ideas and Methods Adopted and Developed by the Nazis in Eastern Europe," *European History Quarterly* 35(3), 429–464, and David Olusoga and Casper W. Erichsen, 2010, *The Kaiser's Holocaust: Germany's Forgotten Genocide and the Colonial Roots of Nazism*, London: Faber.

[11] Schaller, "Genocide," 101.

[12] See the Introduction for an explanation of "fellow travelers."

in some of the most compelling musical moments in *Black Box*, to ask how they destabilize the Enlightenment agenda of Mozart's original, and how they negotiate the intricate politics of representing opera's colonial Other. In this, I expand on existing considerations of *Black Box*, which have focused primarily on the work's visual references.[13] Ultimately, I ask with Serena Guarracino whether opera can (or should) be trusted with the postcolonial work of mourning—and if so, how such mourning transforms the operatic form.[14]

Black Box/*Chambre Noire*

Kentridge describes the relationship between *Black Box* and *The Magic Flute* as follows: "In *Black Box* I wanted to look at the political unconscious of *The Magic Flute*—looking at the damages of colonialism, which described its predations to itself as bringing enlightenment to the Dark Continent."[15] *The Magic Flute*, with its triumphant assessment of Western Enlightenment, becomes a representative of the various forms of positivism that underscored the colonial project. "If *The Magic Flute* suggests the utopian moment of the Enlightenment," Kentridge writes, "*Black Box* represents the other end of the spectrum."[16]

Black Box is set on a model stage, which resembles the maquette used to plan the Brussels production of *The Magic Flute*.[17] According to Kentridge, he returned to this miniature stage after completing *The Magic Flute*, specifically to explore "themes that had emerged while working on the opera, but which [he] had not been able to examine in the opera itself."[18] In other words, *Black Box* is not a preparatory document, or dry run, for the theatrical realization of Mozart's opera. Rather, it is a companion piece that also constitutes a creative response, picking up on some of *The Magic Flute*'s main ideas and subjecting them to critical scrutiny.

[13] See Rosemarie Buikema, 2016, "The Revolt of the Object: Animated Drawings and the Colonial Archive: William Kentridge's *Black Box* Theatre," *Interventions* 18(2), 251–269; Ferdinand de Jong, 2018, "Archive of Darkness: William Kentridge's *Black Box/Chambre Noire*," *african arts* 51(1), 10–23; Serena Guarracino, 2010, "The Dance of the Dead Rhino: William Kentridge's Magic Flute." *Altre Modernità* 4, 268–278; Kristina Hagström-Ståhl, 2010, "Mourning as Method: William Kentridge's *Black Box/Chambre Noire*," *arcadia* 45(2), 339–351; Gerhard Schoeman, 2009, "Thinking in the Dark of William Kentridge's *Black Box/Chambre Noire*: Reflections within Reflections," *Acta Academica* 41(2), 1–49.
[14] Guarracino, "Dance," 275.
[15] Kentridge, 2009 "Sarastro."
[16] William Kentridge, 2005, "Black Box: Between the Lens and the Eyepiece," https://www.kentridge.stu dio/black-box-between-the-lens-and-the-eyepiece/, accessed March 22, 2021.
[17] A complete recording of *Black Box/Chambre Noire* is currently available on composer Philip Miller's YouTube channel, https://www.youtube.com/watch?v=wWZCdpV_Gsk&t=104s (accessed March 12, 2024).
[18] Kentridge, "Sarastro."

96   Postcolonial Opera

The *Black Box* theater itself is made of pinewood, and measures approximately two meters in height, width, and depth (see Figure 3.1). Ferdinand de Jong writes that the box looks like a puppet theater, but that it also resembles "a miniature opera house" with proscenium and (cardboard) curtains. However, if the image of the opera house invokes notions of smooth elegance, *Black Box*'s theater represents something more rugged. The stage accoutrements are roughly hewn, with side curtains and coulisses cut to resemble the shape and texture of rock. Thus, the contraption's appearance draws a connection between the theater space and the gloomy hollow of a cave.[19]

The image of the cave carries special significance for Kentridge. In a lecture on the creation of *The Magic Flute* and *Black Box,* the artist describes his cave imagery by turning, again, to Plato's familiar parable:[20]

> The whole opera is full of the metaphor of moving out of darkness into light. What Mozart is doing, of course, is recreating, in operatic form, the parable that Plato tells in *The Republic*—the allegory of the cave. Now, there are a number of similarities between these two works. The first, obviously, is the common central metaphor of moving from darkness toward light, or from ignorance toward knowledge and justice.... What interests me is the introduction of coercion here. It is the same sense of coercion that is present in *The Magic Flute*. Sarastro never denies that he has kidnapped Pamina against her will. But he believes that he had to rescue her from her mother, and he is determined to bring her into enlightenment, even by force. Plato is saying something very similar: that, by force, people, against their will, can be dragged out of the cave, up toward the blinding light.... This returns us to the question: What is it that one learns from the shadows, from being down in the cave? It's a provocative question, especially if one thinks of the many dark, disastrous consequences that have followed from Plato's allegory and the character of Sarastro.[21]

The imagery of the cave in *Black Box* is a conscious, if ironic, reference to the ideals of the Enlightenment articulated in *The Magic Flute*. Invoking Plato's darkened cavern, Kentridge underlines his conviction that Mozart's opera, like the Enlightenment project as a whole, is about the relationship between truth, power, and control.

Black Box, like Kentridge's *Magic Flute*, is set on a stage configured as something between an old-fashioned classroom blackboard and a *camera obscura*.

---

[19] De Jong, "Archive," 13.
[20] See the Introduction for Plato's cave parable.
[21] Kentridge, "Lens and Eyepiece."

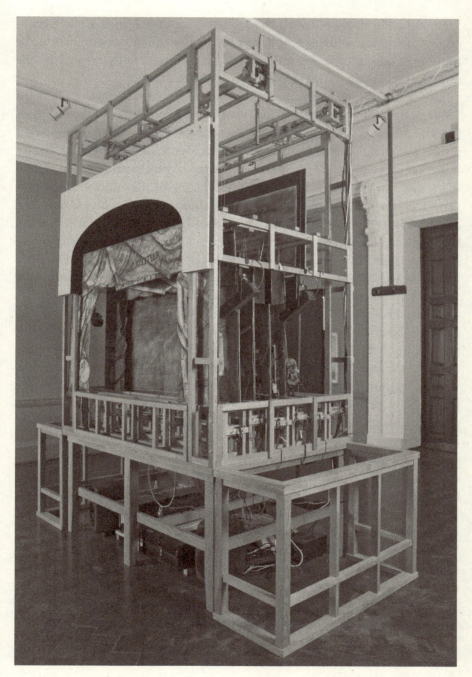

Figure 3.1 Black Box contraption. Photograph: Stella Olivier. Courtesy of William Kentridge Studio.

98   Postcolonial Opera

Predominantly decorated with chalk-like white lines against a black background, the stage settings simultaneously invoke the didactic milieu of the traditional educational institution, and the inverted reality created by the *camera obscura*'s deceptive reproduction of the real world.

Like Plato's cave, the *camera obscura* plays with truth; for Gerhard Schoeman, it offers an optical illusion that, in Kentridge's hands, stands in for "the distorted and distorting ideology of a specular colonialism, itself a product of the distorted and distorting ideology of the eighteenth-century Enlightenment project."[22] Serena Guarracino agrees with Schoeman that *Black Box* and *The Magic Flute*'s settings function as metaphors for the perverse ideals of colonial appropriation and domination. She argues that "the camera and the blackboard both resonate of [*sic*] the themes of power relations and colonial history. The camera was a pivotal instrument of imperial power, used to appropriate the 'virgin lands' and all they included, from landscape to humans and animals; on the other hand, the blackboard is the teacher's instrument and characterizes magician and mentor Sarastro."[23] Cave, blackboard, and *camera obscura*: each of these monochrome settings draws together a complex web of associations conditioned by the ambiguous relationship between knowledge production (and acquisition), representation, and the coercive politics of the colonial civilizing mission.

On this camera-theater-cave stage, a twenty-two-minute performance plays out at regular intervals. Tiny animated figurines, moved by a programmed mechanism similar to that which operates a printer cartridge, enter and exit at various points.[24] The cast is small: an anthropomorphized megaphone bearing a sandwich board with the word *Trauerarbeit* spelled out in capital letters functions as a sort of "narrator," appearing at key moments to broadcast its somber message or to engage in a mournful dance of death. It is joined by a drafting compass which measures skulls; a tall running man apparently assembled from torn scraps of paper, whose legs churn relentlessly while barely moving him forward; a stately Herero woman recognizable by her distinctive headdress; and, in one scene only, a skull that wickedly dismantles and reassembles itself along cranial cracks.[25]

Black Box begins with a lowered curtain, onto which the title is projected in roughly scribbled white chalk. A rapid percussive pattern begins; Megaphone

---

[22] Schoeman, "Thinking in the Dark," 9.

[23] Guarracino, "Dance," 273.

[24] Steven C. Dubin, 2007, "Theater of History," *Art in America*, April, 128-131 and 157, at 128.

[25] Some sources (Buikema; Dubin) mention a second Herero woman instead of a Running Man; pictures of this character form part of printed and digital documentation of the installation. However, none of the versions (live and filmed) I have managed to see contained this configuration of the cast. *Black Box* was produced as an edition of two—it is possible that each version had a slightly different cast.

Man enters stage right and wanders around. As he turns to face the audience, swinging his megaphone head from side to side to broadcast his message of TRAUERARBEIT, three chords sound, resembling a slowed-down version of the opening of *The Magic Flute*'s overture. Like Mozart's chords, they follow a I-vi-I' pattern, but in F major, rather than E-flat.[26] Unlike the lush sonority of the opera orchestra, these chords are articulated in a brass-heavy, synthetic sound; a metallic flute tone rings out at the top, piercing the ear like feedback from speakers in a sound system. After the third set of chords, the music does not proceed to the gentle strings of Mozart's overture; instead, a strangely distorted version of the "March of the Priests," played on a zither, strikes up. On the backdrop, a chaos of white lines appears. They transform into German newspaper headlines, a praying mantis, a shower, a load of "Nobels Dynamit" that explodes in a blinding flash of light, a typewriter that projects the words "Einige Werte an das Volk der Herero" (any value to the Herero people), and finally a rhinoceros. An animated drawing of an old-fashioned box camera snaps a picture, and the screen goes blank in a flash of white, marking the end of the opening sequence.

When the curtain rises and the music begins again—this time a tuneless mixture of brass, zither, and timpani, interspersed with the sound of marching feet—a series of projected scenes with titles such as "Overture," "Berlin Opening," "Measuring," "Fairground," "Rhino," "Dance Macabre," and "Lament from the March of the Priests" is initiated.[27] The automated characters make their entrances and exits against a dizzying array of backdrop projections, which include film footage shot in Namibia, reproductions of archival documents relating to the German imperial project, handwritten text, maps, and replicas of Kentridge's designs for *The Magic Flute*. These visual references to *The Magic Flute* are complemented by musical intertexts from the opera. Philip Miller's score, created specifically for *Black Box*, draws extensively, and with varying levels of recognizability, on Mozart's original composition, thus offering an aural supplement to Kentridge's conceptual critique of the opera's ideals.

[26] Much has been written about the "perfection" of E-flat major, with its three flats, in the context of *The Magic Flute* (which incorporates a whole series of triumvirates, including three chords, three ladies, three boys, and three trials). F major, on the other hand, is associated in Mozart's music with naiveté and "a certain pastoral character" (Alfred Einstein, 1941, "Mozart's Choice of Keys," *Musical Quarterly* 27(4), 415–421, at 420). Though this is most likely unintentional on Miller's part, the use of F major here may be read as an analogy for the "unspoiled natural man" who inhabits pre-colonial (and by extension pre-Enlightenment) lands, as opposed to the "civilized" priests of Mozart's opera.

[27] Kentridge's installation does not contain clearly demarcated scenes. Instead, I refer to tracks and track titles as listed on Philip Miller's CD recording of music for *Black Box* (Miller, n.d., *Music by Philip Miller from the Soundtrack to William Kentridge's* Black Box/Chambre Noir [*sic*], Johannesburg: Artlogic). My analyses are, however, based on the versions heard in the actual installation.

100 Postcolonial Opera

Scholars including Serena Guarracino, Ferdinand de Jong, Gerhard Schoeman, Kristina Hagström-Ståhl, and Rosemarie Buikema have commented extensively on *Black Box* and its condemnation of Enlightenment positivism and colonial technnologies. Guarracino especially focuses on links between the installation and Kentridge's *Magic Flute*; she centers her inquiry on the image of the silent rhino as a symbol of the voiceless feminine subaltern in Western opera. However, like the other authors mentioned above, Guarracino attends almost exclusively to the visual content of *Black Box*, mentioning the sonic only in passing. The scopic register of the piece is indeed compelling, and rewards detailed engagement with its seemingly boundless range of meanings and intertextual references. A reduced list of archival documents incorporated into the piece's background projections would include, for instance, a photocopy of General Lothar von Trotha's 1904 extermination order instructing the German Imperial Army to wipe out all Herero people remaining within German colonial borders; Georg Hartmann's map of South-West Africa, 1904; a 1910 edition of the British handbook, *Mrs. Beeton's Book of Household Management*; lists of mines and shares; copies of advertisements in the satirical German journal *Simplicissimus*; private correspondence from German South-West Africa, 1911; and colonial adventurer and big game hunter Robert Schumann's 1912 film, *Nashornjagd in Deutsch-Ost-Afrika* (Rhinoceros Hunting in German East Africa).[28]

The archival documents, drawn from collections in Namibia, Germany, South Africa, and the Netherlands, shed light on a colonial project that permeates every aspect of public and private life, from the national and international politics of German warfare and fiscal policy, to the intimacy of the domestic sphere, with its letters, magazines, and household management. Kentridge assembles a perspective on coloniality both from the top down (projecting the workings of bureaucracy and officialese) and from the bottom up (tracing the absences and adventures of individuals). In contrast to these records of Western colonial experience, however, no archival documentation representing colonized peoples' perspectives is included. Instead, Kentridge fills the silence of these voices with hand-drawn animations of events that link the history of the Herero to those of other persecuted peoples: lynchings, beatings, eugenic calculations, and the showers of Nazi death camps. In De Jong's assessment, the installation's visual world is an "archival simulacrum" that ponders both "the role [historical documents] have played in the colonial encounter," and "the conditions of possibility of genocide and its remembrance."[29] By juxtaposing the documentary remains of Western

---

[28] De Jong, "Archive," 16.
[29] De Jong, "Archive," 18.

coloniality with the inferences and suppositions of a hand-drawn subaltern history—one literally "traced" with Kentridge's draughtsman's hand—*Black Box* demonstrates a critical engagement with practices of colonial historiography, including neglect, disavowal, self-justification and forgetting.

Despite (or perhaps because of) the excess of historical documentation, *Black Box* does not construct a coherent narrative. In fact, the history of the Herero and Nama massacre is not told explicitly. At most, its presence in the piece is suggested through references to places such as Waterberg (the site of a particularly violent wartime massacre), Berlin, and Windhoek (the capital of Namibia), and decontextualized and truncated quotations from texts such as Trotha's extermination order. Kentridge himself specifies in an artist's statement on the installation that he "will not necessarily describe [the genocide] nor didactically enumerate its stages."[30] Instead, he opts to approach his subject matter allegorically and anamorphically, visiting violence and suffering on various non-specific, nameless characters throughout the piece.

This apparent abstraction of colonial violence is typical of postcolonial narrative. Writing about the works of J. M. Coetzee, Wilson Harris, and Toni Morrison, Sam Durrant argues that these authors' refusal to name time, place, or people directly in some of their postcolonial novels, enacts "a refusal to allow the reader to digest this suffering and then forget it. . . . Precisely because they are not fully individuated characters, they serve as reminders of all those who have been denied humanity, reminders of the history of barbarity that, as Benjamin famously notes, underwrites the history of civilization."[31] In Kentridge's piece, a similar reminder of the universality of exploitative violence emerges, as the elliptical nature of *Black Box*'s historical representation serves to draw connections between various histories of oppression. Nonetheless, for the uninformed audience member, the piece might also just look like an excruciating and extended display of gratuitous violence, much of which happens to be racially coded.

To clarify the specific historical context of the piece, *Black Box* is therefore exhibited alongside a selection of approximately fifty drawings and prints based on archival documents related to the massacre. These are not originals. Rather, they are hand-drawn reproductions or photocopies (see Figure 3.2). For De Jong, it is important that these documents are not originals but art works based on and derived from the archive. He argues that the constructed

---

[30] Kentridge, "Lens and Eyepiece."
[31] Sam Durrant, 2004, *Postcolonial Narrative and the Work of Mourning: J. M. Coetzee, Wilson Harris, and Toni Morrison*, Albany: State University of New York Press, 32.

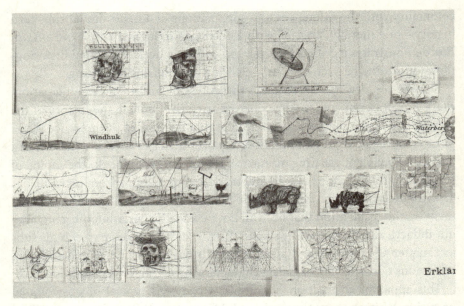

Figure 3.2 A selection of drawings based on archival documentation, displayed alongside the *Black Box* installation. Photograph: Stella Olivier. Courtesy of William Kentridge Studio.

nature of this archival display further complicates the authority of historical documents and ideas of truth or verifiability.[32]

The archival artifice represented by *Black Box*'s display may also be read in light of Roland Barthes's final text, *La chambre claire* (translated as *Camera Lucida*).[33] In this deeply personal essay, Barthes ponders the personal and political affordances of photography. He argues that each photograph generates two planes of meaning: the *studium*, which incorporates the historical, cultural, and political content of the image, and the *punctum*, which evokes something more intimate—a person's own, subjective response to the associative affect of photographic detail. In *Black Box/Chambre Noire*, the image summons both the socio-political valence (the *studium*) of the archive, and the delicate *punctum* of individual memory. Since the documents themselves are not originals but reproductions, their status as testimonies of so-called truth is called into question. Like photographs, they represent, rather than embody, reality. Underscoring the deeply ideological nature of knowledge,

---

[32] De Jong, "Archive," 18.
[33] Roland Barthes, 2000 [1981], *Camera Lucida: Reflections on Photography*, trans. Richard Howard, London: Vintage. Indeed, the *Chambre Noire* of Kentridge's title may itself serve as an inverse reference to *La chambre claire*.

Kentridge's archival reproductions hence reflect the constructed nature of both *studium* and *punctum*.

Together with further paratexts such as exhibition descriptions and catalogues, these visual codes guide the spectator's understanding of *Black Box*. Audience members may engage with the additional material before or after watching the performance: between each showing, a hiatus of approximately twelve minutes allows the audience to examine the art works displayed on the walls of the room in which the stage is installed and to examine up close the mechanism of the miniature theater, which is set away from any walls.

The deliberate exposure of the theater's inner workings may, like the display of not-quite-real archival documents, be interpreted as a comment on the performance and construction of history. For Bronwyn Law-Viljoen, this aspect of the work represents "an invitation to look closely at the skeleton, the bare bones not only of the theater itself, but of the very history [of violence and death] that is gathered in its wings."[34] Rosemarie Buikema concurs, describing the "ominous appearance" of the exposed mechanism as something akin to a torture device and arguing that the visibility of the installation's technical innards focuses the viewer's attention on "the engineered nature of the production process as an inextricable and inescapable part of any performance of memory or truth—or of any erasure of histories of violence from human consciousness, for that matter."[35] In other words, for both authors, the explicit artifice of the installation serves as a reminder that histories— even those based on documentary evidence, like official accounts of Western coloniality—are nothing more than manufactured products, assembled from available materials and human invention.

From an operatic perspective, the visibility of the theater's mechanics is meaningful also for its implicit comment on opera's commitment to illusion and visual effect.[36] Whereas traditional opera often demands the audience member's suspension of disbelief, *Black Box* denies this impulse from the start, insisting instead on a Brechtian reality effect that unmasks the artifice of operatic glamour.[37] Even the most beguiling of art forms, *Black Box* seems to say, is powered by material and ideological machineries of creation and, in the colonial context, exploitation.

---

[34] Bronwyn Law-Viljoen, 2007, "Footnote on Darkness," in *Flute*, ed. Bronwyn Law-Viljoen, Johannesburg: David Krut, 156–191, 188.

[35] Buikema, "Revolt," 259.

[36] See the introduction to Gundula Kreuzer's *Curtain, Gong, Steam: Wagnerian Technologies of Nineteenth-Century Opera*, Berkeley: University of California Press, 2018, for a recent discussion of operatic artifice especially in Wagner, but also more broadly.

[37] On Brechtian realism in theater, see Varun Begley, 2012, "Objects of Realism: Bertold Brecht, Roland Barthes, and Marsha Norman," *Theatre and Material Culture* 64(3), 337–353.

104   Postcolonial Opera

The musical register of *Black Box* joins in this unveiling of opera's artifice. Consisting of an eclectic mix—a kind of collage—of sonic references, the core of the score is constituted by the original music of *The Magic Flute*. Quotations from the opera are presented in a variety of transformations, from unrecognizably distorted to easily identifiable. A few moments from the original opera, including dialogue and some of its most famous arias, appear in unaltered form. Miller lifted these from Sir Thomas Beecham's famous 1937–1938 recording of *The Magic Flute* with the Berlin Philharmonic.

In *Black Box* reception, this recording has acquired its own mythical backstory: one reviewer reported that Miller found it in a thrift shop in Swakopmund—a Namibian harbor town that served as the most important port for German colonial arrivals and exports, and which was also the site of a concentration camp during the German-Herero genocide.[38] The most pervasive myth attached to Miller's *Magic Flute* original is that it is a recording of a performance that was supposedly convened especially for an assembled Nazi elite.[39] I have not been able to find any confirmation that Sir Thomas Beecham's recording was commissioned by the Nazi Party, even though Nazi politics influenced its casting; either way, Beecham's is the first studio recording of *The Magic Flute* and is hence certainly not a document of a special performance for the leaders of the Nazi Party.[40]

Even though they are false, these invented histories reveal the extent to which *Black Box/Chambre Noire*'s political content shaped its reception. Listeners and critics were eager to inscribe the piece's references to both colonialism and genocide onto the circumstances that shaped its production. The close interpolation of histories of Nazism and the geopolitics of the Herero genocide infuses what would otherwise be a simple source text with several layers of painful connotation. Miller's original *Magic Flute* recording therefore presents not only as a rendition of the opera, but as a material artifact that adds its own historical-political significance to the musical register of *Black Box*.

Besides the direct reproduction of Mozart's music, Miller also recomposed some material from the opera for an idiosyncratic ensemble of trombone, euphonium, cello, double bass, zither, keyboard, percussion sampler, and voices. Miller's choice of instruments is strongly evocative of Prussian military

---

[38] Dubin, "Theatre," 131. According to Miller, this story is a fabrication.

[39] See De Jong, "Archive," 16; Buikema, "Revolt," 252, both of whom repeat the claims from reviews of *Black Box/Chambre Noire*.

[40] Thomas Beecham, 1938, *Mozart: Zauberflöte*, Naxos Historical: 8.110127–28. On the influence of Nazi politics on the recording's casting, see Tony Duggan's informative blog review, "Wolfgang Amadeus Mozart: *Die Zauberflöte* (*The Magic Flute*)," 2001, *Classical Music on the Web*, http://www.musicweb-intern ational.com/classrev/2001/apr01/magicflute.htm, accessed May 25, 2021.

music with its janissary influences—a style also mimicked by Mozart in his "Turkish" compositions.[41] Through the configuration of the ensemble, Miller draws an explicit link between the sounds likely to have accompanied German exploration in southern Africa and Mozart's own orientalist compositions. Transposing Mozart's original material for euphonium, trombone, and double bass—instruments associated with outdoor traditions of civic music and marching bands—Miller's score transfers the opera from an imagined theater into the open-air setting of the real-life colonial drama. He incorporates these intertextual references with original material, as well as field recordings of traditional Herero music, collected during a research trip to Namibia, and religious music performed by a Sesotho singer, Alfred Makgalemele.[42] The combination of transfigured Mozart with field recordings performs a critical function not unlike Kentridge's juxtaposition of archival documents with drawn records: it brings directly face-to-face with each other a number of apparently contradictory cultural-historical spheres, embodied by aesthetic traditions that would otherwise hardly meet. This confrontation underscores the silences and exclusions enacted by the so-called pure aesthetic object of Mozart's opera.[43] It exposes the blind spots of a narrative that celebrates one version of history and omits the other.

Black Box poses several interpretative challenges to its audience. Its generic ambiguity—like that of the works under discussion in the rest of the monograph—pushes against conventional definitions of opera, visual art, and performance. Likewise, its score calls into question the boundaries between original and copy, critique and celebration. If mourning is meant to proceed somberly, the ludic moments of the piece seem to contradict its solemn purpose; nonetheless, the violent imagery that accompanies even the most insouciant of sound clips gives the work a troubling, and at times grotesque, character. In what follows, I consider how the piece relates to its self-imposed task of *Trauerarbeit*, and I ask what this might reveal about opera's ability to process trauma in the postcolony.

The Work of Mourning

Kentridge derives his notion of *Trauerarbeit* directly from Freud, who theorized the concept in his 1917 essay, "Mourning and Melancholia." In a 2007

---

[41] See Matthew Head, 2000, *Orientalism, Masquerade, and Mozart's Turkish Music*, Abingdon: Routledge.
[42] Miller, interview with the author, May 25, 2020.
[43] Carolyn Abbate, 2001, *In Search of Opera*, Princeton: Princeton University Press, 104.

106 Postcolonial Opera

interview, Kentridge explains his use of the concept as follows: "I think the term, which is the Freudian term for the work of grief, is in a way saying, 'what is the work needing to be done?'"[44] The "work of grief" to which Kentridge refers is Freud's description of the process of mourning that constitutes a healthy response to loss.[45]

Mourning is goal driven. As Kathleen Woodward notes, the most important feature of Freud's work of mourning is that "it must come to an end."[46] Consequently, the mourning process is not passive; rather, it entails an active process of coming to terms with the loss of the love object.[47] The ultimate outcome of this dynamic—even intentional—project of "working through," is detachment from the lost object and, as a result, healing.

In contrast, melancholia—Freud's alternative to mourning—signals a refusal to accept the loss of the object, ultimately leading to a permanent and pathological internalization of grief. Melancholia is constituted by an ongoing relationship with the lost object; a refusal, as it were, to lay the lost object to rest. In this formulation, mourning may hence be regarded as the restitutive and positive double of melancholia. Freud later adjusted his strict distinction between mourning and melancholia, recognizing instead that the melancholy attachment to the lost object itself constitutes a crucial part of the process of mourning.[48] As an indispensable feature of the work of mourning, melancholia is hence refigured as a potentially positive psychic state—one that may ultimately help to steer the subject toward the endpoint of grief.

For Walter Benjamin and Jacques Derrida, the very act of mourning is a melancholy effort, premised on an ongoing dialogue between a lost past and, crucially, an inevitably disappearing, or shortening, future.[49] Judith Butler likewise refuses a conception of mourning and melancholy as mutually exclusive, arguing that ambivalence—"the struggle that loss occasions between the desire to live and the desire to die"—ties melancholy to the work

---

[44] William Kentridge, in Kristine Bøggild Johannsen and Torben Zenth, 2007, "Interview: William Kentridge," *Kopenhagen Aktuel information om smtidskunst*, July 4.

[45] Freud, "Mourning and Melancholia," 164.

[46] Kathleen Woordward, 1993, "Late Theory, Late Style: Loss and Renewal in Freud and Barthes," in *Aging & Gender in Literature: Studies in Creativity*, ed. Anne Wyatt-Brown and Janice Rossin, Charlottesville: University of Virginia Press, 82–101, 85.

[47] The love object can be a person or an abstraction, such as "the fatherland, liberty, ideal, and so on" (Freud, "Mourning and Melancholia," 164).

[48] Hagström-Ståhl, "Mourning," 345.

[49] See especially Jacques Derrida, 2001, *The Work of Mourning*, ed. Pascale-Anne Brault and Michael Naas, Chicago: University of Chicago Press; and Walter Benjamin, 1977 [1928], *The Origin of German Tragic Drama*, trans. John Osborne, London: NLB. Michael Naas offers a lucid and accessible guide to Derrida's views on mourning in "When It Comes to Mourning," in *Jacques Derrida: Key Concepts*, ed. Claire Colebrook, Abingdon: Routledge, 2015, 113–121.

of mourning.[50] However, unlike Freud, these scholars appear less convinced of the desirability of "successful mourning," which in Sam Durrant's words, "enables the past to be assimilated or digested . . . in order to be consoled, ultimately in order to forget."[51] Benjamin, writing in the context of historiography, views the remains of the past as a series of traces that require continuing reengagement; Derrida, in his late work, views ongoing mourning as "an act of fidelity to the dead"; and Butler figures remembrance as an act of resistance against the political disavowal of commemoration visited upon those regarded as less-than-human.[52] Throughout, these scholars problematize Freud's idea of mourning as a process geared toward resolution—one that must be finished in order to be successful.

Returning to my description of opera as a melancholy form, the genre's recurrent (some might say obsessive) efforts to recover the lost Greek theatrical ideal are evocative of Freud's desperate melancholia. Opera cannot lay its imagined predecessor to rest. The closure afforded by mourning hence remains out of reach. But opera's loss is an existential prerequisite: should the art form abandon its originary ideal, it will cease to exist, reduced to spoken theater or abstract music. Conclusive mourning, in other words, is not an option.

If opera's survival is itself incompatible with the endpoint achieved by successful mourning, then the question arises whether the art form can participate usefully in other mournful projects. Opera can narrate histories and commemorate events. It can create versions of the past that acknowledge injustice and recognize guilt. But can it mourn? Or, in less anthropomorphic terms, can it facilitate the work of mourning? These questions are crucial in any social and political setting where the art form is tasked with historical recovery. This is especially true for opera in the postcolony, where, as I discuss below, the work of mourning is itself ambiguous.

In recent years, the concept of unfinished mourning has had a significant impact on postcolonial scholarship. Though a number of theorists still regard postcolonialism as "a therapeutic retrieval of the colonial past,"[53] the contested nature of historical recovery and assimilation in formerly colonial spaces has led some scholars to cast doubt on the palliative ambitions of the field, its work, and the forms of mourning it appears to advocate. In David Lloyd's view, the future-oriented aim-to-progress implied by postcolonial mourning renders

---

[50] Judith Butler, 1997, *The Psychic Life of Power: Theories in Subjection*, Stanford, CA: Stanford University Press, 193.

[51] Durrant, *Postcolonial Narrative*, 31.

[52] See Benjamin, *Origins*, 1977; Derrida, *Work of Mourning*, 2001; Judith Butler, 2004, *Precarious Life: The Power of Mourning and Violence*, London: Verso.

[53] Leela Gandhi, 1998, *Postcolonial Theory: A Critical Introduction*, New York: Columbia University Press, 5.

108 Postcolonial Opera

the therapeutic project suspect. Lloyd argues that the core aim of postcolonial mourning is a state of recovery that allows the victim of coloniality to (re-) enter modernity as a productive subject.[54] As such, mourning contributes to an oppressive economic order that prioritizes healing simply for the sake of reexploitation.

Like Lloyd, Sam Durrant, Jodi Kanter, and José Esteban Muñoz are uncomfortable with the forward-looking nature of mourning, which enables the mournful subject to leave the past behind.[55] However, for Durrant, Kanter, and Muñoz it is not the postcolonial subject's resultant entry into industrial modernity that is questionable but rather her disloyalty to the past. Alongside Derrida, these scholars argue that "the possibility of a just future lies in our ability to live in remembrance of the victims of injustice, in our ability to conjure the dead rather than bury them."[56] Put differently, the refusal to forget or to move on is itself a way to safeguard the future against a repetition of the past.[57] Kanter, following Muñoz, goes even further, arguing that the retention of grief is an essential component of a just future. "To lose our grief," Kanter writes, "is in a very important sense to lose our historically inflected understanding of who we are and who we might, even should, be."[58] Grief, Kanter asserts, not only historicizes the subject but also calls her into an ethical relationship with both the past and the future. Palliative mourning, on the other hand, enacts a betrayal of history. Moreover, it denies the possibility of a future worth having.

Against the problematics of mourning-as-repair, Lloyd advocates a mode of postcolonial mourning that retains, like Butler's, Benjamin's, and Derrida's models, a strong sense of melancholy. He suggests "a non-therapeutic relation to the past, structured around the notion of survival or living on rather than recovery."[59] Such a work of mourning, Lloyd argues, will transform historiography by shifting the focus from the retrieval of disappeared "facts" or "truths" toward tracing the various ways in which the past endures into the present.[60] In my own reading of Lloyd, I surmise that the type of historical work he proposes is based less on excavatory processes of documentary research and archival digging, and more on close engagement with cultural practices and modes of being that endure across generations. The past's resilient remains

---

[54] David Lloyd, 2000, "Colonial Trauma/Postcolonial Recovery?." *Interventions* 2(2), 212–228, 222.

[55] Jodi Kanter, 2007, *Performing Loss: Rebuilding Community through Theater and Writing*, Carbondale: Southern Illinois University Press; José Esteban Muñoz, 1997, *Disidentifications: Queers of Color and the Performance of Politics*, vol.2, Minneapolis: Minnesota University Press.

[56] Durrant, *Postcolonial Narrative*, 9.

[57] Durrant, *Postcolonial Narrative*, 9.

[58] Kanter, *Performing Loss*, 25, original emphasis.

[59] Lloyd, "Colonial Trauma," 212.

[60] Lloyd, "Colonial Trauma," 212.

may best be found in stories, songs, customs, and superstitions. Here, the dead live on, but without robbing the living of their future.

Kentridge's invocation of the work of mourning does not specify whether the artist is in search of resolution or not. In the statement quoted at the beginning of this section ("I think the term, which is the Freudian term for the work of grief, is in a way saying, 'what is the work needing to be done?'") Kentridge refrains from indicating what "the work needing to be done" is *for*, or what it will achieve.[61] The artist's mournful project is hence pointedly non-teleologic. Nonetheless, given that he derives his conception of mourning directly from Freud, it is not unreasonable to infer that with *Black Box* Kentridge aspires to resolution or healing. But his interrogative formulation around "the work needing to be done"—framing it as a question, rather than a statement—likewise suggests a more speculative approach: that *Black Box* may be read not merely as an attempt at mourning but also (and perhaps more convincingly) as a deliberation on the very question with which scholars such as Lloyd, Kanter, and Durrant grapple, namely, what the postcolonial work of mourning should look (or sound) like. Within this question resides the issue with which this chapter is preoccupied: whether opera may form part of "the work needing to be done," or, indeed, whether the art form can do this work itself. If opera is already incapable of mournful closure in the West, it seems even less likely to achieve such repair in the postcolonial context.

Black Box, Mourning, and *The Magic Flute*

Reading *Black Box* as an examination of the processes and possibilities of postcolonial mourning, rather than an attempt at its successful enactment, opens various avenues for productive enquiry. First, it affords the piece an experimental quality in the tradition of black box theater, which chimes with Kentridge's non-prescriptive approach to the making of meaning.[62] Asking how mourning might happen rather than whether it happens, in other words, liberates the scholar to attend to the mechanisms by which meaning arises rather than being tied to the excavation of these meanings themselves.

Second, from an opera studies perspective, attending to the possible modalities of postcolonial mourning opens the issue of the ethics of form: as stated in the introduction to this chapter, the question of whether the work of

---

[61] Kentridge, "Lens and Eyepiece."
[62] See the Introduction for Kentridge's conception of "Fortuna," or the emergence of meaning through the coincidences of creation and reception.

110 Postcolonial Opera

postcolonial mourning should be entrusted to the operatic form is central to any musicological reading of *Black Box*. By understanding the piece not as a positive statement of mourning but rather as a contemplation on the nature of such mourning, it is possible to answer the question about the viability of postcolonial operatic mourning without ultimately being placed under any obligation to reject the piece should the conclusion be negative. And finally, understanding that *Black Box* seeks to ask what mourning might look like, rather than to achieve such mourning, frees the scholar from having to assess whether or not the piece ultimately succeeds at its task—an undertaking that cannot be assumed in good faith by a white scholar of Western opera.

Kentridge's experiment with possible modalities of postcolonial mourning proceeds first from a direct engagement with cultures of coloniality. Here, Mozart's opera plays a central role. *The Magic Flute* is itself a melancholy opera. Performing what Marianne Tettlebaum calls a "combination of magic and Enlightenment, enchantment and disenchantment," the piece grapples implicitly with a certain loss of innocence brought about by the advent of reason.[63] Expanding on Adorno's classification of *The Magic Flute* as "bourgeois opera," Tettlebaum argues that the opera "reflects the struggle of the bourgeoisie itself to come to terms with an enlightened world 'bereft of magic.'"[64] What Mozart's work offers, then, is a melancholy escape from the disenchantment of rational society—an attempt to preserve in art what has been lost in real life.

In *The Magic Flute*, the objects and characters invested with this magical melancholy are easily identifiable as the enchanted flute and chimes, and the character of Papageno who, with childlike innocence, lives a life of nature rather than culture. Rose Subotnik's important 1991 essay, "Whose 'Magic Flute'" exposes the ambiguity of Papageno's depiction as the embodiment of "natural man" and the exclusionary politics that accompanied this character's portrayal on the operatic stage.[65] For Subotnik, the veneer of equality represented by the Enlightened Brotherhood's acceptance of Papageno "for what he is" in fact excludes the character from the social elite. Moreover, Papageno becomes the "Other" against which this elite defines itself. Like Cheng's identification of race as a melancholy construct, Mozart's portrayal of Papageno serves a negative function: it reminds the Enlightenment elite of what it is not. Thus, social equality emerges in *The Magic Flute* as a melancholy

---

[63] Marianne Tettlebaum, 2008, "Whose Magic Flute?," *Representations* 102(1), 76–93, 87.

[64] Tettlebaum, "Whose," 87.

[65] Rose Rosengard Subotnik, 1991, "Whose *Magic Flute*? Intimations of Reality at the Gates of the Enlightenment," *19th-Century Music* 15(2), 132–150, 142.

Mourning   111

formation—a myth, built on strategic exclusions and disavowals, haunted by the shadows of those it rejects.

In *Black Box*, Mozart's operatic melancholies are transferred to a postcolonial context. Here, matters of nature and magic acquire added significance. Nature is, in this context, not merely desirable as a site for those enchanted fantasies renounced by the Enlightenment project, but it also signifies ownership and profit—a possession that conveys power and wealth. Its magical qualities, associated primarily with pre-Enlightenment society, are no longer a source of bourgeois enchantment. Instead, magic here becomes a superstitious force of incivility—an insurgent but ultimately impotent response to the wounds of coloniality. Likewise, the melancholic object of natural man signifies more malevolently than in Mozart's original, for if Papageno represents Enlightenment Europe's acceptable Other, the Black bodies of the continent's colonial possessions are, like Monostatos, deserving only of punishment, domination, and control. Relocated to a site of imperial history, then, the melancholy inherent in Mozart's Western opera is simultaneously reinforced and transformed, acquiring a more sinister significance in the process.

Fairground

When Kentridge commissioned Miller to compose the music for *Black Box*, he had one requirement: that *The Magic Flute*'s most famous music, the Queen of the Night's so-called rage aria, "Die Hölle Rache," from Act II, should appear in some shape or form in the new piece.[66] Miller complied, but rather than the authoritative and embellished matriarch of Mozart's opera, Miller's Queen is a shadow of her operatic self—a stripped-down and sonically curtailed imprint, rather than a fully realized presence. She appears in a scene titled "Fairground," where she engages in a dialogue that simultaneously reenacts and upends the meeting between European authority and colonial subject.

The track starts with the distinctive sound of the *outa* mouth bow, a traditional Herero instrument. Its delicate, percussive vibrations are joined by the jubilant voices of Herero women, chanting and clapping rhythmically. The pitch of the Herero women's chant is taken up a few octaves higher by an operatic soprano, who sings the interval C_6-F_5. Here, Miller constructs an almost imperceptible intertextual reference to the Queen of the Night's aria, as this interval directly duplicates the falling figure that completes the Queen's

---

[66] Miller, interview with the author, May 25, 2020.

112 Postcolonial Opera

repeated high C's in Mozart's version. After the reference to the Queen, the Herero voices again intone their joyful chants, and again they are followed by the Queen of the Night's interval. All this occurs against a syncopated, percussive strings-and-piano accompaniment on a repeated ostinato. The track is spliced in such a way that a dialogue emerges between the Herero and the Queen of the Night, with the Herero calling and the Queen of the Night responding in an apparent inversion of the distribution of expressive power normally associated with the colonial encounter.

In Miller's treatment, "Die Hölle Rache" is stripped of what Rose Subotnik calls its "ornate and delicate lines"[67] and reduced only to its basic figure: the downward interval. In Subotnik's view, the ornamentation that characterizes the original Queen's vocal lines estranges the character from the social constraints of communication and coherence. Her privileged status exempts her from the obligation to be intelligible and allows her the freedom "to dissolve [into] meaninglessness."[68] The Queen's disregard of etiquette and interaction is a function not only of her narcissism but also of her separation from the realm of the social, and by extension, the human. Singing for no one but herself, Mozart's Queen discards human language in favor of pure, mechanical, sound.

"Fairground" likewise strips the Queen of comprehensible language. Moreover, the absence of her imposing runs and trills further depersonifies her, reducing her vocal presence to nothing but bare bones. If the brittle technicity of Mozart's Queen is what renders her inhuman in Subotnik's assessment, the very removal of these mechanical features further dehumanizes her in *Black Box*. In contrast, the Herero women sound fully alive: though they, like the Queen, articulate an apparently extra-linguistic series of vowels and diphthongs, their singing sounds meaning*ful*, filled with elation, laughter, and the feeling of community. A discrepancy arises between the apparently "natural" voices of the Herero and the artifice of the Queen, here castrated of her more excessive vocal appendages.

This interaction may be interpreted as an ethnocentric realization of the colonial fantasy of "natural (wo)man": pre-linguistic, pre-individual, and pre-developmental—forever entrenched in a state of blissful innocence. In such a reading, the Herero women announce themselves as the melancholy object of opera's racialized Other. They are, as mentioned earlier, the "nature" to opera's "culture"—the negative double that affirms the operatic form's structural exclusivity. But in *Black Box* these melancholy objects move beyond absence;

---

[67] Subotnik, "Whose," 135.
[68] Subotnik, "Whose," 136.

Another interpretation of the dialogue between the Queen of the Night and the Herero women, however, presents itself through Carolyn Abbate's reading of the Queen's coloratura passagework as birdsong. Hearing avian flight rather than automation in the Queen's voice brings the character closer to the realm of "nature."[69] Abbate herself immediately qualifies such an interpretation by dismissing a pure equivalence between nature and wordless vocal flight. Nonetheless, the notion that the Queen represents something closer to irrationality than her male counterpart, Sarastro, is useful for this discussion. It advances an intersectional perspective that reads West/non-West hierarchies through the lens of gender, thereby destabilizing the easy opposition between European "culture" and African "nature."[70] Here, the apparent binary positioning of the Queen and the Herero as hemispheric opposites yields to a more ambiguous collapsing of boundaries between Queen and Herero, north and south, West and non-West. Together, they render permeable the boundary between opera and its others, inserting themselves for the first time into a space whose existence is premised on their exclusion.

Appealing as such an interpretation of Miller's score may be, however, the visual content of the scene suggests the former rather than the latter interpretation. Indeed, the intrusion of the Herero women's voices upon the Queen's operatic sound is ambivalent. Though it appears to suggest a loosening of the limits of formal and aesthetic legitimacy, the encounter cannot be freed from the unequal power relations that continue to determine its outcomes. In *Black Box*, the ominous nature of this unpredictable interaction between North and South, colonizer and colonized, so-called culture and so-called nature, is illustrated in the dialogue between the piece's visual and sonic registers.

On the backdrop, a series of projected drawings—each meaningful in its own right—is systematically destroyed. First, a praying mantis and then a pangolin are shattered by a bullet each. Next, the cover of Heinrich Mann's 1907 novel, *Zwischen den Rassen* (with a glowing endorsement, "Ein glänzender deutscher Roman"),[71] is ruined by a fountain of black ink. Then, a succession

---

[69] Abbate, 2001, *In Search of Opera*, 69–70.

[70] This is, of course, exactly what intersectional feminism is about.

[71] Published in 1907, Heinrich Mann's novel is a love story set mostly in Italy. Despite the book's title, it does not deal explicitly with ideas of race as understood today, though it does gesture toward what later became fascism. Describing the novel for its 1987 edition, Mann's publisher, S. Fischer Verlage, writes: "The title has nothing to do with Nazi ideology. . . . It's about the alleged differences between north and south, between spirit and sensuality. . . . In [main character] Cesare Augusto Pardi, Heinrich Mann draws, as he later indicated himself, a forerunner of the fascists, almost a generation before Mussolini's march on Rome." (https://www.fischerverlage.de/buch/heinrich-mann-zwischen-den-rassen-9783596259229, accessed June 3, 2021).

Figure 3.3 The series of images projected onto the backdrop during "Fairground," including the praying mantis; the cover of Heinrich Mann's novel; three Black victims shot to death; and advertisements for Dr Davidsen's Busen Creme and Voigtländer binoculars. Photograph: Stella Olivier. Courtesy of William Kentridge Studio.

of figures—three prisoners with bags over their heads, a Black woman, and a Black man carrying a bundle on his head—are shot. Their annihilation is followed by an advertisement for Dr. Davidsen's Busen Creme for "Schone Buste," which acquires a more sinister significance when red lines spurt like blood from the pictured lady's bust. Finally, as the automaton of the running man lumbers onto the stage, a pair of Voigtländer Jagdgläser (binoculars) has its lenses blacked out (see Figure 3.3). The projections come to a halt at an advertisement for "Welt-Detektiv/Preiss Berlin."

The violence depicted in this rapid succession of images performs bluntly the brutality of the colonial encounter. Here, the destruction of the praying mantis and the pangolin—both creatures associated with luck in Herero culture—represents allegorically the civilizing mission's devastation of Indigenous knowledge systems and spiritualities.[72] If this reference is lost upon the viewer, the title of Mann's novel, *Zwischen der Rassen* (Between the

---

[72] See Pedzisai Maedza, 2018, "Chains of Memory in the Postcolony: Performing and Remembering the Namibian Genocide," PhD diss., University of Cape Town, 75, for the praying mantis; Rare and Endangered Species Trust for more on the significance of the pangolin: https://www.restnamibia.org/education/, accessed June 9, 2021.

Races), clearly situates the imagery within an encounter between colonized Blackness and imperial whiteness. The subsequent murder of Black figures further reinforces the racialized nature of the preceding violence; however, as the disfigurement of the flawless white bust in Dr. Davidsen's advertisement shows, the colonial project does not leave its perpetrators unmarked. Even domestic pursuits of beauty, leisure, and culture are contaminated by the bloodshed of Empire.

Heard alongside the visual content of this scene, Miller's Queen becomes the musical version of the bullet. Her single, dehumanized interval represents the destructive force of coloniality. Even when reduced to nothing but an outline, her presence remains lethal. The Herero women's joyful song, on the other hand, becomes a poignant reminder of that which has been lost. Thus, the inversion of power suggested by the sonic dialogue between the Queen and the Herero women is unmasked as nothing but make-believe. The fantasy of an equal meeting between colonizer and colonized is a fiction concocted by a self-justifying imperial force. Voices are no match for weapons.

Die Wahrheit

"Fairground" leads without a break into a musical number titled "Die Wahrheit," which further comments on the illusory nature of the truth constructed in the previous scene. Here, a soprano voice repeats the words "die Wahrheit" ("truth") in an ever-rising pattern over a newly composed, percussive piano accompaniment. The vocal part directly copies a moment from Mozart's opera. It is a quotation from the finale of Act I of *The Magic Flute*, where Pamina instructs Papageno that they'll tell Sarastro the truth regarding their attempted escape—"the truth, even if it were a crime."[73] Against Pamina's resolute intervals, Miller juxtaposes a piano part consisting of rapid, insistently repeated chords, marked by sudden interruptions and unpredictable accents. A bassline that marches up and down the keyboard against the unrelenting repetitions of the upper parts creates the impression of a circular parade, at once threatening and jocular. In Mozart's work, Pamina's exhortation captures the opera's central concern with virtue, verity, and valor, the ideals that ultimately allow Tamino and his bride to join the ranks of the

---

[73] "Die Wahrheit! Die Wahrheit, wär die auch Verbrechen!." Burton D. Fisher, ed., 2003, *Mozart's* The Magic Flute: *Translated from German and Including Musical Highlight Transcriptions*, Coral Gables, FL: Opera Journeys Publishing, 33.

116 Postcolonial Opera

enlightened. For Kentridge and Miller, however, the soprano's insistence on truth is more ambivalent.

Chapter 2 has already examined the equivocal nature of confessional truth, especially in the postcolony. In *Confessions of Zeno* such unreliability was explicitly articulated by the character Zeno's own admissions to insincerity, however, in *Black Box* the political, historical, and ideological instability of truth emerges through a process of juxtaposition. Placing Pamina's repeated pledge to veracity directly after the impersonal intervals of the Queen of the Night, Miller compels both Pamina and the audience to ask whose truth they have committed themselves to. This message extends into the visual material that accompanies Pamina's voice: a drawing of the Prussian imperial eagle, representative of Kaiser Wilhelm II's expansionist creed, appears along-side a shadow projection of two hands shaping themselves into the shadow of a bird of prey. Placed adjacently, the two eagles expose one another as constructions—if the shadow bird is real only insofar as it is the product of two living hands, the Prussian eagle exists only as a fabrication of shared ideology. Pamina and her Enlightenment peers, *Black Box* asserts, are committed to an illusion of the knowable. If "die Wahrheit" is an essential component of *The Magic Flute*'s Enlightenment politics, *Black Box* reminds the viewer that the very notion of truth is itself an unstable concept.

Postcolonial mourning acknowledges that there can be no such thing as truth in the wake of colonial violence. A project as thoroughly committed as coloniality to shaping the world in its own image cannot and does not leave room for alternative or supplementary knowledge. Any attempt to come to terms with the losses of colonialism therefore has to proceed from an acknowledgment that what has been lost cannot be known and therefore cannot be recovered. Postcolonial mourning proceeds, like Miller and Kentridge's response to Pamina's "Wahrheit," from shadow, impression, and imagination. Unlike colonial and Enlightenment forms of self-narration, in other words, postcolonial engagements with the past acknowledge the fragility of their own versions of history. Constantly revisiting, re-remembering, and reforming what has been lost, the survivor of colonial violence cannot process and forget; instead, her repetitive retelling of various versions of "truth" acquires a melancholy character. (Returning to *Zeno*'s confessional impulse in Chapter 2, the flimsiness of postcolonial truth therefore also renders practices of testimony and revelation unstable. If the truth cannot be known, the confession cannot be tested.) Juxtaposing this impossible reality with Pamina's demand for veracity, *Black Box* reveals *The Magic Flute*'s commitment to truth as itself a melancholy construct, built on a set of fugitive certainties.

In diesen heil'gen Hallen

Though Pamina is the one who explicitly pledges truthfulness, it is the figure of Sarastro that is most thoroughly associated with this quality in Mozart's opera. In Sarastro's great Act II aria, "In diesen heil'gen Hallen" ("In these holy halls"), this attribute, along with forgiveness and righteousness, is celebrated, as the ruler of the Order of Isis and Osiris assures Pamina that his realm is free from revenge and cruelty. Sarastro's aria sounds out a solemn meditation on mercy and the redemptive possibilities offered by reason, as opposed to superstition. It is perhaps the most candid revelation of the Enlightenment's internal paradoxes; its emphasis on peace and reconciliation belies the vindictiveness of Sarastro's original abduction of Pamina and his violent expulsion of Monostatos and the Queen of the Night from the realm of the enlightened. Kentridge and Miller treat Sarastro's aria as an opportunity to perform unambiguously the contradictions of the colonial project. "In diesen heil'gen Hallen" appears twice in *Black Box*; in each case, the virtue of Sarastro's song plays against a visual allegory of colonial violence.

The first iteration of "In diesen heil'gen Hallen" occurs relatively early on in *Black Box*—about a quarter of the way into the piece. From the outset, Miller approaches the priest's music with heavy irony. He relieves the aria of its vocal line, presenting instead an instrumental transcription for brass band. Whereas Mozart's original composition is infused with earnest dignity, Miller transforms his version into a ragged but bombastic march, noisily peppered with cymbal crashes on every beat. Stripped of its grave authority, Sarastro's aria appears as a pompous, self-congratulatory, and darkly absurd performance.

This moment would be comical were it not for the chilling brutality simultaneously playing out on the backdrop. Here, a pair of shadow projections, metamorphosing between crudely drawn male figures, telegraph poles, and mine shafts, beat each other to death (see Figure 3.4). Again and again, one figure strikes the other until nothing remains but a heap of scraps, only for the victim to resurrect itself and restart the endlessly repeating cycle of violence. The juxtaposition of the animated sequence with Miller's gawky recomposition of "In diesen heil'gen Hallen" is unsettling: on the one hand, the upbeat march rhythm makes it all seem like a ridiculous game; on the other, the bloodthirst performed on screen infuses the music with a sinister hue. Thus, the dignified text of Sarastro's aria acquires a chilling quality: in the holy halls of colonial southern Africa, the interplay between music and image suggests, violence rules.

Figure 3.4 Shadow figures beating each other to death in *Black Box/Chambre Noire*. Photograph: Stella Olivier. Courtesy of William Kentridge Studio.

A similar incongruity between sonic and visual material arises from the second presentation of Sarastro's aria. Rather than Miller's recomposition, the second time the audience hears "In diesen heil'gen Hallen" it is in its original form, lifted in its entirety from the historical recording mentioned earlier. The aria is accompanied by Robert Schumann's film, *Nashornjagd in Deutsch-Ost Afrika*, projected onto the backdrop. While Sarastro sings of brotherhood, mercy, and forgiveness, two early colonial hunters accompanied by a group of Black guides stalk and shoot an African White rhinoceros, then shake hands, hack off the animal's left front foot, and pose for the camera with the carcass. The cruelty of this video clip is brought into sharp relief by its concurrence with Sarastro's conciliatory message. Again, the image of hands—here clasping each other in an expression of congratulatory goodwill—signals a more violent ideology behind the apparent innocence of the gesture. Likewise, it casts doubt on the integrity of Sarastro's agenda by drawing a direct link between Enlightenment progress and a colonial civilizing project that kills for leisure.

Rhino

Several scholars interpret the rhino hunt as the pivotal scene of *Black Box*. Gerhard Schoeman identifies in the rhino an allegory for the ruthless slaughter of the Herero and argues that the entire scene "reflects painfully on colonial desires."[74] Guarracino concurs, writing that "the violence over the helpless body of the rhino works as a reminder of the crude fact that, in Mozart's own time and for some centuries afterwards, some human beings— such as the Herero people in the eyes of Trotha's army—were considered less than human, living beings on which violence could be exerted with little or no moral consequences."[75] Explicitly integrating the idea of mourning, Guarracino further draws on Judith Butler's work to argue that the life of the rhino, like that of the Herero, is not "grievable."[76] Unworthy of the respect for life normally accorded other human lives, these figures are also, by extension, unworthy of respect for the dead—they cannot be mourned because they were never fully alive to begin with.

For Kentridge too, the figure of the rhino is pivotal. An image that recurs throughout his work—often as a reference to Albrecht Dürer's famous rhinoceros woodcut from 1515—it takes on various significations, from symbolizing

---

[74] Schoeman, "Thinking in the Dark," 44.
[75] Guarracino, "Dance," 275.
[76] Guarracino, "Dance," 275.

120 Postcolonial Opera

the orientalist fantasies of early explorers to embodying the precariousness of (post-)modern existence.[77] In his staging of *The Magic Flute*, Kentridge incorporates the rhino as a melancholy bit player suspended between the magical and the real. It first appears in Act I, Scene 3, where it performs an enchanted dance on its hind legs while Tamino plays his magic flute to "delight wild animals."[78] Next, it is hunted down in Schumann's film, which in the opera as in *Black Box*, is projected during "In diesen heil'gen Hallen." In *The Magic Flute*, Sarastro sings this aria while laying a hand on Pamina's shoulder. For Kentridge, this gesture is saturated with the potential for force: "How long and how firmly should this hand be on [Pamina's] shoulder?," he asks. "The shift from the hand being reassuring to its being predatory is a matter of a second, or the slightest resistance from Pamina's shoulder."[79] In Sarastro's singing and conduct, in other words, Kentridge identifies the behavior of a person convinced of his own authority, of the legitimacy of his actions, and of his power over others. Schumann's film demonstrates the cruelty to which such certainty might lead. If Mozart's opera carries a latent risk of violence or coercion, Kentridge's staging executes this possibility.

In *Black Box*, the order of the rhino's appearances is inverted. First seen in Schumann's film, it returns only at the end of the piece for a repetition of its operatic dance. Here, however, the rhino's performance is no longer a joyful response to Tamino's enchanted flute. Instead, it becomes a mournful dance macabre. In this scene, titled "Rhino," a projected drawing of the rhinoceros appears on screen to perform a lopsided waltz with Megaphone Man, who still carries his sandwich board calling for *Trauerarbeit*. The two horned figures reach toward each other across the distance between nature and colonial technicity. Their dance is accompanied by a musical collage: in the foreground, a simple cello line (an original composition by Miller) is accompanied by a weary oom-pah-pah accompaniment on trombone, euphonium, and xylophone. Layered beneath this unassuming dirge is an original recording of Pamina's Act II lament, "Ach, ich fühl's," ("A, I feel it"). In the opera, Pamina sings this aria when she believes that Tamino has forsaken her. Bemoaning the loss of love and future happiness, she threatens to commit suicide.

Miller's combination of Pamina's lament with the rhino's ghostly elegy enacts a transformation of the lost object. As Pamina sings, she seems to mourn not Tamino, who has not made a single sonic appearance in the installation, but the rhinoceros, which in turn symbolizes the Herero. But the

---

[77] See the Introduction for recurring images in Kentridge's work, including the rhino.
[78] Fisher, *Mozart's* The Magic Flute, 30.
[79] Kentridge, "Sarastro."

Mourning **121**

cello solo and Pamina's singing sound discordant, casting doubt upon the easy transposition of Pamina's operatic mourning into a postcolonial register: though Miller casts his own composition in the same key as Pamina's aria (G minor), he misaligns the downbeats of the two waltz forms, thereby disrupting the harmony between the two expressions of grief. Undermining the metric certainty of the dance, the music casts the rhino and Megaphone Man adrift: they appear to be twisting and turning in an irregular attempt at synchronization, unmoored from the grounding power of the downbeat. Here, the melancholy misalignment of different mournful registers—that of Pamina, aimed at the rhino, and that of Megaphone Man, aimed at the destruction wrought by technological progress—underscores the distance from nature introduced by technology. As a result, Pamina's Western operatic mourning and the postcolonial mourning of Kentridge's installation appear at best unsynchronized and at worst incompatible.

The subject material does, however, intimate a certain continuity between operatic and postcolonial mourning. In her original aria, Pamina mourns the Enlightenment man, Tamino; the rhinoceros dance, in turn, mourns the violence inflicted by Enlightenment man's civilizing and colonizing project. Together, these two mournful registers suggest a multidimensional construal of complicity, victimhood, and guilt that reaches beyond the specificity of personal loss or political devastation. What this scene suggests, then, is that Pamina's operatic mourning on its own cannot sufficiently capture or grieve the losses suffered under coloniality. Nor, however, can it be separated from these losses. If the operatic form is to acknowledge and mourn its own complicity in a history of colonial violence and loss, it needs to find expressive forms that can accommodate the contradictions and incommensurability of various, apparently irreconcilable, forms of grief.

Lament from the March of the Priests

Whereas Pamina's rhino lament suggests colonial dissonance, another scene appears to enact a more hopeful form of postcolonial sonic integration. "Lament from the March of the Priests," which appears straight after "Rhino," combines the melody from Mozart's original march with a southern African sonic and linguistic world. In this track, the late gospel singer Alfred Makgalemele—a Johannesburg-based street musician with whom Miller and Kentridge collaborated on a regular basis—improvises words based on Sesotho religious texts to a piano reduction of the March of the Priests. Makgalemele's otherworldly voice defies gender (and genre) classification: sounding within

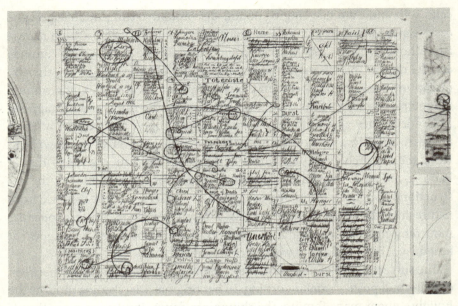

Figure 3.5 "Totenliste," from *Black Box/Chambre Noire*. Photograph: Stella Olivier. Courtesy of William Kentridge Studio.

the alto range, it carries no sonic markers traditionally identified with either male or female vocality in Western art music. This voice, which contradicts the refined projections of operatic singing, is fragile, marked by audible breath, cracks, quivers, and hoarseness. Here, the Black body sounds a foil to the brotherhood of spirit and rationality represented by Mozart's march. Thus, "Lament from the March of the Priests" enacts a sonic encounter between *The Magic Flute* and its excluded Others. The scene's sonic presencing of Black body, Black voice, and by extension, Black historical experience is supported visually: as Makgalemele sings, Kentridge projects onto the backdrop a collage of manufactured "Totenliste" (death lists)—drawings listing names and causes of death based on actual archival inventories of Herero killed in German concentration camps during the genocide (see Figure 3.5).[80]

To create this aria, Miller played a simplified piano reduction of Mozart's march to Makgalamele, who then sang his own words over it. In Miller's description, the whole performance emerged organically—unplanned, but nonetheless in keeping with the aims of the composition and its dramatic scenario. Things "became" freely.[81] This description of the creative process appears to

[80] Similar *Totenliste* also appear in *The Head & the Load*, which is the topic of Chapter 6.
[81] Miller, interview with the author, May 12, 2020.

reinforce clichéd depictions of the racialized subject's apparently "natural," or "free" artistic expression. Miller seems to idealize an image of Makgalemele as authentic musician, unbound by musical convention or the rules of civility. If this reading ignores the inherent unfreedom of the postcolonial subject—of whom Makgalemele, a disabled and economically disenfranchised Black South African, is a striking embodiment—it also reintroduces the nature/culture binary that has haunted all aspects of the piece thus far. Here, however, the binary gives way to a more ambiguous relationality. The improvisatory creative process allows for a certain formal unboundedness: rather than subsuming Makgalemele's singing into a rendition of Mozart's original material, "Lament of the March of the Priests" sounds out something like a "soft collision," if not an integration, between two unrelated musical worlds. Makgalemele's singing is not adapted to suit Mozart's music. Nor, however, does it sound incommensurate with the operatic melody or with the piano accompanying him in simple four-part harmony; rather, the different musical registers complement each other surprisingly well, seeming to suggest that each reaches aesthetic fulfillment through interaction with the others.

The track retains some part of Mozart's original operatic score but welcomes an entirely different genre—gospel—into it with a certain measure of success. Indeed, "Lament of the March of the Priests" is arguably the most moving section of Miller's composition, not only thanks to the charisma of Makgalemele's singing but also due to its compelling interpolation of an unexpected and excluded musical world. "Lament of the March of the Priests" should not be understood as an example of the "Africanisation of Western music"—for instance, in the sense of translating *The Magic Flute*'s libretto into Sesotho and playing it on local instruments. Rather, the track sounds out an easing of the boundaries that define the opera, by drawing in an affective and experiential world unconnected to the original work. Thus, *Black Box* incorporates *The Magic Flute*'s melancholy Others seemingly effortlessly, offering them a form of sonic presence that sounds with, rather than against, the opera.

The Morbidity of Heritage

Makgalemele's transformation of the March of the Priests imagines an operatic structure that makes space for incommensurate or contradictory histories. But this transformation also robs the opera of part of its identity. With the introduction of different forms and figures such as Makgalemele and his gospel singing, *The Magic Flute* ceases to be what it once was. As an adaptation

124 Postcolonial Opera

of Mozart's opera, then, *Black Box* divests the original work of aspects of its meaning and significance—a penalty characteristic of adaptation in general, which, according to performance scholar Jodi Kanter, "always entails some measure of loss."[82] Like all adaptations, *Black Box* itself is built on and marked by loss. Its very form renders the piece melancholy.

In *Black Box*, however, the loss engendered by adaptation is not limited to the forfeiture of the beloved original; it extends also to a loss of operatic innocence. As evidenced by the visibility of the piece's mechanical innards, Kentridge's installation goes to great lengths to unmask the artifice, constructedness, and even brutality that underpin the operatic ideal. Referencing late twentieth- and early twenty-first-century avant-garde theater, the title foregrounds the piece's attempt to react critically to the compromised pasts of the operatic tradition. *Black Box* transforms *The Magic Flute* from a celebration of the cultural, political, and developmental achievements of the Enlightenment to a revelation of its dark underside. Thus, it forces the viewer to acknowledge that opera, like reason, is implicated in the excesses of coloniality, and that the art form can no longer be regarded as merely beautiful, entertaining, or sophisticated. The confrontation with opera's culpability engenders what Paul Gilroy describes as "a sudden and radical loss of moral legitimacy," a realization that in itself becomes a source of melancholy.[83]

Gilroy's theorization of melancholy, which he bases on studies of Germany's post–Second World War attempts to come to terms with the excesses of the Holocaust, applies specifically to the post-imperial nation and its loss of global authority. Faced with both historical culpability and future irrelevance, Gilroy argues, the post-imperial nation turns away from the truths of its shameful past, opting instead for a "neotraditional pathology" that hankers for bygone glories. Until the former empire turns back to acknowledge what Gilroy, after Patrick Wright, calls "the morbidity of heritage," the post-imperial nation will remain a melancholy edifice. But "once . . . a revised account of the nature of imperial statecraft has been folded into critical reflections on national life, the possibility of healing and reconciliation comes into view."[84] *Black Box* appears to perform just the type of recuperative confrontation with a shameful past of which Gilroy speaks. But it also exposes the complicity of opera in this shameful past. In the process, the very form through which the confrontation with the past is enacted is itself brought under suspicion. This complicates the critical labor the piece is supposed to perform.

---

[82] See Kanter, *Performing Loss*, 56, on adaptation and loss.
[83] Paul Gilroy, 2005, *Postcolonial Melancholia*, New York: Columbia University Press, 98.
[84] Gilroy, *Postcolonial Melancholia*, 94.

Though situated in the black box of experimentation—a place idealized as neutral and ostensibly free of value and history—*Black Box* reintroduces, time and again, the operatic form it seeks to critique. As already suggested by its title, the work recognizes that avant-garde ideals can never be shut off entirely from the traditions they appear to resist. The experimental tradition too is part of the history from which it is supposed to distance itself. In *Black Box*, this tradition is both eighteenth-century opera and, by implication, the coloniality that enabled its systems of patronage and circulation. These are the very structures that gave birth to the piece as both concept and performance. Ultimately, *Black Box* itself becomes a victim of the morbidity of heritage—stripped of its innocence by the very story it seeks to tell.

Unlike Gilroy's encounter with the colonial past, which ultimately generates reconciliation, Kentridge's piece does not offer any possibility for healing. Rather, *Black Box* proposes a less future-oriented, or less hopeful, version of melancholy. In this sense, it is not a post-imperial melancholia in Gilroy's sense—one that projects from the metropole outward—but rather a melancholy directed from the postcolony toward the former metropole; one that casts doubt upon the very forms in which the metropole mourns. In *Black Box*, then, *Trauerarbeit* becomes a layered, ambiguous, and ultimately unattainable ideal, which seeks to process not only the trauma of coloniality, or (from the perspective of the former empire) the trauma of the loss of the colony, but also the loss of the operatic form through adaptation, and finally, the loss of the innocence of the operatic form.

Performance, Disembodiment, and Melancholy Form

In *Black Box*, the intrusion of Herero voices and southern African gospel into the sonic world of *The Magic Flute* may be understood to fulfill a function of "historical envoicement." Unlike Kentridge's archival drawings, the musical aspects of the performance are not "exhibited" or repeated outside the installation—they are therefore temporally conditional to a greater extent even than the scopic register of the piece. But they also do more than the visual material to link *Black Box* to both Mozart's opera and the lives of the Herero: thanks to the music, an audience member need not have seen Kentridge's production of *The Magic Flute* to know that the opera is interpolated in the installation (though they must necessarily be familiar with *The Magic Flute* to understand the reference); similarly, the inclusion of Herero music brings these historical figures to life in a way not achievable by means of

126 Postcolonial Opera

drawings and archival references. *Black Box*'s score becomes the ultimate melancholy feature: an ongoing and irresolvable preoccupation with the ghosts of Western high culture and its colonized Others.

Foregrounding the temporally bound register of musical performance, Miller's score embodies a form of ephemerality that contradicts the supposed permanence of historical artifacts such as archival documents and visual records (even when these are, as in Kentridge's work, animated to create the impression of transience). Here, sound deepens the audience member's experience of history and memory *as performance*. This performative register is important: as Kanter notes, performance "may, like narrative, work to compensate, staging unheard voices and unseen bodies."[85] Indeed, Kanter observes, mourning may itself be figured in this context as a form of performance.[86] In other words, the provisional nature of performance creates space for the inclusion of contested, silenced, or archivally neglected perspectives and for the melancholy production of new versions of the past. Through his selection of Herero recordings Miller hence sounds out an alternative take on the experience of colonial history, and by extension, on the afterlives of the Enlightenment.

In the context of a work of mourning, such performativity contributes a melancholy co-presencing of past and present, dead and living. Performance scholars including Joseph Roach, Diana Taylor, and Jermaine Singleton agree that the embodied practice of performance creates scenarios of interaction between experience and memory, self and community, and presence and absence, in a way that "intersects the social and political conditions of the past and present."[87] In the case of the Herero, this form of performative embodiment is crucial: the Herero never make a "live" appearance in the visual material of the piece; instead, they depend fully on the music for a retrospective call to presence. This melancholy sonic enactment suggests a type of resurrection, a way to bring the dead back to life, even if only for a moment. Thus, Miller's score presences both the Herero and *The Magic Flute* in a different way to Kentridge's visual world.

Simultaneously, however, the invisibility of the mournful Black body complicates the politics of representation in *Black Box*. Though the allegorical representation of the Herero in the figure of the rhino helps to avoid the

---

[85] Kanter, *Performing Loss*, 16.

[86] Kanter, *Performing Loss*, 26.

[87] Diana Taylor, 2003, *The Archive and the Repertoire: Performing Cultural Memory in the Americas*, Durham, NC: Duke University Press; Joseph Roach, 1996, *Cities of the Dead: Circum-Atlantic Performance*, New York: Columbia University Press; Jermaine Singleton, 2015, *Cultural Melancholy: Readings of Race, Impossible Mourning, and African American Ritual*, Urbana: University of Illinois Press. The quote is from Singleton, 13.

fetishization of embodied Blackness as visual spectacle, the absence of (Black) human figures does create a disembodied effect at odds with the apparent desire to reinscribe the Herero into colonial history. Makgalemele's improvisation carves out a space for subaltern expression in Mozart's opera; more cynically, though, it might simultaneously be understood to become a stand-in for the fetishized Black body and voice. If "Lament from the March of the Priests" proposes a more optimistic form of multicultural integration, the track also risks usurping Makgalemele's voice and the experiences of those whose names are projected onto Kentridge's *Totenliste* in yet another act of colonial dispossession. Likewise, the apparent nature/culture binary set up between the Herero women and the Queen of the Night suggests that the voice, as cipher for the Black body, merely serves to reinscribe existing stereotypes of pre-colonial incivility rather than fully entering the subaltern perspective into a revisionist account of imperial history.

What voice does offer, though, is greater malleability than body: as archive, Herero voices may furnish a less demanding and less threatening form of historical representation than the Black body. In a way, then, the sonic presence of the Herero may serve simultaneously as representation *and* containment; a way to acknowledge historical injustice without risking the threat of physical confrontation—to incorporate without having to yield space.

The complex dynamics of sonic versus physical presence are demonstrated particularly by the politics surrounding the work's international circulation. Kentridge's installation developed against a backdrop of increasingly fraught diplomatic relations between the former colony of German South-West Africa (Namibia) and its metropole. By the late 1990s, descendants of the Herero began to seek reparations for their suffering and dispossession. In September 2001, Herero representatives belonging to the Chief Hosea Kutako Foundation made the first legal case for restitution when they filed a lawsuit against the German government and three German companies— including Deutsche Bank, one of the sponsors of *Black Box*—in US Federal Court.[88] When *Black Box* opened at the Deutsche Guggenheim in Berlin in 2005, the Herero lawsuit in the United States was still ongoing. The piece cannot be separated from this context, especially given that one of its sponsors was a named defendant in the federal lawsuit for reparations. In conversation with a person involved in the creation of *Black Box*, I learned that Deutsche Bank reacted unenthusiastically to suggestions that the piece be shown in Namibia. According to a representative of the firm, any gesture that might be

---

[88] See Allan D. Cooper, 2006, "Reparations for the Herero Genocide: Defining the Limits of International Litigation," *African Affairs* 116(422), 113–126; the lawsuit was ultimately unsuccessful.

interpreted as a further acknowledgment of responsibility on Germany's part would be "problematic" and "complicated."[89] Thus, Kentridge's piece became simultaneously intertwined in and separated from the restitutive process: if *Black Box* had the potential to offer repair, the installation's imbrication in a political economy of responsibility and recompense rendered any such prospect impotent.[90]

As with Deutsche Bank's refusal to take the installation to Namibia, *Black Box*'s formal configuration plays ambiguously with the politics of inclusion and exclusion. The reparative potential of *Black Box*'s offer of operatic representation hence remains unfulfilled: while Indigenous trauma is allowed to be mourned—by Indigenous voices—on this reconfigured operatic stage, the possibility for restitution is limited to the realm of the symbolic. Even as the disenfranchised voice sounds, the bodies of those actually murdered by coloniality (and figuratively killed by opera) remain buried. As opera, then, *Black Box* cannot offer the resolution demanded by Freud's work of mourning. Rather, the piece's signification remains open, constantly repeating and recirculating the very losses of which it speaks. Defying completion and finality, Kentridge's installation enacts a performative and ambiguous melancholy that resists the finality of mourning—postcolonial or otherwise.

But even if it does not achieve the resolution promised by Megaphone Man and his demand for *Trauerarbeit*, *Black Box* does hold out some hope for opera's capacity to process colonial history. What the piece suggests is that the operatic form, by coming face to face with its colonial history, can expand and "make ethical" its melancholy. This cannot, however, be achieved by conventional opera. As Pamina's lament demonstrates, the individualism of Western operatic mourning remains discordant within the context of colonial loss. Instead, the ethically melancholic operatic form must incorporate its Others or its negatives. This, *Black Box* suggests, can be achieved by loosening the boundaries of what constitutes opera; by welcoming into its realm alternative styles and forms, such as Makgalemele's genderless gospel and the Herero women's song. In this configuration, the operatic form is capable of accommodating its own contradictions; it can simultaneously celebrate

---

[89] This anecdote was shared with me on condition of anonymity.

[90] *Black Box* did not appear in Namibia, but since its first showing in Berlin, the piece has traveled to, among others, Museum der Moderne in Salzburg (2006), Johannesburg Art Gallery (2006), Moderna Museet in Stockholm (2007), Malmö Konsthall in Sweden (2007), San Francisco Museum of Modern Art (2009), the Jewish Historical Museum in Amsterdam (2012), Liebieghaus in Frankfurt-am-Main (2018), Louisiana Museum of Modern Art in Humlebaek, Denmark (2018), and most recently, the Royal Academy in London (2022). As part of its 2018 William Kentridge retrospective, Liebieghaus created a fantastic online introduction (what they call a "digitorial") to *Black Box*: the site is can still be visited at https://kentri dge.liebieghaus.de/en/black-box (accessed May 25, 2021). Louisiana Museum of Modern Art acquired one of the two *Black Box* installations in 2018; the piece is now part of the museum's permanent collection.

the triumph of Western Enlightenment and grieve the dark underside of coloniality. Ultimately, after all, each of these concepts is meaningless without the other: the postcolonial condition is itself, as Homi Bhabha argues, a perpetual state of paradox.[91] Of being both product *and* victim of modernity. The dual nature of the unbounded operatic form renders this subconscious splitting visible and performs it as a form of melancholy perched between indictment and repair.

Through the unbounded form, one that welcomes both opera and the Others against which the genre defines itself, Kentridge refigures operatic melancholy as postcolonial. The idea(l) of postcolonial mourning dissolves before it merges with operatic convention—a move that would itself be nothing short of colonial. Instead, it sounds beyond and against what came before—a melancholy confrontation with opera's past, and a daring wager on its future.

---

[91] Homi K. Bhabha, 2004 [1994], *The Location of Culture*, London: Routledge.

4
Time

On October 1, 1884, a group of scientists, politicians, and military officers from around the world gathered in Washington, DC, for the International Meridian Conference. Their goal: to agree on a prime meridian—a universal zero point—to be adopted by all nations. On October 22, all countries present, with the exception of France, Brazil, and San Domingo (now the Dominican Republic), assented to the adoption of the longitudinal line that passes through Greenwich Observatory as the international prime meridian.[1]

Twenty-four days later, on November 15, 1884, a second group of delegates met in Berlin for the West Africa Conference. This gathering of colonial powers, which would become known as the Berlin Conference, formalized the partitioning and distribution of African territories among European powers. When the conference ended on February 26, 1885, Britain, France, Germany, Belgium, Spain, Portugal, and Italy formally possessed 90 percent of the continent's land.[2]

The near simultaneity of the International Meridian Conference and the Berlin Conference may be coincidental, but it is also symbolic. Time and coloniality were closely interwoven. The universalization of clocks and schedules facilitated transportation and communication, which in turn advanced the trade networks that would form the bedrock of the so-called scramble for Africa. As socio-economic conventions of progress and productivity increasingly guided European modernity, notions of being "in time" came to shape the moral, industrial, and colonial projects of the nineteenth and early twentieth centuries. Western "clock time" was exported to the colonies to fulfill disciplining and civilizing purposes, rehabilitating a sphere represented as primitive and out-of-time. In Peter Galison's assessment, time standardization became one of the defining structures of modernity, an agglomeration of social, scientific, political, and philosophical conventions allied to modernity, which enabled the colonial project both practically and ideologically.[3]

---

[1] For more on the International Meridian Conference, see Charles W. K. Withers, 2017, *Zero Degrees: Geographies of the Prime Meridian*, Cambridge, MA: Harvard University Press, esp. chapter 5.

[2] For more on the Berlin Conference, see Steven Press, 2017, *Rogue Empires: Contracts and Conmen in Europe's Scramble for Africa*, Cambridge, MA: Harvard University Press, chapter 5.

[3] Peter Galison, 2003, *Einstein's Clocks, Poincaré's Maps: Empires of Time*, New York: W. W. Norton, at 328.

Postcolonial Opera. Juliana M. Pistorius, Oxford University Press. © Oxford University Press 2025.
DOI: 10.1093/oso/9780197749203.003.0005

As the "quintessentially temporal art," music, too, is implicated in the nineteenth century's politics of time.[4] Playing "in time" is itself indicative of temporal discipline and homogeneity—ideals that shaped the West's preoccupation with temporal regulation and standardization. Additionally, the musical portrayal of non-Western others as primitive, traditional, or culturally naïve, contributed to the construction of colonial spheres as arrested in a historical past somehow out of sync with the European present.[5]

Nowhere, perhaps, is this as clear as in the manifold operatic depictions of imagined natives that have swarmed European stages since the eighteenth century. With its orientalist fantasies, Western opera contributed to a representation of the colony as occupying, in Keya Ganguly's words, "an 'other' time whose logic and historical expression are incommensurable with the normative temporality of clock and calendar associated with Western modernity."[6] From a postcolonial perspective, the relationship between opera and time is hence significant. It participates in a larger discourse of civic and economic homogeneity shaped by the progressionist principles of modernity.

But opera, with its interplay between action and reflection (or recitative and aria), also complicates linear time. It resists teleology, arresting narrative progress with arias, and dwelling in the past with musical fragments and recollections. The temporal heterogeneity of opera may hence offer an opportunity to break open what Mark Rifkin calls "chrononormativity," or the homogeneity of clock time, and to imagine different ways of being "in time."[7]

Kentridge's 2012 chamber opera, *Refuse the Hour*, places questions of time and coloniality front and center. Growing out of a series of conversations with historian of science Peter Galison, the piece examines temporal unification and its impact on Europe's colonies. Its quasi-improvisatory score combines futuristic blips and glitches with sung reflections on the history of colonial arrival on the African continent. Together, the visual and sonic registers of *Refuse the Hour* produce a ludic archive of time from a variety of cultural and geographical perspectives. This chapter takes *Refuse the Hour* as a starting point to probe the formal limits of the Western temporal order. Attending to the construction of temporality in opera, it speculates on the potential of the

---

[4] Karol Berger, 2007, *Bach's Cycle, Mozart's Arrow: An Essay on the Origins of Musical Modernity*, Berkeley: University of California Press, at 99.

[5] Johannes Fabian, 2014 [1983], *Time and the Other: How Anthropology Makes Its Object*, New York: Columbia University Press.

[6] Keya Ganguly, 2004, "Temporality and Postcolonial Critique," in *The Cambridge Companion to Postcolonial Literary Studies*, ed. Neil Lazarus, Cambridge: Cambridge University Press, 162–180, at 162.

[7] Mark Rifkin, 2017, *Beyond Settler Time: Temporal Sovereignty and Indigenous Self-Determination*, Durham, NC: Duke University Press, 44.

132 Postcolonial Opera

operatic form to refuse the constraints of colonial temporal regimes on the postcolonial stage.

Refuse the Hour

Refuse the Hour premiered on June 18, 2012 at the Holland Festival, Amsterdam. A co-production with Festival d'Avignon, RomaEuropa Festival, and the Onassis Cultural Centre, the ninety-minute chamber opera serves as a fellow traveler to Kentridge's five-channel video installation, *The Refusal of Time* (2012).[8] A team of Kentridge's regular co-workers animated *Refuse the Hour*'s assorted components. Production programs credit Catherine Meybrugh (video editing), Sabine Theunissen (stage design), Luc de Wit (movement), and Greta Goiris (costumes). Philip Miller composed the music, and acclaimed South African dancer Dada Masilo developed and performs the work's extensive choreographic sequences.

Both the opera and the video installation face the topic of chrononormativity head-on. Inspired by conversations between Kentridge and Galison, they develop complementary meditations on the standardization of time, the construction of simultaneity, and the development of relativity. *Refuse the Hour*'s libretto derives from a talk Kentridge gave in advance of *The Refusal of Time*'s premiere at Documenta 13 in Kassel. The text navigates topics as diverse as Greek myth, artistic method, relativity, and string theory. In the opera, Kentridge (playing himself) delivers a near-identical version of the Documenta lecture, interspersed with song and dance numbers and complemented by the artist's animated background projections.

Part 1, " 'He that fled his fate,' narrates the saga of the death of Acrisius, who was killed by his own grandson, Perseus, despite taking all possible measures to avoid this outcome, which had been foretold in advance.[9] Kentridge recalls being told this story by his father while on a train journey from Johannesburg to Port Elizabeth. The artist recounts his younger self's outrage at the senselessness of Acrisius's death: if only the conceited Perseus had not decided to participate in the competition where he threw the discus that killed his grandfather; if only the old king had chosen a different seat at the athletics tournament where his grandson's discus struck him. Kentridge's recollection of the

---

[8] Kentridge and his team refer to related productions by the artist as "fellow travelers." I discuss the term in the Introduction.

[9] For the myth of Acrisius and Perseus, see Joy Tyldesley, 2017, *Stories from Ancient Greece & Rome*, Oxford: Oxbow Books, 62–71.

Time   133

story of Acrisius and Perseus highlights three themes that return throughout the opera. They include the capriciousness of fate, the inevitability of death, and the impossibility of calling back time—of returning the discus to the hand once it has been launched. Subsequent scenes return to these topics, scrutinizing them with an often-humorous mix of exasperation and forbearance.[10]

In part 2, "The universal archive," Kentridge adds two further thematic concerns to the three already highlighted. First, "The universal archive" engages with a topic that recurs throughout Kentridge's oeuvre: the idea of permanence. The artist draws on German jurist and astronomer Felix Eberty's (1812–1884) proposition, derived from the fact that the speed of light is fixed at 186,000 miles per second, that "the image of everything that has happened can be found in space if one could be at the right distance, and so the right point of space to see the image."[11] In other words, if one appraises the earth from a particular number of light-years away, one could see events that have been confined to the past: at thirty light-years away, the first democratic elections in South Africa; at 532 light-years away, the arrival of Christopher Columbus in the Americas; at 2,024 light-years away, the birth of Christ. Based on Eberty's hypothesis, Kentridge concludes that nothing is ever completely lost. Everything can be found back again, if one could travel to the appropriate place in the cosmos. This insight contradicts the inevitability of death articulated in "He that fled his fate."

Second, "The universal archive" introduces the theme of decay. In a closing sequence comprising six repetitions of a scenario titled "Concerning entropy," Kentridge and dancer Dada Masilo together mime the enactment of a series of variations on a short task:

Concerning Entropy no. 1

Take a vase. Use a no. 9 hammer and rap firmly on the rim. Smash the thing. All the pieces with half athletes, the discus, the tree, the maiden—all in pieces. Place shards in a hat. Shake vigorously. Spread the evidence. Read your fortune.[12]

"Concerning entropy" numbers 2 to 6 represent gradual disintegrations of number 1, until the instructions and their performance descend into nonsense:

[10] William Kentridge, 2013, "Refuse the Hour Lecture by W. K.," in *The Refusal of Time*, ed. Peter Galison, William Kentridge, Catherine Meyburgh, and Philip Miller, Paris: Xavier Barral Publishing, I–XVI.
[11] The words are Kentridge's; Eberty developed his thesis in *The Stars and the Earth: Thoughts upon Space, Time, and Eternity*, London: Bailliere, Tindall, and Cox, 1846.
[12] Kentridge, "Refuse the Hour," VII.

134 Postcolonial Opera

<u>Concerning Entropy no. 6</u>
With athletes your read
rap maidens
Place on the discus
Spread rim

The telegraph
The breathing lung
The beating clock
The reel of string
The directory
The atlas
The encyclopaedia
The donkey
the swan
the journey
the wrong chair
the wrong chair
the wrong chair
the wrong chair
the wrong chair
the wrong chair
the wrong chair
the horizon
the perpendicular
the acute
the arcane
the reflex
The shards in a hat and fragmented thing.
Use all fortune.
a vase smash[13]

"Concerning entropy" bears clear intertextual allusions to Ai WeiWei's 1995 work, *Dropping a Han Dynasty Urn*, and LaMonte Young's text-based *Compositions 1960* (1960). Perhaps Kentridge here seeks to invoke the apparent senselessness of both WeiWei's act of destruction and Young's whimsical assignments. But as the tasks fragment and chaos threatens to overwhelm the scene, the artist's closing words shift from elated disorder to regret: "The

---

[13] Kentridge, "Refuse the Hour," IX–X. Original punctuation.

universal archive of images becomes also an overstocked, miserable collection of surplus images. We are caught between wanting to send ourselves out, and hold back, to call back, to annul, and obliterate so many traces and acts. To undo. To unsave. To unsay. To unremember. To unhappen."[14] Permanence can be a burden.

In part 3, "Self-portrait as coffee pot," Kentridge proposes a solution to the challenge of undoing, unsaving, unsaying, unremembering, and unhappening. Visual technologies (photo and video), he says, have the capacity to resist the working of time. Photography, on the one hand, "congeals" time, or turns it "into stone." Film, on the other, allows "successive images [to be] looked at in reverse" by offering the possibility of running events from end to beginning. In what may be regarded as something of a manifesto for his own work in film, the artist celebrates the capacity of these media to "hold time to account."[15] Allowing for time to stop, or even to reverse, the acts of unsaying or undoing become a little more possible.

Ultimately, Kentridge's concern with temporal arrest appears to be about resisting death. "Man is a breathing and talking clock," he says in the final part of scene 3. "Our hearts, our pulse, our lungs—natural clocks, both measuring and counting out the time. One big windup at birth and a slow winding down—and all our actions, attempts to slow the clock down."[16] As he narrates this passage, the artist draws a big breath and holds it (murmuring in a tiny voice, "holding . . . holding . . . still holding") until he no longer can.[17] Attempting to make each allocated breath last as long as possible, Kentridge executes an embodied refusal of temporal encroachment and decay. Thus, the idea of the human body as mechanism—a construct anticipated in the artist's puppet productions, and especially in the anatomical references of his *Ulisse*—traces a connection between the technological preoccupations of modernity and the processes of physical existence.[18]

Part 4, "In praise of bad clocks," develops the metaphor of time as breath. Kentridge describes the pneumatic clocks of nineteenth-century Paris, which regulated time by sending regular bursts of air through a network of pipes under the city's streets, creating, in the artist's description, a city breathing in unison.[19] Here, the artist renders temporal coordination in biomechanical terms. He draws attention to the fact that time is a technology of both the mind and the body, and that it controls as much as it enables.

---

[14] Kentridge, "Refuse the Hour," X.
[15] Kentridge, "Refuse the Hour," X.
[16] Kentridge, "Refuse the Hour," XII.
[17] Kentridge, *Refuse the Hour*, unpublished video recording, courtesy of the artist.
[18] See Chapter 1 for *Ulisse*.
[19] Kentridge, "Refuse the Hour," XII–XIII.

136 Postcolonial Opera

What occurs locally in Part 4 obtains global reach in Part 5, "Productive procrastination," where the topic of temporal coordination is expanded from Paris to the colonies. Kentridge describes how "the clock and the colonial observatory completed the mapping of the world," covering the globe with "a huge dented bird cage of time zones, of lines of agreement of control, all sent out by the clock rooms of Europe." Reflecting on the fact that temporal coordination severed local time from the diurnal rhythms of sunrise and sunset, the artist mentions that "local suns were shifted further and further from local zeniths." This resulted not only in a system of metropolitan control but also in the alienation from the natural world the customs assembled around it.

Kentridge argues that such temporal standardization did not pass unremarked upon in the colonies. Rather, he describes anti-colonial revolts such as the Chilembwe revolt of 1915 and the Herero revolt of 1906 as resistance to colonial time, a demand that the colonizers "give us back our Sun." Finding the materiality of time in the technologies enabled by it, Kentridge remarks on violent attempts to resist temporal domination: "As if blowing up a train line could blow up the pendulum of the European clock, which swung over every head."[20]

The penultimate scene, "Charon at the Event Horizon," offers something of a corrective to the authoritarian force of temporal coordination. Drawing on Einstein's general theory of relativity, Kentridge undermines the ideal of absolute simultaneity. The artist reconstructs Einstein's scenario of two twins, one of whom travels to outer space while the other stays on earth. The twins end up aging at different rates based on their position relative to the center of the earth. In Kentridge's treatment, the earth-bound twin eventually forgets his brother, whose return, much like that of Homer's Ulisse in Chapter 1, becomes not a triumphal homecoming but an anonymous reappearance. Thus, the space brother's triumph over temporal decay yields nothing but emptiness. He has been forgotten; his past consigned to non-existence.

Part 6, "Anti-entropy," once more resists the apparent nothingness of death. Describing (and resisting) the assumption that nothing can escape a black hole ("a black hole the size of a full stop swallows the sentence"), Kentridge turns to string theory: "Entropy forbids all elements from entering the black chasm. As an object approaches a black hole, its wavelength lengthens, slowing down, becomes redder and redder; the information and attributes separate from the object, and remain as strings."[21] Here, Charon, invoked in the title of the previous section, returns—not merely as the usher of the dead, but also

---

[20] Kentridge, "Refuse the Hour," XIII–XIV.
[21] Kentridge, "Refuse the Hour," XVI.

as the keeper of what remains. This Charon appears with a boat full of objects left behind by people as they crossed the river Styx: "a suitcase of teeth and glasses, thoughts, stories, an old stone discus."[22] The opera appears to settle on the conclusion that decay, or entropy, prohibits complete extinction. Time, it claims, does not end. Death is not absolute.

From the lecture's contents the meaning of the opera's title becomes clear. "Refusal," in Kentridge's treatment, is first about resisting the inevitability of fate and, by extension, death. The artist himself acknowledges that "everybody knows that we are going to die; but the resistance to that pressure coming towards us is at the heart of the project. At the individual level, it was about resisting; not resisting mortality in the hope of trying to escape it, but trying to escape the pressure that it puts on us."[23] For Kentridge, the inevitability of death is but one of the certitudes he seeks to put under pressure with his work. He writes, "One of the beginnings was the contrast to *Seize the Day. Refuse the Hour*, like *Seize the Day*, has the implicit confidence and certainty of a revolutionary dictum; but *Refuse the Hour* and *The Refusal of Time* is [sic] also a refusal of that certainty."[24] The notion that time's forward motion places pressure on the present moment—an imperative to make the most of every second—hence inspires Kentridge's conception of individual refusal.

At a structural level, refusal emerges as resistance to temporal systems of order and control. Kentridge states, "In colonial terms, the refusal was a refusal of the European sense of order imposed by time zones; not only literally, but this refusal also referred metaphorically to other forms of control as well."[25] Standing in as a metaphor for the colonial project as a whole, time hence becomes a focal point for the defiance of those upon whom it was imposed. Resistance to time is not only an attempt to escape the pressure of death but also to recoup political self-determination and to reclaim material and cultural properties stamped out by colonialism.

For Vilashini Cooppan, the refusals imagined by Kentridge's opera allow for "(1) the exploration of terrain beyond empire and nation; (2) the chronicling—through alternative chronologies—of places of regional and inherited memory; (3) renewed encounters with the subjective and affective textures of memory; (4) via all of the previous, the ongoing unlocking/ unclocking of the spacetime of the postcolonial; and (5) a related rippling

---

[22] Kentridge, "Refuse the Hour," XVI.

[23] William Kentridge and Peter Galison, 2013, "Give Us Back Our Sun," in *The Refusal of Time*, ed. Peter Galison, William Kentridge, Catherine Meyburgh, and Philip Miller, Paris: Xavier Barral Publishing, 157–164, at 157.

[24] Kentridge, in Kentridge and Galison, "Give Us Back Our Sun," 157.

[25] Kentridge, in Kentridge and Galison, "Give Us Back Our Sun," 157.

138 Postcolonial Opera

forth of a melancholic yet reparative realm that [she calls] oceanic space-time, a field of swells and flows, depths and crests, a wake that demands us to awaken."[26] The anti-colonial possibility of temporal refusal emerges from its capacity to unlock alternative forms of selfhood, alternative imaginaries of place, and alternative modes of historical narration.

As in so many of Kentridge's pieces, history serves as a driving force in *Refuse the Hour*. The central role of the past—as both subject and object—is underlined in the work's production design, which explicitly references the period at the end of the nineteenth century when clocks were being standardized and cinema became available to larger numbers of artists, entertainers, and media institutions. Kentridge identifies 1905 as a key date of the work. This was what the artist describes as "the year of Einstein's special theory of relativity," and a time characterized by new developments in film and cinema.[27] Another central event, more explicitly depicted in *The Refusal of Time* than in *Refuse the Hour*, is Martial Bourdin's attempt on February 15, 1894 to blow up the Greenwich Observatory. Kentridge first learned of this failed historical event from Galison, who describes it in his study of temporal standardization, *Einstein's Clocks, Poincaré's Maps: Empires of Time*.[28] Drawing especially on Joseph Conrad's novel, *The Secret Agent* (1907), which is based on the Greenwich bombing, Galison identifies in this event an attack on the symbolic power of the prime meridian.[29] In *The Refusal of Time* Kentridge relocates the anarchist bombers to Dakar, Senegal, thereby reframing the attack on Greenwich as resistance to colonial rule.[30]

Visual references to the period around Bourdin's failed bombing and Einstein's relativity are amplified by a collection of quirky machines that look like they stepped straight out of a museum of late nineteenth-century inventions. Designed by Kentridge and created by Christoff Wolmarans, Louis Olivier, and Jonas Lundquist, they include a self-playing percussion machine suspended above the stage, a megaphone activated by a bicycle wheel, a dancing telegraph pole, a turntable large enough to carry a human, and a giant set of bellows. The automatons appear to invoke the lumbering but spectacular technologies of early industrialization. Galison reflects as follows: "[We are both fascinated by] the late nineteenth and early twentieth century period,

---

[26] Vilashini Cooppan, 2019, "Time Maps: A Field Guide for the Decolonial Imaginary," *Critical Times* 2(3), 396–415, at 398.

[27] Kentridge, in William Kentridge and Peter Galison, 2013, "Blowing Up the Meridian," in *The Refusal of Time*, ed. Peter Galison, William Kentridge, Catherine Meyburgh, and Philip Miller, Paris: Xavier Barral Publishing, 249–250, at 249.

[28] This event is recounted in Galison, *Einstein's Clocks*, at 159–160.

[29] Galison, *Einstein's Clocks*, 160. See Joseph Conrad, 1960 [1907], *The Secret Agent: A Simple Tale*, London: J. M. Dent and Sons.

[30] Kentridge, in Kentridge and Galison, "Blowing Up the Meridian," 249.

Figure 4.1 A partial view of *Refuse the Hour*'s stage, showing megaphones activated by a bicycle wheel (far left), the giant turntable (next to Kentridge), and projected metronomes. Photograph: Jack de Villiers. Courtesy of William Kentridge Studio.

when the project of modern technology and science had begun, yet everything was visible, or almost visible. It was a time when you could almost see the mechanisms of things working—before they disappeared into a microchip, beyond our grasp."[31] Kentridge confirms, stating that "it relates to an interest in nineteenth century mechanical technology, a mechanical switchboard, a pipe in which you can feel and hear the pulse of air being transferred. Nineteenth century technology rendered visible what are now invisible phenomena in the twenty-first century."[32]

Indeed, as in *Black Box/Chambre Noire*, Kentridge chooses to make visible the technical processes that enable these machines to operate (see Figure 4.1).[33] The contraptions are manipulated and maneuvered by the work's cast of singers, actors, and dancers, challenging viewers and performers alike to reflect on the increasingly tenuous boundary between human and machine. Kentridge himself acknowledges that the relationship between humans and machines is important to him, especially as the automatons occasionally acquire their own agency, directing the movements of the performers rather than the other way around.[34] Here, anxieties about productivity and the

---

[31] Galison, in Kentridge and Galison, "Give Us Back Our Sun," 162.
[32] Kentridge, in Kentridge and Galison, "Give Us Back Our Sun," 162.
[33] See Chapter 3 for *Black Box/Chambre Noire*.
[34] Kentridge, 2012, "Entretien avec William Kentridge," in *Refuse the Hour* [Production Program]. Festival d'Avignon, July 7–13.

140 Postcolonial Opera

automation of human labor are coupled with guileless enchantment at the aesthetics of these technologies.

For composer Philip Miller, who created the score for *Refuse the Hour*, the relationship between humans and machines also offered musical inspiration. In conversation with Kentridge, he describes "the lungs pumping air up through the windpipes, vibrating onto the vocal chords" as "in itself a machine." Kentridge concurs, observing that "the body becomes a machine but also, the machine becomes humanized. The abstract nature of time gets brought into the body."[35] Elsewhere, the artist observes that the music creates "a sense of the body as a clock, the body as a musical instrument, the body as an engine."[36] Miller's description applies literally, of course, to another object of nineteenth-century French pneumatic innovation: the organ.[37] Instead of using an organ, however, Miller foregrounds the metaphor of breath-as-time through music focused especially on wind instruments. Scored for an ensemble comprising trumpet, trombone, tuba, harmonium, violin, piano, and percussion, the composition also includes sound effects such as amplified human breaths, tinny noises processed through megaphones, and the wheezy tones of concertinas.

Miller's music combines a tour of various different musical styles with a meditation on the themes and metaphors explored in Kentridge's lecture. As in other Miller scores discussed in this book, the opera incorporates a multitude of musical intertexts.[38] Berlioz's "Le spectre de la rose" from his song cycle *Les Nuits d'Été* (Op. 7) is something of a refrain, recurring at various moments in the opera. As explored at greater length below, the song's subject matter, as well as Miller's treatment of its lyric and musical content, presents sonic reenactments of some of the most pressing concerns of Kentridge's lecture. The composer combines his references to Berlioz's song with invocations of southern African drumming, isiZulu a-capella singing in the style of *isicathamiya*, sentimental waltzes, lopsided marches, and eerie wails. Miller himself describes his approach to this eclectic score as follows:

> As a composer, in South Africa, I am constantly working across musical genres and languages which jostle up against each other. I am often very curious to see how

[35] William Kentridge and Philip Miller, 2013, "Gathering Sounds and Making Objects Breathe," in *The Refusal of Time*, ed. Peter Galison, William Kentridge, Catherine Meyburgh, and Philip Miller, Paris: Xavier Barral Publishing, 197–212, at 198.

[36] Kentridge, "Give Us Back Our Sun," 161. These mechanistic descriptions of vocality bear a striking resemblance to the Queen of the Night's automated, or machine-like singing, as discussed in Chapter 3.

[37] Thanks to Daniel Grimley for drawing my attention to this point. See Orpha Ochse, 2000, *Organists and Organ Playing in Nineteenth-Century France and Belgium*, Bloomington: Indiana University Press.

[38] See Chapter 3 for *Black Box/Chambre Noire*, Chapter 5 for *Triumphs and Laments*, and Chapter 6 for *The Head and the Load*.

> the barriers break down between the so-called "high art" forms of classical music, and other musical styles, whether it be African drumming or a Zulu a-capella choir. . . . This impetus to mix up different musical languages together is not for the sake of some kind of utopian musical dream. It is rather to play with the way sounds constantly collide with each other in our everyday world. The notion of a discreet musical sound or language seems to me very artificial. Living in a city like Johannesburg, a perfectly normal musical sound world, is me driving in my car listening to Schubert piano sonatas, interrupted by the hooting of irate taxi drivers, cars next to me playing traditional rap music called "kwaito" on the car stereo, a street evangelist preaching in the street to his congregation, and above me I hear the sounds of the raucous hadeda birds in the sky.[39]

The sound world Miller describes here reveals something of the insular, not to mention privileged, sonic subject position of the postcolonizing subject in post-apartheid South Africa.[40] But it also captures an interplay of rhythmic and melodic constructs of both time and place, which influences the composer's experience of his environment and his art. Miller's incorporation of intertexts and cross-temporalities evokes the temporal turmoil of Kentridge's mediations. As critic Mark Swed writes, "Music, being the art of clock time, has here the idiosyncratic task of being an ironic advocate of opposing the clock."[41] The syncopations and metric irregularities of Miller's score, often augmented by giant metronomes beating out of sync on the background projection, or the drum machine suspended above the stage gradually descending into rhythmic disorder, problematize the tidy control idealized by Western chrononormativity. In this sense, the dancing automata on stage serve not only to add a repertoire of uncanny sound effects to the opera's musical texture but also enact a kind of automated uprising against time.

Even in the first ensemble number, titled "Prologue Metronome," temporal anarchy seems inevitable. This piece bears a distinct resemblance to György Ligeti's *Poème Symphonique* for 100 metronomes (1962), thereby reinforcing the link between Kentridge and the European avant-garde—an aspect of the artist's practice I discuss in the Introduction. Actor Bham Ntabeni enters the stage carrying a large bass drum, which he directs at the middle of three enormous projected metronomes. With drumbeats and a melodious chant, he

---

[39] Miller, cited in Lonneke Kok, 2012, "Stopping Time," *Refuse the Hour* [Production Program], Holland Festival, 8–10, at 9–10.

[40] See the Introduction for an explanation of the category of the postcolonizing subject.

[41] Mark Swed, 2017, "Music Review, 'Refuse the Hour' Tinkers with Time; William Kentridge's Transformation of His Installation into Opera Is a Fresh Revelation." *Los Angeles Times*, November 20, https://www-proquest-com.libproxy.ucl.ac.uk/docview/1965998828?pq-origsite=primo.

142 Postcolonial Opera

tries to direct the metronome's tempo. But soon, the instrument seems to lose pace with Ntabeni's directions. The actor directs himself at the metronome on the right, which starts in time but almost immediately strays into a different tempo. When the third metronome enters, Ntabeni's instructions have apparently become irrelevant. Even the band, which at first offered musical support to Ntabeni's temporal directions, succumbs to rhythmic irregularity. Two actors, each carrying a megaphone, join Ntabeni. They shout tempo directions at the metronomes: "lento! . . . lento! . . . presto! . . . presto! . . . moderato! . . . moderato! . . . allegro! . . . allegro!" But the metronomes ignore them, adjusting their tempi apparently at will. Soon, rhythmic chaos ensues. Gradually, the ensemble appears to run out of steam. After a breathless refrain of rhythmic semitone oscillations in the band, the sounds quieten down, until only a series of slightly disjointed ticks remains (see ▶ Clip 4.1).

Time, Modernity, Coloniality

Western practices of temporal discipline, progress, and control developed with the onset of modernity in the eighteenth century.[42] Though scholars disagree about the extent to which "modern" temporal practices supplanted or erased so-called traditional temporality, they agree that the political, scientific, and philosophical changes of the Enlightenment were accompanied by a new conception of historical succession and temporal progression. Karol Berger distinguishes between the time of traditional pre-modern European societies, characterized by "a sense of cyclical or entirely timeless stasis," and modern time, which is shaped by ideas of progressive continuity, linearity, revolutionary breakthrough, and secularism.[43] He ascribes the temporal reorientation of modernity to the changing political and economic practices of eighteenth-century Europe, identifying particularly the shift from subsistence-based agricultural (or seasonal) labor to "a dynamic, growth-oriented, mercantile-industrial economy" as a key contributor to a new valuation of time.[44]

European time is, in other words, shaped by the linear and regulated time of progress. It views time as a commodity, as something that can be used, consumed, and wasted. Manifesting most destructively in the factories of Western

---

[42] Berger, *Bach's Cycle*, 9.

[43] Berger, *Bach's Cycle*, 12. Berger's study paints distinctions between pre-modern and industrialized societies in crude terms. Nonetheless, his arguments do provide a useful starting point from which to think through the histories of Western temporal regimes, especially as they manifest in music.

[44] Berger, *Bach's Cycle*, 172.

industrial cities and on the plantations and mines of colonies, European time is industrial time, labor time, colonial time. It exists to regulate the labor of the subjugated. Time functions first and foremost as a form of control.[45]

The demands of the mercantile-industrial economy ultimately culminated in the universalization of clock time and the adoption of the prime meridian. As trade and travel across borders became ever more ubiquitous, the standardization of measurements, routes, and timetables became crucial. Thus, the changes brought about by eighteenth-century technological and political developments created the circumstances for the adoption of temporal homogeneity between Western trade partners. In Galison's description, these conventions—of length, of weight, of electrical power, war, peace, and price—served to calm the friction generated by collisions between different places, interests, and practices.[46] Time was one such convention, "an agreement like any other that would, depending on the accord, unify cities, lines, zones, countries, or the world."[47]

But temporal standardization was not only for Western countries. Given the close interweaving of modernity with coloniality, it is no surprise that the generalization of clock time played as important a role in the colonies as in the metropole. In colonial terms, time standardization primarily functioned in service of what Galison describes as "a race for symbolic map-possession."[48] The ability to measure time accurately was crucial in establishing exact longitudinal positions for the construction of maps of newly claimed territories. Thus, the master of time became the master of the map. By extension, those who could map could also take ownership of place. Time became crucial for connecting with and claiming control over colonial geographies. Later, as undersea telegraph cables, international shipping routes, and continental train lines turned the globe into a web of interconnecting lines, synchronization integrated colonial territories with metropoles and allowed them to function as temporally unified extensions of the mother country rather than remote, isolated appendages.[49] In *Refuse the Hour*, Kentridge references the centrality of transport and communication structures to time standardization by mentioning that he heard Acrisius's story on a train. Railways served as an

[45] This is what Foucault refers to as the discipline of the timetable, a form of control whose dissemination he traces, in *Discipline and Punish: The Birth of the Prison* (trans. Alan Sheridan, London: Penguin Books, 2020 [1975]), from the monastery to the factory. Dale Southerton, ed., 2020, *Time, Consumption, and the Coordination of Everyday Life*, London: Palgrave Macmillan, gives an up-to-date overview of theories regarding the relationship between time, modernity, and industrial labor.

[46] Galison, *Einstein's Clocks*, 91.

[47] Galison, *Einstein's Clocks*, 125.

[48] Galison, *Einstein's Clocks*, 129.

[49] Giordano Nanni, 2012, *The Colonisation of Time: Ritual, Routine and Resistance in the British Empire*, Manchester: Manchester University Press, 26.

144 Postcolonial Opera

important impetus for the establishment of universal times and timetables. They also served to connect formerly distant geographies, sending people and products to new places.

But time standardization was not only about facilitating trade and communication. The colonial circulation of chrononormativity, or what Cooppan calls "Eurochronology," also formed part of evangelical and civilizing missions that accompanied the colonial project. In his wide-ranging account of Western time standardization in colonial spheres, Giordano Nanni shows the important role colonial missionaries and cultural workers played in bringing European clock time to colonized peoples. Nanni describes this process as "a series of world-wide, localised assaults on alternative cultures of time, whose perceived 'irregularity' threatened the colonisers' dominant notions of order with conflicting attitudes towards life, time, work, order and productivity."[50] Like Berger, who distinguishes between traditional and modern conceptions of temporality, Nanni observes differences between Western and Indigenous time. He ascribes the discrepancy between the two temporal orders to the role of nature in directing temporal awareness. In the eyes of colonizers, Indigenous people replicated the temporal patterns of pre-modern, agricultural communities in Europe. They directed their diurnal rhythms according to seasons, weather patterns, and a host of apparently irrational conventions including rituals, superstitions, myths, and magic.[51] Lacking what colonial agents regarded as the rationality, discipline, and regularity of clock time, Indigenous people appeared to live at the behest of nature and instinct.

In Nanni's description, "the notion of the 'savage' was constructed partly upon the belief that to be 'human' entailed separating man's [*sic*] rituals and routines from the rhythms and cycles of nature."[52] Industrialization had largely achieved this for Western societies. In colonial spheres, however, Indigenous communities had not yet severed time from nature. They hence remained in a pre-human state. It became the task of colonial agents to habilitate Indigenous people into Western time, not only to secure "regular and disciplined labourers for farms, mines and plantations," Nanni argues, but also to civilize subjects, and to usher them into the spiritual order of Christianity.[53] "It was partly by interrupting the cycles of Indigenous and local seasons and calendars, and replacing them with the colonisers' rituals and routines, along with a new calendar for counting the days, months and years, that heathens

---

[50] Nanni, *Colonisation of Time*, 3.

[51] See also Saurabh Dube, 2017, *Subjects of Modernity: Time-Space, Disciplines, Margins*, Manchester: Manchester University Press, in this regard.

[52] Nanni, *Colonisation of Time*, 9.

[53] Nanni, *Colonisation of Time*, 3.

were visibly Christianised, and that idle hands were put to productive work," Nanni writes.[54] Moral and material progress, in other words, were conditioned by adherence to Western temporal conventions.

The imposition of Eurochronology on colonial subjects proceeded along various methods, including supervised work sessions, colonial rituals of labor, rest, and worship, and the imposition of an annual rather than a seasonal calendar. Sound played a vital role in facilitating these everyday practices of timekeeping. In places that often lacked even the most basic infrastructure, the bell was an ever-present marker of time and a crucial tool for control over the actions of colonizer and colonized alike. Bells functioned as "amplifiers" of Western time.[55] In what Nanni describes as "a geographic act of temporal extension," bell sounds reverberated from the Western monasteries, factories, and schools where they marked time, to the far-flung corners of Empire, gathering colonial subjects into a universal temporal order produced by sound.[56] Time hence emerges as a sonic technology above all else. Just as the pneumatic clocks of Europe directed the timetables of city dwellers in Paris, Vienna, and Berlin, so the bell controlled the movements and rituals of those in the colonies.

But sound also played a temporal disciplining role in another way, namely, through the practice of singing. Communal song formed an important part of the daily rhythms of colonial missionary and educational settings. Singing hymns together not only signified colonized people's adherence to conventions of colonial worship, but also participated in the disciplining and ordering of colonized bodies and voices. Singing together and in time required its own temporal discipline, dictated by musical logics that served as metaphorical extensions for notions of self-restraint, orderliness, and obedience.[57] Furthermore, the activity inscribed colonized worshipers into a global Christian order, thereby constructing "a living link between the temporal culture of the medieval monasteries of western Christendom and the colonial outposts of Empire."[58] The politics of temporal control and bodily discipline were hence musically enacted, specifically through the discipline of song.

In the former colony, then, singing cannot be separated from the colonial imposition of Western clock time. But if music served to enter colonial

---

[54] Nanni, *Colonisation of Time*, 3.

[55] Nanni, *Colonisation of Time*, 16

[56] Nanni, *Colonisation of Time*, 16. For the role of bells in Europe, see Alain Corbin, 1999 [1998], *Village Bells: Sound and Meaning in the 19th-Century French Countryside*, trans. Martin Thom, London: Papermac.

[57] Grant Olwage's work is instructive in this regard. Olwage refers to the temporal discipline imposed by colonial choral singing's practices of rhythmic homogeneity and breath management as "hymn-time" (Olwage, 2004, "Discipline and Choralism: The Birth of Musical Colonialism," in *Music, Power, and Politics*, ed. Annie J. Randall, London: Routledge, 25–46, at 35).

[58] Nanni, *Colonisation of Time*, 39.

146 Postcolonial Opera

subjects into Western time, it also kept them out of time. Concurrently with time standardization's expansion throughout the colonies, the primitive, superstitious, and irrational natives Nanni identifies in colonial discourse populated Western stages in Verdi's, Meyerbeer's, Mozart's, and others' works. Opera portrayed the non-Western Other as primitive and out of time. In this regard, it was guided by stereotypical portrayals of Indigenous people authored by explorers, colonizers, missionaries, and other prejudiced observers. Denying the contemporaneity of the non-Western Other, opera fixed Indigenous people in a perpetual past. This musical practice hence refused colonized people the Eurochronology enforced upon them by other sonic means. In the process, opera became an agent of what Johannes Fabian calls "the denial of co-evalness."[59] Fabian directs his comments specifically to the discipline of anthropology, which, he argues, tends to approach its research subjects not as contemporaries, but as if they inhabit a different time, located somewhere in the past. Opera, with its public representation of exotic figures, arguably performed on stage what anthropologists did in their writings: it created a colonized subject incapable of joining the present.

Coloniality hence operated a dual temporal politics in the colony. First, temporal standardization enabled colonial powers to take possession of colonial territories and their people. Second, colonized people were arrested in a perpetual and inescapable past, which alienated them from the affordances of co-eval humanity. Both in the colonies and in the imperial metropole, competing forces of synchronization and arrest trapped colonized people in a temporal double bind. Sound cultures played a crucial role in constructing and maintaining this deadlock, forcing colonized subjects to yield to Eurochronology, and at the same time shutting them out of European time.

Post- and Anti-Colonial Time

Given the sinister history of temporal standardization in the colony, resistance to Western chrononormativity presents a logical form of anticolonial thought and action. As *Refuse the Hour* suggests, a refusal of the Western clock is also a symbolic refusal of Western colonialism. But as several postcolonial scholars have noted, it is no longer possible to enact an anti- or decolonial shift to precolonial time. "There is no way to turn back time," Cooppan writes, and by extension, no way to recoup a temporal order unmarked by modernity.[60]

---

[59] Fabian, *Time and the Other*, 32.
[60] Cooppan, "Time Maps," 397.

Indeed, any attempt to equate anticolonialism with a return to "traditional time" risks another version of Fabian's denial of co-evalness. It reveals a tacit assumption that formerly colonized people need to regain a lost essence that remains calcified in a perpetual past, and that postcolonial recovery means stepping out of the present and returning to a time before modernity.

The postcolonial subject's temporal positionality—what Achille Mbembe calls her "historicity"—is more complex than a simple "before" of tradition, and "after" of modernity.[61] Rather than the neat binary of a lost past and an unbearable present, the postcolonial subject's experience of time is layered, multidimensional, and often contradictory. It navigates between the forward thrust of global capitalism and the lingering traumas and lost selves created by coloniality. Mbembe describes "the peculiar 'historicity' of African societies" as one rooted in "a multiplicity of times, trajectories and rationalities that, although particular and sometimes local, cannot be conceptualized outside a world that is, so to speak, globalized."[62] He calls this postcolonial time "entanglement." Entanglement, for Mbembe, "encloses multiple *durées* made up of discontinuities, reversals, inertias, and swings that overlay one another, interpenetrate one another, and envelope [*sic*] one another."[63] It is a heterogeneous time that cannot be reduced to a single experience of history or to a teleological account of the events of the past. Invoking Henri Bergson with his reference to multiple *durées*, Mbembe emphasizes that postcolonial time is shaped by relationality, not only between people but also between different modes of inhabitation and narration.[64]

Mark Rifkin, writing from an Indigenous American perspective, refers to the same phenomenon as temporal multiplicity.[65] Rifkin concurs with Mbembe that postcolonial historicity necessarily encompasses the time and effects of modernity. He observes that "viewing Natives as being *historical*, in the sense of acknowledging Native existence in and change over time, includes addressing the effects of settler colonialism on Native lifeways, choices, and modes of collective self-expression and organization."[66] Rather than distinguishing between a "before" and an "after" of colonization, Mbembe and Rifkin both propose a conception of postcolonial time as "a combination of several temporalities."[67] Mbembe clarifies as follows: "this time of African

---

[61] Achille Mbembe, 2001, *On the Postcolony*, trans. Laurent Dubois, Los Angeles: University of California Press.

[62] Mbembe, *On the Postcolony*, 9.

[63] Mbembe, *On the Postcolony*, 14.

[64] Henri Bergson, 2003 [1889], *Time and Free Will: An Essay on the Immediate Data of Consciousness*, trans. F. L. Pogson, London: Routledge.

[65] Rifkin, *Beyond Settler Time*, 33.

[66] Rifkin, *Beyond Settler Time*, 6–7.

[67] Mbembe, *On the Postcolony*, 15.

148 Postcolonial Opera

existence is neither a linear time nor a simple sequence in which each moment effaces, annuls, and replaces those that preceded it, to the point where a single age exists within society. This time is not a series but an *interlocking* of presents, pasts, and futures that retain their depths of other presents, pasts, and futures, each age bearing, altering, and maintaining the previous ones."[68] Crucially, Mbembe acknowledges that the time of the postcolony is neither simple teleology nor stable cyclicity. Rather, it is erratic, unforeseen, "all sharp breaks, sudden and abrupt outbursts of volatility."[69] Postcolonial time resists linearity and problematizes the distinction between past, present, and future.

Faced with the impossibility—and undesirability—of a return to precolonial time, postcolonial resistance to Eurochronology hence entails an acknowledgment of the meeting between extra-colonial and modern time, and an engagement with the interlacing persistence of these temporal practices. It is not a reconstruction of primitivist stereotypes of cyclicity, spirituality, and eternity but a negotiation of contradiction, instability, and inconsistency. In practice, accounting for the temporal multiplicity of Indigenous temporalities means taking seriously different modes of temporal narration and experience, including alternative periodicities, intergenerational memory, repetition, simultaneity, and the various forms of lateness pejoratively described as "African time" or "whitefella time."[70] In Rifkin's words, such "patterns of behavior, forms of perception, periodizations, continuities, memories, stories, prophecies" may offer new spheres in which to recognize "political manifestations of peoplehood" in opposition to the dehumanizing politics of coloniality.[71]

The key descriptor in Mbembe's and Rifkin's conception of postcolonial time is, arguably, *complexity*. Complexity acknowledges chaos as one possible result of temporal nonlinearity but also identifies other dynamic systems that may derive from such irregularity.[72] Rather than settling for an account of postcolonial time as unpredictable and confused, in other words, complexity challenges the theorist to find system, structure, and even a new kind of logic in the multiplicities and irregularities of postcolonial time. In *Refuse the Hour*, such alternative order may be detected in Kentridge's depictions of non-linearity and reversal: toward the end of Part 3, the artist describes how he reverses a film of his son throwing paint and pencils around the studio. Starting from chaos, the film ends in pristine order. The child is delighted;

---

[68] Mbembe, *On the Postcolony*, 16, original emphasis.

[69] Mbembe, *On the Postcolony*, 16.

[70] See Nanni, *Colonisation of Time*, especially 227–228, for an incisive account of the development of the stereotypes of "African time" and "whitefella time."

[71] Rifkin, *Beyond Settler Time*, 185.

[72] Rifkin, *Beyond Settler Time*, 17.

he asks to do it again. Here, reversal and the breakdown of linearity produce order rather than disrupting it. Like Mbembe's identification of alternative logics in the complex temporality of the postcolony, Kentridge finds reason in reversal.

Operatic Time

If in Kentridge's description, film offers the most immediate medium for temporal disruption and reordering, *Refuse the Hour* demonstrates that opera too may open productive avenues for processing the temporal multiplicity of the postcolony. The essential relationship between music and time is constituted by complementary truths, namely, that music marks time, and that time is a vital element when realizing a piece of music as sound. In Berger's account of temporal change in Western society between the seventeenth and nineteenth centuries, music emerges strongly as a sonic representative of the socio-cultural shift from the eternity and cyclicity of "God's time" to the progressive continuity of secular universal history.[73] Different compositional structures, Berger observes, offer different temporal orientations. The periodicity of ritornello form, for instance, constructs a sonic equivalent of temporal cyclicity (the "natural" time of pre-modernity), while the teleology of sonata form acts as a counterpart for the goal-directed movement of modern progress. In both, time flows forward in an ordered sequence, allowing events to follow one another in apparently logical and uninterrupted succession.

Opera, however, does not adhere strictly to linear temporality. Traditionally, Berger notes, the genre negotiates between moments of narrative movement and stasis, distributed between recitative and aria.[74] Recitative serves to push the story forward, offering space for important events and actions. Arias, on the other hand, represent moments out of time, where the narrative thrust is arrested to enable characters to react and reflect on the action in song.[75] Generally, arias are not places where things happen. Rather, they represent moments when people think about things that have happened or are happening. Berger argues that the musical construction of arias often supports such temporal suspension: the most common aria structures, such as strophic, binary, ternary, and da capo form, are more episodic than organic. They hence resemble more closely the cyclicity of pre-modern time,

---

[73] Berger, *Bach's Cycle.*
[74] Berger, *Bach's Cycle*, 200.
[75] Berger, *Bach's Cycle*, 200, see also 99 and 106.

150 Postcolonial Opera

"[suggesting] timelessness by bending the linear flow of time from past to future into a circular shape." These sung interventions thus appear to arrest or neutralize forward-moving time.[76]

To be sure, the narrative arc of traditional opera still suggests teleology. The genre's conventional structure, comprising a beginning, at least one climax, and a denouement, serves to steer dramatic tension and character development toward a particular point. But within this overarching adherence to temporal linearity, which in Berger's description signals a victory of time over timelessness, arias perform small interruptions that unsettle the apparent naturalness of such headlong movement.[77] In short, opera's continuous alternation between recitative-led narrative thrust and aria-based stasis disrupts the seamless flow of temporal continuity, creating instead a more ambivalent or multifarious way of being in time.

Of course, not all operas adhere to this generic temporal model. Richard Wagner's through-composed works arguably evade the temporal arrest of the aria model by blurring the distinction between recitative and aria. In its place, the composer creates an alternative temporal experiment shaped around large-scale structures, resurgent histories sounded as leitmotiv and echo, and a narrative arc that culminates in annihilation rather than apotheosis. Time in Wagner's operas is, according to Theodor Adorno, spatialized.[78] The same is true for the operas of Alban Berg. In these works, too, Adorno argues, large-scale structures and leitmotivs disrupt narrative linearity. Palindromes, reversals, negotiation between the micro-structures of tone rows and the macro-structures of compositional forms, all culminate in works that upset opera's temporal conventions.[79] Crucially, though, they also disrupt the conventional chronology and flow of Western clock-time. My discussion of traditional operatic temporality writ large does not account for these works (and others) that move away from operatic convention. Nonetheless, their temporal structures serve to reinforce, rather than undermine the argument that opera disrupts chrononormativity. What interests me here is what happens when such temporal disruption is read from and within a postcolonial perspective.

The negotiation between teleology and arrest represented by opera's musical-narrative balancing act offers a starting point from which to think

---

[76] Berger, *Bach's Cycle*, 106.

[77] Berger, *Bach's Cycle*, 106.

[78] Theodor Adorno, 2006 [1949], *Philosophy of New Music*, trans. Robert Hullot Kentor, Minneapolis: University of Minnesota Press. Adorno derives this description from *Parsifal*, of course, where Gurnemanz describes Monsalvat as the sphere where time turns to space. I return to Wagner and his spatial-temporal dynamics in Chapter 6, to discuss their reverberation in Kentridge's opera, *The Head & the Load*.

[79] In this regard, see Stephen Decatur Smith, 2013, "'Even Money Decays': Transience and Hope in Adorno, Benjamin, and *Wozzeck*," *Opera Quarterly* 29(3), 212–243.

through the postcolonial potentialities of operatic temporality. Put differently, the fact that opera complicates Eurochronology potentially makes it an ideal art from through which to resist Western clock time and experiment with postcolonial forms of being-in-time. This places opera in an equivocal position: on the one hand, the genre is, as discussed earlier, implicated in the more sinister temporal politics of civility and othering deployed as part of the colonial project. On the other, it offers an opportunity to act against the time of coloniality.

By now, this ambiguity should be familiar: it is the same ambiguity I describe in chapter 2 of this book, where opera sounds out the postcolonizing subject's confession, only to reveal its impotence; or the ambiguity of operatic mourning in chapter 3, where the art form both amplifies and disrupts the colonial politics of sonic (dis)possession and representation. It is an ambiguity that returns also in the next chapters, in discussions of opera's relationship to place and mobility (chapter 5) and its enactment of forms of fragmentation and totality (chapter 6). In short, it is an ambiguity that is characteristic of opera's position in the postcolony, where the art form serves simultaneously to reinscribe and to disrupt the enduring relationship between the former colony and the former metropole.

Postcoloniality and Operatic Time in *Refuse the Hour*

In *Refuse the Hour*, the postcolonial ambiguity of operatic time emerges from the complex interplay between creatively deployed musical and visual intertexts, overt political statements, and an idiosyncratic approach to narrative. The opera's combination of image, text, and sound figures time in several different ways. Time is breath, echoing the pneumatic clocks of the late 1800s and galvanizing the primarily wind-based score. Time is also the position of the sun, prompting the anticolonial entreaty to "give us back our sun." Time is decay and permanence, movement and stasis, process and reversal, fate and chance.

None of the work's temporal imaginaries adheres strictly to historical continuity or teleology, though they all incorporate principles of chronology in unique ways. The very fact that the opera's narration is based around a lecture, rather than a story, automatically disrupts the narrative convention of the genre. In the Western operatic repertoire, perhaps the closest equivalent of a lecture-opera is Philip Glass's *Einstein on the Beach* (1975), which like *Refuse the Hour* trades chronology for episodic non-linearity. Unlike *Einstein*

152 Postcolonial Opera

on the Beach, however, *Refuse the Hour* is anchored to a text which, however rambling and disjointed, lends a degree of coherence to the work. The lecture meanders, working with free association and resisting conclusive statements. It challenges the point-driven approach normally associated with a lecture. Whereas the inclusion of a lecture might hence invite a reading of the opera as didactic art, Kentridge subverts any compulsion toward instruction.

Silvana Carotenuto describes Kentridge's lecture as "a montage of autobiography, wordplay, and literary quotations."[80] Indeed, the text seems to dart randomly between scenes from the artist's past and a selection of made-up or quoted aphorisms. When exposed to musical and choreographic treatment, these catchphrases take on lives of their own, acquiring new meanings of becoming altogether meaningless. For instance, the maxim, "Truth is Beauty, Beauty Truth," adapted from John Keats's "Ode on a Grecian Urn," becomes a repetitive rhythmic refrain chanted over a marching beat, as the performers follow each other around the stage in an absurd conga line. Keats's poem, where the quoted lines appear as "Beauty is truth / truth beauty," is a meditation on arrested time. It describes figures on a Grecian urn who, frozen in their pursuits, are forever suspended between life and death.[81] If Keats uses his poem to evoke timelessness and inertia, Kentridge and Miller's treatment of the citation infuses it with a dynamism that resembles something between a protest march and a party game. Thus, the sonic treatment of the line subverts the meaning of the original text. Stasis becomes movement, movement stasis.

Disjunctions between music and text abound throughout *Refuse the Hour*. In the jaunty dance number, "Slow quick quick slow," a trio of singers repeat the words of the title to a recurring foxtrot box rhythm (slow-quick-quick), with the second pair of "quicks" remaining silent (see ▶ Clip 4.2). They sing over a syncopated band accompaniment marked "light and playful," and articulate every "quick" with a staccato, while the "slows" are sung portato. Dada Masilo, against a background projection of an animated dancer assembled from newspaper shreds, performs rapid, flailing choreography over the music.

Midway through the song, the singers switch the text around. Now, the box rhythm is accompanied by the words, "quick slow slow quick," causing the words and the rhythm to contradict each other. However, the text's articulation remains the same, creating a pattern of staccato-portato-portato-staccato. The interplay between the pattern's articulation and duration creates the uncanny impression that the singers are performing a short-long-long-short rhythm

---

[80] Silvana Carotenuto, 2018, "Writing 'Time': The (Late) *Oeuvres* of Jacques Derrida and William Kentridge," *English Academy Review* 35(1), 73–95, at 80.

[81] John Keats, 1982 [1819], "Ode on a Grecian Urn," in *Complete Poems*, ed. Jack Stillinger, Cambridge, MA: Harvard University Press, 282–283.

(echoing the words) rather than the actual foxtrot box (slow-quick-quick). In this moment, the interplay between words and music constructs a multivalent and contradictory temporal experience. Pitch, duration, articulation, and language interact to expose the contingency of the listener's perception of time. Sound, here in contradistinction to its colonial function, can undermine chronos. It can stretch time or condense it, reverse it, or make it rush forward.

Music also enacts time at a larger scale. Periodicity and genre inscribe sound with history. A piece created in the twenty-first century, for instance, may invoke the nineteenth century by revisiting the compositional conventions of Romanticism. This temporal transposition (which is of course also achievable by other means, including clothing, language, or imagery) lies at the heart of movements such as Neoclassicism and Neoromanticism. In *Refuse the Hour*, Miller and Kentridge play with sound's historical affordance through the recurring intertextual incorporation of Berlioz's "Le spectre de la rose." The song, here rendered in D major, is first introduced in a number titled "Berlioz breakdown," which opens with Berlioz's haunting melody performed on a Stroh violin (see ⏵ Clip 4.3).

The Stroh violin is a string instrument invented by John Matthias Augustus Stroh in 1899, with a large metal amplifier, not unlike the horn of a phonograph, attached to the fingerboard. Held and bowed like a normal violin, the instrument generates a more resonant but also slightly more metallic sound than its unamplified counterpart. The Stroh violin's piping tone has something of an inhuman quality, which is enhanced in *Refuse the Hour* by means of digitally added reverberation. Performed on this curious instrument, Berlioz's tune strikes the ear as a forlorn melody from outer space—an impression supported by the black background projection, upon which white paint marks appear like flickering stars. During the Stroh violin's brief solo, then, the audience encounters a visual reference recognizably evocative of the sound technologies of the late nineteenth century, while sonically, they are confronted with a futuristic sound palette. These contradictory sensory inputs seem to pit nostalgia against expectation, the vivid imagery of bygone mechanics brushing up against the possibilities afforded by technological development.

When the soprano enters, carried by Berlioz's distinctive rolling piano accompaniment, the confrontation between past and future intensifies. At first, the song proceeds as expected. But soon, strange noises begin to infiltrate the warm vocal lines. While the soprano holds the sustained C# on the final syllable of the line, "des pleurs d'argent," a bizarre trilling tone emerges on the same pitch. It gets louder, before breaking into a pair of hollow wails. Onomatopoeically scripted, the sounds approach something along the lines of

154 Postcolonial Opera

"trrrrrrr – au-wau." They have a mechanical quality, situated somewhere between human vocality and extra-terrestrial automation. As the song proceeds, these interjections become more frequent. Sometimes they interrupt the soprano line, at other times they repeat the soloist's pitches in mocking tones. The mechanistic sounds are created by voice artist and frequent Kentridge collaborator Joanna Dudley. Their alien character, enhanced by digital manipulation, summon the sounds of futurism. They are the hums, echoes, and clangs of developmental zeal, of the exhilaration of technological progress first activated by the Stroh violin.

Berlioz's song is a rumination on death and its numerous afterlives. The specter of the rose, appearing at the bedside of the one who picked it, promises a haunting that is both exquisite and terrible. It will dance forever before its executioner, not as an indictment, but as a celebration of the beauty of its death. Dudley's futuristic tones, however, undercut the romantic melancholy of Berlioz's composition, allowing the song's profoundly human reflection on mortality to be usurped by the impersonal agency of the machine. Notwithstanding their inhuman character, however, these sounds are not mechanical products. Rather, they are the embodied outcome of human effort. Apart from enacting a collision between romantic nostalgia and futuristic invention, Dudley's otherworldly sounds thus expose the "dark underside" of the machine—the fact that even advanced technologies rely on human labor.[82] Futurism, "Berlioz breakdown" seems to suggest, is dependent on fallible humans, even as it seeks to exceed or circumvent mortality.

"Le spectre de la rose" returns toward the end of *Refuse the Hour*, this time devoid of the soprano solo. Now, only Dudley's broken-down version rings out over the piano accompaniment. Background projections suggest that this time the song functions as a recapitulation: behind Dudley, references appear to previous scenes from the opera. A self-portrait of the artist runs in place; Dada pirouettes, first in one direction, then in the other (as if she, too, seeks to reverse her actions); words materialize, referring to the artist's eccentric ruminations ("the wrong chair"; "particular collisions"). Stripped of Romantic idealism, the song retraces what came before, enacting an ambivalent play between "redoing" and "undoing," "resaying" and "unsaying," "reremembering" and "unremembering."

Devoid of meaningful text, the mechanistic reprise of "Le spectre de la rose" represents either destruction or fulfillment. It may be interpreted as either the complete disintegration of Berlioz's composition, or it may represent the technological apotheosis of a future in which the human is rendered

---

[82] I return to this point in Chapter 6.

obsolete. In Kentridge and Miller's hands, "Le spectre de la rose" hence enacts two ways of approaching the same moment. Nostalgia and progress accumulate around a single musical instant, as sonic reversals and anticipations intermingle. The interface between different sounds and media offers a chance to look at and listen to the same moment from different angles, or for multiple events to take place at once. Thus, temporal alterity becomes a product of operatic intermediality. From a postcolonial perspective, the number may be understood to enact a subversion of a particular instant in European history: as the Romanticism of the nineteenth century develops into imperial self-assurance and industrial fervor, chaos, human breakdown, and eventually, self-destruction loom.

The compositional devices Miller employs in the examples discussed here are neither new nor unusual. They are, as the composer acknowledges, "the staple tools of any composer: slowing something down, speeding it up, repetition, augmentation, breaking it up."[83] What Kentridge and Miller achieve is not, in other words, an altogether new way of making opera or of making time. Rather, they use opera's existing capacities to think differently about time in the postcolony. This approach resembles the tactics used by colonized persons to resist the imposition of Eurochronology. Nanni observes that "colonial timetables, rituals, clocks and bells always remained prone to their observers' tardiness, sluggishness, dissent, defiance, resistance and procrastinations."[84] Being late, being slow, putting off unwelcome tasks: these are not modes of temporal resistance unique to colonized people. But in the particular circumstances created by colonial exploitation, extraction, and Western cultural-spiritual encroachment, these ordinary modes of temporal misalignment transform from ostensible indolence to defiant self-assertion.

Apart from subtler forms of rejection, the anti-colonial repertoire of temporal refusals also included explicit expressions of resistance. Nanni observes that "the history of colonialism is littered with damaged bells, broken curfews and desecrated Sabbaths—suggestive of the fact that time was a cultural arena in which the colonial struggle was consciously fought out."[85] *Refuse the Hour* displays such overt resistance in two pieces, both of which may be described as protest songs. The first, a soprano aria titled "Colonial Invasions," comprises a vocal call-and-response over a rapid, aggressive accompaniment (see ⏵ Clip 4.4). Singing in an alto register, the soprano rehearses a series of incantations, some of which are based on traditional African proverbs. She starts with a

---

[83] Miller, in Kentridge and Miller, "Gathering Sounds," 209.
[84] Nanni, *Colonisation of Time*, 4.
[85] Nanni, *Colonisation of Time*, 20.

Ghanaian maxim: "The head and the load are the troubles of the neck."[86] The chorus responds in isiXhosa with a reference to Eurochronology's disruption of circadian time: "Buyisilanga lethu! ("It is our sun!"). Next, the soloist intones, "My witness is in Europe, says the liar," followed by the same chorus response. Then, an apparently unrelated statement from the soprano: "Being thin is not dying," again followed by the chorus laying claim to the sun. After the soloist's next phrase, a Setswana proverb suggesting, "If the good doctor can't cure you, find the less good doctor," the chorus adopts a new isiXhosa rallying cry: "Phum'ezwe nila lami" ("Get out of my country!"). The dialogue between soloist and chorus continues with further such statements, until the group finally alights on its specific demand: "Give us back our sun!" Above this repeated exclamation, the soprano soloist names possessions she has lost: her cow with a wet nose, her goat in a circle of grass, her sun. "Let the rich man, the banker, the shopkeeper go die," she sings in a damning downward scale, before joining the chorus for a final, percussive refrain: "Give us back our sun!."

"Colonial invasions" examines the inventory of losses visited upon Indigenous people by the process of colonization. Apart from material dispossession, the aria suggests, colonized people also suffered disease (referenced by the metaphor of the doctor), starvation ("being thin is not dying"), and the imposition of a socio-economic order that created and nurtured inequality (represented by the rich man, the banker, and the shopkeeper).

The music enacts the apparent incongruity between Indigenous and colonial ways of being by means of a now-familiar temporal inconsistency: while the accompaniment and the chorus parts are rapid (with a metronome marking of 127 to a quarter note), and punctuated by accented crash chords and aggressive trumpet exclamations, the soprano soloist sings in a slow, portentous style. There seems to be little relation between the soloist's music and the surrounding figurations; sonically, the musicians seem to occupy different spheres. At a superficial level, the slowness of the soprano's song may be interpreted as a depiction of a precolonial time as yet unmarked by the industrial accelerationism represented by the accompaniment. But this is too easy an interpretive binary. Rather, the aria's competing temporal frames seem to suggest something of the struggle to reconcile the competing demands of cultural and physical survival in the colonial present. Unable to escape the decimating demands and temporal drive of imperial invasion, the colonized subject compromises. She finds the less good doctor, mourns her

---

[86] This proverb is a favorite Kentridge phrase and the title of his 2018 First World War commemoration opera. I discuss it at some length in Chapter 6.

lost possessions, and curses the agents of inequality with impotent damnation. Ultimately, however, she yields to the colonial clock, ends the song at the double bar, and remains silent as the trumpet and trombone launch a final, triumphant rising flourish.

There is an underlying irony to using a protest song to resist Western temporality. The protest song is designed with a purely teleological intent. It pursues a goal, and that goal is liberation. If successful, its outcome is both the arrival and the return of a state of freedom. The teleology of this protest, in other words, is itself circular: its end point is recovery rather than discovery. As a musical genre and an operatic device, protest song can thus enact formally the entanglement of past, present, and future, of desire and actuality, and of history and memory.

Entanglement

In *Refuse the Hour*, sound, image, and movement interact to produce an intricate temporal play marked by contradiction, discontinuity, reversal, and multiplicity. The work generates a complex simultaneity of tangled futures and pasts. Sometimes, the opera creates the impression of several different moments happening at once. At other times, it performs multiple ways of occupying the same instant. Together, these devices raise the question not of where we are, but of "when" we are. The answer, if it does appear, is ambiguous. In the postcolonial moment, "now" is both before and after, present infused with past, future with present. The work's returns and repetitions, accelerations and delays, resist the simple teleology of Eurochronology. Indeed, as Cooppan writes, *Refuse the Hour* stages "the condition of a continuity that need not be mapped as line, indeed, which exceeds linearity through a dazzling concert of repetition, replay, and reversal, all subtended by an eschatology not of progress, but of change—the postcolony's promise of a future still to come."[87]

The postcolonial future of which Cooppan writes may be one in which temporal heterogeneity is allowed to co-exist with post-industrial teleology—without the resulting collisions immediately being reduced to chaos or incoherence. Returning to Mbembe's description of entanglement, it is a future that embraces both the Indigenous and the modern, allowing for inconsistency, rupture, inertia, and overlap. It recognizes the haunted time of ghosts and roses, the spectral afterlives of memories, the accelerations of hope and prediction, and the simultaneity of now, never, and forever. Change, in this

[87] Cooppan, "Time Maps," 403.

158 Postcolonial Opera

conception, is not necessarily movement but (r)evolution; a process of expansion and contraction, rather than backward or forward motion. Thus, the postcolonial future becomes one of multiple durations marked by clock time but not produced by it, just as operatic time may be guided by a metronome but is not generated by its beats. Relativity emerges as multiplicity: not multiple ways of measuring a single time, but multiple times saturating a single moment.

Exploiting opera's capacity to play with time offers an opportunity for postcolonial resistance to colonial chrononormativity. Rather than just being part of Western imperial temporality—feeding it with disciplined singing and images of primitive natives—opera may offer a reparative or even resistant engagement with the complex temporalities of postcoloniality. Inscribed with the rituals of Europe, but open to the heterochronologies of the postcolony, opera can navigate the complex interplay of temporal existence demanded of the postcolonial subject. Like time, the art form is itself poised "between empowerment and acculturation, resistance and negotiation."[88] The complex and occasionally contradictory interplay of sound, sight, and motion enabled by operatic intermediality becomes a proving ground for multiple temporalities. Thus, the art form offers a way for colonial and postcolonial subjects to participate in the Western order of modernity while retaining space for cultural and temporal identities that precede, exceed, and outlive the narrow frame of colonial civility.

---

[88] Nanni, *Colonisation of Time*, 212.

5
Place

This is the age of mobility. Poverty, climate crisis, violence, and conflict have conspired to produce what UN Secretary General António Guterres has described as "the highest levels of forced displacement in recorded history."[1] Alongside these tragic regimes of destitution, a growing proportion of the global middle class has embraced habits of travel and movement both produced by and productive of an increasingly interconnected world. Together, forcibly and voluntarily itinerant people embody what Mimi Sheller and John Urry call "the new mobilities paradigm"—a regime of existence conditioned not by placement and permanence, but by transience, rootlessness, and motion.[2]

In the context of this global proliferation of mobility, certain forms of permanence begin to appear suspicious. Establishments and traditions with claims to physical intransience and formal endurance appear at odds with the irresistible flow of bodies, ideas, and objects that characterizes the late capitalist global order of mobility. The tradition of Western opera, with its institutional consolidation and its historical presence in opera houses and other large-scale venues, participates in an imaginary of cultural and physical permanence. Tethered to the revivalist impulses of the Florentine Camerata, as I discuss in Chapters 1 and 3, the art form's heritage is founded on an aspiration toward perpetuity and monumentality. Even as people and practices shift, opera stays.

This is the case in both the formal construction of the genre and in its geographical and institutional consolidation. Rebekah Ahrendt observes that opera has, since the turn of the eighteenth century, been associated with "a tradition of enduring urban opera houses" with increasingly stable companies.[3] Housed in tailor-made structures (both physical and musical)

---

[1] António Guterres, 2015, "Opening Remarks at the 66th Session of the Executive Committee of the High Commissioner's Programme," Geneva, October 5, https://www.unhcr.org/news/news-releases/opening-remarks-66th-session-executive-committee-high-commissioners-programme, accessed May 20, 2021. Guterres made this comment when he was UN High Commissioner for Refugees.

[2] Mimi Sheller and John Urry, 2006, "The New Mobilities Paradigm," *Environment and Planning A* 38, 207–226.

[3] Rebekah Ahrendt, 2019, "The Legal Spaces of Opera in the Hague," in *Operatic Geographies: The Place of Opera and the Opera House*, ed. Suzanne Aspden, Chicago, IL: University of Chicago Press, 12–25, at 13.

Postcolonial Opera. Juliana M. Pistorius, Oxford University Press. © Oxford University Press 2025.
DOI: 10.1093/oso/9780197749203.003.0006

160 Postcolonial Opera

optimistically fashioned to withstand the tests of time, the art form lays claim to intransience. Opera has been built to last.

But in a postcolonial sphere marked by continuing legacies of uncertainty and displacement—whether due to war, poverty, or climate crisis—the idea of operatic permanence seems both alien and unjustifiable. Indeed, the art form's often self-assured, if not self-congratulatory, physical and ideological presence sometimes bears something akin to colonial regimes of settlement. With claims to continuity, solidity, and tradition, opera seems to assume an immutable entitlement to space, place, time, significance, and relevance within the global cultural arena. If this posture is consistent with the durational politics that underscores operatic survival, it also estranges the art form from the stories of those forced into movement in order to survive. One form of survival, in other words, excludes the other.

This chapter asks whether a postcolonial operatic form may be able to capture something of the provisional and mobile nature of postcoloniality. Pushing back against the genre's more prevalent ideals of physical and formal constancy, it asks if opera could be reimagined as an alternative site of dwelling and home-making for the displaced subject. The central case study is a 2016 performance, *Triumphs and Laments*, created by Kentridge as a site-specific installation for the nineteenth-century travertine embankment along the river Tiber in Rome. In *Triumphs and Laments* I trace an intermedial engagement with the question of mobility, both as image and as practice, as suffering and as empowerment. The performance's multifarious musical and visual references invite the spectator to reflect anew on the nature of belonging, especially as it affects migrants, refugees, and other mobile peoples.

I take as a starting point recorded documentation of *Triumphs and Laments* as well as the original unpublished score of the performance, to ask how the piece reflects opera's relationship with contemporary and postcolonial forms of mobility.[4] Through an examination of the piece's intertextual and intermedial integration, I present new arguments regarding opera's participation in various forms of dwelling and place-making, before returning to the question of whether a newly conceived operatic form may offer an opportunity for alternative forms of inhabiting and self-presencing in the postcolonial present.

---

[4] My thanks to Philip Miller for making the score available to me.

Background

Triumphs and Laments is a collaboration between Kentridge and Tevereterno, a multidisciplinary arts initiative headed by American artist Kristin Jones. Tevereterno was created to revitalize the spaces around Rome's Tiber River and to reintegrate the river with the city. The collective, whose name is a conjunction of "Tevere" (Tiber in Latin) and "eterno" (eternal), responds to the urban decay surrounding the river by creating and promoting public art installations on the Piazza Tevere and the Tiber's embankment. The embankment was built between 1880 and 1900 to protect Rome from floods such as the one that devastated the city in December 1870. It rises approximately 13 meters above the riverside footpath, thus effectively segregating the urban landscape and the river from each other.[5] According to Kay Bea Jones, the construction of the Tiber embankment changed the relationship between Romans and the river, detaching them from one another and effectively turning the Tiber into a peripheral and abandoned part of the city.[6]

Tevereterno's aim is to regenerate the banks of the Tiber as a site of civic participation and enjoyment. It was as part of this project that Jones approached Kentridge in 2002 with an invitation to contribute to their activities.[7] The artist agreed in principle, and after an extended period of negotiations—not only between Tevereterno and Kentridge, but also between the creative parties and the Roman municipality—the project was finally completed more than a decade later.[8]

Kentridge's installation faces head-on questions of monumentality, (im)permanence, and displacement, both in form and in content. At its heart is a 550-meter-long frieze comprising fifty-one figural groupings that recall—and occasionally deconstruct—the history of the city. Applied to the stretch of river bank between Ponte Sisto and Ponte Mazzini (a site chosen for the fact that it follows an almost-straight line), the frieze evokes the ancient Roman ceremony of the *triumphus*, which celebrated the victorious return to the

---

[5] See Tom Rankin, 2019, "Culture Meets Ecology in the Public Space: *Triumphs and Laments* on the Tiber," in *Art and Economics in the City: New Cultural Maps*, ed. Caterina Benincasa, Gianfranco Neri, and Michele Trimarchi, Bielefeld: transcript Verlag, 49–67, and Pamela Allara, 2019, "William Kentridge's *Triumphs and Laments*: The Challenges and Pleasures of Collaboration," *de arte* 54(1), 60–85, for details on the 1870 flood and the effect of the construction of the Tiber embankment on the city's geography.

[6] Kay Bea Jones, 2009, "Rome's Uncertain Tiberscape: Tevereterno and the Urban Commons," *The Waters of Rome* 6, 1–12.

[7] Kentridge recounts the circumstances of the invitation and the development of the work in "Triumphs and Laments: A Talk," 2016, https://www.kentridge.studio/triumphs-laments-a-talk/, accessed October 31, 2022.

[8] Rankin, "Culture," documents in detail the various bureaucratic and administrative obstacles the project faced as well as the almost farcical ineptitude of fundraising efforts and managerial structures at various organizations involved in the project.

162 Postcolonial Opera

city of war heroes and their loot.[9] Kentridge mentions that his idea for the frieze was inspired by Trajan's Column, which was erected in 100 CE to celebrate Emperor Trajan's victory over the Dacians. On Trajan's Column, the triumphant history of the war appears engraved in a winding relief, spiraling upward along the length of the structure. Kentridge imagined unrolling this ascending scroll and being confronted with the processional frieze structure he ultimately employed for *Triumphs and Laments*.[10]

For Kentridge, however, the frieze is not only celebratory. In an interview with curator Carlos Basualdo, the artist states explicitly that his installation is intended as a reminder of the dark underside of triumph: "Overall I suppose it's not just to say history is problematic and complicated, but that inside one person's triumph is someone else's disaster."[11] In other words, the primary message of *Triumphs and Laments* refers to the multifaceted nature of history—the fact that, as the work's title suggests, each triumph is also a lament, each gain also a loss.

Concomitantly, the piece reflects on the shifting and contested nature of place. Referring explicitly to the ambiguous history of the "eternal city," *Triumphs and Laments* emphasizes the selective practices of narration and remembrance that produce place—practices always in flux, as populations and contexts shift. Indeed, the whole of *Triumphs and Laments* is about place. Not only the place of Rome but also of a series of geographical areas farther afield, which are evoked through visual and sonic intertexts. These include places as varied as the island of Lampedusa, the southern Italian regions of Campania and Salenta, the southern African areas of South Africa and Zimbabwe, and the city of Jerusalem. Each of these physical spheres participates in a complex discourse animated by questions of movement and belonging. Their presence in *Triumphs and Laments* reflects not only the integrated nature of twenty-first-century place—each place is always already connected to and routed through several others—but also shows the contested nature of notions of origin and arrival. "Coming from" and "going to" are activities destabilized by the interconnected and impermanent nature of physical presence in a globalized world. In Kentridge's frieze, this uncertainty about the nature of "here" and "there" becomes a critical lens through which to reappraise not only ideals of operatic tradition or permanence, but also paradigms of vocal presence and embodiment.

---

[9] Salvatore Settis, 2017, "Drawing, Memory, and the City: William Kentridge's Rome," in *William Kentridge: Triumphs and Laments*, ed. Carlos Basualdo, Berlin: Buchhandlung Walther Koenig, 161–207, at 162.

[10] Kentridge, "Triumphs and Laments: A Talk."

[11] Kentridge, in Carlos Basualdo and William Kentridge, 2017, "In People's Memory: Carlos Basualdo in Conversation with William Kentridge," in *William Kentridge: Triumphs and Laments*, 49–96, at 51.

Much has been written about Kentridge's Rome frieze and the source material to which it refers. Such work engages especially with the visual manifestation of Kentridge's piece, including the physical art works applied to the riverbank and the intertextual references contained in these images. But *Triumphs and Laments* also comprises a second dimension, one arguably as important, if not more so, than the drawings on the banks of the Tiber. The frieze was inaugurated on the holiday of Natale di Roma on April 21, 2016—according to legend, the date in 735 BC on which Rome was founded was April 21—with a processional performance comprising shadow projections, sculptural props, dance, song, and live instrumental music. Designed by Kentridge, with music by Philip Miller and Thuthuka Sibisi, the *Triumphs and Laments* performance offers a live and embodied reflection on the monumental, but often troubled, history imagined on the riverbank (see ⏵ Clip 5.1).

For Kentridge, it is arguably the performance, rather than the frieze images, that constitutes the core of *Triumphs and Laments*. Responding to a question about the work's circulation, he remarks, "I am not interested in redoing the frieze anywhere else. Redoing the concert and shadow procession performance is what I'm really interested in. I want to see those shadows on a variety of different walls and hear that music at that scale again."[12] For Kentridge, then, the essence of the work lies in the "concert and shadow procession performance"—the elements that transform the work from permanence to impermanence. Indeed, the very act of looking at the frieze anticipates something of the performative core of Kentridge's creation: stretching over 550 meters along the river, and scaled to fit the bank's 13-meter-high walls, the range of the frieze is such that it cannot be experienced in a single glance. Instead, it invites a measured appraisal guided by the rhythm of movement along the riverbank. Ideas (and practices) of mobility constitute the heart of *Triumphs and Laments*.

The Frieze

Pamela Allara and Michael Godby, among others, have documented in great detail the complex artistic process that underpinned the creation of Kentridge's frieze.[13] The project started with exploratory archival research conducted by two Rome-based assistants, and proceeded through an

---

[12] Basualdo, in Basualdo and Kentridge, "In People's Memory," 69.
[13] Allara, "Challenges and Pleasures"; Michael Godby, 2019, "Unwritten History: William Kentridge's *Triumphs and Laments*, Piazza Tevere, Rome, 2016," in *What Was History Painting and What Is It Now?*, ed. Mark Salber Phillips and Jordan Bear, Montreal: McGill-Queen's University Press, 215–233.

Figure 5.1 Frieze figures showing the contrast between dark organic matter and the washed embankment wall. Photograph: Sebastiano Luciano. Reproduced with permission.

elaborate process of drawing, copying, redrawing, and enlarging, involving many collaborators both in Rome and in South Africa. Fifty-one images created by Kentridge make up the final processional series. These were applied to the embankment wall using a process called "reverse graffiti," which involved the removal of accumulated dirt from the stone. Plastic stencils produced from enlargements of Kentridge's drawings were attached to the embankment, which had been darkened by over a century's worth of grime and organic matter. Municipal workers then cleared the exposed areas between the stencils with high-pressure hoses pumping water from the Tiber. Once the stencils were removed, they left behind shadowy impressions that stood out against the lightened canvas of the washed embankment (see Figure 5.1).

Each image in the series derives from an existing visual reference. Starting with an adaptation of Trajan's Winged Victory—a figure that returns at the midpoint of the frieze (Figures 26–28) in a state of collapse—the procession advances through iconic images such as the she-wolf that suckled Romulus and Remus, the bust of Cicero (also revisited in fractured form later on), King Victor Emmanuel II and Mussolini, both on horseback, the body of Italian prime minister Aldo Moro after his murder in 1978, and Pope Gregory VII, fleeing from Rome after his deposition in 1084.[14] In the second half of the frieze, iconographic references to various forms of displacement pile

---

[14] For a complete list of figures in the frieze as well as the visual sources on which they are based, see Tommaso Speretta and Lucia Franchi Viceré, 2017, "*Triumphs & Laments*: Sources for the Frieze Figures," in *William Kentridge: Triumphs and Laments*, 257–271.

up. Figures 31 ("Spoils from Jerusalem"), 33 ("Deportees"), 36 ("Finding Refuge from the Flood of the Tiber, 1937"), 37 ("Migrants and Prisoners"), 39 ("Procession of Migrants"), and 41 ("Women Weeping for a Lampedusa Shipwreck"), all depict the desperate movements of victims of persecution and dislocation (see Figure 5.2).

As a whole, the frieze affords an unusually tragic view of the history of Rome and its empire. Allara notes that "the repeated motifs of dead bodies, fractured statues, and displaced peoples systematically undercut Rome's triumphal history to expose its violent underbelly."[15] Indeed, the cynical (though often humorous) references to dark episodes in the city's past and present—all presented in Kentridge's distinct, rough-hewn visual register—create an image of history marked as much by catastrophe as by conquest. Like so many of the artist's creations, *Triumphs and Laments* is what Gabriele Guercio calls "a work of paradoxical monumentality."[16] Grandiose in scale and conception, the frieze's iconography undermines the delusions of greatness suggested by the form.

The paradoxical monumentality of Kentridge's frieze is underscored by the precarity of its medium. Reverse graffiti, as used for *Triumphs and Laments*, relies on the reversal of a natural process of biological contamination by which grime, accumulated over centuries of exposure, yields to the eradicating force of water. The stenciled figures emerge from the embankment wall through a process not of application but of removal. Inevitably, this intervention is temporary. The embankment walls, perpetually exposed to environmental forces such as pollution and organic recolonization, cannot offer an eternally clear canvas for Kentridge's figures.[17] As such, the disappearance of the art work was preordained from the start.

Kentridge himself resisted calls to expose the frieze to treatments that could delay the environmental blackening of the embankment. Instead, he chose to allow the work to dissolve naturally.[18] By September 2020, the frieze had disappeared completely.[19] As I write, nothing remains of it but a series of visual documents including book publications, sculptures, and tapestries based on the frieze drawings. In a way, then, the very medium of the work undercut its epic intent. Rather than memorializing Rome in a permanent form, the "eternal city" was reduced to ephemerality—to what Guercio describes as "an

[15] Allara, "Challenges and Pleasures," 65.
[16] Gabriele Guercio, 2017, "A Paradoxical Monumentality," in *William Kentridge: Triumphs and Laments*, 129–143, at 129.
[17] See Flavia Bartoli et al., 2021, "Biological Recolonization Dynamics: Kentridge's Artwork Disappearing along the Tiber Embankments (Rome, Italy)," *International Biodeterioration & Biodegradation* 160, 1–10, for a study of the biological recontamination of Kentridge's frieze.
[18] Bartoli et al., "Biological Recolonization," 8.
[19] Bartoli et al., "Biological Recolonization," 8.

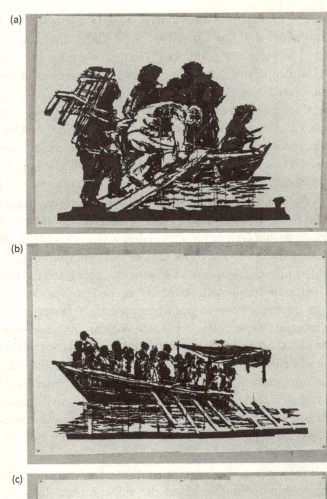

Figure 5.2 Figures 36, 37, and 39 from *Triumphs and Laments*. Courtesy of William Kentridge Studio.

art of decay and entropy."[20] The tension between the figures' scale, which for Settis signifies their triumph, and their precarious state (or, as Settis argues, their lament), thus turns the frieze's "powerful evocation of people and events into a quiet lament for its own fate."[21]

The Performance

Given that impermanence is central to both the form and the function of the frieze, it is perhaps unsurprising that Kentridge chose to celebrate the official opening of the installation with a performance—itself a manifestation of artistic transience. The *Triumphs and Laments* performance involved some of Kentridge's regular collaborators, including Philip Miller, Joanna Dudley, Ann Masina, and Bham Ntabeni, as well as a cast of 101 performers including musicians, singers, dancers, actors, and ushers. Across the 550-meter stretch of embankment, the performers—split into two groups, one called Triumphs and the other Laments—realized a dual procession. The two troupes started at opposite ends of the concourse and marched toward each other accompanied by a hybrid score of instrumental and vocal music. At the mid-point, they met. After engaging one another in an aggressive exchange of song and dance, they continued on their journeys until each arrived at the other's point of origin.

Kentridge derived the idea for the structure of *Triumphs and Laments* from Charles Ives's father George, a bandmaster in Danbury, Connecticut, whose experiments with contrapuntal musical marching likely inspired Ives junior.[22] Kentridge recycled a notorious episode from Ives senior's career as bandleader of Danbury, in which the conductor led several bands in a simultaneous performance of different pieces. As the bands marched toward each other, the cacophonic interaction of the different tunes created bewilderment and chaos.

In *Triumphs and Laments*, Kentridge adopted the idea of steering two marching groups toward each other, ultimately "[going] through each other."[23] Based on the artist's split processional model, Miller started the compositional process with two separate pieces of music to be played simultaneously, one belonging to the Triumphs band and the other to Laments.[24] However, due to the risk of producing what Kentridge preemptively called "a nasty clash," the composer ultimately opted to base the two processional groupings' music

---

[20] Guercio, "Paradoxical Monumentality," 130. See Kenneth J. Pratt, 1965, "Rome as Eternal," *Journal of the History of Ideas* 26(1), 25–44, for an exploration of the idea of Rome as eternal city.

[21] Settis, "Drawing," 175.

[22] Stuart Feder, 1999, *The Life of Charles Ives*, Cambridge: Cambridge University Press, 72.

[23] Kentridge, in Basualdo and Kentridge, "In People's Memory," 66.

[24] Miller, interview with the author, May 13, 2020.

168 Postcolonial Opera

on the same primary material, a motet by Jewish Italian composer Salamone Rossi (c. 1570–1630).[25]

Miller's description of the composition reveals much about the musical source material for the work. It also divulges the political and ethical framework within which the composer and his creative collaborator, Thuthuka Sibisi, conceived the piece. The program note, which is reproduced on Kentridge's website, offers crucial perspective on the work's structure, instrumentation, and intertextual references. It further reasserts the complex interplay between joy and pain already articulated in Kentridge's description of the frieze:

> The music for *Triumphs and Laments* is inspired by the masses of migrants trudging across Europe and the images we carry of them: mothers, fathers, children, brothers, sisters, and friends dragging their scant belongings from a place of terrible violence to a place of imagined sanctuary, a place that might become "home." The migrants are, of course, not the first exiles, nor will they be the last. These are the processions of the 21st century.
>
> As a starting point for my [*sic*] composition, I examined the liturgical songs of the late Renaissance Italian Jewish composer Salamone Rossi of Mantua. His madrigal [*sic*] *Al Naharot Bavel,* which is based on the text of Psalm 137 of the Book of Exodus [*sic*],[26] speaks to me not only of oppressed peoples forced into exile but also of the nationalism and violence that surrounds this exile. The structure of my composition came from re-imagining Rossi's score being played stereophonically by two musical processions of singers along the waters of the Tiber. One procession is an expression of triumph, the other of lament, as the narratives of migration are tragic, but they can also be redemptive. I was imagining brass players and percussionists walking toward each other along the rivers of Babylon, or along the edges of the Red Sea, or indeed along the edges of Africa and Lampedusa, and encountering one another across great bodies of water.
>
> As migrants leave loved ones behind, or make it to the hopeful "promised land" only to find a new world of difficulties, *Triumphs and Laments* speaks across the water. Exploring the dissonances, harmonic shifts, and mottos of Rossi's work, together with my co-composer Thuthuka Sibisi, I have broken down the composition into fragments, loops, and rhythmical motifs. I have extended moments of both dissonance and resolution, which evoke both lamentation and triumph that emerge from the two musical processions. Every triumphant musical phrase is answered by its counterpoint: music of mourning and darkness. I have also allowed

---

[25] Miller, interview with the author, May 13, 2020. Miller and Kentridge both refer to "Al naharot Bavel" as a madrigal. However, given the piece's sacred content it is best described as a motet.
[26] Psalm 137 is from the Book of Psalms, not Exodus.

the elaboration of Rossi to give way to eruptions where voices from both past and present come together to resonate within the sound-world of the processions: a Mandinkan slave song from West Africa combines with an ancient Southern Italian melismatic folk song and a battle-song of the Zulu warriors.

In the city of Rome, as in all European metropolises, the narratives of migration are inscribed in its stones. As we walked and played this music along the Tiber, I chose not to ignore the graffiti written on the embankment wall behind us, much of which has been erased in preparation for the project. Rather, I chose to incorporate these slogans—even if they were sometimes foreign or unclear and indecipherable—into a "call and response" chant between the two musical processions. This "sounding" of the erased graffiti brings visual traces into the musical palimpsest that shapes the composition, reminding us of the triumphs and laments of the present-day city that these inscriptions mark.

Finally, I chose the words of the poet Rainer Maria Rilke from his book *Die frühen Gedichte* (1909), to be recited and sung during the procession: "That is the longing: to dwell amidst the waves / and have no homeland in time."[27]

Miller's program note foregrounds the displacement highlighted in Kentridge's iconography. The composer emphasizes that his and Sibisi's score proceeds from a concern with migration. This topic is represented by original source materials and intertexts (such as Rossi's motet), and by the structure of the composition, which reflects motifs of spatiality, movement, and circulation.

The score's formal and intertextual preoccupations integrate the procession's music with the visual content displayed on the embankment. They also draw attention to the complex interaction between sound and place, not only in *Triumphs and Laments* but also in sonic events more generally. As already implied by Miller's reference to Salamone Rossi, sound has the capacity to evoke geographically determined histories of location and dislocation—of belonging or, in the case of "Al Naharot Bavel," exile. It conjures specific places and the stories of those who dwell (or dwelt) in them. Sound also inhabits place, filling it and impressing upon the environment the presence of the sound source. Thus, it serves as a means of physical and historical orientation and of occupation. The music of *Triumphs and Laments* is hence significant not only as an auditory accompaniment to the launch of Kentridge's frieze, but also, as Miller acknowledges, for its sonic engagement with regimes of place and displacement in the past and the present.

---

[27] Philip Miller, 2018, "The Music of Triumphs and Laments." Document supplied by the author, also available online at https://www.kentridge.studio/the-music-of-triumphs-and-laments/, accessed March 31, 2022.

170 Postcolonial Opera

Miller and Sibisi's main source text, Rossi's setting of the psalm known as "By the rivers of Babylon," is a lament for the city of Jerusalem. It remembers the Babylonian capture and destruction of Jerusalem in 587 BCE and articulates Israel's desire to return to their homeland while in exile in Babylon:[28]

Hebrew text (transliteration) set by Rossi	English text, *King James* version
`Al naharót bavel	By the rivers of Babylon
sham yashavnu gam bachinu	There we sat down, yea, we wept
b'zochrénu et tsiyyón.	When we remembered Zion.
`Al `aravim b'tóchah	We hanged our harps upon the willows
talinu kinnróteinu.	In the midst thereof.
Ki sham sh'elunu shóveinu divrei shir	For there they that carried us away captive required of us a song
v'tólaleinu simcha	And those that wasted us required of us
shiru lanu mishshir tsiyyón.	mirth, saying,
Ech nashir et shir adónai	Sing us one of the songs of Zion.
`al admat néchar.	How shall we sing the Lord's song
Im eshkachéch y'rushalayim	In a foreign land?
tishkach y'mini.	If I forget thee, O Jerusalem,
Tidbaz l'shóni l'chiki im ló ezk'réchi	Let my right hand forget her cunning. If I do not remember thee
im ló a`ale et y'rushalayim	Let my tongue cleave to the roof of my
`al rósh simchati.	mouth
Z'chor adónai livnei edóm	If I prefer not Jerusalem above my chief joy.
et yóm y'rushalayim	Remember, O Lord, the children of Edom
haóm'rim `aru `aru	in the day of Jerusalem
`ad hay'sód bah.	who said, "Raze it, raze it,
Bat bavel hashsh'duda	even to the foundation thereof."
ashrei shey'shallém lach et g'muléch	O daughter of Babylon, who art to be destroyed
shegamalt lanu.	Happy shall he be, that rewardeth thee
Ashrei sheyóchéz v'nipéts	as thou hast served us.
et `ólalayich el hassala![29]	Happy shall he be, that taketh and dasheth thy little ones against the stones.[30]

[28] See Daniel Simango, 2018, "A Comprehensive Reading of Psalm 137," *Old Testament Essays* 31(1), 217–242.

[29] Salomon Rossi, 1876 [1622], "Aux bords des fleuves de Babylone: Psaume 137 à 4 voix," *Cantiques de Salomon Rossi: Psaumes, Chants et Hymnes à 3, 4, 5, 6, 7 et 8 voix*, transcribed and edited by Samuel Naubourg, Paris, 27–29.

[30] BibleGateway, n.d., "Psalm 137," https://www.biblegateway.com/passage/?search=Psalm%20137&version=KJV, accessed May 9, 2022.

In *Triumphs and Laments*, "Al Naharot Bavel" serves as a kind of cantus firmus or perpetually present leitmotiv. Never silent for long, Rossi's motet ties together the wide range of musical material distributed between the two marching bands that approach each other along the embankment. The Triumph ensemble is scored for violin, clarinet, two trumpets, two trombones, tuba, bass drum, tambourine, accordion, SATB chorus, and three vocal soloists (two sopranos and a tenor). Lament is similarly scored, though slightly smaller; it comprises bass flute, clarinet, viola, horn, trombones, tuba, bass drum, SATB chorus, and two solo sopranos. The two ensembles interact with each other both harmoniously and contrapuntally. The musical material for Lament is clearly tied to "Al Naharot Bavel" throughout: the ensemble never veers from the original Hebrew text, and its melodic content is identifiably based on Rossi's motet. In dialogue with the uniform thematic design of Lament, Triumph introduces several rhythmic, melodic, and textual countertexts. These include a traditional Zulu song from South Africa, a Ndebele song from Zimbabwe, and references to two southern Italian folk forms, the *tammurriata* and the *pizzica*. I return to these intertexts and their individual interactions with regimes of mobility and ideas of place below.

Triumphs and Laments starts with an ominous introduction, played by Lament's bass drum. The rhythm, a simple statement of two quarter notes—the second of which is accented—on the first two beats of the bar in a 4/4 time signature, evokes the melancholy cadence of funeral processions. With the two bands still at extreme ends of the processional stage, the embankment appears dark, illuminated only at intervals by spotlights that will later highlight the movements of the live performers. From the gloom, the rest of the Lament band joins in with a first statement of the theme from Rossi's motet. The key is C minor, but in the absence of a minor third, the music obtains a modal rather than tonal character. After four instrumental statements of the theme—the last of which is slightly curtailed—the marching chorus finally joins in with a vocal rendition of Rossi's text.

Miller and Sibisi decorate the original music subtly by introducing semi-tone and whole-tone intervals between voices. These soft but jarring dissonances add to a sense of tension already captured by the relentless bass drum and the pressing, nasal timbre of the brass. It is a tension sustained throughout the performance through a combination of abrupt dynamic contrasts, registral shifts, harmonic irresolution, and rhythmic syncopation.

When the front lines of the two marching troupes meet, the performers begin to interact face-to-face. They exchange spoken and sung statements, gesturing aggressively toward each other as if conducting a vocal duel. Behind them, walking bodies amble along, carrying large cutouts that cast moving silhouettes on the riverbank. Against a desiccated and pointillistic

172 Postcolonial Opera

instrumental backdrop, the five soloists from the two ensembles face each other in a hostile exchange of unscripted sounds. The singers provoke each other with vocal clicks, trills, shrieks, and slides. They loom over one another threateningly, waving their arms, swaying, and intimidating their opponents with the sheer force of their physical and sonic presence.

After an aggressive interruption on the words "aru" ("Raze it"), repeated in a rising (and rousing) crescendo exchange between instruments and chorus, the entire ensemble arrives on the statement, "shey'shallém lach et g'muléch shegamalt lanu" ("happy shall he be, that rewardeth thee as thou hast served us," or "happy shall he be that has avenged us").[31] This forceful call for retribution, articulated by the assembled forces of both ensembles, captures neatly the complex relationship between conquest and devastation. For both groups—the one representing triumph and the one representing lament—violence may generate elation, even as it initiates misery for another.

Following their climactic demand for the joy of suffering, the two marching troupes continue on their journey along the riverbank. As the bands approach their points of arrival at opposite ends of the causeway, the music settles into a coda based on the opening material of the work. The Laments group returns to long, static chordal lines that replicate the melodic and lyric lines that launched the composition, while the Triumphs group performs rapid triplet movements undercut by a sixteenth note violin ostinato. The coda repeats until both groups have completed their processions. Rather than arriving decisively on a triumphant final cadence, the music peters out uncertainly, limping away into silence as the deserted riverbank is left empty but for the shadowy frieze.

Procession

Triumphs and Laments' processional structure is typical of Kentridge's work. The artist first used the procession as a theme in his animation, *Johannesburg, 2nd Greatest City after Paris* (1989). Since then, processions have marched across his static drawings (*Arc/Procession: Develop, Catch Up, Even Surpass*, 1990), films (*Drawings for Projection*, 1989–2020) and live-action video installations (including *Notes towards a Model Opera*, 2015, and *More Sweetly Play the Dance*, 2015).[32] In *Triumphs and Laments*, Kentridge removed the

---

[31] BibleGateway, "Psalm 137."

[32] See Leora Maltz-Leca, 2013, "Process/Procession: William Kentridge and the Process of Change," *Art Bulletin* 95(1), 139–165, for an overview of Kentridge's processions. Chapter 3 ("Process/Procession: Processing Regime Change") in Leora Maltz-Leca, 2018, *William Kentridge: Process as Metaphor and Other Doubtful Enterprises*, Oakland: University of California Press, 131–193, offers an expanded version of the 2013 article.

mediating technologies of the frame and the screen to produce his first live processional performance. With the Rome piece, Kentridge's processional practice hence metamorphoses from depiction to performance. This ties the work to a longer tradition of processional performance, first comprehensively theorized by Barbara Kirshenblatt-Gimblett and Brooks McNamara in 1985.[33] Kirshenblatt-Gimblett and McNamara describe processional performance as "basically . . . performance in motion through space."[34] They further stipulate that the procession offers "a means of getting [from Place A to Place B] in ways that have ceremonial and symbolic importance," and that it is hence distinct from "everyday movement through space."[35] Emma Cox expands on this definition by tracing the roots of the word *procession* to the Latin *procedere*, which means "to go forward, advance, or proceed." For Cox, *procession* "bears the semantic trace of its derived terms *process* and *procedure* to connote movement that is framed, predictable, sanctioned."[36] Processional performance therefore refers to a form of mobility that is geographically delineated, directional, and intentional.

In *Triumphs and Laments*, Kentridge's processional practice weaves together longer traditions of parades and pageantry to raise questions about the aesthetic and political significance of the image of the mobile subject in performance. Leora Maltz-Leca's instructive overview of Kentridge's processions identifies various historical precedents for this thematic concern and the visual language in which it is codified.[37] These include Western epistemological constructions of the sequential nature of thought (the "stream of consciousness") and of linear narrative structures, or in Godby's words, "the idea of the flow of history."[38] Maltz-Leca further identifies in Kentridge's processions a Western conception of political emancipation, which finds its ultimate representation in the French Revolution.[39] Crucially, however, the artist's use of the processional form also points to an experience of freedom unlocked by manumission. Thus, they reach back to what Maltz-Leca describes as "African rituals of masked processions."[40] In other words, Kentridge's processions invoke temporal and geographical regions encompassing both the West and

---

[33] Barbara Kirshenblatt-Gimblett and Brooks McNamara, 1985, "Processional Performance: An Introduction," *Drama Review: TDR* 29(3), 2–5.

[34] Kirshenblatt-Gimblett and McNamara, "Processional Performance," 2.

[35] Kirshenblatt Gimblett and McNamara, "Processional Performance," 2.

[36] Emma Cox, 2017, "Processional Aesthetics and Irregular Transit: Envisioning Refugees in Europe," *Theatre Journal* 69(4), 477–496, at 477.

[37] Maltz-Leca, 2013, "Process/Procession."

[38] Godby, "Unwritten History," 220.

[39] Maltz-Leca, 2013, "Process/Procession," 155.

[40] Maltz-Leca, 2013, "Process/Procession," 155.

174   Postcolonial Opera

the so-called global South. They mark people's shifting physical and political positions in the world, both across and between history and place.

Given the contested nature of concepts such as emancipation and empowerment, especially as they play out in the contrasting histories of Western modernity and anti-colonial resistance, it is not surprising that Kentridge's processions resist straightforwardly triumphant narratives. Rather, they juxtapose depictions of privilege with scenes of abjection. Figures adorned with the accoutrements of power find themselves marching alongside the shuffling bodies of the disempowered. In the context of *Triumphs and Laments*, this combination is meaningful. As I mention above, the inspiration for Kentridge's frieze and the accompanying performance is the Roman tradition of *triumphus*. In the antique ritual, performed to celebrate military success, it was not only the victorious combatants who participated in the procession (*pompus*). Instead, they were preceded and accompanied by the humiliated figures of their captives.[41] The imagery of the *triumphus* hence did not consist purely of jubilant and consensual participation. Kentridge channels this ambiguity and amplifies it by drawing attention to the anguish of the defeated. Complicating the legacy of the Roman *triumphus*, the artist portrays viscerally Walter Benjamin's observation that the triumphal procession is also a scene of horror, an event in which "the present rulers [step] over those who are lying prostrate."[42]

As in so many of Kentridge's works under discussion in this book, *Triumphs and Laments* draws attention to the darker side of progress; "a foil," in Maltz-Leca's words, "to triumphant nationalisms and the colonialism they fostered."[43] In Kentridge's realization of these mobile scenes, in other words, Western progression toward late-capitalist liberal democracy comes face to face with the experiences of those dispossessed and displaced by the modernizing impulse. By bringing together these contrasting representations, Kentridge's processions become a meeting point for incommensurate histories.

Homi Bhabha, in a discussion of Kentridge's video installation, *More Sweetly Play the Dance* (2015), describes Kentridge's processions as "acts of hospitality, ongoing gatherings of people and things on the move."[44] Focusing especially on the artist's depictions of displaced people, Bhabha uses the

---

[41] See Mary Beard, 2007, *The Roman Triumph*, Cambridge, MA: Harvard University Press, for more on this ritual. Chapter 4 of Beard's study (107–142) describes the practice of parading prisoners and loot as part of the victory procession.

[42] Walter Benjamin, 2007 [1942], "Theses on the Philosophy of History," paragraph vii, in *Illuminations*, ed. Hannah Arendt, trans. Harry Zohn, New York: Schocken Books, 256.

[43] Maltz-Leca, 2013, "Process/Procession," 157.

[44] Homi Bhabha, 2016, "Processional Ethics: Homi K. Bhabha on William Kentridge's *More Sweetly Play the Dance*," *Artforum International* 55(2), 230–292.

term "foot power" as a descriptor of the ambulatory nature of contemporary mobilities. In the twenty-first century, Bhabha remarks, "foot power remains ... the motor of movement."[45] His moving description of the "aesthetic drive" and "ethical measure" of foot power bears repeating in full:

> The flickering projections we see in the news of people fleeing floods, civil war, refugees, migrations, refugees returning, displacement—still, two and a half thousand years later, so largely on foot, individual human power still the central means of locomotion, handcarts, wheelbarrows. . . . Foot power is as much an aesthetic drive as it is an ethical measure. The footstep is a sign of the singular fate of each member of each oppressed group while serving as a symbol of the collective condition of dispossession and diaspora.[46]

For Bhabha, foot power inscribes contemporary displacements onto longer histories of devastation. Shifting between the anonymity of crowds ("the large scale of the muchness of people in the world") and the specificity of individual action ("the small-scale shifting and shuffling of the body in locomotion"), the procession, for Bhabha, captures both the singularity of suffering, and the shared burden of history.[47] Kentridge's processions hence become a measure not of progress, but of stasis. They draw attention to the fact that displacement retains its form across millennia. Kentridge's subjects do not tread lightly. Anything but triumphant, their procession is a lament for the enduring and abject spectacle of physical displacement.

While Bhabha identifies in the processional depiction of refugees a restorative form of representation, Cox argues that the same visual regime may also risk dehumanizing its subject. For Cox, the processional depiction of displaced people is a trope "central to the visual economy associated with refugee transit."[48] Observing that "the movements of asylum-seekers and migrants into and across Europe are more intensively imaged and spectated than ever," Cox agrees with Bhabha that the processional form offers an opportunity to observe the displaced person both as individual object and as unit of a larger superstructure. Whereas Bhabha identifies in this negotiation between individual and collective a form of shared history, however, Cox argues that it may also depersonalize the mobile figure.

The processional "mode of looking and responding," which renders a figure that is at once animate and mechanical, results in a sensory regime Cox

---

[45] Bhabha, "Processional Ethics," n.p.
[46] Bhabha, "Processional Ethics," n.p.
[47] Bhabha, "Processional Ethics," n.p.
[48] Cox, "Processional Aesthetics," 479.

classifies as "processional aesthetics."[49] As a visual regime, it describes the portrayal of the migrant caught in constant, repetitive forward motion. Both human and machine, sufferer and automaton, the processional figure of the migrant is an Other configured by their simultaneous humanity and inhumanity. Thus, processional aesthetics shapes (and represents) both an optical and a political orientation to refugees. It may produce a shared sense of humanity, but it may just as well strip the mobile subject of that which makes it human.

In *Triumphs and Laments*, the contradiction between these contrasting observational ethics is again mediated through Kentridge's use of shadow projections. As described in Chapter 2 ("Confession"), Kentridge's shadows negotiate between the depiction of the subject as individual and as type. In *Triumphs and Laments*, this mediating element plays an important role in the practical realization of the piece. The scale of the work—with audiences observing events from across the river—diminishes the distinctiveness of the individual performers, even though each marching body is clad in a unique costume and performs personalized movements. As marching collectives observed at a distance, the two bands usurp their constitutive parts into a slightly chaotic whole. Only the large shadows projected onto the riverbank (combined with the singing voices of the two bands' soloists) remind the viewer that each group is comprised of singular figures. Thus, *Triumphs and Laments* exemplifies the contradiction of Cox's processional aesthetics. Even as, following Bhabha, it performs a gesture of hospitality toward the mobile subject, the piece simultaneously underscores the potentially dehumanizing effect of such depiction.

Apart from the processional aesthetics of refugee depictions, *Triumphs and Laments* also links with the processional form as deployed in opera. Here, procession is perhaps most closely associated with the grand operas of the Romantic period, though Michael Burden identifies spectacular processions on British stages as early as the mid-eighteenth century.[50] In Burden's description, these scenes functioned as vehicles for "operatic extravagance"; they offered an opportunity to showcase to full effect the theater's technological, scenographic, and artistic capabilities.[51] Processions also, Burden notes, counteracted the distancing effect generated by the expansion of theaters during the 1700s. Where audiences felt themselves detached, or

---

[49] Cox, "Processional Aesthetics," 479.

[50] Michael Burden, 2009, "The Lure of Aria, Procession and Spectacle: Opera in Eighteenth-Century London," in *The Cambridge History of Eighteenth-Century Music*, ed. Simon P. Keefe, Cambridge: Cambridge University Press, 385–401, at 396.

[51] Burden, "Lure," 400.

even alienated, from the stages of these new, supersized theaters, processional scenes offered an instance of sensory immensity that overwhelmed the listener-spectator and reintegrated her into the performance.[52] Processional scenes hence mitigated the very impulses to monumentality and physical permanence that characterize Western opera, as described at the beginning of this chapter.

Perhaps the most evocative example is the triumphal march from the second act of Verdi's *Aïda*, which still serves—with few exceptions—as a chance for directorial teams to unleash their most excessive scenographic fantasies. Other operatic processions may be less rousing, for instance, the march of Sarastro's priests in Mozart's *Magic Flute* (Act II), or the many mobile-crowd scenes by Wagner (I think here especially of the "Procession of the Knights of the Holy Grail" in Act III of *Parsifal* and Elsa's procession to the cathedral in *Lohengrin* Act II), or they may appear to be permanently consigned to the realm of brass band showstoppers (as in the case of Rimsky Korsakov's Wagner-inspired "Procession of the Nobles" from *Mlada*, Act II), but they nonetheless contribute to a processional tradition inescapably bound up with ideals of operatic extravagance and grandeur.

Triumphs and Laments gestures to the tradition of operatic procession. Like its operatic counterparts, Kentridge's procession relies on an imposing visual effect not only to mitigate the sheer scale of the performance site, but also to conjure the triumphant aspects of the tale being told. Whereas operatic processions are usually restricted to single scenes, however, Kentridge turns his entire piece into a procession. This formal decision, inspired as discussed above by the Roman tradition of the *triumphus*, transforms the procession from embellishment to objective—from a decorative spectacle to the main event.

The operatic procession, contained both physically and temporally (on the opera house stage and in a dedicated scene from the work), is essentially static. It arrests both time and place, despite the impression of mobility created by bodies in transit.[53] Kentridge's processional opera, in contrast, incorporates walking as a formal feature that transforms the very nature of the operatic event. Here, the centralization of motion as aesthetic practice produces a musical form that is adaptable, improvisatory, site-specific, and mobile. *Triumphs and Laments'* processional structure hence complicates traditional opera's emplacement to generate a performance practice that is more responsive to the instability of contemporary practices of settlement and habitation. In the

---

[52] Burden, "Lure," 400.
[53] On opera's ambiguous play with temporal arrest and progress, see Chapter 4.

178 Postcolonial Opera

process, Kentridge's work offers new perspective on the relationship between opera and place, especially in postcolonial and migratory contexts.

Opera and Place

Opera participates in the making of place across a number of practical and ideological registers. First, the genre literally "takes place," not only in the sense of occurring but also in its occupation of physical place. Whether in designated opera houses, repurposed theater spaces, or (increasingly) in alternative sites, both indoors and outdoors, the art form's realization requires the material inhabitation—both physical and sonic—of particular places. Through the sheer weight of its musical volume, it demands attention, occupying its immediate surroundings with an irresistible insistence. "Taking place" hence refers both to the physically situated occurrence of the performance, and to the genre's usurpation of its environment: opera takes in and takes charge of its physical settings.

Apart from taking place—as performance and as physical inhabitation—opera also imagines place. Both musically and through visual realizations on stage, the art form represents particular settings and locations in performance. Thus, it contributes to contemporaneous ideas about the nature of local and distant geographical and historical locations. For Susan Rutherford, this operatic depiction of physical locations plays an important role in the social construction of place. Rutherford argues that operatic scenography disseminates particular images of places both near and far, to contribute to audiences' perceptions of these settings, their history, and their culture.[54] In this sense, opera helps to make place as idea and ideal. Even as it takes inspiration from particular locations, the genre shapes the way these locations are imagined and experienced by its consumers.

But opera also "makes" place by inscribing certain cultural and class values upon a specific context. The siting of opera houses within urban settings is meaningful for the way it influences the perceived reputation and status of a particular neighborhood and its inhabitants.[55] Suzanne Aspden observes that

---

[54] Susan Rutherford, 2019, "The City Onstage: Re-Presenting Venice in Italian Opera," in *Operatic Geographies*, 88–104.

[55] See Rebekah Ahrendt, Michael Burden, and Klaus van den Berg in Aspden's *Operatic Geographies* for insightful accounts of the cultural and class politics that underpinned planning for opera houses in the cities of The Hague, London, and Paris. Rebekah Ahrendt, 2019, "The Legal Spaces of Opera in The Hague," in *Operatic Geographies*, 12–25; Michael Burden, 2019, "London's Opera House in the Urban Landscape," in *Operatic Geographies*, 39–56; Klaus van den Berg, 2019, "The Opera House as Urban Exhibition Space," in *Operatic Geographies*, 213–233.

since the eighteenth century the opera house has been viewed as a structure with potential to "manifest and broadcast civic ambition." The perceived prestige of the operatic form enabled the opera house to "aestheticize the city in structural terms and thereby affirm elite control of the civic environment."[56] Rebekah Ahrendt concurs, observing that the establishment of opera houses in The Hague contributed greatly to public views of the morality, cultural accomplishment, and class status of the neighborhoods in which these theaters were built.[57] Even so-called country house opera with its enactment of a rural idyll, contributes to a valuation of physical place. Here, the tradition's inscription in a cultural and class context dominated by nostalgia for the pursuits of the leisured classes, (re)constructs the countryside not as a site of physical labor but as a bucolic setting for sophisticated enjoyment. Thus, opera literally "cultivates" the rural sphere, transforming it from rustic land to aristocratic institution.[58]

In colonial spheres, opera's cultural validation of place acquires additional political weight. The colonial context maintains a delicate relationship with the metropole, simultaneously emulating and deviating from the European motherland. Within this frame, Aspden notes, opera was exported to the colonies "as a marker in various ways of European 'civilization' and power, as well as a means of resisting and complicating it—in turn 'provincializing' Europe."[59] As I noted especially in Chapter 1, operatic participation inscribes citizens into European regimes of class and culture. It also serves as a vehicle of aspirational self-improvement, allowing patrons to become part of a European cultural community, and to imagine themselves as active participants in the global project of Western modernity.[60] A city with opera is not merely a clearing in the wilderness but a place with culture. As a symbol of civility and power, in other words, opera endows the colonial location with social and cultural identity, transforming it from territory into place.

Histories of opera's sites—including opera houses in Cairo, Cape Town, Buenos Aires, and New Orleans (among others)—show how closely the cultural project of colonial opera is tied up with physical place.[61] Colonial

[56] Suzanne Aspden, 2019, "Opera and the (Urban) Geography of Culture," in *Operatic Geographies*, 1–11, at 5 and 6.

[57] Ahrendt, "Legal Spaces."

[58] See Suzannee Aspden, 2019, "Pastoral Retreats: Playing at Arcadia in Modern Britain," in *Operatic Geographies*, 195–212.

[59] Aspden, "Opera," 9.

[60] See Chapter 1.

[61] I think here especially of Donato Somma, 2022, "A Tale of Two Houses: Opera Houses in Cairo and Cape Town," *Cambridge Opera Journal* 33(1–2), 129–160; Juliana M. Pistorius and Hilde Roos, 2021, "Burgerskap onder konstruksie: *Rigoletto* en *Aida* by die Suid-Afrikaanse Republiekfeesvieringe, 1971," *Litnet Akademies* 18(2), 102–131; Charlotte Bentley, 2018, "Resituating Transatlantic Opera: The Case of the Théâtre d'Orléans, New Orleans, 1819–1859," PhD diss., University of Cambridge; Ronald Dolkart,

180 Postcolonial Opera

regimes built opera houses as symbols of their nations' cultural accomplishment and participation in Western modernity.[62] The locations they chose for these structures were themselves sites for contested power dynamics and the curation of political and cultural legacies: in Cairo, for instance, the Khedivial opera house opened in 1869 was located in the new, westernized district of Attaba—the hub of Khedive Ismail's quest to modernize the city.[63] And in Cape Town, the apartheid regime opted to construct its opera house in a location on the outskirts of the original colonial city center as a means to distinguish the new political establishment from its colonial predecessor. The Nico Malan Opera House, which opened in 1971, was built on land reclaimed from the ocean, and was designated to become the focal point of a new administrative center for the city—a plan that ultimately came to nothing.[64]

The process of choosing and preparing land for the construction of opera houses further entails the erasure of certain forms of inhabiting in favor of others. Often, communities must be cleared to make space for the new building—as in the case of New York's Metropolitan Opera House (completed in 1966), which was built on the site of a largely African American and Puerto Rican neighborhood.[65] Alternatively, opera houses transform particular areas from sites of transit—spaces through which people move on their way to other destinations—to sites of arrival, upon which people converge with the express purpose of obtaining meaningful and esteemed social and cultural experiences. Opera may hence participate unwittingly in regimes of displacement by which some publics are removed to make place for others.

By curating the types of publics that converge upon particular settings, opera and its places partake in a broader culture of exclusion. Hierarchical valuations of the perceived desirability of persons yield a mode of place-making whereby certain bodies and voices, rather than others, are admitted into specific spheres. In opera, this is particularly evident in the often-strident policing not only of audience behavior but also of performance style. Voice types and singing techniques become a cipher through which certain persons and their forms of musicianship may be kept off the operatic stage. As Aspden writes, opera could, "through its attendant social rituals as well as its music, create a penumbra of exclusivity that appeared to reinforce social hierarchies

1983, 'Elitelore at the Opera: The Teatro Colón of Buenos Aires," *Journal of Latin American Lore* 9(2), 231–250.

[62] See Dolkart, "Elitelore," 240.
[63] See Somma, "Two Houses."
[64] See Somma, "Two Houses," 150–151.
[65] Van den Berg, "Urban Exhibition Space," 213–224.

just as effectively as military muscle might do."[66] Often, then, opera functions as an art of exclusion. It makes place by admitting some people and rejecting others.

Ironically, however, opera occasionally serves as a vehicle for structurally excluded bodies to obtain admission to inaccessible places. Just as the art form locks out those who do not conform to its cultural requirements, it may sometimes offer a way in for those who possess the necessary cultural qualifications but not the attendant racial, social, or political credentials. An example from apartheid South Africa is the Eoan Group, whose singers belonged to the so-called Colored racial grouping.[67] The Eoan Group was the first South African company to produce Italian opera in the original language on a regular basis. In recognition of their artistic accomplishments, the apartheid government allowed these singers to perform in venues reserved by law for the white population. Opera hence became a channel for sonic and physical presence—a vehicle for excluded bodies to occupy places in which they would otherwise not appear.[68]

In summary, then, opera participates in the making of place by several means: it occupies places, portrays them, curates their accessibility, and infuses them with social and cultural signification. The effects of opera's emplacement are largely determined by the conventions of the form and the political context within which it circulates. In these circumstances, the art form leaves little room for reflection on the experiences of those who perpetually find themselves out of place. Refugees and other migrant subjects do not fit in the places opera traditionally makes. Nor do their itinerant lives—unmoored from place and the values it represents—fit with operatic principles of institutional stability and cultural consolidation. As a form that is fundamentally *placed*, opera hence appears ill equipped to engage ethically with the experiences of the displaced.

In *Triumphs and Laments*, however, the displaced experience becomes the very substance of the operatic work. This casts into sharp relief the art form's place-making tendencies and asks the viewer to reconsider the relationship between the operatic form and the displaced subject. In what follows, I reflect

---

[66] Aspden, "Opera," 6–7.

[67] A racial label invented by the apartheid regime, "Colored" referred to those South Africans who did not neatly fit into Black or white classifications. In contemporary South Africa, the term and its use are contested—some citizens embrace it as a racial identity, while others reject the term due to its apartheid connotations. I use "Colored" here not to reinforce a particular racial classification system but as a historical referent that conditioned the details of a series of events under apartheid.

[68] See Juliana M. Pistorius, 2017, "Coloured Opera as Subversive Forgetting," *Social Dynamics: A Journal of African Studies* 43(2), 230–242, and Pistorius, 2019, "Inhabiting Whiteness: The Eoan Group *La Traviata, 1956*," *Cambridge Opera Journal* 31(1), 63–84, for more on the Eoan Group and its ambiguous participation in apartheid's politics of place.

Postcolonial Opera

on the ways in which Kentridge's work complicates and resists the dislocation of refugees and other migrant subjects. Under the headings of "location" and "movement," I investigate *Triumphs and Laments*' multifarious modes of place-making and inhabitation before asking how this reimagined operatic form responds to the experiences of those who find themselves outside opera's permanences.

Location

As a site-specific installation, the very substance of *Triumphs and Laments* is dictated by place. Both the structure and the medium of the piece are direct results of the location Kentridge chose for his project. The black grime that makes up the artist's embankment figures consist of a number of bacterial communities called biopatinas. As Bartoli et al. show, these communities are determined by the particular combination of elements, including building materials (travertine stone), climatic conditions (Mediterranean), directional aspect (North-West), and exposure (including to water and sunlight) that characterizes the section of the riverbank.[69] The work's medium—grime—is hence a residue of the natural processes of time and place specific to that part of the city and the river. As the stone surfaces yield to bacterial recolonization, the medium also becomes the source of the work's destruction. Dirt and moss quickly returned to the cleared areas on the embankment walls, resulting in the gradual filling-in of the frieze. By September 2020 this process was complete, and the riverbank was once again covered by an even layer of grime. Thus, *Triumphs and Laments* became both a product and a victim of place—created and destroyed by the site in which it was located. The ecological makeup of Kentridge's chosen site turned the frieze into a physical representative of the intersecting particularities of time and place, of history and geography.[70]

Like its visual register, the work's musical configuration is a product of its riverside setting. Filling the entire stretch of riverbank with a constant, if shifting, wash of sound, the procession emphasized the acoustic qualities of the site, while the antiphonal construction of the piece drew attention to the physical composition of the performing groups and the improvised stage on which they found themselves. Given the expansive concourse on which the performance played out, the binaural effect of advancing and departing sounds created a geographically determined musical narrative of approach,

[69] Bartoli et al, "Biological Recolonization."
[70] Guercio, "Paradoxical Monumentality," 130.

Place **183**

through arrival (the meeting of the two marching bands at the midpoint of the performance) to departure. However, the climax suggested by arrival was not entirely stable: rather, it shifted along with the positions of its audience members. Depending on where they were stationed on the opposite riverbank, viewers would have seen and heard different portions of the performance as more sensorially immersive. Their visual and acoustic perspectives were hence impacted by the material they consumed directly versus what they experienced from afar. As a result, the nature of the theater product consumed at every point in the performance was different from any other. This is of course the case for every live musical experience, especially in performance spaces with less sophisticated acoustic design: what one hears is impacted by one's position in the venue. *Triumphs and Laments* amplifies this aspect of live performance by turning the place-specific nature of aesthetic experience into a structural feature of the work.

As if to underscore the importance of the performance site, Miller and Sibisi employ subtle text painting to illustrate the movement of the Tiber. Small instrumental wave formations accompany each lyric reference to the river, as Triumphs repeats the words "al naharot" ("by the river") in a syncopated rhythmic contraction of Laments' melodic line, which is strongly suggestive of uneven fluvial movement. Text and music thus combine to focus the attention on the river as performance site. This not only underlines the importance of place for Kentridge's piece but also creates a link with the original source material.

Joshua Jacobson's description of the compositional techniques Rossi employed for "Al naharot Bavel" identifies "gentle melismatic lines [to] suggest the flowing of rivers."[71] In both Rossi's and Miller and Sibisi's compositions, the Tiber and the two Babylonian rivers—the Tigris and the Euphrates—thus emerge as sonic constructs. They become sources of and sites for musical performance.

If place seems predominantly to be a structural feature in Miller and Sibisi's composition, their choice of intertexts introduces the politics of location to the work's musical content. The main source text for the music of *Triumphs and Laments*, "Al naharot Bavel," invokes two distant places: Babylon and Jerusalem. But it also sets up a geopolitical relationship between Jerusalem and Rome—one that in turn introduces to *Triumphs and Laments* a range of historical and intercultural significations centered around the figure of Salamone Rossi.

---

[71] Joshua Jacobson, 1988, "The Choral Music of Salamone Rossi," *American Choral Review* 30(4), n.p., https://zamir.org/resources/music-of-salamone-rossi/rossi-monograph/, accessed May 9, 2022.

184 Postcolonial Opera

For Rossi, Psalm 137 may have had personal meaning. Though composed as a reflection on Babylonian exile, the psalm's lyrical content also conjures the more recent sacking of Jerusalem by Rome in 70 CE, during the first Jewish-Roman War.[72] Rossi, who was a respected violinist and composer active in Mantua at the turn of the seventeenth century, traced his ancestry back to the exiles from Jerusalem who had been transported to Rome as captives after the Jewish-Roman War.[73] The composer's Italian identity was hence itself a product of displacement.

It appears that Rossi's dual Jewish and Italian heritage served as both impediment and resource for the composer. Due to widespread anti-Semitism directed by the Catholic Church, Rossi was accorded less respect and professional acclaim than his contemporary (and likely colleague), Claudio Monteverdi. The composer was forced to navigate social and legal structures that excluded him from formal employment at the Court of Mantua based on his Jewish identity. Nonetheless, his reputation as an accomplished musician was sufficient for the composer to be exempt by ducal decree (in 1606 and 1612) from wearing the yellow star used to identify Jews in Mantua.[74]

Rossi's dual cultural heritage also served as a source of musical experimentation. Though the composer is perhaps best known for his contributions to the development of Renaissance chamber music, his vocal works demonstrate a uniquely intercultural perspective on seventeenth-century secular and sacred musicality.[75] Apart from numerous collections of madrigals (six books in total), Rossi's compositions for voice included what Jacobson describes as "a path-breaking collection" of Hebrew motets for the synagogue.[76] It is in this collection, published in 1622 and titled *Hashirim Asher Lish'lomo* (The Songs of Solomon, in a witty play on the composer's own name) that "Al naharot Bavel" appears. *Hashirim Asher Lish'lomo* comprises thirty-three polyphonic settings of Hebrew psalms, hymns, and synagogal songs. Musically, it combines contemporary compositional conventions with traditional Jewish chants and verse forms. The result, according to Ian Fenlon, is "novel in its fusion of different cultural traditions," even if it did not represent great musical invention.[77] The collection is widely held to be the first example of concerted

[72] David W. Stowe, 2016, *Song of Exile: The Enduring Mystery of Psalm 137*, Oxford: Oxford University Press, 41–43.

[73] Jacobson, "Salamone Rossi." See also Stowe, *Song of Exile*, 42.

[74] Ian Fenlon, 2001, "Rossi, Salamone," *Grove Music Online*, https://doi-org.libaccess.hud.ac.uk/10.1093/gmo/9781561592630.article.23896.

[75] Fenlon, "Rossi."

[76] Jacobson, "Salamone Rossi." For Rossi's madrigals, see Alfred Einstein, 1950–1951, "Salamone Rossi as Composer of Madrigals," *Hebrew Union College Annual* 23(2), 383–396.

[77] Fenlon, "Rossi." See also Jacobson, "Salamone Rossi," who argues that the collection "represented a bold innovation for the synagogue," but "did not differ greatly from the conventions of early Baroque music."

music composed specifically for Jewish worship.[78] Thus, it represents an unusual—if not unique—instance of integration between Italian-Late Renaissance musical practice and Jewish liturgy.

If Rossi's musical presence paints a sonic picture of the incorporation of Jews into European culture and society, the images in Kentridge's frieze evoke a more sinister history. Among the frieze figures the artist includes a series of images referencing various moments from the two-millennia-long Jewish past in Europe. These include "Spoils from Jerusalem," in which four carriers transport treasures (including a menorah and the Table of Shew Bread) raided from the Temple of Jerusalem; "Mockery of the Condemned at the Carnival of Rome," which shows the custom of parading Jewish prisoners through the city on a donkey during the Roman carnival; and a pair of images referencing the brutal atrocities of fascism and the Second World War ("Deportees" and "Partisans").[79] Together, the score and the frieze present an intermedial engagement with the history of *Triumphs and Laments*' site, to highlight the ambiguity and multivalence of place. Rome emerges as a location of intercultural exchange but also of violent racism.

Between Figures 33 and 35 of the frieze ("Deportees" and "Partisans"), an anomalous image appears in the form of a large, black rectangle inscribed with the words, "Quello che non ricordo" ("that which I do not remember") (see Figure 5.3). This is the only item in Kentridge's frieze that does not refer to an existing archival source. Instead, "Quello che non ricordo" disrupts the flow of documentary reproduction and remembrance articulated in the frieze. Its reference to amnesia highlights the fact that the events depicted on the embankment wall are partial reconstructions of the past. Thus, the image captures the unreliability of historical accounts and recollections. Like the dark square of *Black Box/Chambre Noire*, it is a reference to the work of memory.[80] However, whereas the earlier piece invokes the black box as witness, here it refers to the power of erasure and forgetting. Situated among portrayals directly referencing Jewish history, the image draws attention to various forms of historical contestation, including the deliberate mis-remembering of Holocaust deniers, the loss of historical completeness through archival and narrative neglect, and the strategic forgetfulness of survivors of trauma.[81]

---

[78] This claim is advanced by Don Harrán, 2009, "A Tale as Yet Untold: Salamone Rossi in Venice, 1622," *Sixteenth-Century Journal* 40(4), 1091–1107; Michelene Wandor, 2002, "Salamone Rossi, Judaism and the Musical Canon," *European Judaism: A Journal for the New Europe* 35(2), 26–35; and Jacobson, "Salamone Rossi," among others; however, it is disputed by Ian Fenlon, who argues that the importance of Rossi's collection "has perhaps been overemphasized by Jewish liturgists."

[79] Allara, "Challenges and Pleasures," 66; Speretta and Viceré, "Sources," at 266–267.

[80] See Chapter 3 for *Black Box/Chambre Noire*.

[81] See Chapter 2 for the role of forgetting in trauma and mourning.

Figure 5.3 "Quello che non ricordo," number 34 of the *Triumphs and Laments* frieze. Courtesy of William Kentridge Studio.

"Quello che non ricordo" obtains sonic realization in Miller and Sibisi's score. In the only direct musical reference to Kentridge's frieze, Soprano 1 of the Triumphs ensemble pronounces the image's words fourteen times to a repeated single-pitched triplet pattern. She is accompanied by Soprano 2 of Laments, who launches into a series of slow glissandi, described in the score as "crying, wailing." As these mournful sounds attest, historical amnesia both produces and conceals pain—it dispossesses history's underdogs of their version of the past and obscures the suffering that is the inevitable byproduct of conquest. "Quello che non ricordo" arguably captures the very essence of *Triumphs and Laments*, namely, that place and history are contested and contestable, inhabited as much by what is forgotten as by what is remembered.

If the incorporation of Jewish intertexts—both musical and visual—draw attention to the ambivalent legacies of the city of Rome specifically, another series of musical references expands *Triumphs and Laments'* geographical scope to situate the piece (and the city) within a broader political-historical perspective on place and displacement. These references circle outward in an ever-widening cartographic sweep, imagining hidden connections between the fortunes of Italy's first city and the modes of survival enacted in locations near and far.

Staying, first, within the borders of the country, Miller and Sibisi incorporate two traditional dance forms associated with the Italian south: *tammurriata* and *pizzica*. These are folk forms from the Campania and the Salento regions, respectively, and are strongly associated with agrarian societies convened around the cultivation of land. For Incoronata Inserra, both *tammurriata* and *pizzica* are "place-specific music tradition[s]."[82] They are inseparable from rural imaginaries congregated around the people of Campania and Salento, and they remain tied up with practices of inhabitation and belonging typical of these areas.

Dancer and educator Pia Vicinanza describes *tammurriata* as a tradition that "expresses a distinctive ethnic identity, a much localized sense of geographical and cultural belonging: it is a rite, a feast where once the peasant told the story of his life, of his faith, of his labor in the fields, his love, through the sound of the drum, the singing, and the dance."[83] Inserra concurs, explaining that *tammuriata* songs "are born in the fields as work songs and thus recount the peasants' labor and express their worldview." *Tammurriata*, in other words, is a form of self-narration that articulates the relationship between subject and land. It situates the singer in a particular geographical and cultural context, and it communicates the extent to which this context shapes the subject's sense of self. Indeed, according to Augusto Ferraiuolo, the relation between *tammurriata* and land is so strong that the tradition is also known as "dance of the earth."[84]

---

[82] Incoronata Inserra, 2017, *Global Tarantella: Reinventing Southern Italian Folk Music and Dances*, Champaign: University of Illinois Press, 24.

[83] Vicinanza, quoted and translated in Inserra, *Global Tarantella*, 15.

[84] Augusto Ferraiuolo, 2015, "The Tammorra Displaced: Music and Body Politics from Churchyards to Glocal Arenas in the Neapolitan Area," *Cultural Analysis* 14, 1–22, at 8.

188 Postcolonial Opera

While *tammurriata* expresses the profound integration between the peasant's identity and his environment, *pizzica* articulates a more spiritual aspect of the rural imaginary. The musical form, which like *tammurriata* incorporates rapid drumming, singing, and dance, forms part of tarantism—the system of cultural-religious rituals associated with the bite of the tarantula spider. (*Pizzica* itself is derived from the Italian *pizzicare*—to bite).[85] Inserra observes that *pizzica*, which is characterized by frenetic drum rhythms and a dance incorporating extensive motion of the arms, forms part of southern Italian healing rituals. Early studies most frequently described the practice as part of a trance-inducing ritual intended to rid the dancer of the poison of the tarantula's bite. Since the publication of Italian anthropologist Ernesto De Martino's *La terra del rimorso* (The Land of Remorse, 1961), however, scholars have accepted that the tradition may also serve a more symbolic therapeutic function, intended to mend sufferers of heartbreak, depression, or anxiety. Nonetheless, the mystical power of *pizzica* to treat illness—whether medical or psychological—remains part of the tradition's characterization.[86]

Traditionally, both *tammurriata* and *pizzica* are performed by ensembles combining sung chants with distinctive instruments: the *tammorra* drum and *castagnole* castanets for *tammurriata*, and a small tambourine (sometimes called the Lecce tambourine) for *pizzica*. Both traditions may also incorporate other instruments, such as guitars, mandolins, violins, flutes, and accordions. Formally, they rely on a metrical interplay between instrumental and sung parts. In *tammurriata*, a slow binary drum rhythm accompanies long, rapid chants of hendecasyllabic distiches in an irregular meter. *Pizzica*, on the other hand, combines a rapid ternary meter in the instrumental part with binary-meter vocal chants.[87]

Miller and Sibisi incorporate the tambourine and accordion into their score and treat both *tammurriata* and *pizzica* as an energetic foil to the somber material of Rossi's motet. First appearing as a rapid, syncopated ostinato in violin, trombones, tambourine, and accordion, the references to these folk traditions appear to undercut the grave nature of the thematic content.

The apparent exuberance of the Italian folk reference is not, however, unequivocal. Indeed, both *tammurriata* and *pizzica* also articulate a more somber interplay of place and cultural significance. The places evoked by these sonic references are themselves inscribed in the fraught politics of migration and displacement summoned by *Triumphs and Laments*. As Inserra notes, the

---

[85] Inserra, *Global Tarantella*, 11.
[86] Inserra, *Global Tarantella*, 12.
[87] Inserra, *Global Tarantella*, at 7, 9, and 11.

Italian South is a poor region, which plays host to large numbers of migrants and refugees from North Africa and the Middle East.[88] In the popular Italian imaginary, it is a sphere of social and economic deprivation—a place from which people seek to escape.

Internal migration of southern Italians to the north of the country poses challenges for citizens, politicians, and policymakers alike. For northern Italians, the influx of southerners into towns and cities in the wealthy north raises perceived threats of moral and social instability, as well as an erosion of living standards and employment opportunities. As a result, the arrival of southern Italians in the north of the country frequently spurs separatist and self-preservationist impulses based on a form of internal xenophobia.[89]

These socio-political responses are, of course, familiar from broader concerns about migration between the countries of the global South and the wealthier economies of the West. As with Italy's internal migration, the international movement of people stimulates nationalist and preservationist movements aimed at protecting the integrity of the social fabric, and at keeping strangers out. It plays a crucial role in the rise of populist movements in countries such as the United States, the United Kingdom, Sweden, Finland, and several European nations, including Italy, Austria, Hungary, Germany, and France.

The north-south problem in Italy may in other words be regarded as a local microcosm of broader challenges relating to the displacement of people. Indeed, for Inserra, the imbalance of power between the Italian north and south replicates larger colonial and orientalist relationships.[90] It results in the unequal distribution of rights and resources, and in a discourse of division built on alienation and cultural Othering. In this context, *tammurriata* and *pizzica* become representative of the politics of place and belonging both in Italy and across the global north-south divide. As musical forms emblematic of the rural economies and pre-industrialized cultural traditions of the south, their intertextual reproduction invokes the problematics of internal and foreign migration, displacement, and socio-cultural estrangement.

The politics of displacement articulated by the southern Italian intertexts may be read in conversation with a second set of musical quotations, these from southern Africa. "Wena ukhuluma kanjani" ("How do you speak") and "Sayiwela" ("We crossed over") are songs originating with the isiZulu people of South Africa and the Ndebele people of Zimbabwe, respectively. Miller and

---

[88] Inserra, *Global Tarantella*, 16–17.
[89] Inserra, *Global Tarantella*, 19.
[90] Inserra, *Global Tarantella*, 17.

190   Postcolonial Opera

Sibisi introduce the strains of these songs at various points in *Triumphs and Laments*, thereby expanding the geographical purview of the work to the so-called global South. Southern Italy thus emerges as one part of a dual "south"—the other being the southern hemisphere, and southern Africa specifically.

The first of the "African intertexts," "Wena ukhuluma kanjani," makes its appearance against a syncopated and polyrhythmic accompaniment of interlocking triplet figurations. It is sung as a rapid call and response between the second soprano soloist of the Triumph ensemble, Ann Masina, and Bham Ntabeni, the same group's tenor soloist. Replicating the traditional distribution of musical material between a song leader and chorus, Masina and Ntabeni exchange rapid sixteenth-note statements in a simple melodic figuration revolving around the interval of a major third.

Wena ukhuluma kanjani	English translation
Call:	*Call:*
Wen' ukhuluma kanjan'	How do you speak
Response:	
Wen' ukhuluma kanjan' simanxeba sinje	How do you speak with such wounds like this?
Wen' ukhulu makanjan'	How do you speak

Against Masina and Ntabeni's dialogue, the Triumphs chorus repeats a fragment of Rossi's motet on the words "talinu kinnóróteinu" ("we hung up our lyres"). Both the chorus and the soloists sing in a straightforward 4/4 meter, which sits uncomfortably atop the 12/8 triplet instrumental parts, and the 6/8 figurations of the bass drum. Here, metrical instability appears to underscore the disparate nature of the musical intertexts, which denote distinct cultural, historical, and geographic spheres. In this brief moment, the intercultural estrangement of the displaced subject makes itself heard through rhythmic and melodic incommensurability.

"Wena ukhuluma kanjani" is a traditional isiZulu warriors' song, forming part of the *ingoma* performance tradition.[91] It originates in the Zulu kingdom, situated in the KwaZulu-Natal province of South Africa. As a battle song, it interpolates the isiZulu people's celebrated history as a military force, which

---

[91] On *ingoma*, see Veit Erlmann, 1991, *African Stars: Studies in Black South African Performance*, Chicago, IL: University of Chicago Press, esp. chapter 4.

reached its apex under the leadership of Shaka kaSenzangakhona (c. 1787–1828), and which led to the rapid territorial expansion of the Zulu Empire. The battle histories of the isiZulu themselves led to the mass displacement of other Indigenous tribes, including the Nguni, the Hlubi, and the Ngwane.[92] By incorporating "Wena ukhuluma kanjani" into *Triumphs and Laments*, Miller and Sibisi hence invoke not only the strong relationship between place, ethnic identity, and musical practice in isiZulu culture and history, but also the dislocations enacted by this history. Sounding "Wena ukhuluma kanjani" in Triumphs, while locating the implied silence of "we hung up our lyres" in Laments, sets up a binary opposition between military conquest and defeat. It performs the conflict between experiences of triumphal destruction and the lament of vanquishment and displacement.

Triumphs and Laments' second African intertext also refers to a specific region of southern Africa. Here, place is explicitly named, as the song refers to the Limpopo River, which acts as a border between Zimbabwe and South Africa. The quoted material is from "Sayiwela," an *imbube* song of the Ndebele people of Zimbabwe.[93] "Sayiwela" describes the journey across the Limpopo River made by Ndebele laborers to work in the gold mines of South Africa. Miller and Sibisi only quote the first strophe of the song, which reflects on the reality of the journey and its ultimate goal:

Sayiwela	We crossed over
Sayiwela, sayiwela	We crossed over, we crossed over
sayiwela sibili	We really crossed over
Sayiwela Ingulukudela	We crossed the Limpopo River
siyofuna imali	To look for money

"Sayiwela" is again sung by Bham Ntabeni for the Triumphs ensemble. The fact that this song, with its gloomy description of economic migration, forms part of Triumphs' music incorporates a measure of ambiguity into the work's portrayal of dislocation. Whereas the other musical intertexts depict place as a privileged location of identity and belonging, one which, as "Wena ukhuluma kanjani" suggests, needs to be expanded by force, "Sayiwela" suggests that the loss of place need not necessarily be harmful. Instead, it may also act as a first

---

[92] For more on Shaka and his military campaigns, see Elizabeth A. Eldredge, 2014, *The Creation of the Zulu Kingdom, 1815–1828: War, Shaka, and the Consolidation of Power*, New York: Cambridge University Press.

[93] For *imbube* (or *mbube*), see Erlmann, *African Stars*, esp. Chapter 6.

step toward empowerment. I return to the ambivalent construction of displacement in *Triumphs and Laments'* music in the next section.

"Wena ukhuluma kanjani" and "Sayiwela" introduce the African continent as geographical sphere into *Triumphs and Laments*. Each quotation invokes a particular location, not only as place but also as an assemblage of precarious forms of being and belonging. Like its Italian counterpart, the African south here emerges as Other. It is far removed from the triumphant beauty of Rome. Appearing only in fragments and snatches of song, it seems forever half-remembered, more fractured than whole. Miller and Sibisi's repetition of the word "there" (e.g. 84–108; 146–151) underscores exactly how distant these Other places are, both physically and culturally. Not here, but there, they emerge as locations that are as much imagined (or remembered) as real.

Both the Italian South and African South are places from which people depart, rather than places of arrival. Instead of traditional Western opera's celebratory, assertive, or even colonial construction and appropriation of place—its insistent *here*-ness—*Triumphs and Laments* hence evokes place as something more ambiguous. It is both a site of self-assertion and a form of loss or a starting point for departure. Place emerges as both ideal and constraint: a site to mourn, but also a sphere to leave behind in search of better lives. This is not the monumental place of the opera house or Rome, the Eternal City. Rather than fixed, it appears mobile and mutable—a product of embodied practice, memory, and movement.

Movement

If movement in *Triumphs and Laments* is constitutive of a particular conception of place, it also articulates a visceral embodiment of displacement. Trapped in processional monotony, the work's performers draw attention to the perpetual motion of those who find themselves in voluntary or enforced homelessness. The piece embraces movement as an essential feature of both form and content. Indeed, as a processional opera, the work itself relies on locomotion for its realization. Despite its solemn onward trudge, however, I trace in *Triumphs and Laments* a more equivocal interpretation of the meaning and possibilities afforded by motion. The piece arguably imagines the ambulatory movement of its physical and projected bodies as both an articulation of dislocation and as a newly conceived form of postcolonial habitation.

Triumphs and Laments relies on different regimes of mobility to articulate the meaning of the places it remembers and (re)constructs. This is first and foremost a function of the performance site: stretching over 550 meters, the elongated "stage" left Kentridge and his collaborators with few alternatives other than to incorporate lateral movement—either by the audience or the performers—into the work. In other words, just as the performance creates a particular sense of place, the place itself also influences the form and content of the performance.

The most characteristic movement of the performance is the slow shuffle of the processional bodies. Though the bass drum rhythm that directs the cadence of the performance suggests something closer to a regulated funeral march, the assembled actors and musicians lumber forward in a haphazard, almost listless manner. Kentridge describes the particular type of movement articulated by the performers as a directorial decision spurred by earlier failed attempts at marching uniformity:

> [Working on the shadow procession] helped me understand why sacramental processions are so slow and measured: because this is what allows them to be controllable and manageable. . . . At first we tried to keep everyone walking in time, but it became so authoritarian, all steps moving and moving in sync. In the end, walking out of time in a slightly chaotic way became an important corrective.[94]

The shuffling movement of the performers, in other words, was a response to the sheer intractable scale of the performance. During the creative process, however, it also became an articulation of freedom—a reaction against the rigid and despotic connotations of enforced synchronicity. The very form of mobility in *Triumphs and Laments* hence resists simplistic readings of dislocation as oppressive or disempowering. Instead, the hobbling bodies appear to suggest that disorderly forward motion may also be a reclamation of agency and individuality.

Apart from asserting identity, the movement of the processing performers also produces a particular relationship with their environment. According to Tim Edensor, "Walking rhythms accommodate the contingencies of the ground underfoot, continuously becoming attuned to changing gradients, surfaces and textures."[95] From this intimate interaction with the pedestrian surface arises what Edensor describes as "a distinct, embodied material and sociable "dwelling-in-motion"," which may in turn result in "mobile homeliness."[96]

---

[94] Kentridge, in Basualdo and Kentridge, "In People's Memory," 67.
[95] Tim Edensor, 2010, "Walking in Rhythms: Place, Regulation, Style and the Flow of Experience," *Visual Studies* 25(1), 69–79, at 73.
[96] Edensor, "Walking," at 70.

Edensor's description echoes that of Tim Ingold, who argues that the feet are a source of knowledge and belonging. By walking, the subject makes sense of her surroundings.[97] In other words, ambulatory movement such as that performed in *Triumphs and Laments* becomes a form of quasi-improvisatory meaning-making, responsive to the specificities of the site and productive of a relationship between walker and ground. It is a form of inhabiting that produces its own rhythms.

Edensor's theorization of walking expands Martin Heidegger's notion of "dwelling," as developed by the philosopher in his 1951 lecture *Building Dwelling Thinking*.[98] Heideggerian dwelling captures the idea that mortal life is structured by the creation and inhabitation of meaningful places. Home— or any place for which one cares—becomes a site of spiritual and embodied presence and of intentional occupation. To dwell is to have a relationship with place. It is essential not only for well-being, but for the construction and articulation of the self. In short, for Heidegger, existence is itself a form of being-in-place.

For Mimi Sheller and John Urry, Heideggerian dwelling is misaligned with contemporary mobilities.[99] Sheller and Urry argue that Heidegger's theorization of dwelling foregrounds stasis, or what they call "sedentarism," as opposed to movement.[100] The philosopher hence appears to privilege the experiences of those who already enjoy access to stable sites of belonging. Heidegger himself writes that "the basic character of dwelling is to spare, to preserve.... [D]welling itself is always a staying with things."[101] Dwelling, in other words, entails remaining in place. The displaced person, caught in a cycle of arrival and departure, does not qualify for Heidegger's dwelling. Given the apparent placelessness of the refugee or the migrant, they only ever "move through," incapable of enacting meaning "in place." Only people who have already arrived get to dwell.

Louise Platt et al., however, resist interpretations of Heideggerian dwelling as necessarily static or enclosed. Expanding on Edensor's conception of the "mobile homeliness produced through walking," they argue that "it is movement in place, rather than merely through space, that enables a sense of dwelling to form and be maintained."[102] For Platt et al., movement is itself

---

[97] Tim Ingold, 2004, "Culture on the Ground: The World Perceived through the Feet," *Journal of Material Culture* 9(3), 315–340.

[98] Martin Heidegger, 1971, "Building, Dwelling, Thinking," in *Poetry, Language Thought*, trans. Albert Hostadter, New York: Harper Perennial, 141–160.

[99] Sheller and Urry, "New Mobilities Paradigm," 209.

[100] Sheller and Urry, "New Mobilities Paradigm," 209.

[101] Heidegger, "Building, Dwelling, Thinking," 150.

[102] Louise Platt, Dominic Medway, and Chloe Steadman, 2021, "Processional Walking: Theorising the 'Place' of Movement in Notions of Dwelling." *Geographical Research* 59(1), 106–117, at 115.

"a form of dwelling work" which produces a sense of being in place, whether by creating community, by fostering the interaction between sole and soil, or by allowing the environment to emerge as a product of sensory exploration and interaction. Dwelling, in other words, "can be conceived via the body and can be dynamic."[103] For Platt et al., as for Edensor, a more local conception of dwelling allows for a meaningful inhabitation of place to emerge simply in the act of setting foot to stone. Walking, as a form of meaning-making and a means of fostering relationships with place, thus offers a kind of mobile dwelling—a way of creating a home, even without staying. In this light, *Triumphs and Laments'* processional motion becomes more than just a depiction of refugees in transit. Rather, it suggests an inhabitation of place that is neither possessive nor permanent.

The notion of dwelling-in-motion, or mobile homeliness, complicates simplistic constructions of mobility as abject. In *Triumphs and Laments*, the embodied movements of the performers support a more multifaceted interpretation of the procession. Within the overwhelmingly wretched drudgery of the processional figures' shuffling march, actors occasionally break into frenzied dance, at once aggressive and ecstatic. Their gestures invoke the frantic movements of *pizzica*, while alleviating the monotony of the slow procession. The dancers' twirling bodies complicate overwhelmingly negative constructions of migration by offering glimpses of more jubilant and assertive forms of presence (a point to which I return below) and even—in the flailing limbs and unhindered motion of the figures—freedom.

Together with the dancers, the various sonic intertexts upon which Miller and Sibisi draw foreground distinct regimes of and approaches to movement. The southern Italian and southern African traditions quoted in *Triumphs and Laments* depict diverse places and cultures of inhabitation. Each of these frames mobility differently. In *pizzica*, movement becomes healing. The dancer engages in the agitated gestures of the *pizzica* to rid herself of physical or psychological affliction. In *tammurriata*, on the other hand, movement represents a form of labor—of inhabiting and cultivating land. "Wena ukhuluma kanjani" frames movement as conflict. Here, motion carries the potential for territorial expansion and conquest. Finally, in "Sayiwela," movement carries the possibility of empowerment, as migrant laborers seek work and income elsewhere. Traversing all these regimes of mobility is "Al naharot bavel," with its evocation of movement as displacement and loss. Musically, Miller and Sibisi thus cast *Triumphs and Laments'* procession in an equivocal

---

[103] Platt et al., "Processional Walking," 109.

196 Postcolonial Opera

light. Exposing the conflict between the desire to remain in place versus the desire to leave as a false contradiction, the score challenges the traditional portrayal of the migrant as victim. Like history, the music suggests, migration is neither a triumph nor a lament, but a bit of both.

If *Triumphs and Laments* frames displacement ambiguously, it also complicates the idea of migration as goal-directed movement. The procession, with its two bands moving in opposite directions, resists the teleology of departure and arrival. Both groups are on their way somewhere, but the goal is undefined—they are both coming and going at once. Andreas Huyssen describes this destabilization of directionality as "indetermination," and recognizes it as characteristic of Kentridge's processional works.[104] Whereas processions and marches normally "always have a goal," Huyssen argues, Kentridge's pieces acknowledge that "after a century of murderous utopias and the often violent waning of colonialism, . . . it is just not possible to name a goal or telos of the procession."[105] Maltz-Leca concurs, writing that Kentridge "portrays his processions as deeply ambiguous journeys, with numerous obstacles and multiple reversals."[106]

On the frieze itself, the reversals of which Maltz-Leca writes play out in the bearing of Kentridge's figures. Godby observes that the "general right-to-left movement towards the Ponte Sisto from the Ponte Mazzini is actually reversed halfway with . . . the Winged Victory that herself is turned around and now faces to the right."[107] Following the reversal of Winged Victory, directional movement appears to break down, with figures facing toward both Ponte Mazzini and Ponte Sisto apparently at random (though, in Godby's observation, with a predominant orientation back toward Ponte Mazzini).[108] Visually, then, forward and backward movement become undefined. They emerge as a function of perspective (depending on the direction from which the viewer approaches) rather than being structurally determined by a fixed beginning and endpoint. The destabilization of directionality thus allows the frieze to be experienced from right to left and from left to right without creating the impression that one course captures the artist's intentions better than the other. It also undercuts the notion of arrival, leaving the frieze suspended between coming and going.

---

[104] Andreas Huyssen, 2018, "Memories of Europe in the Art from Elsewhere," *Stedelijk Studies* 6, 1–10, at 8.

[105] Andreas Huyssen, 2017, "The Shadow Play as Medium of Memory in William Kentridge," in *William Kentridge*, October Files 21, ed. Rosalind Krauss, Cambridge, MA.: MIT Press, 77–98, at 80.

[106] Maltz-Leca, 2013, "Process/Procession," 179.

[107] Godby, "Unwritten History," 217.

[108] Godby, "Unwritten History," 217.

In the *Triumphs and Laments* performance, directionless movement is evoked especially by the formal features of the composition's musical intertexts, which rely on cyclicity and repetition rather than the harmonic development characteristic of much traditional Western opera. *Pizzica* and *tammurriata*, like traditional isiZulu and Ndebele call and response vocal traditions, work with durational forms that allow for improvisation and reiteration, resulting, in Inserra's observation, in "a trancelike obsessive quality" appropriate for the social and spiritual objectives of the music.[109]

Like the musical traditions it references, Miller and Sibisi's score also retains a cyclical character. The piece foregrounds non-teleology through its unwillingness to develop toward a triumphant finale, or indeed toward any point of arrival at all. Instead, in a coda based on the opening material of the work, the composition reiterates the irresolution and cyclicity of Kentridge's drawn procession. The Laments ensemble returns to long, static chordal lines that replicate the melodies and lyrics that launched the composition, while Triumphs performs rapid triplet movements undercut by a sixteenth-note violin ostinato. The Triumphs chorus repeats the words "al naharot" ("by the river") in a syncopated rhythmic contraction of Laments' melodic line. Rather than arriving, the piece seems to remain suspended in place, forever caught between "here" and "there."

The regimes of mobility enacted in *Triumphs and Laments* portray movement as a goal in itself—a form of dwelling that results in the meaningful inhabitation of place. The piece's foregrounding of locomotion complicates constructions of migration as a symptom of deprivation or disempowerment. Instead, *Triumphs and Laments* reiterates the perception that dwelling-in-motion may itself engender a form of indeterminate, but powerful, belonging.

Presence

In migratory contexts, the politics of inhabitation is fraught. As Mains et al. observe, migrants are often regarded as being "out of place." They are liminal figures vulnerable to deportation and displacement.[110] Their lack of citizenship and the impermanence of their being-in-place rob them of personhood

---

[109] On the cyclical nature of *tammurriata*, *pizzica*, and other musical traditions associated with tarantism, see Inserra, *Global Tarantella*, esp. 11–12.

[110] Susan P. Mains et al., 2013, "Postcolonial Migrations," *Social & Cultural Geography* 14(2), 131–144, at 132. See also Stephen E. Wilmer, 2018, *Performing Statelessness in Europe*, Cham: Springer, especially at 5.

198 Postcolonial Opera

and its concomitant rights and privileges.[111] But in *Triumphs and Laments*, this literal displacement is countered by what I would like to call an active form of "performative presencing." The artists parading along the bank of the Tiber impress themselves upon the processional site with an insistent sonic and visual presence. Thus, they assert both their own personhood and their right to be there.

In critic Michael Godby's description, *Triumphs and Laments'* music, lights, and performers combined "to express some demotic urge symbolically to re-claim and re-possess urban space."[112] This description echoes Judith Butler's assertion, in *Who Sings the Nation-State? Language, Politics, and Belonging*, that song "exposes the street as the site for free assembly." In Butler's description, "the song can be understood not only as the expression of freedom or the longing for enfranchisement—though it is, clearly, both those things—but also as restaging the street, enacting freedom of assembly precisely when and where it is explicitly prohibited by law."[113] Butler refers specifically to author-itarian contexts where the right to assemble in public is curtailed or legally controlled. However, the basic thrust of her argument remains relevant be-yond authoritarian contexts: the practice of collective singing, or of any form of sonic self-presencing, serves to reclaim place for those who would not nor-mally enjoy the privilege of unencumbered dwelling.

Where displaced persons are concerned, the act of impressing themselves physically or sonically on a particular site becomes a means of reclaiming per-sonhood, even where the host state denies it. In *Triumphs and Laments*, the shuffling, singing, dancing, and shouting bodies of the processional subjects hence enact a form of presencing that is itself politically empowering: through sound and movement, the marching groups reclaim their own subjectivity.

To be sure, this enactment of presence is not unique to Kentridge's piece. In recent years, migrant theater has become something of a genre, with nu-merous projects launched especially in continental Europe to allow displaced persons (including refugees and asylum seekers) to appear onstage, telling not only their own stories but also those belonging to Western canonical reper-toire.[114] These projects, some critics argue, award subjects with new forms of dignity and creative expression.[115] Thus, theatrical performance becomes a site of political empowerment.

---

[111] Wilmer, *Performing Statelessness*, 5.

[112] Godby, "Unwritten History," 221.

[113] Judith Butler, 2007, *Who Sings the Nation-State? Language, Politics, and Belonging*, London: Seagull Books, 62.

[114] See Wilmer, *Performing Statelessness*.

[115] See, Wilmer, *Performing Statelessness*, for a nuanced discussion of such views.

Triumphs and Laments is not simply another piece of migrant theater, however. Its generic framing as a processional opera inscribes the work into a specifically operatic rather than broadly theatrical tradition. In this context, the politics of performative presencing holds implications for the form. As discussed earlier, opera and its places are themselves constructed around practices of exclusion: the types of bodies permitted to sound on the operatic stage, the types of sounds these bodies are allowed to make, and the types of audiences permitted to listen are all defined by a set of implicit valuations that cohere around ideals of cultural citizenship and belonging. *Triumphs and Laments*, however, challenges the rules of operatic presence. Its range of voice types, singing styles, and musical traditions, all of which are presented in a public place reconfigured as an operatic stage, reach beyond the places and practices normally associated with the form. Allowing its subjects to claim physical and sonic presence by means of a reconfigured music-theatrical imaginary, the piece impresses the figure of the displaced subject not only onto the site of Rome but also onto the site of opera.

The disconnect between what happens in the theater and outside of it remains an obstacle to the practical realization of the rights and freedoms imagined for the migrant subject on stage. Theaters and opera houses remain insular spaces, enclosed in relative privilege, and insulated from the realities of intolerance by strictly enforced codes of behavior and rules regarding who is allowed entry. As Pieter Verstraete shows, the enactment of migrant stories on stage does little to curb the perceived hostility of the outside world.[116] Here, the outward orientation of *Triumphs and Laments*—appearing outdoors, in a public place—serves as a very real instance of "claiming the streets," not only symbolically, but also practically. In the form of processional opera, the mobile performers recast the public walkway as a theatre-for-all; an endorsement of cultural, social, and geographical belonging that exceeds the confines of legal citizenship.

But this is a split belonging. The sonic intertexts, with their evocation of places far from Rome, inscribe performers and listeners in two places at once. Referencing diverse styles and cultural formations, the hybrid score offers multiple belongings beyond the singular constructions of place and identity associated with citizenship. Singing of Jerusalem while exiled in Babylon, singing of the countryside while shuffling through the city: each song brings together the different places and inhabitations that make the subject who she is.

---

[116] Pieter Verstraete, 2013, "Turkish Post-Migrant 'Opera' in Europe: A Socio-Historical Perspective on Aurality," in *The Legacy of Opera: Reading Music Theatre as Experience and Performance*, ed. Dominic Symonds and Pamela Karantonis, Boston: Brill, 185–207.

200 Postcolonial Opera

It is difficult not to interpret the multifaceted construction of domicile and occupancy in *Triumphs and Laments* as a foil to the singular belonging required by nationalist responses to migration. As Mains et al. argue, the politics of belonging has become "increasingly territorialized, securitized and penalized in receiving contexts."[117] Prospective residents must prove that they belong and that they are worthy (and trustworthy) occupants of the national domain. In this climate of territorial defensiveness, Mains et al. continue, "multiple identifications and contested affiliation are to be muffled; congealed into a publicly expressed singular narrative of belonging." Those who do not form part of the unitary formation are necessarily deprived of subjectivity and presence.

Triumphs and Laments challenges the singularity of citizenship. With its multiple identifications and belongings, the piece defies what Sara Ahmed et al. call "the immediacy of location as a discrete entity."[118] Rather, multiplicity constitutes presence. Kentridge's work resists portraying the migrant experience as a function of movement "between two distinct national formations, 'here' and 'there.'"[119] Instead, it opts to find "here" everywhere.

If *Triumphs and Laments* offers its subjects a form of presence in opposition to territorial and nationalist narratives of citizenship, the piece nonetheless acknowledges that such belonging is fleeting. Both the performance and the frieze are ephemeral. The procession peters out after approximately forty minutes. The frieze disappeared after four years. Despite their monumental and immersive occupation of visual and sonic space, both remained subject to the forces of time that ultimately turned them into nothing more than memories. But this evanescence need not necessarily be negative. Guercio interprets it instead as an explicit incorporation of time into the historical project. "With Kentridge," Guercio writes, "the memory or *monumentum* no longer alludes to the presence of a majestic, indelible identity, with the superlative capacity to endure now and forever. . . . Rather than aspiring to stably occupy space, Kentridge's Roman project expresses and fosters a desire to experience both the unfolding of time, and time itself as an unfolding."[120] Whereas *Refuse the Hour* articulates, or even critiques time, then, *Triumphs and Laments* marks its progression as a natural occurrence that shapes the subject's relationship with place.[121] The transitory nature of the piece resists the fetishization of

---

[117] Mains et al., "Postcolonial Migrations," 134.

[118] Sara Ahmed et al., eds., 2003, *Uprootings/Regroundings: Questions of Home and Migration*, Oxford: Berg, 4.

[119] Ahmed et al., *Uprootings*, 4.

[120] Guercio, "Paradoxical Monumentality," 135.

[121] See Chapter 4 for a discussion *Refuse the Hour* and the construction of time.

rootedness or duration, revealing instead that being and belonging do not require permanence.

As a processional opera, *Triumphs and Laments* draws together issues relating to physical and cultural displacement, the politics of belonging, and the territoriality of both the nation and the operatic form. The work's engagement with place and its depiction of different kinds of mobility—both abject and empowering—invite critical consideration of the role of performance in subaltern dwelling. Additionally, the processional form of the performance compels the viewer to "walk alongside" the Other and to listen not as stranger but as a fellow traveler. In Bhabha's words, "To perceive that we come after an other whoever he may be—that is ethics."[122] Or as Cox argues, in a statement that echoes Bhabha's notion of "processional ethics," "The relationship between looker and looked-upon within these aestheticized contexts is mediated by processional codes that make lookers visible as both presentational and representational bodies—both activist and symbolic."[123] In other words, the performative procession initiates an exchange between the mobile and the static subject, which ultimately reiterates the mutuality and reciprocity of the processional event.

Engaging issues of mobility and marginalization from a site itself become marginalized by the forces of nature that are currently responsible for mass displacement, Kentridge's processional opera imagines a way of making place with and for the displaced. By combining different regimes of mobility and sonic inhabitation, *Triumphs and Laments* reconfigures opera's participation in the making of place. Imprinting the embodied presence of the mobile subject upon the revered site of both city and opera, the piece reconsiders the politics of belonging and suggests that even the apparently homeless subject may get to dwell.

[122] Bhabha, "Processional Ethics," n.p.
[123] Cox, "Processional Aesthetics," 496.

6
Totality

Colonialism may be regarded as a form of totalitarianism. The colonial agenda pursued total territorial control: it sought to map the entire globe and to bring it under the power of a small group of economic, religious, and political rulers. In its simplest articulation, colonial totality was an initiative to become masters of all lands and seas.[1] Along the way, it became an all-consuming force, bringing under total domination not only physical geographies but also persons, histories, cultures, and ways of knowing. As I have observed repeatedly throughout this book, nothing escaped the effects of colonialism. Its consequences were felt in metropole and colony alike. As a political and economic regime, colonialism was everywhere.

However, even as colonizers claimed total control over reality, memory, the past, and the future, their actions resulted in fragmentation. Geographical control broke up land, and cultural control splintered communal and individual identities. Rather than integration and unification, colonialism hence engendered disintegration. The colonial project may have been shaped by totalitarianism, but its effect was less coalescent than anticipated. Colonialism spread as an uncomfortable, and often uncontainable, interplay between unity and division; control and unruliness; completeness and fissure.

In the postcolony, the interplay between totality and fragmentation remains. The totalitarian ambitions of the colonial project persist into the postcolonial present, where competing political and economic interests rely on inherited practices of totality to produce and consolidate power.[2] As Achille Mbembe observes, postcolonial regimes (*commandement*), pursue and enact a totality that, in its complete control over time, space, ritual, and bodies, effects a politics of excess, enchantment, virility, and grand theater.[3] Seeking to consolidate its power in the wake of independence from colonial rule, *commandement* dramatizes its own magnificence. It constructs an all-encompassing social order governed by itself; one in which those in power aggregate to themselves

[1] See Eve Tuck and K. Wayne Yang, 2012, "Decolonization Is not a Metaphor," *Decolonization: Indigeneity, Education & Society* 1(1), 1–40 on colonialism as primarily a geopolitical project.

[2] See Achille Mbembe, 2001, *On the Postcolony*, trans. Laurent Dubois, Los Angeles: University of California Press.

[3] Mbembe, *On the Postcolony*, 104.

Postcolonial Opera. Juliana M. Pistorius, Oxford University Press. © Oxford University Press 2025.
DOI: 10.1093/oso/9780197749203.003.0007

absolute authority over both life and death. Simultaneously, however, the "chaotically pluralistic" nature of the postcolonial sphere makes it impossible to create "a single, permanently stable system out of all the signs, images, and markers current in the postcolony."[4] The effect is of a society, much like the colony, governed by competing forces of integration and fracture, of control and instability. In the postcolonial present, totality is both an ideal and a curse.

Opera carries its own histories of totality. In the West, these are inextricably intertwined with Richard Wagner and his vision of a unified artwork of the future. Ever since the German composer articulated his dream of a society consolidated within the total aesthetic experience of *Gesamtkunstwerk*, opera has been unable to escape discourses of totality. Exceeding the very practical intermedial integration of the genre's constitutive arts, Western operatic totality summons an ambivalent discourse of political control, historical curation, and aesthetic de-hierarchization.[5] As the thorny legacy of Wagner's *Gesamtkunstwerk* attests, narratives of operatic totality cannot easily be separated from more sinister political histories of totality and totalitarianism.

In large swaths of both the West and the so-called Global South, Wagner's *Gesamtkunstwerk* and twentieth-century artists' attempts either to resist or to rehabilitate the form remain the touchstone for integrative theater practices. But operatic totality may also be approached from an Indigenous framework. Here, the total work of art translates into an integrative approach to traditional performance, which combines different artistic genres into communal acts of celebration, narration, and cultural identification.

I gestured toward the tradition of African total theater in Chapter 1, where I discussed extra-colonial genealogies of musical storytelling on the African continent. In this chapter, I return to the concept of African total theater, to read it in dialogue with Wagnerian and post-Wagnerian aesthetic practices and discourses. African total theater offers an opportunity to expand discussions of operatic totality beyond a purely Western perspective. It also, I would like to argue, complicates the relationship between histories of colonial totality and operatic totality in the postcolonial present. If operatic totality serves, first, as an aesthetic counterpart to the integrative (and exclusionary) ideal of political totality, and second as a remnant of extra-colonial cultural traditions, then total theater must have a role to play in processing the ongoing negotiation between totality and fracture that characterizes the postcolony.

---

[4] Mbembe, *On the Postcolony*, 108.
[5] Matthew Wilson Smith, 2007, *The Total Work of Art: From Bayreuth to Cyberspace*, New York: Routledge, offers a compelling analysis of the extra-musical valences that attach to the total work of art in contemporary discourse.

The complex dynamic of (post)colonial totality and fragmentation raises intractable questions regarding the social and political significance of opera and the total work of art in the postcolony. What does it mean to think of operatic totality in a postcolonial sphere that still bears the wounds of colonial totality? What does total theater do in a political sphere marked by fracture? The relationship between opera and political legacies of totalitarianism compels the researcher to ask whether the art form can recover the fragmented histories produced by colonial totality. By extension, it bears asking whether the total work of art can reintegrate those persons, cultures, and epistemologies excluded from the social unit by a colonial system built on dehumanization.

In this chapter, I examine the postcolonial affordance of operatic totality through the lens of Kentridge's First World War commemoration piece, *The Head & the Load*. Kentridge has emerged as something of an emblematic figure in current discourses of the total work of art.[6] As I mentioned in the Introduction to this book, the artist's name often appears in discussions of contemporary *Gesamtkunstwerk*, and individual works (as well as his oeuvre as a whole) have been characterized as instances of the form. A 2019–2020 exhibition on the topic of *Gesamtkunstwerk* at the Centre Pompidou-Metz, titled *Opera as the World: The Quest for a Total Work of Art*, held up Kentridge's work as paradigmatic of operatic totality.[7]

The Head & the Load itself has, since its first performance in 2018, been described as a *Gesamtkunstwerk* by several critics.[8] But the work also draws attention, in both its form and its content, to the various types of fracture visited upon the colony and postcolony by the colonial project. I approach *The Head & the Load* as a theater piece that simultaneously engages and destabilizes legacies of operatic totality—both African and Western. The work's overwhelming, almost all-consuming scope, alongside its integrative approach to visual and sonic performance, contrasts with a fragmented narrative structure

[6] I follow Matthew Wilson Smith in using "total work of art" and "*Gesamtkunstwerk*" interchangeably. See Smith, *Total Work of Art*.

[7] Centre Pompidou-Metz, "Opera as the World," https://www.centrepompidou-metz.fr/en/programme/categorie/opera-as-the-world.

[8] See, for instance, Eileen Blumenthal, 2018, "What One Show Can Carry: William Kentridge's *The Head and the Load*," *American Theatre*, December 14, https://www.americantheatre.org/2018/12/14/what-one-show-can-carry-william-kentridges-the-head-and-the-load/; Hein Janssen, 2018, "William Kentridge snijdt een cruciaal onderwerp aan in *The Head and the Load*, maar een duidelijke dramatische lijn ontbreekt (drie sterren)," *de Volkskrant*, August 12, https://www.volkskrant.nl/cultuur-media/william-kentridge-snijdt-een-cruciaal-onderwerp-aan-in-the-head-and-the-load-maar-een-duidelijke-dramatische-lijn-ontbreekt-drie-sterren~b6dcdd6f/?referer=https%3A%2F%2Fwww.google.com%2F; John Rockwell, 2018, "In a Vast Space, Tragic Spectacle Floods the Senses," *Classical Voice North America*, October 12, https://classicalvoiceamerica.org/2018/12/10/in-a-vast-space-an-epic-spectacle-to-beguile-senses/; and Louisa Buck, "William Kentridge Outplays the England Match with Tate Premiere of Performance The Head and the Load," *Art Newspaper*, July 12, 2018, https://www.theartnewspaper.com/blog/william-kentridge-outplays-the-england-match-with-tate-premiere-of-the-head-and-the-load.

and a disparate geographical and historical frame of reference. Thus, the piece simultaneously enacts and undermines histories of operatic totality.

Like the other works analyzed in this book, *The Head & the Load* engages directly with colonial history. But indirectly, it also contemplates the political and ethical work of an artistic form such as *Gesamtkunstwerk* in the postcolony. Contrasting diverse histories and theories of artistic totality from European and African perspectives and putting these in dialogue with the legacies of political totality in colonial and postcolonial spaces, I follow *The Head & the Load*'s lead to think about opera's role in processing colonial histories of totalitarianism.

Background

The Head & the Load was co-commissioned by 14-18 NOW: WWI Centenary Commissions (UK), Park Avenue Armory (New York City), Ruhrtriennale (Germany), and MASS MoCa (North Adams, Massachusetts) as part of a program of events commemorating the centenary of the First World War.[9] Collaboratively developed by William Kentridge (concept and director), Philip Miller (composer), Thuthuka Sibisi (co-composer and music director), Gregory Maqoma (choreographer), Sabine Theunissen (set designer), and Greta Goiris (costume designer), the ninety-minute multimedia spectacle, set on a 55-meter-long stage and featuring a cast of twenty, with an additional fourteen musicians all on stage, premiered at the Tate Modern museum in London on July 11, 2018.

Played out over three acts (titled "Manifestos," "Paradox," and "War"), *The Head & the Load* combines dance, music, speech, video projections, and processional motion. The piece is performed by a cast of mobile sculptures, shadows, singers, dancers, and musicians. Behind them, a colossal backdrop is brought alive throughout with projections of text, images, archival footage, and shadow figures. Like most of Kentridge's productions, the piece does not follow a narrative trajectory. Instead, it offers a series of impressions assembled as if at random to form a vast, confrontational warscape.

Kentridge's work trains its gaze on those who carried—literally—the war effort in Africa. It depicts the experiences of Black Africans forcefully recruited as porters in service of the British, French, and German colonial armies. These men accompanied troops across the African continent, carrying supplies, weapons, and other forms of cargo required for the ongoing

---

[9] See *The Head & the Load*'s website, https://www.theheadandtheload.com.

conflict. *The Head & the Load*'s title refers explicitly to the labor of these forgotten subjects. Derived from a Ghanaian proverb, "The head and the load are the troubles of the neck," it refers to the burdened existence of those tasked with carrying. The proverb also invokes the integration between the mental and the physical, implying that what goes on in the mind burdens the body. For Homi Bhabha, the title's metaphorical affordance gestures toward "the load of history, the head-load of carrier labor, the burden of the war, the psychic load of colonial humiliation, racism and indignity."[10] It hence combines the physical conditions of war and colonialism with the psychological effects and historical impacts of these systems of conquest and exploitation.

Little is known about the First World War's African porters. Forcefully recruited from local communities to stand in for the continent's insufficient transport infrastructures, they were little more than human freightage, responsible for conveying the cargo of war. Historians are unable to measure accurately the number of men conscripted to such service by the French, British, and German colonial powers, but they do know that these subjects were deprived of sufficient nutrition, clothing, and shelter; forced to traverse vast stretches of inhospitable terrain carrying inhumanly heavy loads on their backs; and often used as cannon fodder during skirmishes.[11] Estimates place the figure of fatalities associated with carrying well in excess of 200,000.[12]

Kentridge regards the First World War as a culminating episode of the colonial project. The artist describes the conflict as "the completion of the Conference of Berlin and the rearrangement of the map of Africa."[13] At the end of the war, German colonies were reallocated to French, British, Portuguese, and Belgian control. Thus, Europe's conflict enabled the redistribution of Africa. *The Head & the Load*'s engagement with the history and legacy of the First World War is therefore also an engagement with the history and legacy of European colonialism.

When he started work on *The Head & the Load*, the artist had just completed *Triumphs and Laments* (2016).[14] At first, Kentridge and his team planned to replicate the processional format of the Rome piece, albeit on a smaller scale. Two bands, one representing Europe and the other Africa, would march

[10] Homi K. Bhabha, 2020, "Theater of War: *Din und Drang* in *The Head & the Load*," in *The Head & the Load*, ed. William Kentridge, Paris: Éditions Xavier Barral, 301–316, at 303.

[11] See David Killingray and James Matthews, 1979, "Beasts of Burden: British West African Carriers in the First World War," *Canadian Journal of African Studies* 13(1–2), 5–23; Michèle Barrett, 2017, "Dehumanization and the War in East Africa," *Journal of War & Culture Studies* 10(3), 238–252.

[12] David Olusoga, 2018, Program note, *The Head & the Load*, 13.

[13] William Kentridge, 2020, "Thirty Thoughts on *The Head & the Load*," in *The Head & the Load*, ed. William Kentridge, Paris: Éditions Xavier Barral, 283–293, at 283. For more on the Berlin Conference, see Chapter 4.

[14] See Chapter 5 for *Triumphs and Laments*.

toward each other across the 50-meter stage, culminating in a confrontation between the opposing forces. However, the processional format did not provide sufficient scope for variety over the span of ninety minutes, so it was replaced by a series of tightly structured set pieces incorporating movement, music, and spoken word.[15] Ultimately, the procession was limited to one scene in which porters carrying cardboard cutouts traverse the stage from left to right, casting huge shadows onto the backdrop. This scene, titled "Procession to War," functions as something of a centerpiece of the production and offers a visual realization of the work's historical subject matter. It also sets up a link between *The Head & the Load* and Kentridge's other processional pieces such as *Triumphs and Laments* (see Chapter 5), *More Sweetly Play the Dance* (2015), and *Notes Towards a Model Opera* (2015), thereby contributing to the sense of intertextual integration that characterizes the artist's oeuvre.

The Head & the Load's libretto is assembled from a variety of fragments derived from European and African sources. These bits of text include quotes from Frantz Fanon's *The Wretched of the Earth* (1961), the Reverend John Chilembwe's famed open letter protesting Africans' involvement in the war (1914), Setswana proverbs from Sol Plaatje's 1916 collection, and fragments from a Swahili phrase book.[16] They also incorporate notes from an English colonial marching handbook, sections from a war speech by Germany's Kaiser Wilhelm II, a French translation of Wilfred Owen's "Anthem for Doomed Youth" (1917), quotations from Tristan Tzara's *Dada Manifesto 1918*, and Kurt Schwitters's *Ursonate* (1932).[17] The intertexts appear unattributed and are often translated or altered beyond easy recognition. In Kentridge's description, the source material is "cut-up, interleaved and expanded" to create a collage of discrepant statements performed in English, Swahili, Siswati, German, French, and nonsense.[18] Citing recognizable (though often disguised) signifiers from European high modernism and African independence struggles, the work paints a historical canvas that spans discrepant aesthetic, temporal, and political worlds.

Visually, the piece develops a sense of collage. On the backdrop, drawings in Kentridge's characteristic black and white charcoal style are overlaid onto maps and pages of books. Torn pieces of paper, reassembled into new forms,

---

[15] Philip Miller, interview with the author, May 13, 2020.

[16] Chilembwe's letter, "The Voice of African Natives in the Present War," was published in the *Nyasaland Times* on November 26, 1914; the full text can be found in Kenneth R. Ross, ed., 2020, *Christianity in Malawi: A Source Reader*, Mzuzu: Mzuni Press, 247–249. Sol Plaatje's collection of Setswana proverbs is published as *Sechuana Proverbs, with Literal Translations and Their European Equivalents; Diane Tsa Secoana le Maele a Sekgooa a a Dumalanang naco*, London: K. Paul, Trench, Trubner and Co., 1916.

[17] The war speech is Kaiser Wilhelm's call to war, delivered on August 6, 1914.

[18] Kentridge, 2018, Program Note, *The Head & the Load*, 3.

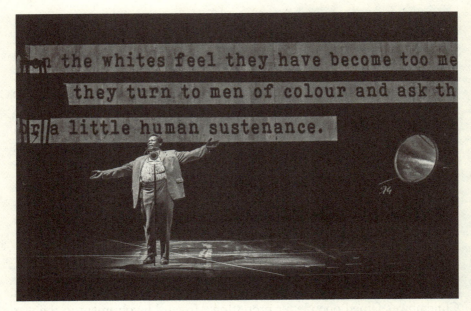

Figure 6.1 Mncedisi Shabangu in *The Head & the Load.* Photograph: Stella Olivier. Courtesy of William Kentridge Studio.

and bits of typewritten text pasted apparently haphazardly onto drawings of idealized landscapes all contribute to an impression of cluttered assemblage rather than unified coherence. Kentridge also incorporates archival footage of African conscripts completing military training and transcripts of archival documents bearing lists of names and goods involved in the conflict.

Contrasting with the monochrome background, Sabine Theunissen's and Greta Goiris's props and costumes fill the stage with bright colors and exaggerated shapes. The props incorporate Kentridge's familiar visual codes, including telegraph poles, megaphones, gramophone horns, and various uncanny automata. These sculptural creations shift around the stage to serve as platforms, lookout posts, containers, and carriages bearing colonial officers, yoked to the backs of Black porters.

Like the props, the actors embody a selection of larger-than-life figures. Mncedisi Shabangu, clad in a yellow corduroy jacket, represents resistance to war and to the colonial project (see Figure 6.1).[19] Incorporating Chilembwe's and Fanon's words, he reflects on wartime recruitment practices, porters'

---

[19] In *The Head & the Load*'s published libretto, performers' names, rather than their characters, are used in the designation of dialogue. I replicate this practice here. See William Kentridge, ed., 2020, *The Head & the Load*, Paris: Éditions Xavier Barral.

Figure 6.2 Hamilton Dlamini in *The Head & the Load*. Photograph: Stella Olivier. Courtesy of William Kentridge Studio.

experiences, and, finally, death. Against Shabangu's harrowing testimonies, Hamilton Dlamini and Luc De Wit appear as farcical villains. Dlamini, wearing a bright blue uniform with exaggerated golden epaulettes and a cap perched at a jaunty angle, embraces war with self-indulgent satisfaction (see Figure 6.2). "I sit down to a good German breakfast," he claims, "good beer, plenty of eggs, cream and asparagus. If you don't get rich in this war, you don't

Figure 6.3 Nhlanhla Mahlangu, Hamilton Dlamini, and Luc De Wit in *The Head & the Load*. Photograph: Stella Olivier. Courtesy of William Kentridge Studio.

deserve to live through it."[20] De Wit, as a bare-legged, khaki-clad French general, insists on safeguarding the lavish colonial aesthetic of his country (see Figure 6.3). Speaking in French, he dreams of "mak[ing] a tower of the opulence of words, made from the diamonds and oil, the silk and cotton, from all the exotic produce of the colonies." Nhlanhla Mahlangu appears first as a military officer, but later as a bare-chested, barefoot porter wearing a pleated paper skirt (see Figure 6.4). Voice artist Joanna Dudley performs as Kaiser Wilhelm II with an eagle-shaped helmet on her head (a sardonic reference to the *Pickelhaube*) (see Figure 6.5).

Musically, composers Philip Miller and Thuthuka Sibisi replicate Kentridge's juxtaposition of modernist references with colonial artifacts. Quotations from a cohort of composers as diverse as Wagner, Fritz Kreisler, Paul Hindemith, Arnold Schoenberg, and Eric Satie ring out against sonic signifiers evocative of an African imaginary, broadly conceived. Miller and Sibisi describe their composition as follows:

> Using collage as a tool we move from a cabaret song by Schoenberg, intercut with percussive slaps on hymn books, to a Viennese waltz by Fritz Kreisler. Amidst this

---

[20] Kentridge, dir., 2018, *The Head & the Load*, Recorded: London, Tate Modern, July 2018 (public performance), video recording, private archive of William Kentridge.

Figure 6.4 Nhlanhla Mahlangu in *The Head & the Load*. Photograph: Stella Olivier. Courtesy of William Kentridge Studio.

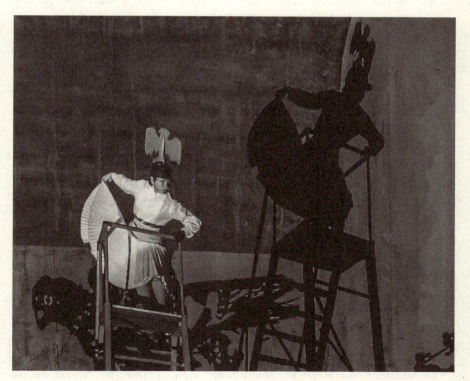

Figure 6.5 Joanna Dudley in *The Head & the Load*. Photograph: Stella Olivier. Courtesy of William Kentridge Studio.

212 Postcolonial Opera

tension and instability, Africa talks back to Europe through rhythmic war songs and chants, deliberately resisting the raucous musical soundscapes of the European avant-garde.[21]

Each section confronts the audience with a near-incomprehensible cacophony of sounds and images (see Table 6.1). During Act 2, "Einleitung und Lied: Breite Halbe" and "Ziemlich Lebhafte Viertel," numbers 1 and 8 from Paul Hindemith's *Klaviermusik* Op. 37, Vol. 2 (1926), are transformed into extensive ensemble pieces. In the first act, military exercises are accompanied by a rousing rendition of "Nachtwandler" from Arnold Schoenberg's *Brettl-Lieder* (1901).

In between, sirens, shots, and explosions intermingle with the pointillistic sounds of morse code, the operatic strains of soprano Ann Masina's voice, and the quiet reverberations of a Guinean kora. Juxtaposing an imagined soundscape of colonial Africa with archetypical signifiers of European late Romanticism and early modernism, the piece thus launches its own sonic assault on unitary accounts of early twentieth-century aesthetics and politics.

Despite the fractured nature of *The Head & The Load*'s collage impulse, several critics eagerly described the piece as a twenty-first-century *Gesamtkunstwerk*. This comparison is not entirely arbitrary. The intermedial integration of text, score, and scenography, and even the construction of a special stage large enough to accommodate the action, all resemble a Wagnerian ethos of aesthetic absoluteness. Moreover, Kentridge's application of techniques more readily associated with twentieth-century theatrical plurality, such as Bernd Alois Zimmermann's "virtual simultaneity," and Laszlo Moholy-Nagy's "mechanized eccentric," clearly invokes the heritage of the total work of art.[22]

But if the description of *The Head & the Load* as a total work of art is characteristic of Kentridge reception, it nonetheless seems unable to account for the piece's fragmented aesthetic. *The Head & the Load* resists totality. Rather than integration, the work foregrounds contradiction, juxtaposition, and dissolution. It constructs an intermedial form assembled from splinters and coarsely-sutured shreds; the overall impression is of disintegration rather than unification. If, as critics argue, *The Head & the Load* is a total work of art, it is one that complicates the very notion of totality. Kentridge's piece

---

[21] Philip Miller and Thuthuka Sibisi, 2018, Program Note, *The Head & the Load*, 5.
[22] See Schröder, "Total Theatre and Music Theatre," especially 37–45, for Zimmermann and Moholy-Nagy.

Totality **213**

Table 6.1 Schematic Outline of *The Head & the Load*'s Structure

Act	Scene	Sonic content
1. Manifestos	Manifestos	Vocal siren; spoken word
	Morsecode/Swahili Phrasebook	Spoken word; high-pitched strings; rhythmic clicking; followed spoken call and response accompanied by rhythmic violin figure
	Ursonate	Kurt Schwitters, *Ursonate*, performed as trio
	Orders and Commands	Arnold Schoenberg, "Nachtwandler" from *Brettl-Lieder* (1901)
	Recruiting	Spoken word; rhythmic scraping sound on string instrument
	Procession to war	Kora ostinato; opera; brass band; chorus; mounting sonic chaos
2. Paradox	Eight things	Spoken word accompanied by Paul Hindemith, "Einleitung und Lied" from *Klaviermusik* Op. 37
	Troubles of the body	Paul Hindemith, "Ziemlich lebhafte Viertel" from *Klaviermusik* Op.37, arranged for piano, brass and percussion; mosquito sounds
	Chilembwe's letter	Spoken word interspersed with descending chorus exclamations and orchestral punctuation
	Playing against history	Foot stomping, clapping, whistle, in the style of *isicathulo* (gumboot dancing), accompanied by snare drum
	God Save the King	Fragmented rendition of "God Save the King"
	Amakatsi	Loud percussion; shouting; kwela chord progression on the accordion; chorus
3. War	Kaiser Waltz	Fritz Kreisler, "Liebesleid" (1905), accompanied by spoken word and bird-like shrieks
	Running	Spoken word; panting; breathing and scratching sounds from orchestra
	Running and Falling	Call and response between soprano and chorus on the words "Ngo-damn abelungu" (White people be damned!)
	Je te veux	Eric Satie, "Je te veux," accompanied by warbling bird sounds
	Wounded man	Kora lament
	Advanced arithmetic	Spoken word; looped string figures; eventually shouts, vocal gun sounds, brass exclamations; mounting sonic chaos
	Return from war procession	Traditional Mpondo song, "Kwanukimpi"
	Independence	Spoken word
	Coda/Death list	Spoken word

therefore offers an opportunity to reconsider what operatic totality might mean. Moreover, given its thematic engagement with a history of colonial exploitation, the work invites the viewer to ask what the tension between operatic integration and breakdown might represent in a postcolonial context.

Operatic Totality

In 2017 the online publication *artnet* proclaimed the return of the *Gesamtkunstwerk*.[23] Observing a surge in visual artists turning to the operatic stage, critic Naomi Rea heralded a renaissance of the integrative ideals championed by Wagner and his "artwork of the future." Rea identified two key factors driving the apparent reawakening of a Wagnerian aesthetics of totality in opera. The first: a new appetite for scenographic experimentation among an aging opera establishment. The second: the financial and material possibilities the genre offers for artists relying on an increasingly insecure economic environment.

Of course, rather than seeing a resurgence, some commentators may argue that the *Gesamtkunstwerk* never really went away. Indeed, experiments with totality have preoccupied Euro-American musical avant-gardes throughout the twentieth and twenty-first centuries.[24] On the popular front, increasingly elaborate recording practices and stadium-filling world tours by megastars from Meatloaf to Beyoncé have inspired critics to reach for Wagnerian terms when describing their subjects' multimedia experiments.[25] And in traditional opera, the phenomenon of visual artists working on productions—a criterion, it seems, for critics interested in *Gesamtkunstwerk*—has been a mainstay of institutions since the nineteenth century.[26]

Today, new forms of theatrical multimedia generate greater possibilities than ever for scenographic experimentation and spectacle. The surge in digital arts and immersive technologies on the operatic stage has enabled directors

[23] Naomi Rea, 2017, "The Return of the Gesamtkunstwerk? Why Contemporary Artists Are Flocking to the Opera House," *artnet*, August 23. https://news.artnet.com/art-world/opera-contemporary-art-1047605.

[24] Julia H. Schröder, 2019, "Total Theatre and Music Theatre: Tracing Influences from Pre- to Post-War Avant-Gardes," in *New Music Theatre in Europe: Transformation Between 1955–1975*, ed. Robert Adlington, London: Routledge, 33–51.

[25] On Beyoncé and *Gesamtkunstwerk*, see Sahanika Ratnayake, 2018, "Beyoncé and the New Gesamtkunstwerk," *3:am magazine*, October 1, https://www.3ammagazine.com/3am/beyonce-and-the-new-gesamtkunstwerk/; on Meatloaf, see Rakewell, 2022, "A Total Artist—In Memoriam Meatloaf," *Apollo*, January 21, https://www.apollo-magazine.com/meat-loaf-bat-out-of-hell-gesamtkunstwerk/.

[26] Denise Wendel Poray's *Painting the Stage: Artists as Stage Designers* (2018, Milan: Skira) offers a lavishly illustrated survey of the relationship between opera and visual artists.

and designers to reach beyond the simple integration of sound and scenery to create immersive experiences that complicate already fraught notions of liveness, authenticity, and embodiment. These technologies and the directorial prospects they offer doubtlessly play a role in the resurgence of interest in the total work of art.

Alongside preoccupations with *Gesamtkunstwerk* in European theater, a discourse of total theater on the African continent has begun to draw the attention of scholars and practitioners working in opera and theater across cultural and geographical settings.[27] Though not new, the notion of the African total work of art is gradually drawing engagement as an Indigenous counterpart to Wagner's legacy.

According to theater historian Praise Zenenga, the concept of African total theater characterizes discourse on theater practices across the continent. Zenenga describes the genre as "a cohesive integration of cross-disciplinary expressive forms where theater, dance, and music do not exist in isolation but in a continuum that combines multiple performance modes into a unified whole."[28] This description applies just as well to the genre's Western counterpart. The difference, Zenenga argues, is in the uniqueness of the historical experiences that give rise to African theater, as well as "the perpetuation of a predominantly integrative aesthetic paradigm," rather than an approach that conceives of music, dance, and acting as separate traditions.[29]

South African author and librettist Zakes Mda reiterates a conception of performance that does not distinguish between different art forms. Describing African total theater as "the Common Festival," Mda confirms that local cultural traditions approach music, dancing, acting, sculpture, painting, performance and spectatorship as one single, integrated expressive practice. He calls this assemblage by the Sesotho word, *bonunu*, or "art."[30]

Meanwhile, celebrated Ghanaian playwright and director, Mohammed Ben Abdallah, speaks of "Abibigro," which literally means "African play" but

---

[27] A selection includes Joel Adedeji, 1969, "Traditional Yoruba Theatre," *African Arts* 3(1), 60–63; Adedeji, 1971, "A Profile of Nigerian Theatre 1960–1970," *Nigeria Magazine* No. 107–109 (December–August), 3–14; Dapo Adelugba and Olu Obafemi, 2004, "Anglophone West Africa: Nigeria," in *A History of Theatre in Africa*, ed. Martin Banham, Cambridge: Cambridge University Press, 138–158; Praise Zenenga, 2015, "The Total Theater Aesthetic Paradigm in African Theater," in *The Oxford Handbook of Dance and Theater*, ed. Nadine George-Graves, New York: Oxford University Press, 236–251; Bode Omojola, 2020, "Towards an African Operatic Voice: Composition, Dramaturgy, and Identity Strategies in New Yorùbá Opera," in *African Theatre 19: Opera and Music Theatre*, ed. Christine Matzke et al., Woodbridge: James Currey, 107–135, at 107; Samuel Kasule, 2020, ""I Smoked Them Out": Perspectives on the Emergence of Folk Opera or 'Musical Plays' in Uganda," in *African Theatre 19*, ed. Christine Matzke et al., 183–193, at 184.

[28] Zenenga, "Total Theater," 242.

[29] Zenenga, "Total Theater," 236.

[30] Hilde Roos, n.d., "In Conversation with Zakes Mda: "The Full Story Must Be Told," *herri* 7, https://herri.org.za/7/hilde-roos/.

is normally translated as "total African theater." According to Jesse Weaver Shipley, Abibigro is reflective of Ghanaian storytelling traditions that unite different artistic disciplines, social classes, and ritual practices.[31] The notion of total theater is hence not limited to one geographical, linguistic or cultural grouping on the African continent. Rather, it recurs among diverse communities while retaining remarkable consistency in the meaning of the concept and its associated practices.

African total theater represents a complex interrelation between extracolonial, colonial, and postcolonial performance practices. With growing academic interest in opera and music theater on the African continent, the history and practice of African total theater opens unusual avenues for examining the relationship between local and Western opera, as well as the sometimes uncanny coincidences and correspondences between performance practices in different times and places.

Intriguingly, the concept of African total theater shares pronounced similarities with the Wagnerian model of *Gesamtkunstwerk*. Specifically, the two traditions share an ideal of organic unity, characterized by integration between nature and society. In an article titled "African Theatre and the West," theater practitioner Donald Baker identifies ideals of physical and spiritual integration between humans and nature as a formative aspect of African theater practices. Although dated in some more essentialist assessments regarding "the nature of theater in general and what the Western world might learn from African theatrical forms in particular," Baker's article does offer a fascinating perspective on the role of theater in an environment where little distinction historically existed between art and life. The author quotes Yoruba writer Adebayo Adesanya, who describes "the harmony between man, nature, and the gods which is fundamental to African societies" as follows: "Philosophy, theology, politics, social theory, land law, medicine, psychology, birth and burial all find themselves logically concatenated in a system so tight that to abstract one item from the whole is to paralyse the structure of the whole."[32] In this integrated metaphysics, theater emerges as a ritualized articulation of the relationality of things. It marks moments of natural or spiritual significance, including cycles of labor and worship and serves to constitute social structures within communal formations.

Since the publication of Baker's article in 1977, much has changed, of course, not only for theater practitioners but also for scholars seeking to

---

[31] Jesse Weaver Shipley, 2015, *Trickster Theatre: The Poetics of Freedom in Urban Africa*, Bloomington: Indiana University Press, 122.

[32] Donald Baker, 1977, "African Theatre and the West," *Comparative Drama* 11(3), 227–251, at 241; the original is at Adebayo Adesanya, 1958, "Yoruba Metaphysical Thinking," *Odù* 5, at 39.

Totality   **217**

study these models. The barely concealed ethnic essentialism contained in Baker's remarks has since made way for more careful engagements with the continent's performance traditions, including in work that acknowledges the strong impact of industrialization, urbanization, and globalization on African theater.[33] But while it is, as Wole Soyinka writes, no longer possible to speak of an African theater practice untouched by the rhythms and practices of modernity, the tradition of total performance does continue to reflect a hereditary relationship with rituals that structured the spiritual and physical coherence of the subject and her environment. Whether explicitly or implicitly, organic unity remains a formative principle in African total theater.

The same ideal shapes Wagner's conception of *Gesamtkunstwerk*, which, according to Smith, "implies not only an intermingling of art-forms but also an attempt to create an organic synthesis of arts that recovers supposedly original, lost, organic unities: unity of the individual subject, unity of the social body, unity of life and art."[34] For Wagner, the total work of art should recover a utopian version of "natural man"; a person who exists in a mode of social, aesthetic, and ecological harmony that renders politics, culture, and industrialized labor obsolete. Wagner's ritual theater hence pursues a state of being that does not distinguish between life and art or between leisure and labor.[35]

Traditional African theater, particularly what Baker calls the "festive or dramatic phase" in terms that echo Mda, similarly reflects this unified worldview: performance is as part of the "structure of the whole" as labor in the fields or practices of law, since it ritualizes these practices. Theater hence mediates a cosmic unity among labor, leisure, and ceremony, or between body, mind, and spirit. Moreover, like Mda, Wagner describes this integrated performance model as a festival rather than an opera. Wagner's *Bühnenweihfestspiel* exposes the spiritual and ritual significance of total theater. It articulates an aesthetic worldview that regards performance as the consolidation of man's (and woman's, though Wagner is less explicit about her position in the festive fabric) transcendent natural state.

Despite these correspondences, important differences do exist between African total theater and Wagner's *Gesamtkunstwerk*. For instance, Wagner seems to prefer—despite his own statements to the contrary—a single-authored artistic model whereby the auteur figure retains control over all constitutive parts of the production. In African total theater, labor is more

---

[33] Shipley's work cited above, and the volume *African Theatre 19*, edited by Matzke et al., are exemplary in this regard.

[34] Smith, *Total Work of Art*, 11.

[35] My description here relies heavily on Matthew Wilson Smith's account of the Wagnerian *Gesamtkunstwerk*. See Smith, *Total Work of Art*, especially chapters 1 and 2.

dispersed, with various agents working together to create performance events.[36] These participants include audience members, who contribute to the musical and dramatic action with sound interjections (calling, clapping, singing, chanting) and movement. Wagner, on the other hand, welcomes the spectator into the performance only insofar as she remains a silent witness, seated in a darkened hall and usurped into the actions on stage. These differences reveal distinctive approaches to the role of the performance within the social body. Wagner appears unable to shed the notion of theatrical performance as sacred; in his conception, the theater event reaches its apotheosis through exclusion of the outside world rather than by welcoming it in.

Wagner's pursuit of a sacred total performance, severed from the actualities of physical and socio-political context, relies on various mechanics of obfuscation. Scholars including Gundula Kreuzer, Matthew Wilson Smith, and Anthony J. Steinhoff have remarked on the irony of Wagner's dependence on increasingly sophisticated technological innovations in his quest for naturalistic fantasy.[37] The composer required all kinds of mechanical interventions to realize his spectacular shows; however, he insisted on a staging practice that sought to hide all evidence of this mechanization. Extraordinary effects were meant to take place as if supernaturally, without any disclosure of the creaking machines, brittle materials, and laboring bodies behind them. More often than not, the reality fell short of Wagner's enchanted intentions.[38] But the objective remained: *Gesamtkunstwerk* was meant to hide the effects of industrial modernity to give the spectator the illusion of a return to pure and wondrous nature.

Just as the mechanics of Wagner's stage were intended to stay hidden, the conditions upon which those technologies were developed likewise remained obscure. Here again, Walter Mignolo's modernity/coloniality bind is relevant.[39] Wagner's stage technologies were part and parcel of a modernity built on systems of colonial labor and extraction—what Achille Mbembe calls "the nocturnal face of capitalism," and Mignolo describes as "the dark underside of modernity."[40] By hiding the mechanics that enabled his stage

---

[36] Shipley, *Trickster Theatre*.

[37] Gundula Kreuzer, 2018, *Curtain Gong Steam: Wagnerian Technologies of Nineteenth-Century Opera*, Oakland: University of California Press; Smith, *Total Work of Art*; Anthony J. Steinhoff, 2016, "Richard Wagner, *Parsifal*, and the Pursuit of Gesamtkunstwerk," in *The Total Work of Art: Foundations, Articulations, Inspirations*, ed. David Imhoof, Margaret Eleanor Menninger, and Anthony J. Steinhoff, New York: Berghahn Books, 56–77.

[38] See Kreuzer, *Curtain, Gong, Steam*.

[39] Walter D. Mignolo, 2011, *The Darker Side of Western Modernity: Global Futures, Decolonial Options*, Durham, NC: Duke University Press. See the Introduction for a discussion of this concept.

[40] Achille Mbembe, 2017 [2013], *Critique of Black Reason*, trans. Laurent Dubois, Durham, NC: Duke University Press, 129. My thanks to William Fourie for reminding me of Mbembe's concept. Mignolo's "dark underside of modernity" is developed in *Darker Side*.

experiments, Wagner implicitly obscured the colonial labor that produced these tools. The Eurocentric experience of modernity reflected in Wagner's *Gesamtkunstwerk*—one that embraces modernity by rendering it invisible—hence remained unconscious of its nocturnal underside.

Wagner's *Gesamtkunstwerk* operated by means of exclusion. It excluded the outside world, the signs of industrial modernity, the labor of those who produced it, and those who did not fit within a unified social body. Thus, colonized people, racial others, and anybody who did not meet the exacting standards of an idealized German *Volk*, became the "necessary Other"—an outsider whose outsideness confirmed the coherence of the "inside."[41] The total work of art's "necessary Other" bears a distinct resemblance to the "melancholy object" of racial difference examined in Chapter 3. Both concepts underscore the importance of differentiation to the creation of coherent socio-political and aesthetic identities. Whereas the melancholy object implies a sense of loss, however, the necessary Other of Wagner's ideal constructs exclusion as a form of liberation: it frees the unified and sacred socio-aesthetic body from the abject encumbrances of toil, technology, and disparity.

In the twentieth century, discomfort about the alignment of this restricted aesthetic practice with the totalitarian politics of Nazism stirred artists and theater makers to seek new models of total performance, ones that also integrate diverse artistic disciplines but without the search for an idealized social body devoid of difference.[42] Rather than Wagnerian naturalism, many of these theater models—which included not only such practices as Zimmermann's "pluralistic music theater" and Luigi Nono's "azione scenica," but also the experiments of the Bauhaus—foregrounded and celebrated mechanization.[43] They sought to incorporate the technologies of industry into a sacred union between human and machine. In Smith's analysis, the architects of these forms believed that their versions of theatrical totality would render a utopia built on the elimination of human labor, resulting in a perfectly capable, radically equal society.

The totalizing theater experiments of the twentieth-century Euro-American avant-garde could arguably not be further from the African total work of art as described by Zenenga and others. Nonetheless, in their quest for the unification of different artistic disciplines, as well as their pursuit of a spiritually unified social body (whether this spirituality is represented by the

---

[41] Smith, *Total Work of Art*, 41.

[42] Schröder, "Total Theatre and Music Theatre."

[43] Schröder, "Total Theatre and Music Theatre"; Smith, *Total Work of Art*; David Roberts, 2011, *The Total Work of Art in European Modernism*, Ithaca: Cornell University Press.

220 Postcolonial Opera

creed of technological progress or of natural harmony), the two traditions do share a basic organizing principle. They both seek to exceed the formal limits of the work of art, to reach into the realm of the social.

Despite this interrelatedness, Zenenga emphasizes that African total theater exists independently from parallel Western traditions.[44] His insistence on the distinction between these practices appears to function as a form of reparative acknowledgment: recognizing African total theater as a separate ontological category grants it an individual critical and aesthetic identity that is neither derivative of nor supplementary to Western theater.

Framed as such, the distinctiveness of African total theater is partly a result of and response to the history of colonialism. Both the art form's practitioners and the stories they seek to tell have been shaped by coloniality in a way that Western forms of total theater have not. To be sure, Western total theater, in its reliance on technologies produced by colonial labor and extraction, also bears the mark of colonialism. But the difference between the colonized person's experience of colonial extraction and that of the Western recipient of colonially enabled modernity cannot be denied. African total theater and Western total theater hence reflect different conceptions of the notion of totality. For Western practitioners, totality frames technology as empowerment; for African practitioners, technology is domination. By extension, the art that springs from these different experiences necessarily differs.

In *The Head & the Load*, the interplay between the cultural products of Western modernity and the colonial conditions that enabled them manifests especially by means of discrepant juxtapositions. As with traditional European and African total theater, Kentridge distributes his performance across a range of artistic disciplines. Rather than coherent communication, however, the different media contradict or complicate each other. The piece hence uses a total structure to communicate fracture rather than consolidation.

I do not wish to frame Kentridge's production as either a Western or an African total work of art. Rather, I trace in the piece an engagement with the colonial practices that enable Western theatrical totality and result in the obliteration of the spiritual and social unification that underpins African communal performance. Put differently, while *The Head & the Load* possesses characteristics belonging to both European and African total theater, it is especially interesting for the way in which it breaks open the idea of totality that informs both these traditions. In the process, it draws attention to the fact that colonialism shaped theatrical totality, just as political totality shaped the colonial project.

---

[44] Zenenga, "Total Theater Aesthetic Paradigm," 249.

Coloniality, Totality, Fracture

Colonial totality was a twofold project. Its main feature was control: colonizers combined total control over land and resources with attempts at total control over the people who inhabited those territories. This human control occurred on various fronts and by various means. Perhaps the most important sphere of colonial domination was, as suggested above, labor: colonial territories possessed resources that could be extracted for capital gain. Colonizers needed workers to cultivate their plantations and farms, to excavate their mines, and to dig their roads and build their rails. To enable this extraction, colonized people were forced into forms of servitude that ranged from slavery and indentured labor to penal labor and requisition. Those who refused to work for the colonizers had their labor colonized by the imposition of taxation and enterprise legislation, which compelled them into a system of work in exchange for money.[45]

Apart from controlling people's labor, the colonial project also took control over their bodies. Colonizers decided how the bodies of colonized people were to be used, dictating not only the types of work available to different subjects but also which types of behavior constituted civilized, legal, or acceptable conduct. Laws and conventions determined how people were to behave both in private and in public, and they governed even the most basic functions such as feeding, resting, worship and leisure.[46]

Most troublingly, the colonial project controlled which kinds of bodies qualified for personhood. In a cumulative totalitarian project that started with the control of land and eventually filtered down to the total psychological and physiological control of the subject, the colonial agenda created and applied race categories designed to deprive colonized persons of personhood. As Fanon observes in *Black Skin White Masks*, colonial logic assumes that white bodies qualify for personhood; black bodies do not.[47] Good only for hard labor in support of Western industrial progress, Black colonized subjects were denied spiritual or intellectual existence. They were, in Mbembe's description, "useful things when needed."[48] In the view of the colonizer, Mbembe continues, "the colonised does not exist as a self; the colonised *is*, but in the

---

[45] Salvaing, Bernard. 2020. "Forced Labour in European Colonies," *Encyclopédie d'histoire numérique de l'Europe*. https://ehne.fr/en/node/12505.

[46] This constitutes not only control over bodies but also over colonized people's temporality. For more on this topic, see Chapter 4.

[47] Frantz Fanon, 2008 [1952], *Black Skin, White Masks*, translated by Charles Lam Markmann, London: Pluto.

[48] Mbembe, *On the Postcolony*, 187.

same way as a rock *is*—that is, as nothing more."[49] Or, as Dlamini states in *The Head & the Load*, "They are not men, because they have no name. They are not soldiers, because they have no number. You do not call them, you count them."[50] Little more than a thing, colonized subjects are deemed incapable of personhood. They fall short of subjectivity, intentionality, and rationality.

While people's bodies—especially their skin color—determined the extent to which they qualified for personhood, the colonial project did not limit its reach to the physical attributes of humanness. Instead, it also took total control over culture. Black subjects who aimed to qualify for personhood in the eyes of empire were required to reject their own traditions and to adopt those of the colonizer. Colonial forces reshaped education, religion, familial relations, and judicial systems in the image of European conventions. In the process, they threatened to wipe out forms of cultural difference that could produce resistance or safeguard identities beyond the absolute control of the colonizer. Not unlike the utopian ideal imagined by Wagner, the colonial project hence set out to fashion a society sanitized of cultural and political heterogeneity. By taking control of colonized people's practices and traditions, the colonial project sought to create a compliant, "civilized" populace comprising subjects dominated both physically and spiritually. Along the way, it devastated the organic totality between communities and their environment, and between labor, worship, and culture that underpinned African total theater practices. Here, then, one form of social integration developed from the exclusion and destruction of another.

To be sure, the cultural domination of colonized peoples was not successful throughout. I do not wish to portray all colonized people as a homogenous mass of exploited victims. That would itself entail a continuation of the totalitarian domination of colonized persons' histories and agency. Across the colonized world, individuals and groups resisted assimilation and exploitation. They found creative ways to safeguard traditions, and challenged colonial control both secretly and openly.[51] The rich history of anticolonial thought, action, and literature bears testimony to the forceful self-assertion of these agents. Nonetheless, the power of colonial regimes to punish those who resisted, and to reward those who complied, reinforces the argument that persons who challenged colonial totality were not merely battling a form of settlement but a system of absolutist control. This was not only about land but about total domination—of people, of place, and of history.

---

[49] Mbembe, *On the Postcolony*, 187.
[50] Kentridge, *The Head & the Load*, 169.
[51] See Priyamvada Gopal, 2019, *Insurgent Empire: Anticolonial Resistance and British Dissent*, London: Verso.

Until recently, the colonial pasts constructed in history books and national memory have been ones that celebrate the interventions of colonizers. Even now, large swaths of the populations of former imperial powers believe that colonialism benefited those it affected.[52] The prevalence of these self-congratulatory narratives offer evidence of the extent to which the colonial project managed to control not only lands and their inhabitants but also knowledge. It did this by regulating colonized subjects' access to literacy, and by implementing record keeping and archival practices that captured only one side of colonial history. Thus, the past itself became a casualty of colonial totality.

Paradoxically, the pursuit of totality resulted in various forms of geopolitical and historical fragmentation. As imperial forces united expanding swaths of land under their rule, the continent fractured. It was carved up arbitrarily into bordered possessions and distributed between competing political and economic claimants. In the process, enormous geographical areas, which used to host shifting patterns of seasonal inhabitation, or functioned as migrant zones, ancestral homelands, or communal lands, splintered into separate national domains. Movement, ownership, and belonging fragmented.

The colonial project likewise produced a fragmentation of Indigenous pasts. For Mbembe, colonial denial of the historiographical experience of the Black subject creates an epistemological problem. In a passage I have already cited in the Introduction to this volume, Mbembe writes, "Where the kinds of traces that serve as sources for historiographical fact are absent, it becomes clear that the history of Blacks [can] be written only from fragments brought together to give an account of an experience that itself was fragmented, that of a pointillist people struggling to define itself not as a disparate composite but as a community whose blood stains the entire surface of modernity."[53] Colonized subjects' historical experiences were not accorded the dignity of archival or narrative preservation: where information about the lives and experiences of colonized subjects survives, it is often in the form of administrative documents such as lists, tables, and figures. From these incomplete records, what Mbembe calls "fragments," the histories of colonized subjects emerge as sutured and disjointed assemblages, manufactured as much from fissures as from facts. Historical knowledge, then, emerges as collage, rather than unity.

---

[52] In 2020, a YouGov poll found that 30 percent of British people still think colonialism benefited former colonies. See Robert Booth, 2020, "UK More Nostalgic for Empire than Other Ex-Colonial Powers," *The Guardian,* March 11, https://www.theguardian.com/world/2020/mar/11/uk-more-nostalgic-for-empire-than-other-ex-colonial-powers.

[53] Mbembe, *Critique,* 28–29.

224 Postcolonial Opera

Colonizers' efforts at historical and epistemological totality hence resulted in a form of fracture that placed the historical experience of the colonized subject always out of reach. In what may be regarded as a curative mode of historical self-possession, these fugitive pasts remain, ironically, beyond the control of the colonizer. At the moment of historical destruction, the colonizer loses its grip on the very thing it seeks to control. Coloniality thereby emerges as a simultaneous project of totality and disintegration—a complex interplay between consolidation and dissolution not unlike the splintered structure of *The Head & the Load*.

Kentridge states clearly his interest in a recovery of broken history by disjointed means. In a description of *The Head & the Load*, the artist articulates a desire to "show whether, in the technique and process of making *The Head & the Load*, we can find an understanding of the history itself as a provisional construction of reconfigured fragments."[54] Kentridge's understanding of history as an assemblage of splintered residues echoes Mbembe's description of Black pasts as "disparate composite." The notion of fractured history becomes both an epistemological preoccupation and an aesthetic code in Kentridge's piece: "Can one find the truth in the fragmented and incomplete?" the artist asks. "Can one think about history as collage, rather than as narrative?"[55] In other words, Kentridge's collage aesthetic exchanges a totalitarian approach to knowledge—one governed by paradigms of certitude and completeness—for a more provisional attitude in keeping with the fragmentation of colonized persons' making of history. It is an approach shaped by incoherence, contradiction, and uncertainty.

Totality and Fragmentation in *The Head & the Load*

The Head & the Load's constitutive formal aesthetic is one of fragmentation. Here, the fragmented form refers to the non-integrative assembly of constituent parts, as effected by collage. For Bhabha, Kentridge's use of collage is the only appropriate way to capture this history. "If not a collage or a montage, what other form could the fragments assume?" Bhabha asks. Describing fragments as "relational forms, attempts at assemblage," Bhabha argues that *The Head & the Load* achieves a form of "grafting" that creates a new, reassembled version of the past. "A grafting is an active insertion of an element, a movement or sign, from within the structure of one work implanted into another system,"

---

[54] Kentridge, *The Head & the Load*, 283.
[55] Kentridge, Program Note, 3.

Bhabha writes. "The 'cut' of the graft displaces the disposition of both entities, and along the suture created by the art of *making fragments* begins the work of reframing and rescaling the 'topic' in question."[56] What Bhabha describes here is a mode of assemblage that creates new, "hybrid" entities marked by breaks, seams, and irregularities. Not organic unity but constructed togetherness.

The Head & the Load's collage form brings face to face with each other anticolonial and imperial texts. As fragments and intertexts are overlaid, sutured, and juxtaposed, contradictory messages emerge from the action on stage. For instance, while Shabangu quotes John Chilembwe's letter opposing the Africans' participation in the war, Dlamini offers a conflicting point of view: "We demand the right to serve in the army as all French citizens do," he states, quoting Blaise Diagne, the first Black deputy in the Chamber of Deputies in Paris. "We offer a harvest of devotion."[57] Kentridge remarks that such moments of juxtaposition were designed to capture the paradoxes that characterize colonial subjectivity, especially "the desire of Africans to be part of Europe, to share in the wealth and the richness of Europe, while wanting to resist Europe and its depredations."[58] In other words, the confrontation between the contradictory content of the spoken and projected texts stands in for the apparent incoherence of Africans' response to colonialism.

But the collage form also creates uncanny resemblances and conspicuous unmaskings. Suturing together disparate threads across media, visual and sonic codes frequently seem to undermine each other. What the audience sees and what it hears are often violently discrepant. A performance of Eric Satie's popular love song, "Je te veux" (1903), is accompanied by projections of carrier pigeons, which explode one by one (see ⏵ Clip 6.1). The effect is jarring. At a surface level, the scene refers most obviously to the disjuncture between romanticized accounts of patriotic self-sacrifice and the very real horror of war. But heard within the broader context of the work, it also gestures toward the almost dissociative nature of coloniality: beauty and prosperity at the heart of Empire, unthinkable violence and exploitation at its margins.

Despite the apparent disjointedness of a scene such as "Je te veux," Kentridge's piece still exists, in Bhabha's description, as a whole. The paradoxical or self-contradictory nature of the piece may undercut its coherence, but the work nonetheless retains a hybrid congruence. This is the result of the "grafting" Bhabha describes—the suturing together of discrepant strands of

---

[56] Bhabha, "Theater of War," 315, original emphasis.
[57] Kentridge, *The Head & the Load*, 140.
[58] Kentridge, *The Head & the Load*, 284.

meaning into a constructed assemblage of which the stitches and seams remain visible.

What Bhabha characterizes as grafting is, in essence, a feature of Kentridge's "unbounded work of art."[59] For Kentridge, unboundedness describes a theater practice that allows different traditions and histories to cohabit without succumbing to the chaos of formlessness. It is the artist's answer to both Wagnerian *Gesamtkunstwerk* and to the interdisciplinary ideal of African total theater. The unbounded work of art incorporates different artistic disciplines and media technologies, not to achieve coherence but to show up the gaps and inconsistencies that shape history and the present. Allowing for disjunction, such performance welcomes a multitude of perspectives and experiences into the same frame, rendering the pointillist subjectivity of which Mbembe writes.

Bhabha's metaphors of transplantation and suture highlight an important aspect of this newly integrative practice: the grafted or unbounded work of art relies on an initial break, the disintegration of a former whole, from which it may assemble its constituent fragments. Kentridge's pieces do not collect together random splinters of information. Rather, the artist constructs operas such as *The Head & the Load* from pre-existing histories, practices, or artifacts. As with the vase in *Refuse the Hour*, he breaks apart these units and reassembles them in combination with pieces from other broken wholes.[60] The result is a new accumulation of information, which yields an altered perspective on what came before. Kentridge's assemblages do not hide their scars; rather, the seams, ridges, and joints serve to unmask the illusion of completeness that characterizes unitary perspectives. It follows, then, that these works rely on an essential condition of fracture. Before reassembly, there is breakdown. Fragmentation, in other words, serves a generative purpose in Kentridge's work.

Linguistic Breakdown

For Kentridge, the aesthetics of unboundedness is tied to Dadaism. The artist states that he is inspired by the movement's recognition that anything can be art and that things' meanings often change when they are presented alongside or in combination with other things.[61] Given that Dada was itself a response

---

[59] See the Introduction for a more detailed discussion of the concept.
[60] See Chapter 4.
[61] Kentridge, interview with the author, February 15, 2021.

to war, Kentridge's incorporation of the movement complements *The Head & the Load*'s historical subject matter.

But Kentridge extends Dada's anti-war ethics to enact a critique of colonialism. Referencing his own understanding of the First World War as the culmination of the colonial project, he couples Kurt Schwitters's *Ursonate*, an emblematic piece of Dadaist poetry, with the Berlin Conference of 1884. Dlamini, De Wit, and Mahlangu, huddled over clipboards and official documents, squabble using extracts from Schwitters's poem. On the backdrop, a projected map of Africa is systematically carved into smaller pieces, until nothing is left but a muddle of frenzied lines and barbed wire (see Figure 6.6). The men trade territory in a parodied performance of the Berlin Conference. They address each other as if Schwitters's syllables have semantic meaning. When Mahlangu stuffs a document in his mouth, literally consuming—and becoming consumed by—the colonial agenda, the projected map rips apart. Its torn fragments flail about in the aftermath of Dlamini, De Wit, and Mahlangu's senseless assault. Then Shabangu appears with an order: "Stop! Do it again."

The performance of *Ursonate* here encapsulates the unreason of the colonial project, or, as Kentridge describes it, "the sound of a rational argument

Figure 6.6 "Ursonate," with Dlamini, De Wit, and Mahlangu in the foreground and the map of Africa projected onto the background. Photograph: Stella Olivier. Courtesy of William Kentridge Studio.

228 Postcolonial Opera

hiding a deep irrationality."[62] Equating territorial negotiations to nonsense poetry, the scene shows up the preposterousness of an endeavor founded entirely upon the distribution of goods among those who do not own them. Apart from setting up a clear link between war, colonialism, and absurdity, this scene also captures two crucial forms of colonial fragmentation: in pairing Schwitters's poem with geopolitical wranglings, Kentridge maps the fragmentation of language directly onto the fragmentation of territory.

Ursonate's provocative representation of irrationality is but one part of a larger play with linguistic fragmentation and incoherence in Kentridge's piece. *The Head & the Load* incorporates several different languages, often at the same time. Occasionally, actors' words are projected in translation onto the backdrop; often, they are not. For audience members, the result is a chaotic dynamic of incomprehension: one is never entirely sure if one understood what has just been said. Kentridge himself describes the piece's linguistic interplay as "a kind of broken telephone along the length of the stage, English into isiZulu into French back into English, translations and mistranslations projected onto the screen."[63]

In a war setting, the frenzied interplay of different tongues would have been characteristic of conscripts' sound world. From a colonial perspective, there is something more humorous, but potentially also more threatening about this tumult. Danger lurks where language breaks down into mistranslation, incomprehension, or nonsense. Trickery, subterfuge, and duplicity become possible, for colonizers and colonized alike. It is in the cracks and fissures of linguistic interaction, in other words, that both the implementation and the destabilization of totalitarian control becomes possible.

Language never breaks down more elegantly than in opera. The most obvious scenes of incomprehension are of course generated by foreign-language libretti. Even when works are performed with surtitles, operatic bewilderment shows itself in audience members' frantically dashing glances, trying to take in stage and text at once. Nuances and insinuations go unmarked, jokes elicit nothing but scattered chuckles. But beyond the challenge of translation, operatic singing itself also functions as a force of linguistic breakdown. With their embellished vowels, overdone consonants, and breathless syntax, operatic voices push intelligibility to the limit. The most consummate articulators cannot undo the fact that opera complicates the ability of language to communicate clearly and directly.

In many contexts, opera's linguistic awkwardness may be a drawback. However, as *The Head & the Load* shows, the breakdown of language also

---

[62] Kentridge, *The Head & the Load*, 290.
[63] Kentridge, *The Head & the Load*, 290.

Totality   229

offers an opportunity to engage more fully with colonial conditions of incomprehension and misarticulation. From a postcolonial perspective, opera's linguistic malfunction is hence an aesthetic device: it underscores the unruly interplay of communication, miscommunication, control, and resistance that emerges when languages meet.

The Head & the Load's use of multiple languages in and out of translation constructs a colonial sphere of competing logics. In a scene titled "Kaiser Waltz," such logic is pushed to its limits. Here, linguistic breakdown reaches beyond the boundaries of reason, into absolute disorder. As a violist performs the popular "Liebesleid" from Fritz Kreisler's *Alt-Wiener Tanzweisen* (1905), voice artist Joanna Dudley, performing as Kaiser Wilhelm II, quotes from the German emperor's call to arms, delivered on August, 1914. Wilhelm reflects on Germany's authority as an empire, urging his soldiers to fight not only for the survival of their homeland but also for its legacy as a world power. Dudley, however, inverts Wilhelm's compulsion toward language, instead descending, irresistibly, into bird-like shrieks. The Kaiser's exhortations remain unintelligible (see ▶ Clip 6.2).

Dudley's screeching questions the apparent logic of a resolution that privileges hubris over reason. Just as the unreason of amorous yearning interrupts the logic of the implied subject in Kreisler's "Liebesleid," the irrationality of wartime arrogance undoes the coherence of Dudley's language. The scene inverts the colonial conflation of rationality with whiteness, rendering the monarch—a figure of absolute authority—incomprehensible.

This moment appears straightforwardly to upend entrenched stereotypes of white logic. However, it also gestures to something more sinister: the racialized rupture of reason effected by the colonial encounter. In *Critique of Black Reason*, Mbembe observes a dark underside to coloniality's binary distribution of reason and incoherence. He remarks: "Every time it confronted the question of Blacks and Africa, reason found itself ruined and emptied, turning constantly in on itself, shipwrecked in a seemingly inaccessible place where language was destroyed and words themselves no longer had memory."[64] What Mbembe describes here is the idea that white reason breaks down when brought face to face with Blackness. The threat of the racialized other is such that it consumes everything in its path, rendering even language meaningless. Such assumptions are familiar even now, from global discourses around the distribution of aid and infrastructural support to the African continent, where everything, apparently, is on an irreversible path to destruction. Bearing this in mind, Dudley's descent into disorder as she ruminates on the

---

[64] Mbembe, *Critique*, 13.

230 Postcolonial Opera

future of the German empire becomes altogether more ambiguous. On stage, brought into contact with the chaotic irrationality of the colonies, the Kaiser loses his reason.[65]

Fractured Subjectivity

Colonial conditions of linguistic breakdown affect both colonizer and colonized. If the colonizer descends into madness when confronted with Blackness, the colonized is understood to possess no reason to begin with. As my discussion of colonial totality and totalitarianism made clear, coloniality fragments the colonized subject, turning her into no more than an object. Devoid of subjectivity, colonized persons are deemed incapable of reason, understood instead to act from animal instinct or coercion. Or, as Dlamini, quoted above, states, "You do not call them, you count them."

The denial of the colonized subject's personhood is reiterated in the final scene of *The Head & the Load*, in which a young carrier slowly perishes. As the boy dies, Shabangu recites the objects on which his fading mind comes to rest: "Mountain. Tree. Haversack. Biscuit."[66] In the background, a traditional Mpondomise song, "Kwanukimpi" (translated as "The Smell of War"), laments the account of the death of conscripts.[67] Interspersed with Shabangu's recitation, Dlamini reads out a "list of the dead," projected onto the backdrop. The two orations intertwine, until from the muddled dialogue the names emerge of carriers such as "Geelbooi Dinokee," "Saucepan Moake," "Whisky Mahlaba," "Paraffin Makilitshi," "Transvaal Masilo," and "Thousand Matupu."[68] These names, devised by combining everyday items with clan names, not only reflect colonial nomenclature but also reinforce the objectification enacted by imperial practices.

Colonial subjects were thought of, for the most part, as no more than objects. However, they were person enough to be considered a threat. Colonizers sought to neutralize this threat by means of control over colonized persons' leisure and culture. In *The Head & the Load*, colonial attempts

---

[65] Arguably the most visceral account of the breakdown of white reason in confrontation with colonized Blackness is, of course, Joseph Conrad's *Heart of Darkness* (1899).

[66] Kentridge, *The Head & the Load*, 259.

[67] A field card containing Hugh Tracey's collector's notes on the song is projected on the backdrop during its performance. It specifies the language of the song as Xhosa, its type as "Old fighting song," its place of origin as "Pondoland, Eastern Cape, South Africa," and its recording date as 23 May 1957. This particular field card forms part of the Hugh Tracey Fieldwork Collection and the Sound of Africa Series, TR061 (1957) at the International Library of African Music (ILAM), Grahamstown, South Africa.

[68] Kentridge, *The Head & the Load*, 276.

Totality **231**

to estrange colonized subjects from their own culture are captured by yet another list, one that demonstrates not only the educational properties ascribed to objects of leisure but also the war effort's ability to usurp practices that have nothing to do with combat. Dudley recites a catalogue of "goods sent to the troops by the Committee for the Welfare of African Troops." It reads like an inventory of ambitions:

> 26 gramophones, 634 records, 600 mouth organs, 2 guitars complete with cases and extra strings, 3 concertinas, 1 coronet, 1 portable organ, 2 footballs, 1 football pump, 1 bagatelle board, 21 sets of ludo, 17 cricket bats, 5 sets of cricket stumps, 6 cricket balls, 12 dumbbells, 6 sets of boxing gloves, 30 sets of dominoes, 30 sets of draughts, . . . 600 hymn and prayer books, 111 song books, 12 union jacks, 108 coloured handkerchiefs, 1250 school primers, 3000 slate pencils, 1440 pen holders, 4320 pens, 120 packets of ink powder, 13 tuning forks and pipes.[69]

A collection of seemingly innocuous objects, but also an act of sinister altruism. The list of objects sent to the colonies hints at colonizers' attempts to control and civilize colonized subjects by directing how they occupied themselves in their moments of rest.

Dudley's list sheds light on the refining properties ascribed to musical practice: named alongside the sporting equipment and educational tools of empire, the gramophones, mouth organs, guitars, and concertinas were evidently intended to encourage wholesome recreation and to initiate recruits into the protocols of colonial subjecthood. Their presence suggests a sphere in which the customary sonic selfhood of Black conscripts was policed—smoothed over and refined—even as the brutal clamor of war raged around them. Thus, sound became a means of converting colonial people from bodies into persons. Total control over their activities reunited their fractured being, transfiguring them from objects into subjects.

The items listed above not only signified total control over colonized persons' cultural or psychic lives; they were also objects that had to be carried. The labor of carrying tyrannized porters' bodies. Bhabha describes the control over carriers' nutrition (limited to 2 lb. of maize meal per day), their sleep, their clothing, and their movements.[70] Whereas, in the eyes of their masters, wholesome recreation could potentially recuperate personhood for colonized subjects, porterage turned them back into nothing more than animals.

---

[69] Kentridge, *The Head & the Load*, 245.
[70] Bhabha, "Theater of War," 304.

232   Postcolonial Opera

Scene 6, "Procession to War," captures the abjection of carrying and its effect on colonial subjectivity. Occurring at almost the exact midpoint of the performance, the procession is a visceral reenactment of the burdened march undertaken by Black porters. It starts with Scene 5, "Recruiting," in which Shabangu recites a desperate account of colonial conveyance:

> I assure you this is the truth. We had to move a boat from Cape Town to Lake Tanganyika. The engineers took the boat apart. First it was carried by train. When the train line ended, it was pulled by tractor. When the road defeated the tractor, it was put on the backs of oxen. When the tsetse fly killed all the oxen, it was put on the backs of men.[71]

The first porter enters, carrying a silhouetted flag. Shabangu, meanwhile, returns with another set of figures in this exercise in "arithmetic for those who should know better":

> From the Congo, 200 000 carriers. From Nigeria, 4 000 carriers each month. For every soldier, 3 carriers. For every officer, 9 carriers. For every machine gun, 12 carriers. For every cannon, 300 carriers. If a man dies, another remains. If a hundred die, a hundred remain. If a thousand die, a thousand carry the boat to the lake.[72]

As Shabangu narrates these figures, a seemingly never-ending parade stumbles across the stage. They carry burdens reminiscent of the cargos in *Triumphs and Laments*. Here, however, the shadowy loads do not represent the ambivalent glories of Rome. Rather, the carriers bear evidence of war: on their heads and shoulders they balance airplanes, cannons, ammunition, wooden structures, piles of war detritus tied into precarious bundles, the heads of African freedom fighters, and, in reference to Shabangu's recitation, a boat. A marching band joins the convoy, but instead of marching, it stumbles along with the slow gait of prisoners. Occasionally, the players lift their instruments into position for a tune.

When a carrier reaches the right end of the stage, they exit and walk back to the starting point stage left, where they rejoin the procession. As they retrace their steps over and over again, their loads become increasingly disheveled. The flag is torn—by the end it hangs in limp shreds. Airplanes turn into barely recognizable bundles of metal. The freedom fighters' heads are scarred and bandaged. War has taken its toll.

---

[71] Kentridge, *The Head & the Load*, 74.
[72] Kentridge, *The Head & the Load*, 91.

Totality   233

The carriers themselves are markedly depersonalized. As they march, the shadows they cast on the backdrop render them indistinguishable from their loads. They become objects of transport, existing only insofar as they fulfill a structural function (see ▶ Clip 6.3).

While Shabangu describes the dehumanized numbers of carriers at the beginning of the procession, Mahlangu interjects with his own account of the war experience. Barefoot and bare-chested, and carrying a gramophone on his head, Mahlangu faces the audience with a promise spoken in Zulu and projected onto the backdrop in translation: "They hope we will die and not return home. That I will not do. But will go back home to enjoy the company of beautiful women."[73] As Mahlangu turns the crank of his gramophone, a rhythmic creaking reverberates, produced by a bow scraping on a viola, like a record run out. Accompanied by this noise, the actor slowly staggers off stage to the right.

For Bhabha, Mahlangu's statement is one instance of *The Head & the Load*'s "portrayal of the turning force of carrier agency from reluctance to resistance within the military orders of obedience."[74] Citing a quotation from Frantz Fanon's essay, "On Violence," Bhabha asserts that the porters are "dominated, but not domesticated."[75] This, he contends, is "everywhere audible and visible in the performance of [*The Head & the Load*], in the sound-systems of colonial power relations."[76] Though colonized people are denied personhood on a physical level, in other words, they refuse to yield psychic control to the totality of the colonial project. Again, totality fractures, rendering a colonized subject divided between physical subjection and mental defiance.

Bhabha's reference to "the sound-systems of colonial power relations" suggests that the tension between colonial totality and fractured subjectivity presents itself sonically. This is certainly the case in the procession, where conflicting sound signifiers allow the scene to perform a simultaneous consolidation and rupture. While carriers' individuality dissolves into a great, undifferentiated plodding mass, the sound world accompanying their movements shatters. It assaults the ears with an incommensurate collection of statements, advancing as a series of sonic waves.

The parade in its entirety is underpinned by N'faly Kouyaté's delicate kora lament, "Keleni tanta ye / hamba nhliziyo yami / uye ezulwini" ("leave now, my heart, to the heavens").[77] The kora rarely sounds alone: if not accompanied

---

[73] Kentridge, *The Head & the Load*, 74.
[74] Bhabha, "Theater of War," 310.
[75] Fanon, 2004 [1961], *The Wretched of the Earth*, trans. Richard Pilcox, New York: Grove Press.
[76] Bhabha, "Theater of War," 311.
[77] Kentridge, *The Head & the Load*, 91.

234 Postcolonial Opera

by Kouyaté's own voice, it contends with the rasping grind of the gramophone; with the ragged chorus repeating Kouyaté's words in a war-like monotone; the marching band vacillating between dance-like syncopations and bright trumpet fanfares; frustrated string tremolos and angry flute flourishes; and soprano Ann Masina's mesmerizing operatic incantations of the Zulu phrase, "Europe umsebenzi wethu ngithi" ("Europe is our work").[78] Again and again, the disparate sounds wash over each other, threatening to erupt into cacophony—an anarchic uproar strongly evocative of the chaos of war. But each time, an unexpected and ominous calm disrupts the escalating commotion. The result is an uneasy stasis. Dry timbres drag at the heels of musical lines, refusing to let them move. Attempts to reach for novel sounds collapse back into endless repetition. Against the forced mobility of the work's historical subjects, the music appears stuck. Time itself seems to stand still and move simultaneously.

A Broken Record, or a Wagnerian Intertext

The procession's paradoxical impression of concurrent mobility and stasis arises most obviously from the sheer size of the parade. Playing out across the whole of the 55-meter-long stage, the carriers' forward motion is countered both by the unchanging nature of their effort as they cross the vast walkway and by the monochrome anonymity of the silhouette projections against the backdrop. Likewise, musical repetition extends the action to meet the requirements of spatial immensity, allowing the same actions to be seen (and heard) in multiple sites at once.

If the size of the stage is the main cause for the procession's disruption of teleology, however, it does not erase the ideological potency of this device, one amplified by a Wagnerian intertext. At the ostensibly superficial level of thematic figuration, *The Head & the Load*'s procession gestures clearly toward Wagner's *Parsifal*. Specifically, Miller and Sibisi's music invokes material from the opera's procession scenes, in which the Knights of the Grail gather to insist on the ritualized gratification of their Grail cravings. *Parsifal*'s Grail march, with its jaunty dotted rhythm, initiates a tense motivic interplay between secular celebration and pious sobriety: constructed on a repetitive brass iteration of the pitches C-G-A, the processional motif becomes the basis of the Grail Temple's bells, which outline the fourths C-G and A-E in a perpetual downward figuration, now with the dotted rhythm removed.[79]

---

[78] Kentridge, *The Head & the Load*, 92.
[79] See William Kinderman, 2013, *Wagner's Parsifal*, New York: Oxford University Press, 187.

Totality 235

The correspondence between this music and *The Head & the Load*'s processional ostinato is striking. From the outset, Kouyaté's kora replicates the pitch classes of Wagner's bells, albeit transposed a tone higher and with a single alteration: rather than presenting two fourth intervals, Kouyaté inverts the final fourth to produce an outline of a falling fourth followed by a rising fifth on D–A–B–F-sharp. The result of this inversion is significant: whereas the downward arc of the majestic bell theme suggests pendulous oscillation, Kouyaté's motif sounds circular. Like the gramophone that turns on its central axis, and the procession that keeps turning back on itself, the kora ostinato is trapped in an eternal loop. If the *Parsifal* motif is majestic, the *Head & the Load* motif seems destitute and mournful.

Throughout the procession, Kouyaté's desolate kora emerges repeatedly as a gloomy reminder of the agony that underpins the parade's more animated exhortations. The juxtaposition of this lethargic refrain against the marching band's swinging rhythms is jarring from the start, but never more so than when Kouyaté's ostinato is given a similar martial treatment as that unleashed on Wagner's bells: having abandoned their syncopated responses to Ann Masina's operatic incantations, the brass take up Kouyaté's ostinato on D–A–B–F-sharp and turn it into an energetic fanfare, sounding first in high trumpet, then echoed an octave lower on the trombone.

The dotted fanfare rhythm represents an exact replication of the *Parsifal* march. It also follows a similar pitch contour (leap down, step up, though with an additional tone to complete the figure) and is articulated with similar instrumentation. Both rhythmically and texturally, the reference is unmistakable. The insular loop of the kora motif now makes way for confident exteriority: if Kouyaté's simple, self-generating perpetuum mobile suggests the dejected plodding of a people turned inward upon their own suffering, the brass fanfare gazes outward, asserting itself in imprudent celebration. However, unlike *Parsifal*'s fanfare, which traces a teleological route toward fulfillment by reiterating the motif in an ever-rising trajectory, *The Head & the Load*'s fanfare never takes off. Instead, it remains stuck in its original position, bellowing its rowdy tune a few times before giving up and disappearing into futility. Underneath, Kouyaté's kora ambles along despondently, acutely aware of the impossibility of resolution. Though both Wagner's and Miller and Sibisi's processions seem uneasily perched between solemnity and martial exuberance, the outcome of this tension is different in each case: Wagner's procession reaches a goal; Miller and Sibisi's keeps circling back on itself until it is suddenly cut off by a series of siren-like vocal glissandi that abruptly drops into silence.

Alongside the Wagnerian tones of the kora and the brass band, the creaking noise of Mahlangu's gramophone sounds a constant reminder of the speaker's

236 Postcolonial Opera

desperate promise to defy colonial annihilation, spoken at the start of the procession. Symbolically, the gramophone itself embodies circularity: forever
turning on a central axis, mirrored by the hand forever winding the crank,
it repeats in the same way that Kouyaté's ostinato repeats. In its circularity, it
echoes the apparent endlessness of colonial subjection. Mahlangu's gramophone symbolizes the goal-less procession that never seems to end.

But the rasping gramophone also represents portable modern technology
and by extension, modern culture. It is the means by which such artifacts as
Wagner's *Parsifal* may reach into the supposedly unenlightened colonial hin-
terland. The porters literally carry modernity on their heads.

The Head & the Load's procession explicitly visualizes Mignolo's mo-
dernity/coloniality world system. Here, the Black subject's experience of
coloniality is exposed as a simultaneous experience of modernity. Whereas in
Europe, however, the objects and processes representative of this modernity
are experienced as empowering, in the colony they appear as an oppressive
force, weighing on the heads and backs of those tasked with the production
of a future from which they remain excluded. Colonial subjects' experience of
modernity is, in other words, discrepant: the sonic and visual symbols of the
West—like the items listed in Dudley's catalogue of "goods sent to the troops
by the Committee for the Welfare of African Troops"—refuse integration,
appearing instead as alien objects unceremoniously dumped where they do
not belong.

The procession's Wagnerian intertext generates a sonic connection between
one artist's total work of art and another's fragmented collage. Inviting the listener to hear *The Head & the Load* through *Parsifal* (or, indeed, the other way
round), the reconfigured marches suggest that it should no longer be possible
to think of artistic totality without acknowledging the colonial conditions that
enable it. What was concealed in Monsalvat becomes a central focus in *The
Head & the Load*. While Wagner seeks to hide the labor that produces this totality, Kentridge's procession exposes it. Thus, the procession scene presents
a disclosure of the biomechanics of both operatic and political totality. *The
Head & the Load* invokes Wagner's *Gesamtkunstwerk* but unmasks it.

Totality and Fragmentation in Postcolonial Opera

Amid fears of resurgent political totalitarianism around the globe,
predicaments of social, political, and artistic unity are rapidly acquiring an
urgency reaching well beyond the walls of the opera house. Given the socio-
political complexities surrounding contemporary forms of totality, the

resurrection of the total work of art invites engagement with questions regarding the political, artistic, social, and ideological role of ideas of integration and synthesis. From a postcolonial point of view, renewed engagement with the pitfalls and potentialities of total performance offers an opportunity to combine narratives of Indigenous tradition with perspectives on technological progress. It also invites engagement with *Gesamtkunstwerk*'s capacity to deal with difference and to process the competing forces of totality and fracture that characterize both the colony and the postcolony. In short, engagement with practices of operatic totality in the postcolony afford an opportunity to examine anew the relationship between stage and society, politics and performance.

If the total work of art is, as David Roberts argues, about finding an ideal union of the arts through which to transform society into an aesthetic-social utopia, then Kentridge's creation represents the opposite.[80] Rather than harmony, everything about *The Head & the Load* signifies conflict: the piece represents viscerally not only the conflict of war but also the conflicting forces of subjection and defiance, of body and mind, and of logic and unreason. Simultaneously, however, the piece plays with a range of practices and principles related to totality, from Wagnerian synthesis to twentieth-century simultaneity. It invokes metaphors of technological, artistic, political, and sensorial integration only to explode these into a tumult of apparently contradictory signifiers. The deliberate disruption of any tendency to coherence alienates the work from traditional understandings of the total work of art. Not unity but fracture, not collaboration but disjuncture: each aspect of *The Head & the Load* acquires its meaning in opposition to another.

Kentridge's piece extends some of the practices associated with the twentieth-century total work of art, specifically the use of counterpoint, collage, fragmentation, and juxtaposition. But importantly, in *The Head & the Load* these techniques are not coupled with a romanticized view of mechanization nor with a utopian depiction of labor-free mechanized totality. Rather, *The Head & the Load* exposes explicitly the "dark underside" of totality, namely, the exploitative labor and exclusionary politics that are required to produce the impression of idealized homogeneity. Language, reason, subjectivity, and history become the shattered remains from which Kentridge grafts a new perspective on the relationship between performance, coloniality, and artistic totality.

The Head & the Load's tense interplay between totality and fracture is representative of both colonial history and the postcolonial present, where attempts

---

[80] Roberts, 2011, *Total Work of Art*, 7.

238 Postcolonial Opera

at totalitarian control continue, paradoxically, to yield fragmentation. In the face of this complex dynamic, totality obtains contradictory meanings. While it reflects the abjection of the colonial system, it may also represent an anti-colonial recovery of wholeness in the wake of disintegration. Read alongside histories of African total theater, the pursuit of theatrical totality may reinvigorate a more integrative approach to the relationship between work, worship, and leisure, between self and society, and between the social and the environmental. In this sense, the practice may also signify repair, recovery, and reconstruction of a ruptured self and a splintered society. Theatrical totality may, in other words, perform one version of the cultural return examined in Chapter 1 of this book.

The theatrical embrace of total form is ambiguous: it heads toward a totality that has been shown to be dangerous, but it also recovers what was lost. Opera can capture and enact this ambivalence. The art form's incorporation of diverse media enables a mode of theatrical communication that captures multiple perspectives at once. As *The Head & the Load* shows, the genre is capable of staging simultaneous agreement and disagreement; it corroborates and contradicts in one fluid motion. Operatic totality thus enables a multidimensional recovery of fragmented histories, offering an opportunity to recount the competing facts, memories, and experiences that constitute these pasts. Rather than recovering the idealized organic unity of Wagnerian *Gesamtkunstwerk* and African total theater, such work constructs a more makeshift form of aesthetic assemblage. Grafting, suturing, stitching together: the fragmented totality of postcolonial opera discards a conception of wholeness conditioned by coloniality, in favor of attachments that may be little more than accidental, disparate, or contradictory.

In the postcolonial sphere, opera's capacity for simultaneous synthesis and disruption may be employed to powerful effect, to reflect the paradoxes characteristic of colonial and postcolonial subjectivity and history. The art form's reliance on vocal performance enables a mediation between linguistic coherence and incomprehension, thus capturing the various breaks, miscommunications, and contradictory messages characteristic of coloniality. Moreover, through singing, the colonized subject reintegrates her body with the history she narrates. Recovering the coherence of a fractured selfhood, opera returns the colonized subject to herself.

With its spectacular multimedia effects, *The Head & the Load* foregrounds opera's interaction between music, stage, screen, and text. In the process, the work gives rise to interpretations that not only augment the work's intertextual treatment of source material but also enriches existing theoretical framings of the interaction between modernity, African performance traditions, Western aesthetic experimentalism, and postcoloniality. It enacts a collision rather than a reconciliation, for the fractures of the past cannot be resolved. Rather, they need grafting, into a multidimensional reckoning with the competing forces of colonial totality and fragmentation.

Conclusion

Future

In September 2019, Kentridge's forty-two-minute chamber opera, *Waiting for the Sibyl*, premiered at the Teatro dell'Opera di Roma in Italy. *Sibyl* was commissioned to accompany the theater's revival of *Work in Progress*, a 1968 piece by American sculptor Alexander Calder. Kentridge's response to Calder was an ensemble production for nine performers, based on the legend of the Cumaean Sibyl. The artist recounts the Sibyl's story as follows:

> The story of the Cumaean Sibyl was that you would go and ask her a question. She would write your fate on an oak leaf and place the leaf at the mouth of her cave, accumulating a pile of oak leaves. But as you went to retrieve your particular oak leaf, a breeze would blow up and swirl the leaves about, so that you never knew if you were getting your fate or someone else's fate. The fact that your fate would be known, but you couldn't know it, is the deep theme of our relationship of dread, of expectation, or foreboding towards the future.[1]

In *Sibyl*, as in so many of Kentridge's works, uncertainty is a central preoccupation. The prophetess's visitors cannot be sure that they've obtained their own fate from the swirling oak leaves. The future, even as they hold it in their hands, remains a mystery. Kentridge imagines a series of Sibyllean prophecies for his opera. These become the basis for the libretto. The Sibyl's imagined instructions are clear, if innocuous: "Beware the age of 73," she predicts, and "You will never see that city." Or:

> Resist: frenzied action on behalf of homeless cats
> the third cup of coffee
> the third martini

---

[1] William Kentridge, 2019, "Waiting for the Sibyl: Programme Note," https://www.kentridge.studio/waiting-for-the-sibyl-programme-note/, accessed May 31, 2023. Kentridge bases his version of the Sibyllean myth on Virgil's *Aeneid*, which describes her arboreal practice. See Ilaria Ottra, 2017, "'Ne saevi, magna sacerdos': L'ethos della Sibilla Virgiliana," *Studi Classici e Orientali* 63, 163–186.

Postcolonial Opera. Juliana M. Pistorius, Oxford University Press. © Oxford University Press 2025.
DOI: 10.1093/oso/9780197749203.003.0008

Conclusion **241**

the stroking of her knees
the smell of the starched shirt[2]

These phrases, based on fragments of text, translated proverbs, and half-remembered poems assembled by Kentridge over several years, accompany the onstage action in the form of painted projections.[3] They flicker onto the backdrop alongside Kentridge's drawings, functioning as surtitles (sometimes synchronized, at other times not) to the performers' songs.

Sibyl's music was devised by regular Kentridge collaborator, Nhlanhla Mahlangu, and celebrated South African jazz pianist, Kyle Shepherd. The score combines traditional southern African choral singing, performed live, with Shepherd's free improvisations, which are overlaid onto the opera as a recorded track. Musically, the production reaches beyond the conventions of Western opera to construct a piece rooted in South African song and dance (see ▶ Clip 7.1).

The opera's staging initiates a dialogue between Kentridge and Calder, and between Kentridge's own works for stage and screen. Kentridge recognized in Calder's mobile sculptures, which form the centerpiece of *Work in Progress*, a correspondence with his own fanciful stage mechanisms. He developed this connection to create a response to Calder that incorporates the whimsical props and eccentric technologies characteristic of his work. The artist writes that Calder's piece reminded him specifically of a series of "two-dimensional sculptures" he had created for Venice's La Fenice Opera House.[4] These sculptures, collectively titled *Return* (2008), comprise several disconnected shards, which combine into a coherent image from one particular point of view. As the sculpture rotates, its individual sections appear to shift into chaos, only to reassemble into intelligible form once the proper angle has been reached. Kentridge projected a video of these rotations onto the Venice opera house's fire curtain while the orchestra tuned for each night's performance, creating a visual realization of the sonic undulations of the players, as they settle on the oboe's "A," before collapsing back into musical chaos.[5]

For *Sibyl*, Kentridge returned to his rotating sculptures. Again, he incorporated them as projections—this time, onto the front stage curtain, which came down between each of the opera's six short scenes. The *Return* sculptures play,

---

[2] William Kentridge, 2020, *Waiting for the Sibyl* [libretto], London: Koenig Books.
[3] Kentridge, "Programme Note."
[4] Kentridge, "Programme Note."
[5] See Kentridge's discussion of the process in the video, "William Kentridge: 'Return,'" published by Art21. Art21, 2010, *Return: William Kentridge* [film], https://art21.org/watch/extended-play/william-kentridge-return-short/.

in Kentridge's words, with ideas of disintegration and regathering: they descend into chaos, only to reassemble into coherent form, much like the Sibyl's flying oak leaves, which swirl around before returning to their pile.[6] Crucially, this coherence is subject to perspective. Only from a particular place, at a particular time, can the true image embodied by the sculpture be discerned. *Return*, hence, brings themes of serendipity, perspectivalism, fracture, and recovery to bear on Kentridge's chamber opera. It also summons the thread of operatic return that weaves throughout this study: *Return* recalls opera's perpetual attempts to recover its imagined origins.

Sibyl embodies several of the topics I considered throughout this book. The piece enacts a dialogue between Kentridge and the Euro-American avant-garde; it incorporates non-operatic music into a work explicitly framed as opera; it constructs a ludic interplay between the sonic and the scopic; it resists narrative coherence; and it presents an accumulation of technological apparatus in a subversive meditation on anti-utilitarianism and purposeless mechanism.

With its incorporation of themes of doubt, generic ambiguity, and intermedial communication, *Sibyl* offers an ideal lens through which to revisit the themes that weave throughout this study. Though the production is worthy of detailed consideration in its own right, I use *Sibyl* here as an anchor for concluding remarks about the Kentridge works I addressed in previous chapters. Along with the prophetess, I also look to future prospects for scholarship on postcolonial opera and to further options for the study of Kentridge's work in music and theater. The subheadings I use in this concluding chapter are drawn from *Sibyl*'s libretto.

* * *

All So Different from What You Expected

I recently spoke to a friend who had seen *Sibyl* at its showing in Berkeley, California.[7] This had been his first encounter with a Kentridge production. My friend's initial reaction was confusion. Though he appreciated the beauty and humor of the opera's visual and textual construction, he told me, he felt that he must have missed some kind of deeper meaning to the work. He had

---

[6] Kentridge, 2010, in *Return: William Kentridge* [film], *art21*, https://art21.org/watch/extended-play/will iam-kentridge-return-short/.

[7] *Sibyl* was staged by Cal Performances in March 2023 as part of Kentridge's six-month-long campus residency at UC Berkeley.

studied the artist's statement in the production program, so he had an idea of the provenance and thematic content of the work; but nonetheless he felt at sea amid the multitude of musical, visual, and textual referents presented on stage.

This effect is not unusual. I, too, felt it when I first saw a piece by Kentridge—his video installation, *I am not me, the horse is not mine* (2008) at the Tate Modern in London. And I felt it again when I saw the production that brought me to this project: *The Head & the Load* (2018). Kentridge's works do not reveal their secrets readily. Instead, they invite deeper engagement, investigation, and a subjective bringing-together of information and insights. Even then, the meanings yielded by such exploration remain no more than options, a set of insights snatched from a swirling assortment of possible interpretations.

Alongside their own referential indeterminacy, Kentridge's operatic experiments subvert expectations that attach to opera as genre. They play with the limits of the form, inviting unusual settings, foreign musical practices, new performers (including machines), and a host of non-operatic narrative approaches into the generic fold. These manifestations of Kentridge's notion of unboundedness may be unsettling for audiences more familiar with the artist's major opera house productions. In their unpredictability and instability, however, these works become part of a performance practice that asks piercing questions about what opera is, what it can be, how it may function, and what purpose it serves at different times and in different places.

At the outset of this volume, I specified that I wished to approach Kentridge's experimental performance pieces as operas, specifically to examine what they might reveal about the expectations and conventions that attach to the genre. I started with an examination of *Il Ritorno d'Ulisse in Patria*, the most conventional of the Kentridge productions discussed here. Ulisse is a stranger wherever he lands; he has become the itinerant subject that reappears in Chapter 5, "Place." Like Ulisse, Chapter 1 argues, opera returns to various sites, all of which can be construed as either origin or destination. But it is a transformed return. Estranged from both its European and its Indigenous inheritance, the art form changes as it meets the demands of the postcolonial present. Juxtaposing the places and traditions that attach to the form, postcolonial opera incorporates a range of epistemologies anchored in both Enlightenment and extra-colonial thought, and subverts the genre's preoccupation with liveness and embodiment. In *Ulisse*, Kentridge performs this multiplicity through the ambiguous disembodiment of Handspring Puppet Company's wooden figures. The puppets, simultaneously persons and things, silent and singing, become a cipher for the fractured subjectivity of the postcolonial

244 Postcolonial Opera

subject. Opera returns to the postcolonial present, Chapter 1 suggests, but it is a transformed opera—changed by its journeys and encounters.

In *Ulisse*, the puppet-protagonist's operatic reminiscences guide the character toward his death. The displaced subjects of *Triumphs and Laments*, on the contrary, use operatic enunciation to enact a return to some form of presence. In *Triumphs and Laments*, Kentridge subverts several of opera's most entrenched expectations, including the art form's reliance on a particular style of singing, its narrative thrust, and its spatial-temporal unification. The production further undermines the genre's attempts at permanence and its inscription in regimes of territorial exceptionalism, to imagine an ambulatory performance practice that enables the migrant subject to construct a sonically enabled form of mobile homeliness. *Triumphs and Laments'* ambulatory form transposes opera from the opera house to the public walkways of Rome, where it allows its performers to occupy both place and space. Along the way, the opera's songs and imagery complicate simplistic constructions of history, monumentality, and belonging.

Triumphs and Laments' processional form plays out on a smaller scale in *The Head & the Load*. Whereas the former work imagines walking as a potentially empowering activity, however, the latter recounts a history of ambulatory abjection. In *The Head & the Load*, Black First World War porters' experiences of dispossession, dehumanization, and disenfranchisement become the basis for a multifarious engagement with Western modernity and its colonial underside. Kentridge's work constructs a "total world," in which the advancements of Europe are directly enabled by the exploitation of the colonies. This is an ambiguous totality: it gestures both to Western totalitarianism and to Indigenous ideals of social and spiritual integration. But even as it reflects the integrated nature of a "total world" conditioned by Walter Mignolo's modernity/coloniality bind, *The Head & the Load* undercuts any attempt at aesthetic or theatrical totality.[8] Its collage form, which grafts references to Western modernity onto scenes of colonial misery, fragments both history and the present. Exposing the contradictions that underpin the idealized total work of art, the piece imagines an operatic form capable of sounding out both the disjunction and the will-to-coherence of the postcolonial present.

If *The Head & the Load* exposes coloniality's worst excesses, *Black Box/Chambre Noire* seeks to mourn them. The automated installation, designed to

---

[8] Walter D. Mignolo, 2011, *The Darker Side of Western Modernity: Global Futures, Decolonial Options*, Durham, NC: Duke University Press. See the Introduction for a discussion of the modernity/coloniality bind.

Conclusion **245**

accompany Kentridge's production of *The Magic Flute*, examines the false hierarchy between Western Enlightenment and colonial darkness, to expose the close relationship between civility and cruelty. Remembering the victims of German extermination efforts in colonial South West Africa (now Namibia), *Black Box/Chambre Noire* asks how opera may participate in a project of memorialization and recovery. Crucially, the project does not perform its restitutive efforts on a traditional stage. Nor does it employ live performers to do so. Rather, it captures the ambiguity of postcolonial mourning by means of miniaturized automation. Portable and programmable, the opera exists somehow out of time and place—it is both universal and specific, bearing the weight of ethical representation by means of a contradictory interplay between disembodiment and envoicement. *Black Box/Chambre Noire*'s tiny, automated performers may symbolize the victims of colonial violence, but they also point to the technologies enabled by colonial extraction. These mechanical referents, which, in various forms, populate all of Kentridge's stages, are both whimsical and wretched—the nostalgic signifiers of a European future built on exclusion.

The history revisited in both *Black Box/Chambre Noire* and *The Head & the Load* coincides temporally with the events narrated in Italo Svevo's *Confessions of Zeno*. Svevo situates his novel in the years immediately preceding the First World War, as the Austro-Hungarian Empire rushed toward disintegration. Kentridge, in his operatic realization of *Confessions of Zeno*, transposes the novel's events to late apartheid and early post-apartheid South Africa. The titular character, fretting about the trivial misdemeanors of an inconsequential life, becomes a cipher for the bourgeois postcolonizing subject, enclosed in a haze of egocentric narcissism. Zeno's confessional practice is both self-serving and unreliable; it reflects the ambiguous position of an individual innocent of specific crimes, but implicated in the guilt of a generation. For Kentridge, Zeno is both individual and type—a person and a kind, whose presence signifies a doubling of Europe in Africa. The artist realizes this dual signification by means of shadow puppetry, which strips the protagonist of his defining features and turns him into an anonymous everyman. Zeno's puppets, parading in counterpoint to the main character's revelations, join composer Kevin Volans's heterogeneous score in enacting an intermedial destabilization of postcolonial confession.

Confessions of Zeno, like *Black Box/Chambre Noire*, casts doubt on the potency of opera's reparative practices in the postcolony. In both works, the art form's ambiguous politics of representation and subject-formation complicate any attempts at ethical engagement with the past—whether through confession or through mourning. Nonetheless, I argue, Kentridge's formal

246 Postcolonial Opera

unboundedness holds out some hope for a reconstituted operatic form capable of meeting the challenges of postcolonial restitution. In *Refuse the Hour*, such promise comes close to fulfillment. This lecture-opera demonstrates that the genre's capacity for temporal subversion turns it into a potent device for the destabilization of Western temporal regimes and their participation in coloniality. As in all of Kentridge's operatic experiments, however, the shadow of opera's complicity in the colonial project remains. The genre cannot free itself from this history. But, as *Refuse the Hour* shows, the art form's colonial collusion may strengthen opera's capacity to reflect on the contradictions that make up the postcolonial present.

The operatic works considered in this monograph demonstrate the potential of multimedia formal experiments to address opera's uneasy relationship with issues of race, representation, and coloniality. But the possibilities imagined in these productions are not conclusive. Instead, return, confession, mourning, time, displacement, and totality emerge in these chapters as equivocal manifestations of the postcolonial condition. Doubt and ambiguity, Kentridge's productions demonstrate, are central to the work of opera in the postcolony. In their play with convention and expectation, these works resist the clarity of certitude, developing instead a compelling perspective on the contradictions and compromises that anchor the genre's position in the postcolony.

* * *

It Is Not Enough

Postcolonial Opera shapes its theories and arguments around six of Kentridge's operatic works (seven, if *Sibyl* is counted too). My selection was informed partly by the availability of source materials, partly by chronology, and partly by the thematic concerns I wished to explore. Several other Kentridge works could have been part of this book. The artist has created a large number of pieces that could fit into my expanded conception of (postcolonial) opera. These include *I Am not Me, the Horse Is not Mine* and *Telegrams from the Nose* (2011), both of which are fellow travelers created alongside Kentridge's production of Shostakovich's opera, *The Nose*. Other multimedia installations that could yield compelling insights are *Paper Music* (2014), a multimedia song cycle with music by Philip Miller; *Notes Towards a Model Opera* (2015), which engages with the history of the Chinese Cultural Revolution, and *A Guided Tour of the Exhibition: for Soprano with Handbag* (2016), which reflects on

Conclusion 247

the "museumification" of contemporary artistic practice. Each of these works could ignite further areas of inquiry related to postcolonial opera, including the role of political authoritarianism on the one hand, or capitalist economies on the other, in the construction and dissemination of the genre.

They could also initiate a more expansive examination of Kentridge's engagement with sound technologies (both as images and as media) throughout his oeuvre. Installations such as *Almost Don't Tremble* (2019), *Singer Trio* (2019), and the drum machine from *Refuse the Hour*, which has also been exhibited as a self-contained automated sound sculpture, are realizations of an aesthetic practice conditioned by a deep fascination with the mechanics of sound production. Sound technologies pepper Kentridge's work, from the metronomes of *Refuse the Hour* and *The Refusal of Time*, to the megaphones, gramophones, telephones, and phonographs of works such as *Receiver* (2006), *Phenakistoscope* (2000), and the films that make up the *Drawings for Projection* series (1989–2020). Apart from their visual manifestation, these sound technologies also signify a concern with the interplay between the sonic and the scopic. For Kentridge, sound is not simply soundtrack, but medium—an integrated and meaningful register of the work as a whole. It can support or contradict, expand or contract, the visual dimensions of a piece.

If sound has the capacity to complicate sight, then the inverse is also true. In recent years, the artist has embarked on a number of projects that join his drawings and projections to existing musical compositions. These include a visual realization of Franz Schubert's song cycle, *Die Winterreise* (2014), and a film, *Oh, to Believe in Another World* (2022), to accompany Dmitri Shostakovich's tenth symphony.[9] In each instance, Kentridge's graphics serve as a complement—commentary, counterpoint, and illumination—to the music.

The *Winterreise* and Shostakovich symphony projects underscore Kentridge's integrative approach to theatrical and artistic multimedia. They also form part of a performance practice that sees the artist experiment with creative realizations of standard forms and experimental texts. Kentridge's public lectures (such as his *Six Drawing Lessons* series at Harvard University, his *Refuse the Hour* and *Notes Towards a Model Opera* talks, and the Slade Lectures in Oxford) are highly curated performance pieces. They often present a mixture of video art, performance, and ironic self-reflection, leading the spectator to question where Kentridge the artist ends and Kentridge the

---

[9] For Kentridge's *Winterreise*, see http://quaternaire.org/william-kentridge/winterreise; for *Oh, to Believe in Another World*, see https://www.kentridge.studio/projects/oh-to-believe-in-another-world/.

248 Postcolonial Opera

stage actor begins. Like the artist's live presentation of Kurt Schwitters's sound poem, *Ursonate* (1932), a performance Kentridge first realized in 2017, these public addresses bear witness to the lasting impact of the artist's training in physical theater at the École Jacques Lecoq in Paris.[10] Kentridge often claims that his Paris education convinced him that he was ill-suited to a career as an actor. Nonetheless, the training he received there continues to guide his work as a draughtsman, director, and performer.[11]

Together, the projects I mention here reveal that there is much left to say about Kentridge's work with sound and about his experiments with theater. Disciplinary approaches grounded in performance studies, theater studies, and contemporary scenography (which would, of course, also benefit from engagement with the artist's stagings of repertoire operas) may all productively be brought to bear on Kentridge's heterogeneous practice. Such work would likely yield fascinating perspectives on the critical capacities of intermedial performance, and the generic limits of the visual and sonic arts.

(But It Is Not Nothing)

Despite the limited nature of this book's engagement with Kentridge's operas, it nonetheless offers a first corrective to the dearth of scholarship around the artist's work with sound. More important, *Postcolonial Opera* signifies a first attempt to develop a coherent critical-theoretical frame for postcolonial opera—one centered around a delimited body of work, and animated by thematic concerns central to the postcolonial present.

If opera is to play a role in postcolonial recovery, it cannot be opera as usual. The art form must find a way to accommodate its own ambiguity, especially where its presence in the postcolony is concerned. *Postcolonial Opera* reads the possibilities afforded by formal experimentation against the critical interests that structure postcolonial subjectivity, to offer provisional insights into the art form's capacity for meaningful work in the postcolony.

* * *

[10] Kentridge's performance of *Ursonate* can be viewed on The Centre for the Less Good Idea's *Vimeo* channel, at https://vimeo.com/301783578.

[11] On Kentridge's training in Paris and its impact on his work, see In Terms of Performance, n.d., "Interview—William Kentridge," http://intermsofperformance.site/interviews/william-kentridge, accessed May 20, 2023.

Conclusion **249**

I No Longer Believe What I Once Believed

When I first embarked on this project, I intended to examine opera's capacity to accommodate the decolonial agenda. I set out from the premise that opera itself can function as a decolonial form. My thinking, guided by the Western academy's belated discovery of the value of Indigenous epistemologies, sought to uncover the ways in which opera may subvert conventional hierarchies of creation, consumption, and cultural exchange. As I reach the end of my project, I feel compelled to revisit my initial critical plan.

Despite their innovative and at times disruptive engagement with the operatic form, the productions discussed in this book remain inscribed in traditional, Western networks of patronage and circulation. They rely on funders and competitive promotional strategies to enable their development and transmission. They seek recognition in venues associated with local and/or international prestige. Their success, moreover, is still largely measured by what Thembela Vokwana calls "entry of the previously marginalized into the global arena," whether through the securement of lucrative international touring contracts, endorsement by high-profile brands or individuals, or recognition in the international press.[12]

Kentridge's works are not alone in this. Rather, they are representative of the majority of new and experimental opera created both in former colonies and in former imperial metropoles. Funding, circulation, and institutional support remain crucial concerns for an art form vulnerable to the vagaries of economic uncertainty and neoliberalism. In other words, opera remains tied to networks firmly embedded in modernity.

For Sarah Hegenbart, the fact that even the most reformist of operatic endeavors relies for its survival on asymmetrical sponsorship structures, creates an existential dilemma for the form. She writes, "Given that opera as institution can only exist within a system enabling the infrastructures needed for its operation, e.g. salaries for the cast, costs for the venue etc., the question arises of how fierce the institutional self-reflection of opera can be without gaining the support of the very system sustaining its infrastructures."[13] Opera, Hegenbart argues, cannot change unless it seeks a new set of enabling structures free from Western economic models, even when these are

---

[12] Thembela Vokwana, 2006–2007, "Opera in Africa: Music of the People, for the People, by the People," *New Music SA Bulletin* 5–6, 12–16, at 15–16.

[13] Sarah Hegenbart, 2020, "Decolonising Opera: Interrogating the Genre of Opera in the Sahel and Other Regions in the Global South," in *"Gefühle sind von Hausa us Rebellen," Musiktheater als Katalysator und Reflexionsagentur für gesellschaftliche Entwicklungsprozesse*, ed. Dominik Frank, Ulrike Hartung, and Kornelius Paede, Würzburg: Königshausen & Neumann, 169–196, 179.

250 Postcolonial Opera

philanthropic. Put differently, comprehensive transformation requires a reassessment of the art form's participation in the late capitalist and neoliberal systems of exchange that constitute modernity.

From a decolonial point of view, opera's reliance on the structures of modernity is awkward. If, as Mignolo argues, the decolonial project is a pursuit of "alternatives to modernity," then opera seems to fall at the first hurdle. Rather than circumventing the modernity/coloniality bind, opera embodies it. The tension between decolonization and participation in the systems and structures of modernity undermines the art form's capacity to decolonize. Regardless of its provenance (Indigenous or colonial), opera, like other institutions including the university, the court of law, and the hospital, is too firmly embedded within international networks of patronage, circulation, and cross-pollination—themselves products and producers of modernity—to decouple entirely from the current world order.

A further challenge to operatic decolonization may be found in the fact that the decolonial project is itself a shifting and variegated pursuit. Despite a long history of decolonial thought developed in different domains, the decolonial agenda remains mutable, its aims and methods as varied as the geographical and historical contexts it incorporates.[14] There is no blueprint for decolonization.

The openness of the decolonial project is representative of its rejection of dogma, and its adaptability to the particularities of time and place. However, this radical refusal of fixed delineation also leaves the meaning of the term always up for grabs, ready to be populated with fluctuating perspectives and ideals. Operatic decolonization will hence manifest differently depending on the place from which it originates. This creates an ontological challenge. If opera relies on reiteration to recognize itself as form, genre, or institution, then the differential decolonization of the practice risks insufficiently addressing the very foundations of the genre—namely, a reiterative return to, or recovery of, an imagined tradition. Put differently, a radically localized decolonial practice risks not being recognized as opera, thereby rendering its subversive or reconstitutive endeavors unresolved.

As I grappled with these challenges, I realized again and again that a far greater range of racial, ethnic, cultural, gender, and economic identities must become part of the conversation on operatic decolonization. It is impossible to theorize conclusively about the decolonial affordances of the operatic form

---

[14] For a historical overview of decolonial thought on the African continent, see Raymond F. Betts, 2012, "Decolonization: A Brief History of the Word," in *Beyond Empire and Nation: The Decolonization of African and Asian Societies, 1930s–1970s*, edited by Els Bogaerts and Remco Raben, Leiden: KITLV Press, 23–38.

Conclusion **251**

on the basis of one, white South African creative agent's work. Decolonization cannot and will not emerge from the singular vision of one artist (even if his works are radically collaborative). Nor can Kentridge and his works be regarded as fully representative of the vast array of operatic experiments and practitioners currently operating in South Africa and the rest of the post- and decolonial world.

The diversity of views and experiences that can find a home on the operatic stage—wherever that stage may be—is potentially limitless. Likewise, the various forms of creativity, expression, and collaboration that may contribute to the creation of the operatic event reach far beyond opera's prevailing institutions and hierarchies. One cannot theorize decolonization without taking into account these small, often hidden or neglected practices and experiments. Indeed, perhaps operatic decolonization is best searched for at the margins, rather than on the internationally acclaimed stages of blockbuster artists. Kentridge's operas, in short, do not answer the decolonial question; in fact, they only raise more questions.

What Kentridge's works do offer, however, is an unusually clear perspective on the structures, possibilities, and limits that shape institutional operatic practice in the present moment. When I speak of opera as form, genre, or convention, it is especially these factors which I have in mind. The expectations that attach to the idea of opera still shape how the art form circulates and how it is received. Kentridge's works, even (or perhaps especially) when they subvert these expectations, reveal not only the power of opera's institutional legacy but also the unexpected flexibility of this legacy and the critical force that flows from disrupting it.

I still believe that opera may complicate existing power relations between the West and the so-called rest. The genre, I have shown throughout this book, possesses enormous capacity for anticolonial critique. Even as it partakes in the compromised networks of modernity, it can draw attention to, comment upon, and ultimately destabilize the coherence of these systems. This, to me, is consistent with the work of postcolonialism. I therefore wish to reiterate my reading of Kentridge's works as examples of postcolonial, rather than decolonial, opera.

With its intermedial composition, opera has the capacity to show and to subvert, to enact and to critique. That is exactly what Kentridge achieves with his sonic-scopic juxtapositions. Appearing to contradict himself across registers, the artist simultaneously emulates and undercuts the signifiers of Western modernity.

* * *

Where Shall We Put Our Hope?

In *Sibyl*'s fifth scene, a performer tries to sit down. Around him, the stage is filled with an assortment of chairs. However, whenever the actor tries to lower himself onto one of them, the chair moves or collapses. The performer is perplexed; the audience is not. The rope with which an off-stage performer pulls the chair from under the sitter is clearly visible: there is no magic trick here. Which chair should the performer trust? Which is the chair that will hold him? How is he to identify "the wrong chair"? Like Perseus's grandfather in *Refuse the Hour*, the actor in *Sibyl* must decide where to place his hope. Get it wrong, and he may end up sprawled on the ground, feeling ridiculous. Get it right, and he may live to embrace his grandson.

Postcolonial opera's future directions may not literally be a matter of life or death. They are, nonetheless, consequential, especially as they relate to matters of ethical representation, cultural self-actualization, and anticolonial rehabilitation. Where the genre is to place its hope remains open to debate. In this volume, I proposed formal unboundedness as a possible practice on which to wager the art form's future. This is not the only way in which opera may meet the challenges of the postcolonial present. Nor is Kentridge necessarily the essential or emblematic figure around which such a project may cohere.

Several companies and practitioners, operating across the Global North and South, have developed powerful operatic responses to the predicaments of coloniality. I think, for instance, of the Los Angeles-based company The Industry's *Sweet Land*, or South African composer neo muyanga's experimental productions, such as *Heart of Redness* (Cape Town, 2015). Other projects include British composer Shirley J. Thompson's *Women of the Windrush: An Opera* (2023); Indigenous Australian singer Deborah Cheetham's opera, *Pecan Summer* (Short Black Opera, 2010); and Ghanaian composer Gorges Ocloo's *The Golden Stool, or the Story of Nana Ya Asantewaa* (Opera Ballet Vlaanderen, 2023).

Each of these works addresses the challenges of representation and historical narration differently; they also respond in diverse ways to the expectations and conventions that adhere to the genre. Crucially, they all develop compelling perspectives on coloniality and its afterlives. The creators and performers involved in these works bring different experiences of coloniality to their practice; the result is a diverse constellation of operatic engagements with postcolonial subjectivity. Challenging conventional assumptions about what opera is and how it should function, these artists and their works make a compelling case, alongside Kentridge's pieces, for a flexible and expansive conception of the form.

The pieces I examine in this book show that the worth of postcolonial opera lies not in its achievement of an impossible future but in its capacity to revisit and reconfigure both past and present. Even as they address the challenges of contemporary life, Kentridge's pieces function most powerfully as contemplations of history. The artist's operas revisit the past both as inspiration and indictment. They allow new versions of history to emerge from the cracks between dislocated certainties, fractured masterworks, and deconstructed narratives. Kentridge's operas offer humor, beauty, and catalytic opportunities to reimagine the form and function of opera in the postcolony.

This book is not the last word on postcolonial opera. Its conclusions are partial and provisional. As a critical-theoretical framework, however, it offers a starting point from which to examine the different chairs upon which the genre may balance its hopes. I anticipate that postcolonial opera will continue to generate ever-more searching and creative dialogues with different traditions of Indigenous performance and historical self-narration; in the process, the art form may enact a new form of return, based not on a search for a lost, premodern and precolonial essence, but in a more responsive and responsible engagement with a transfigured present.

Bibliography

Abbate, Carolyn. 2001. *In Search of Opera*. Princeton, NJ: Princeton University Press.

Abbate, Carolyn and Roger Parker. 2012. *A History of Opera: The Last Four Hundred Years*. London: Penguin.

Adedeji, Joel. 1969. "Traditional Yoruba Theatre." *African Arts* 3(1), 60–63.

Adedeji, Joel. 1971. "A Profile of Nigerian Theatre 1960–1970." *Nigeria Magazine* 107–109, 3–14.

Adelugba, Dapo and Olu Obafemi. 2004. "Anglophone West Africa: Nigeria." In *A History of Theatre in Africa*, ed. Martin Banham. Cambridge: Cambridge University Press, 138–158.

Adesanya, Adebayo. 1958. "Yoruba Metaphysical Thinking." *Odù* 5, 36–41.

Adlington, Robert, ed. 2019. *New Music Theatre in Europe: Transformation between 1955–1975*. London: Routledge.

Adorno, Theodor. 2006 [1949]. *Philosophy of New Music*, trans. Robert Hullot Kentor. Minneapolis: University of Minnesota Press.

Agamben, Giorgio. 1998 [1995]. *Homo Sacer: Sovereign Power and Bare Life*, trans. Daniel Heller-Roazen. Stanford, CA: Stanford University Press.

Agawu, V. Kofi. 2016. *The African Imagination in Music*. New York: Oxford University Press.

Agawu, V. Kofi. 2001. "Chaka: An Opera in Two Chants." *Research in African Literatures* 32(2), 196–198.

Agbamu, Samuel. 2022. "Smash the Thing: William Kentridge, Classical Antiquity, and His Refusal of Time in O Sentimental Machine." *Classical Receptions Journal* 14(2), 264–287.

Ahmed, Sara, Claudia Castañeda, Anne-Marie Fortier, and Mimi Sheller, eds. 2003. *Uprootings/Regroundings: Questions of Home and Migration*. Oxford: Berg.

Ahrendt, Rebekah. 2019. "The Legal Spaces of Opera in the Hague." In *Operatic Geographies*, 12–25.

Allara, Pamela. 2019. "William Kentridge's *Triumphs and Laments*: The Challenges and Pleasures of Collaboration." *de arte* 54(1), 60–85.

Amberson, Deborah. 2016. "Zeno's Dissonant Violin: Italo Svevo, Judaism, and Western Art Music." *Italian Studies* 71(1), 98–114.

André, Naomi. 2018. *Black Opera: History, Power, Engagement*. Champaign: University of Illinois Press.

André, Naomi, Donato Somma, and Innocentia J. Mhlambi. 2016. "*Winnie, the Opera* and Embodying South African Opera." *African Studies* 75(1), 1–9.

Apthorp, Shirley. 2017. "Wozzeck at Salzburg—a Breathtaking Reassessment." *Financial Times*, August 9. https://www.ft.com/content/9b8814c2-7c63-11e7-ab01-a13271d1ee9c.

"Arrival, N., Sense I.3.a." 2023. *Oxford English Dictionary*. Oxford: Oxford University Press. https://doi.org/10.1093/OED/8712077064.

Ashcroft, Bill, Gareth Griffiths, and Helen Tiffin, eds. 2002 [1989]. *The Empire Writes Back: Theory and Practice in Post-Colonial Literatures*. London: Routledge.

Aspden, Suzanne, ed. 2019. *Operatic Geographies: The Place of Opera and the Opera House*. Chicago, IL: University of Chicago Press.

Aspden, Suzanne. 2019. "Opera and the (Urban) Geography of Culture." In *Operatic Geographies*, 1–11.

Aspden, Suzanne. 2019. "Pastoral Retreats: Playing at Arcadia in Modern Britain." In *Operatic Geographies*, 195–212.

256 Bibliography

Baker, Donald. 1977. "African Theatre and the West." *Comparative Drama* 11(3), 227–251.

Ballantine, Christopher. 2019. "Opera and the South African Political." In *The Oxford Handbook of Sound and Imagination*, ed. Mark Grimshaw-Aagaard, Mads Walther-Hansen, and Martin Knakkergaard. Oxford: Oxford University Press, 291–311.

Barrett, Michèle. 2017. "Dehumanization and the War in East Africa." *Journal of War & Culture Studies* 10(3), 238–252.

Barthes, Roland. 2000 [1981]. *Camera Lucida: Reflections on Photography*, trans. Richard Howard. London: Vintage.

Bartoli, Flavia, Annalaura Casanova Municchia, Marcello Leotta, Sebastiano Luciano, and Giulia Caneva. 2021. "Biological Recolonization Dynamics: Kentridge's Artwork Disappearing along the Tiber Embankments (Rome, Italy)." *International Biodeterioration & Biodegradation* 160, 1–10.

Bartolini, Paolo. 2012. "Zeno's Thingness: On Fetishism and Bodies in Svevo's *La coscienza di Zeno*." *Italianist* 32(3), 399–414.

Bashford, Christina. 2003. "The String Quartet and Society." In *The Cambridge Companion to the String Quartet*, ed. Robin Stowell and Jonathan Cross. Cambridge: Cambridge University Press, 3–18.

Basualdo, Carlos, ed. 2017. *William Kentridge: Triumphs and Laments*. Berlin: Buchhandlung Walther Koenig.

Basualdo, Carlos and William Kentridge. 2017. "In People's Memory: Carlos Basualdo in Conversation with William Kentridge." In *William Kentridge: Triumphs and Laments*, 49–96.

Beard, Mary. 2007. *The Roman Triumph*. Cambridge, MA: Harvard University Press.

Beecham, Thomas. 1938. *Mozart: Zauberflöte*. Naxos Historical: 8.110127–28.

Begley, Varun. 2012. "Objects of Realism: Bertold Brecht, Roland Barthes, and Marsha Norman." *Theatre and Material Culture* 64(3), 337–353.

Benjamin, Walter. 2007 [1942]. *Illuminations*, ed. Hannah Arendt, trans. Harry Zohn. New York: Schocken Books.

Benjamin, Walter. 1977 [1928]. *The Origin of German Tragic Drama*, trans. John Osborne. London: NLB.

Bentley, Charlotte. 2022. *New Orleans and the Creation of Transatlantic Opera, 1819–1859*. Chicago, IL: University of Chicago Press.

Bentley, Charlotte. 2018. "Resituating Transatlantic Opera: The Case of the Théâtre d'Orléans, New Orleans, 1819–1859." PhD diss., University of Cambridge.

Bereson, Ruth. 2002. *The Operatic State: Cultural Policy and the Opera House*. New York: Routledge.

Berger, Karol. 2007. *Bach's Cycle, Mozart's Arrow: An Essay on the Origins of Musical Modernity*. Berkeley: University of California Press.

Bergeron, Katherine. 1992. "Prologue: Disciplining Music." In *Disciplining Music: Musicology and Its Canons*, ed. Katherine Bergeron and Philip V. Bohlman. Chicago, IL: University of Chicago Press, 1–9.

Bergson, Henri. 2003 [1889]. *Time and Free Will: An Essay on the Immediate Data of Consciousness*, trans. F. L. Pogson. London: Routledge.

Beschara, Karam. 2014. "William Kentridge's Animated *Drawings for Projection* as Postmemorial Aesthetic." *De arte* 49(90), 4–23.

Betts, Raymond F. 2012. "Decolonization: A Brief History of the Word." In *Beyond Empire and Nation: The Decolonization of African and Asian Societies, 1930s–1970s*, ed. Els Bogaerts and Remco Raben. Leiden: KITLV Press, 23–38.

Bhabha, Homi K. 2020. "Theater of War: *Din und Drang* in *The Head & the Load*." In *The Head & the Load*, ed. William Kentridge. Paris: Éditions Xavier Barral, 301–316.

Bhabha, Homi K. 2016. "Processional Ethics: Homi K. Bhabha on William Kentridge's *More Sweetly Play the Dance*." *Artforum International* 55(2), 230–292.

Bibliography 257

Bhabha, Homi K. 2004 [1994]. *The Location of Culture*. London: Routledge.

BibleGateway. n.d. "Psalm 137." https://www.biblegateway.com/passage/?search=Psalm%20 137&version=KJV.

Bloechl, Olivia. 2019. *Opera and the Political Imaginary in Old Regime France*. Chicago:, IL University of Chicago Press.

Blumenthal, Eileen. 2018. "What One Show Can Carry: William Kentridge's *The Head and the Load*." *American Theatre*, December 14. https://www.americantheatre.org/2018/12/14/ what-one-show-can-carry-william-kentridges-the-head-and-the-load/.

Booth, Robert. 2020. "UK More Nostalgic for Empire than Other Ex-Colonial Powers." *The Guardian*, March 11. https://www.theguardian.com/world/2020/mar/11/uk-more-nostal gic-for-empire-than-other-ex-colonial-powers.

Braidotti, Rosi. 2011. *Nomadic Subjects*. New York: Columbia University Press.

Bräuninger, Jürgen. 1998. "Gumboots to the Rescue." *South African Journal of Musicology: SAMUS* 18, 1–16.

Buck, Louisa. 2018. "William Kentridge Outplays the England Match with Tate Premiere of Performance The Head and the Load." *Art Newspaper*, July 12. https://www.theartne wspaper.com/blog/william-kentridge-outplays-the-england-match-with-tate-premi ere-of-the-head-and-the-load.

Budasz, Rogério. 2019. *Opera in the Tropics: Music and Theater in Early Modern Brazil*. Oxford: Oxford University Press.

Buikema, Rosemarie. 2016. "The Revolt of the Object: Animated Drawings and the Colonial Archive: William Kentridge's *Black Box* Theatre." *Interventions* 18(2), 251–269.

Burden, Michael. 2019. "London's Opera House in the Urban Landscape." In *Operatic Geographies*, 39–56.

Burden, Michael. 2009. "The Lure of Aria, Procession and Spectacle: Opera in Eighteenth-Century London." In *The Cambridge History of Eighteenth-Century Music*, ed. Simon P. Keefe. Cambridge: Cambridge University Press, 385–401.

Butler, Judith. 2007. *Who Sings the Nation-State? Language, Politics, and Belonging*. London: Seagull Books.

Butler, Judith. 2005. *Giving an Account of Oneself*. New York: Fordham University Press.

Butler, Judith. 2004. *Precarious Life: The Power of Mourning and Violence*. London: Verso.

Butler, Judith. 1997. *The Psychic Life of Power: Theories in Subjection*. Stanford, CT: Stanford University Press.

Calico, Joy H. 2018. "Genre Designation as Ambiguating Force: Olga Neuwirth's *Lost Highway* as Opera." In *Ambiguity in Contemporary Art and Theory*, ed. Frauke Berndt and Lutz Koepnick. Hamburg: Felix Meiner Verlag, 151–164.

Cameron, Dan. 2001. "An Interview with William Kentridge." In *William Kentridge*, ed. Michel Sittenfeld. Chicago, IL: Museum of Contemporary Art, 67–74.

Cameron, Dan. 1999. "A Procession of the Dispossessed." In *William Kentridge*, ed. Michel Sittenfeld. Chicago, IL: Museum of Contemporary Art, 36–81.

Cameron, Dan, Carolyn Christov-Bakargiev, and J. M. Coetzee, eds. 1999. *William Kentridge*. London: Phaidon.

Campbell, Patricia J. 2000. "The Truth and Reconciliation Commission (TRC): Human Rights and State Transitions—The South Africa Model." *African Studies Quarterly* 4(3), 41–63.

Carotenuto, Silvana. 2018. "Writing 'Time': The (Late) *Oeuvres* of Jacques Derrida and William Kentridge." *English Academy Review* 35(1), 73–95.

Cavarero, Adriana. 2005. *For More than One Voice: Toward a Philosophy of Vocal Expression*. Stanford, CA.: Stanford University Press.

Cavell, Stanley. 1994. *A Pitch of Philosophy: Autobiographical Exercises*. Cambridge: Cambridge University Press.

258 Bibliography

Centre Pompidou. n.d. "Opera as the World: The Quest for a Total Work of Art." https://www.centrepompidou.fr/en/program/calendar/event/cBrLzdg.

Centre Pompidou-Metz. n.d. "Opera as the World." https://www.centrepompidou-metz.fr/en/programme/categorie/opera-as-the-world.

Charlton, Ed. 2021. *Improvising Reconciliation: Confession after the Truth Commission*. Liverpool: Liverpool University Press.

Cheng, Anne Anlin. 2001. *The Melancholy of Race: Psychoanalysis, Assimilation, and Hidden Grief*. Oxford: Oxford University Press.

Chilembwe, John. 2020 [1914]. "The Voice of African Natives in the Present War." In *Christianity in Malawi: A Source Reader*, ed. Kenneth R. Ross. Mzuzu: Mzuni Press, 247–249.

Christiansë, Yvette. 1996. "At the Fault Line—Writers in the Shadow of Truth and Reconciliation." *New Coin Poetry* 32(2), 70–75.

Christov-Bakargiev, Carolyn. 1998. *William Kentridge*. Exhibition catalogue: Palais des Beaux-Arts de Bruxelles.

Coetzee, J. M, 1992 [1985]. "Confession and Double Thoughts: Tolstoy, Rousseau, Dostoevsky." In *Doubling the Point: Essays and Interviews*, ed. David Attwell. Cambridge, MA: Harvard University Press, 251–293.

Connor, Steven. 2000. *Dumbstruck: A Cultural History of Ventriloquism*. Oxford: Oxford University Press.

Conrad, Joseph. 1960 [1907]. *The Secret Agent: A Simple Tale*. London: J. M. Dent.

Cooper, Allan D. 2006. "Reparations for the Herero Genocide: Defining the Limits of International Litigation." *African Affairs* 116(422), 113–126.

Cooppan, Vilashini. 2019. "Time Maps: A Field Guide for the Decolonial Imaginary." *Critical Times* 2(3), 396–415.

Corbin, Alain. 1999 [1998]. *Village Bells: Sound and Meaning in the 19th-Century French Countryside*, trans. Martin Thom. London: Papermac.

Cox, Emma. 2017. "Processional Aesthetics and Irregular Transit: Envisioning Refugees in Europe." *Theatre Journal* 69(4), 477–496.

Davies, Geoffrey and Anne Fuchs. 1996. "'An Interest in the Making of Things': An Interview with William Kentridge." In *Theatre and Change in South Africa*, ed. Geoffrey Davis and Anne Fuchs. Amsterdam: Harwood, 140–153.

Davies, Sheila Boniface and J. Q. Davies. 2012. "'So Take This Magic Flute and Blow. It Will Protect Us as We Go': *Impempe Yomlingo* (2011) and South Africas Ongoing Transition." *Opera Quarterly* 28(1–2), 54–71.

Davison, Neil. 1996. *James Joyce, Ulysses and the Construction of Jewish Identity: Culture, Biography, and "the Jew" in Modernist Europe*. Cambridge: Cambridge University Press.

De Jong, Ferdinand. 2018. "Archive of Darkness: William Kentridge's *Black Box/Chambre Noire*." *african arts* 51(1), 10–23.

Derrida, Jacques. 2001. *The Work of Mourning*, ed. Pascale-Anne Brault and Michael Naas. Chicago, IL: University of Chicago Press.

Diamond, Beverly. 2011. "Decentering Opera: Early Twenty First Century Indigenous Production." In *Opera Indigene: Re/presenting First Nations and Indigenous Cultures*, 31–56.

Dlamini, Jacob. 2016. "Apartheid Confessions." *interventions* 18(6), 772–785.

Dolkart, Ronald. 1983. "Elitelore at the Opera: The Teatro Colón of Buenos Aires." *Journal of Latin American Lore* 9(2), 231–250.

Dospinescu, Liviu. 2006. "Vers un nouveau théâtre politique: William Kentridge et les discours transculturels." *ANADISS* 2(2), 95–116.

Drott, Eric. 2013. "The End(s) of Genre." *Journal of Music Theory* 57(1), 1–45.

Dube, Saurabh. 2017. *Subjects of Modernity: Time-Space, Disciplines, Margins*. Manchester: Manchester University Press.

Dubin, Steven C. 2007. "Theater of History." *Art in America*, April, 128–131 and 157.

Dubow, Jessica and Ruth Rosengarten. 2004. "History as the Main Complaint: William Kentridge and the Making of Post-Apartheid South Africa." *Art History* 27(4), 671–690.

Duggan, Tony. 2001. "Wolfgang Amadeus Mozart: *Die Zauberflöte* (*The Magic Flute*)." *Classical Music on the Web*. http://www.musicweb-international.com/classrev/2001/apr01/magicflute.htm.

Durrant, Sam. 2004. *Postcolonial Narrative and the Work of Mourning: J. M. Coetzee, Wilson Harris, and Toni Morrison*. Albany: State University of New York Press.

Eberty, Felix. 1846. *The Stars and the Earth: Thoughts upon Space, Time, and Eternity*. London: Bailliere, Tindall, and Cox.

Edensor, Tim. 2010. "Walking in Rhythms: Place, Regulation, Style and the Flow of Experience." *Visual Studies* 25(1), 69–79.

Einstein, Alfred. 1950–51. "Salamone Rossi as Composer of Madrigals." *Hebrew Union College Annual* 23(2), 383–396.

Einstein, Alfred. 1941. "Mozart's Choice of Keys." *Musical Quarterly* 27(4), 415–421.

Eldredge, Elizabeth A. 2014. *The Creation of the Zulu Kingdom, 1815–1828: War, Shaka, and the Consolidation of Power*. New York: Cambridge University Press.

Ellis, Katharine. 2021. *French Musical Life: Local Dynamics in the Century to World War II*. New York: Oxford University Press.

Erlmann, Veit. 1991. *African Stars: Studies in Black South African Performance*. Chicago, IL: University of Chicago Press.

Fabian, Johannes. 2014 [1983]. *Time and the Other: How Anthropology Makes Its Object*. New York: Columbia University Press.

Fanon, Frantz. 2014. "The Conduct of Confession in North Africa." In *Decolonizing Madness: The Psychiatric Writings of Frantz Fanon*, ed. Nigel Gibson. New York: Palgrave Macmillan, 87–89.

Fanon, Frantz. 2008 [1952]. *Black Skin, White Masks*, trans. Charles Lam Markmann. London: Pluto.

Fanon, Frantz. 2004 [1961]. *The Wretched of the Earth*, trans. Richard Pilcox. New York: Grove Press.

Feder, Stuart. 1999. *The Life of Charles Ives*. Cambridge: Cambridge University Press.

Fenlon, Ian. 2001. "Rossi, Salamone." *Grove Music Online*. https://doi-org.libaccess.hud.ac.uk/10.1093/gmo/9781561592630.article.23896.

Fenn, Hayley. 2021. "Puppets That Sing or Scenery That Breathes: Phelim McDermott's Satyagraha." In *Experiencing Music and Visual Cultures: Threshold, Intermediality, Synchresis*. London: Routledge, 64–78.

Fenn, Hayley. 2019. "Big Marionette, Little Marionette." *Opera Quarterly* 35(4), 335–349.

Fensham, Rachel. 2008. "Operating Theatres: Body-Bits and a Post-Apartheid Aesthetics." In *Anatomy Live: Performance and the Operating Theatre*, ed. Maaike Bleeker. Amsterdam: Amsterdam University Press, 251–261.

Ferraiuolo, Augusto. 2015. "The Tammorra Displaced: Music and Body Politics from Churchyards to Glocal Arenas in the Neapolitan Area." *Cultural Analysis* 14, 1–22.

Fischer, Burton D., ed. 2003. *Mozart's* The Magic Flute: *Translated from German and Including Musical Highlight Transcriptions*. Coral Gables, FL: Opera Journeys Publishing.

Foucault, Michel. 2020 [1975]. *Discipline and Punish: The Birth of the Prison*, trans. Alan Sheridan. London: Penguin Books.

Foucault, Michel. 2014 [1981]. *Wrong-Doing, Truth-Telling: The Function of Avowal in Justice*, trans. Stephen W. Sawyer. Chicago, IL: University of Chicago Press.

Foucault, Michel. 2007 [1997]. *The Politics of Truth*, ed. Sylvère Lotringer, trans. Lysa Hochroth and Catherine Porter. Los Angeles, CA: Semiotext(e)

Foucault, Michel. 1990 [1976]. *The History of Sexuality*, vol. 1, *An Introduction*, trans. Robert Hurley. New York: Pantheon Books.

260 Bibliography

Fourie, William. 2020. "Musicology and Decolonial Analysis in the Age of Brexit." *Twentieth-Century Music* 17(2), 197–211.

Fourie, William. 2020. "On the Fragile Joys of Interpretation: A Response to Kevin Volans." *SAMUS: South African Music Studies* 40, 23–28.

Fourie, William. 2019. "Between the Musical Anti- and Post-Apartheid: Structures of Crisis in Kevin Volans's String Quartet No.5, Dancers on a Plane." *SAMUS: South African Music Studies* 39, 134–174.

Frank, Peter. 2023. "William Kentridge: In Praise of Shadows at the Broad Museum, Los Angeles." *White Hot Magazine.* https://whitehotmagazine.com/articles/at-broad-museum-los-angeles/5705.

Freud, Sigmund. 1963 [1917]. "Mourning and Melancholia," trans. Joan Riviere. In *General Psychological Theory: Papers on Metapsychology*, ed. Philip Rieff. New York: Macmillan, 161–178.

Galison, Peter. 2003. *Einstein's Clocks, Poincaré's Maps: Empires of Time*. New York: W.W. Norton.

Galison, Peter, William Kentridge, Catherine Meyburgh, and Philip Miller, eds. 2013. *The Refusal of Time*. Paris: Xavier Barral Publishing.

Gandhi, Leela. 1998. *Postcolonial Theory: A Critical Introduction*. Edinburgh: Edinburgh University Press.

Ganguly, Keya. 2004. "Temporality and Postcolonial Critique." In *The Cambridge Companion to Postcolonial Literary Studies*, ed. Neil Lazarus. Cambridge: Cambridge University Press, 162–180.

Gatt-Rutter, John. 1988. *Italo Svevo: A Double Life*. Oxford: Clarendon Press.

Gerber, Melissa. 2021. "(De)coding Contemporary South African Opera: Multimodality and the Creation of Meaning, 2010–2018." PhD diss., University of the Free State.

Gerber, Melissa. 2020. "Postcards from the Platteland: Avant-garde Aesthetics and Nostalgia in *Poskantoor*'s (2014) Paratexts." *SAMUS: South African Music Studies* 40, 239–268.

Gilroy, Paul. 2005. *Postcolonial Melancholia*. New York: Columbia University Press.

Godby, Michael. 2019. "Unwritten History: William Kentridge's *Triumphs and Laments*, Piazza Tevere, Rome, 2016." In *What Was History Painting and What Is It Now?*, ed. Mark Salber Phillips and Jordan Bear. Montreal: McGill-Queen's University Press, 215–223.

Goloubeva, Irina Rasmussen. 2013. "'That's the Music of the Future': James Joyce's *Ulysses* and the Writing of a Difficult History." *Modernism/Modernity* 20(4), 685–708.

Gopal, Priyamvada. 2019. *Insurgent Empire: Anticolonial Resistance and British Dissent*. London: Verso.

Gough, Maria. 2010. "Kentridge's Nose." *October* 134, 3–27.

Grobe, Christopher. 2014. *The Art of Confession: The Performance of Self from Robert Lowell to Reality TV*. New York: New York University Press.

Gross, Kenneth. 2012. *Puppet: An Essay on Uncanny Life*. Chicago, IL: University of Chicago Press.

Guarracino, Serena. 2010. "The Dance of the Dead Rhino: William Kentridge's Magic Flute." *Altre Modernità: Rivista di studi letterari e culturali* 4, 268–278.

Guercio, Gabriele. 2017. "A Paradoxical Monumentality." In *William Kentridge: Triumphs and Laments*, 129–143.

Guterres, António. 2015. "Opening Remarks at the 66th Session of the Executive Committee of the High Commissioner's Programme," Geneva, October 5. https://www.unhcr.org/news/news-releases/opening-remarks-66th-session-executive-committee-high-commissioners-programme.

Hagström-Ståhl, Kristina. 2010. "Mourning as Method: William Kentridge's *Black Box/Chambre Noire*." *arcadia* 45(2), 339–351.

Harding, Frances. 1998. "'To Present the Self in a Special Way': Disguise and Display in Tiv *Kwagh-hir* Performance." *African Arts* 31(1), 56–67.

Bibliography 261

Harrán, Don. 2009. "A Tale as Yet Untold: Salamone Rossi in Venice, 1622." *Sixteenth-Century Journal* 40(4), 1091–1107.

Head, Matthew. 2000. *Orientalism, Masquerade, and Mozart's Turkish Music*. Abingdon: Routledge.

Hegenbart, Sarah. 2020. "Decolonising Opera: Interrogating the Genre of Opera in the Sahel and Other Regions in the Global South." In *"Gefühle sind von Hausa us Rebellen," Musiktheater als Katalysator und Reflexionsagentur für gesellschaftliche Entwicklungsprozesse*, ed. Dominik Frank, Ulrike Hartung, and Kornelius Paede. Würzburg: Königshausen and Neumann, 169–196.

Heidegger, Martin. 2002 [1930]. *The Essence of Truth: On Plato's Parable of the Cave Allegory and Theaetetus*, trans. Ted Sadler. London: Continuum.

Heidegger, Martin. 1971. "Building, Dwelling, Thinking." In *Poetry, Language Thought*, trans. Albert Hofstadter. New York: Harper Perennial, 141–160.

Hoxby, Blair. 2005. "The Doleful Airs of Euripides: The Origins of Opera and the Spirit of Tragedy Reconsidered." *Cambridge Opera Journal* 17(3), 253–269.

Huggett, Nick. 2018. "Zeno's Paradoxes." *Stanford Encyclopedia of Philosophy*. https://plato.stanford.edu/entries/paradox-zeno/.

Hutchison, Yvette. 2013. *South African Performance and Archives of Memory*. Manchester: Manchester University Press.

Hutchison, Yvette. 2010. "The 'Dark Continent' Goes North: An Exploration of Intercultural Theatre Practice through Handspring and Sogolon Puppet Companies' Production of *Tall Horse*." *Theatre Journal* 62(1), 57–73.

Huyssen, Andreas. 2018. "Memories of Europe in the Art from Elsewhere." *Stedelijk Studies* 6, 1–10.

Huyssen, Andreas. 2017. "The Shadow Play as Medium of Memory in William Kentridge." In *William Kentridge*, October Files 21, ed. Rosalind Krauss. Cambridge, MA: MIT Press, 77–98.

Imhoof, David, Margaret Eleanor Menninger, and Anthony J. Steinhoff, eds. 2016. *The Total Work of Art: Foundations, Articulations, Inspirations*. New York: Berghahn Books.

Ingold, Tim. 2004. "Culture on the Ground: The World Perceived through the Feet." *Journal of Material Culture* 9(3), 315–340.

Ingraham, Mary I., Joseph K. So, and Roy Moodley, eds. 2016. *Opera in a Multicultural World: Coloniality, Culture, Performance*. Abingdon: Routledge.

Inserra, Incoronata. 2017. *Global Tarantella: Reinventing Southern Italian Folk Music and Dances*. Champaign: University of Illinois Press.

In Terms of Performance. n.d. "Interview—William Kentridge." http://intermsofperformance.site/interviews/william-kentridge.

Jacobson, Joshua. 1988. "The Choral Music of Salamone Rossi." *American Choral Review* 30(4), n.p. https://zamir.org/resources/music-of-salamone-rossi/rossi-monograph/.

Janssen, Hein. 2018. "William Kentridge snijdt een cruciaal onderwerp aan in *The Head and the Load*, maar een duidelijke dramatische lijn ontbreekt (drie sterren)." *de Volkskrant*, August 12. https://www.volkskrant.nl/cultuur-media/william-kentridge-snijdt-een-cruciaal-onderwerp-aan-in-the-head-and-the-load-maar-een-duidelijke-dramatische-lijn-ontbreekt-drie-sterren~b6dcdd6f/?referer=https%3A%2F%2Fwww.google.com%2F.

Johannsen, Kristine Bøggild and Torben Zenth. 2007. "Interview: William Kentridge." *Kopenhagen Aktuel information om smtidskunst*, July 4.

Jones, Basil. 2014. "Puppetry, Authorship and the Ur-Narrative." In *The Routledge Companion to Puppetry and Material Performance*, ed. Dassia N. Posner, Claudia Orenstein, and John Bell. London: Routledge, 61–68.

Jones, Kay Bea. 2009. "Rome's Uncertain Tiberscape: Tevereterno and the Urban Commons." *The Waters of Rome* 6, 1–12.

262 Bibliography

Kanter, Jodi. 2007. *Performing Loss: Rebuilding Community through Theater and Writing*. Carbondale: Southern Illinois University Press.

Karantonis, Pamela and Dylan Robinson, eds. 2011. *Opera Indigene: Re/presenting First Nations and Indigenous Cultures*. Farnham: Ashgate.

Kastnelson, Anna. 2015. "A Real 'Lulu' of a Tale." *Forward*, November 27, 28–29.

Kasule, Samuel. 2020. "'I Smoked Them Out': Perspectives on the Emergence of Folk Opera or 'Musical Plays' in Uganda." In *African Theatre 19*, 183–193.

Keats, John. 1982 [1819]. "Ode on a Grecian Urn." In *Complete Poems*, ed. Jack Stillinger. Cambridge, MA: Harvard University Press, 282–283.

Kentridge, William. n.d. "The Head & the Load." https://www.theheadandtheload.com.

Kentridge, William. 2022. "To What End: A Visual Lecture by William Kentridge." Berkeley Art Museum and Pacific Film Archive. https://www.youtube.com/watch?v=iWy45ahrTtI.

Kentridge, William. 2020. *Waiting for the Sibyl*. London: Koenig Books.

Kentridge, William, ed. 2020. *The Head and the Load*. Paris: Éditions Xavier Barral.

Kentridge, William. 2019. "Waiting for the Sibyl: Programme Note." https://www.kentridge.studio/waiting-for-the-sibyl-programme-note/.

Kentridge, William. 2018. Program Note. In *The Head & the Load* [production program]. Tate Modern, 3.

Kentridge, William, dir. 2018. *The Head & the Load* [video recording]. Unpublished.

Kentridge, William. 2016. "Triumphs and Laments: A Talk." https://www.kentridge.studio/triumphs-laments-a-talk/.

Kentridge, William. 2014. *Six Drawing Lessons*. Cambridge, MA: Harvard University Press.

Kentridge, William. 2013. "Refuse the Hour Lecture by W.K.." In *The Refusal of Time*, I-XVI.

Kentridge, William. 2012. "Entretien avec William Kentridge." In *Refuse the Hour* [production program]. Festival d'Avignon, July 7–13, n.p.

Kentridge, William. 2010. *William Kentridge: Anything Is Possible* [film]. *art21*. https://art21.org/watch/william-kentridge-anything-is-possible/full-program-william-kentridge-anything-is-possible/.

Kentridge, William. 2010. *Return: William Kentridge* [film]. *art21*. https://art21.org/watch/extended-play/william-kentridge-return-short/.

Kentridge, William. 2009. "Magic Flute and Black Box: Sarastro and the Master's Voice." https://www.kentridge.studio/magic-flute-and-black-box-sarastro-and-the-masters-voice/.

Kentridge, William. 2005. "Black Box: Between the Lens and the Eyepiece." https://www.kentridge.studio/black-box-between-the-lens-and-the-eyepiece/.

Kentridge, William. 2002. "Confessions of Zeno: Regieanmerkungen von William Kentridge." In *Confessions of Zeno* [production program], Programmheft Nr. 21. Frankfurt am Main: schauspielfrankfurt.

Kentridge, William. 2001. "Zeno at 4 am: Director's Note." https://www.kentridge.studio/confessions-of-zeno-directors-note/.

Kentridge, William. 2001. "The Art of William Kentridge." *Transition* 10(4), 85–86.

Kentridge, William. 2001. "In Praise of Shadows." https://www.kentridge.studio/in-praise-of-shadows/.

Kentridge, William and Peter Galison. 2013. "Give Us Back Our Sun." In *The Refusal of Time*, 157–164.

Kentridge, William and Peter Galison. 2013. "Blowing Up the Meridian." In *The Refusal of Time*, 249–250.

Kentridge, William and Philip Miller. 2013. "Gathering Sounds and Making Objects Breathe." In *The Refusal of Time*, 197–212.

Killingray, David and James Matthews. 1979. "Beasts of Burden: British West African Carriers in the First World War." *Canadian Journal of African Studies* 13(1–2), 5–23.

Kinderman, William. 2013. *Wagner's Parsifal*. New York: Oxford University Press.

Kirshenblatt-Gimblett, Barbara and Brooks McNamara. 1985. "Processional Performance: An Introduction." *Drama Review: TDR* 29(3), 2–5.

Klein, Tobias Robert. 2020. "The Phantom of the West African Opera: A *tour d'horizon.*" In *African Theatre 19: Opera & Music Theatre*, 136–158.

Kok, Lonneke. 2012. "Stopping Time." In *Refuse the Hour* [production program]. Holland Festival, 8–10.

Kramer, Lawrence. 2014. "The Voice of/in Opera." In *On Voice*, eds. Walter Bernhart and Lawrence Kramer. Amsterdam: Rodopi, 43–58.

Krauss, Rosalind. 2000. "'The Rock': William Kentridge's *Drawings for Projection.*" *October* 92, 3–35.

Kreuzer, Gundula. 2018. *Curtain Gong Steam: Wagnerian Technologies of Nineteenth-Century Opera*. Oakland, CA: University of California Press.

Kruger, Marie. 2011. "Puppets and Adult Entertainment in South Africa: A Tale of a Tentative Start, Evolving Prejudices, New and Lost Opportunities, and a Fresh Momentum." *South African Theatre Journal* 25(1), 13–34.

Kruger, Marie. 2010. "Social Dynamics in African Puppetry." *Contemporary Theatre Review* 20(3), 316–328.

Kruger, Marie. 2009. "The Relationship between Theatre and Ritual in the *Sogo bò* of the Bamana from Mali." *New Theatre Quarterly* 25(3), 233–240.

Law-Viljoen, Bronwyn. ed. 2007. *William Kentridge: Flute*. Johannesburg: David Krut.

Law-Viljoen, Bronwyn. 2007. "Footnote on Darkness." In *Flute*, 156–191.

Levine, Caroline. 2015. *Forms: Whole, Rhythm, Hierarchy, Network*. Princeton, NJ: Princeton University Press.

Lindenberger, Herbert. 2010. *Situating Opera: Period, Genre, Reception*. Cambridge: Cambridge University Press.

Lloyd, David. 2000. "Colonial Trauma/Postcolonial Recovery?" *Interventions* 2(2), 212–228.

López, Alfred J., ed. 2005. *Postcolonial Whiteness: A Critical Reader on Race and Empire*. New York: State University of New York Press.

López, Alfred J. 2005. "Introduction: Whiteness after Empire." In *Postcolonial Whiteness: A Critical Reader on Race and Empire*. New York: State University of New York Press, 1–30.

Lorenzini, Daniele and Martina Tazzioli. 2018. "Confessional Subjects and Conducts of Non-Truth: Foucault, Fanon, and the Making of the Subject." *Theory, Culture & Society* 35(1), 71–90.

Lucia, Christine. 2009. "The Landscape Within: Kevin Volans and the String Quartet." *SAMUS: South African Music Studies* 29, 1–30.

Madley, Benjamin. 2005. "From Africa to Auschwitz: How German South West Africa Incubated Ideas and Methods Adopted and Developed by the Nazis in Eastern Europe." *European History Quarterly* 35(3), 429–464.

Maedza, Pedzisai. 2018. "Chains of Memory in the Postcolony: Performing and Remembering the Namibian Genocide." PhD diss., University of Cape Town.

Mains, Susan P., Mary Gilmartin, Declan Cullen, Robina Mohammad, Divya P. Tolia-Kelly, Parvati Raghuram, and Jamie Winders. 2013. "Postcolonial Migrations." *Social & Cultural Geography* 14(2), 131–144.

Maltz-Leca, Leora. 2018. *William Kentridge: Process as Metaphor and Other Doubtful Enterprises*. Oakland: University of California Press.

Maltz-Leca, Leora. 2013. "Process/Procession: William Kentridge and the Process of Change." *Art Bulletin* 95(1), 139–165.

Matzke, Christine, Lena van der Hoven, Christopher Odhiambo, and Hilde Roos, eds. 2020. *African Theatre 19: Opera & Music Theatre*. Woodbridge: James Currey.

Mbembe, Achille. 2017 [2013]. *Critique of Black Reason*, trans. Laurent Dubois. Durham, NC: Duke University Press.

264 Bibliography

Mbembe, Achille. 2001. *On the Postcolony*. Berkeley: University of California Press.

Michaels, Bianca. 2013. "Is This Still Opera? Media Opera as Productive Provocations." In *The Legacy of Opera: Reading Music Theatre as Experience and Performance*. Boston: Brill, 25–38.

Mignolo, Walter D. 2011. *The Darker Side of Western Modernity: Global Futures, Decolonial Options*. Durham, NC: Duke University Press.

Miller, Philip. n.d. *Music by Philip Miller from the Soundtrack to William Kentridge's Black Box/ Chambre Noir* [audio recording]. Johannesburg: Artlogic.

Miller, Philip. 2018. "The Music of Triumphs and Laments." https://www.kentridge.studio/the-music-of-triumphs-and-laments/.

Miller, Philip and Thuthuka Sibisi. 2018. Program Note. In *The Head & the Load* [production programme]. Tate Modern, 5.

Moderna Museet. 2007. "Black Box/Chambre Noire." https://www.modernamuseet.se/stockh olm/en/exhibitions/william-kentridge/black-boxchambre-noire/.

Monteverdi, Claudio. 2018 [1640]. *Il Ritorno d'Ulisse in Patria* [recording insert], dir. John Eliot Gardiner, libretto trans. Boston Baroque. London: Monteverdi Productions SDG730.

Muller, Stephanus. 2022. "Michael Blake's String Quartets and the Idea of an African Art Music." *Tempo* 76(300), 6–17.

Muñoz, José Esteban. 1997. *Disidentifications: Queers of Color and the Performance of Politics*, vol. 2. Minneapolis: Minnesota University Press.

Muyanga, Neo. 2020. "A Revolt in (more than just) Four Parts." In *African Theatre 19: Opera & Music Theatre*, 17–28.

Naas, Michael. 2015. "When It Comes to Mourning." In *Jacques Derrida: Key Concepts*, ed. Claire Colebrook. Abingdon: Routledge, 113–121.

Nanni, Giordano. 2012. *The Colonisation of Time: Ritual, Routine and Resistance in the British Empire*. Manchester: Manchester University Press.

Ndebele, Njabulo. 1998. "Memory, Metaphor, and the Triumphs of Narrative." In *Negotiating the Past: The Making of Memory in South Africa*, ed. Sarah Nuttall and Carli Coetzee. Oxford: Oxford University Press, 19–28.

Nedbal, Martin. 2012. "Live Marionettes and Divas on the Strings: *Die Zauberflöte*'s Interactions with Puppet Theater." *Opera Quarterly* 28(1–2), 20–36.

Ngcoya, Mvuselelo. 2015. "Ubuntu: Toward an Emancipatory Cosmopolitanism?" *International Political Sociology* 9(3), 248–262.

Novak, Jelena. 2016. *Postopera: Reinventing the Voice-Body*. Abingdon: Routledge.

Ochs, Orpha. 2000. *Organists and Organ Playing in Nineteenth-Century France and Belgium*. Bloomington: Indiana University Press.

Okui, Haruka. 2020. "Deformation of the Human Body: Bunraku Puppetry Technique and the Collaborative Body Schema." *Chiasmi International* 22, 351–366.

Olsen, Andrew. 2012. "Mozart's African Jacket: *Die Zauberflöte* and Its Localisation in *The Magic Flute (Impempe Yomlingo)*." *Journal of the Musical Arts in Africa* 9(1), 67–80.

Olusoga, David. 2018. Program note. In *The Head & the Load* [production program]. Tate Modern, 13.

Olusoga, David and Casper W. Erichsen. 2010. *The Kaiser's Holocaust: Germany's Forgotten Genocide and the Colonial Roots of Nazism*. London: Faber.

Olwage, Grant. 2004. "Discipline and Choralism: The Birth of Musical Colonialism." In *Music, Power, and Politics*, ed. Annie J. Randall. London: Routledge, 25–46.

Olwage, Grant. 2002. "Scriptions of the Choral: The Historiography of Black South African Choralism." *SAMUS: South African Journal of Musicology* 22, 29–45.

Olwage, Grant. 1999–2000. "Who Needs Rescuing? A Reply to 'Gumboots to the Rescue.'" *South African Journal of Musicology: SAMUS* 19, 105–108.

Omojola, Bode. 2020. "Towards an African Operatic Voice: Composition, Dramaturgy, and Identity Strategies in New Yorùbá Opera." In *African Theatre 19: Opera & Music Theatre*, 107–135.

Ottra, Ilaria. 2017. "'Ne saevi, magna sacerdos': L'ethos della Sibilla Virgiliana." *Studi Classici e Orientali* 63, 163–186.

Parry, Michael. 2019. "William Kentridge: That Which We Do Not Remember." *Medium*. https://medium.com/@vaguelym/william-kentridge-that-which-we-do-not-remember-347f02e367b5.

Pistorius, Juliana M. 2023. "A Modern-Day Florestan: *Fidelio on Robben Island* and South Africa's Early Democratic Project." *Twentieth-Century Music* 20(1), 107–125.

Pistorius, Juliana M. 2019. "Inhabiting Whiteness: The Eoan Group *La Traviata*, 1956." *Cambridge Opera Journal* 31(1), 63–84.

Pistorius, Juliana M. 2017. "Coloured Opera as Subversive Forgetting." *Social Dynamics: A Journal of African Studies* 43(2), 230–242.

Pistorius, Juliana M. and Hilde Roos. 2021. "Burgerskap onder konstruksie: *Rigoletto* en *Aida* by die Suid-Afrikaanse Republiekfeesvieringe, 1971." *Litnet Akademies* 18(2), 102–131.

Plaatje, Sol. 1916. *Sechuana Proverbs, with Literal Translations and Their European Equivalents; Diane Tsa Secoana le Maele a Sekgooa a a Dumalanang naco*. London: K. Paul, Trench, Trubner and Co.

Platt, Louise, Dominic Medway, and Chloe Steadman. 2021. "Processional Walking: Theorising the 'Place' of Movement in Notions of Dwelling." *Geographical Research* 59(1), 106–117.

Poray, Denise Wendel. 2018. *Painting the Stage: Artists as Stage Designers*. Milan: Skira.

Pratt, Kenneth J. 1965. "Rome as Eternal." *Journal of the History of Ideas* 26(1), 25–44.

Press, Steven. 2017. *Rogue Empires: Contracts and Conmen in Europe's Scramble for Africa*. Cambridge, MA: Harvard University Press.

Rakewell. 2022. "A Total Artist—In Memoriam Meatloaf." *Apollo*, 21 January. https://www.apollo-magazine.com/meat-loaf-bat-out-of-hell-gesamtkunstwerk/.

Rankin, Tom. 2019. "Culture Meets Ecology in the Public Space: *Triumphs and Laments* on the Tiber." In *Art and Economics in the City: New Cultural Maps*, ed. Caterina Benincasa, Gianfranco Neri, and Michele Trimarchi. Bielefeld: transcript Verlag, 49–67.

Ratnayake, Sahanika. 2018. "Beyoncé and the New Gesamtkunstwerk." *3:am magazine*, 1 October. https://www.3ammagazine.com/3am/beyonce-and-the-new-gesamtkunstwerk.

Rea, Naomi. 2017. "The Return of the Gesamtkunstwerk? Why Contemporary Artists are Flocking to the Opera House." *artnet*, 23 August. https://news.artnet.com/art-world/opera-contemporary-art-1047605.

Renihan, Colleen L. 2016. "The Politics of Genre: Exposing Historical Tensions in Harry Somers's *Louis Riel*." In *Opera Indigene: Re/Presenting First Nations and Indigenous Cultures*, ed. Dylan Robinson and Pamela Karantonis. Abingdon: Routledge, 259–276.

"Return, N., Sense II.7.a." 2024. *Oxford English Dictionary*. Oxford: Oxford University Press. https://doi.org/10.1093/OED/1188994751.

Rifkin, Mark. 2017. *Beyond Settler Time: Temporal Sovereignty and Indigenous Self-Determination*. Durham, NC: Duke University Press.

Roach, Joseph. 1996. *Cities of the Dead: Circum-Atlantic Performance*. New York: Columbia University Press.

Roberts, David. 2011. *The Total Work of Art in European Modernism*. Ithaca, NY: Cornell University Press.

Rockwell, John. 2018. "In a Vast Space, Tragic Spectacle Floods the Senses." *Classical Voice North America*, October 12. https://classicalvoiceamerica.org/2018/12/10/in-a-vast-space-an-epic-spectacle-to-beguile-senses/.

Roos, Hilde. n.d. "In Conversation with Zakes Mda: 'The Full Story Must Be Told.'" *herri* 7. https://herri.org.za/7/hilde-roos/.

Roos, Hilde. 2018. *The La Traviata Affair: Opera in the Age of Apartheid*. Berkeley: University of California Press.

Roos, Hilde. 2010. "Opera Production in the Western Cape: Strategies in Search of Indigenisation." PhD diss., Stellenbosch University.

266 Bibliography

Rossi, Salomone. 1876 [1622]. "Aux bords des fleuves de Babylone: Psaume 137 à 4 voix." In *Càntiques de Salomon Rossi: Psaumes, Chants et Hymnes à 3, 4, 5, 6, 7 et 8 voix*, transcribed and edited by Samuel Naubourg. Paris, 27–29.

Rutherford, Susan. 2019. "The City Onstage: Re-Presenting Venice in Italian Opera." In *Operatic Geographies*, 88–104.

Saavedra, Leonora. 2008. "Staging the Nation: Race, Religion, and History in Mexican Opera of the 1940s." *Opera Quarterly* 23(1), 1–21.

Said, Edward. 1994 [1993]. *Culture and Imperialism*. New York: Knopf.

Salvaing, Bernard. 2020. "Forced Labour in European Colonies." *Encyclopédie d'histoire numérique de l'Europe.*" https://ehne.fr/en/node/12505.

Schaller, Dominik J. 2013 [1997]. "The Genocide of the Herero and Nama in German South-West Africa, 1904–1907." In *Centuries of Genocide: Essays and Eyewitness Accounts*, ed. Samuel Totten and William S. Parsons. New York: Routledge, 89–116.

Scherzinger, Martin. 2008. "Whose 'White Man Sleeps'? Aesthetics and Politics in the Early Work of Kevin Volans." In *Composing Apartheid: Music for and against Apartheid*, ed. Grant Olwage. Johannesburg: Wits University Press, 209–235.

Schipper, Mineke. 1982. *Theatre and Society in Africa*, trans. Ampie Coetzee. Johannesburg: Ravan Press.

Schoeman, Gerhard. 2009. "Thinking in the Dark of William Kentridge's *Black Box/Chambre Noire*: Reflections within Reflections." *Acta Academica* 41(2), 1–49.

Schröder, Julia H. 2019. "Total Theatre and Music Theatre: Tracing Influences from Pre- to Post-War Avant-Gardes." In *New Music Theatre in Europe: Transformation between 1955–1975*, ed. Robert Adlington. London: Routledge, 33–51.

Settis, Salvatore. 2017. "Drawing, Memory, and the City: William Kentridge's Rome." In *William Kentridge: Triumphs and Laments*, 161–207.

Sheller, Mimi and John Urry. 2006. "The New Mobilities Paradigm." *Environment and Planning A* 38, 207–226.

Shipley, Jesse Weaver. 2015. *Trickster Theatre: The Poetics of Freedom in Urban Africa*. Bloomington: Indiana University Press.

Siisiäinen, Lauri. 2012. "Confession, Voice and the Sensualization of Power: The Significance of Michel Foucault's 1962 Encounter with Jean-Jacques Rousseau." *Foucault Studies* 14, 138–153.

Simango, Daniel. 2018. "A Comprehensive Reading of Psalm 137." *Old Testament Essays* 31(1), 217–242.

Singleton, Jermaine. 2015. *Cultural Melancholy: Readings of Race, Impossible Mourning, and African American Ritual*. Urbana: University of Illinois Press.

Smith, Matthew Wilson. 2007. *The Total Work of Art: From Bayreuth to Cyberspace*. New York: Routledge.

Smith, Stephen Decatur. 2013. "'Even Money Decays': Transience and Hope in Adorno, Benjamin, and *Wozzeck*." *Opera Quarterly* 29(3), 212–243.

Somma, Donato. 2022. "A Tale of Two Houses: Opera Houses in Cairo and Cape Town." *Cambridge Opera Journal* 33(1–2), 129–160.

Southerton, Dale, ed. 2020. *Time, Consumption, and the Coordination of Everyday Life*. London: Palgrave Macmillan.

Soyinka, Wole. 1999. "African Traditions at Home in the Opera House." *New York Times*, 25 April. www.nytimes.com/1999/04/25/arts/african-traditions-at-home-in-the-opera-house.html?searchResultPosition=1.

Speretta, Tommaso and Lucia Franchi Viceré. 2017. "*Triumphs & Laments*: Sources for the Frieze Figures." In *William Kentridge: Triumphs and Laments*, 257–271.

Steinhoff, Anthony J. 2016. "Richard Wagner, *Parsifal*, and the Pursuit of Gesamtkunstwerk." In *The Total Work of Art: Foundations, Articulations, Inspirations*, ed. David Imhoof, Margaret Eleanor Menninger, and Anthony J. Steinhoff. New York: Berghahn Books, 56–77.

Bibliography 267

Steyn, Melissa. 2005. "'White Talk': White South Africans and the Management of Diasporic Whiteness." In *Postcolonial Whiteness: A Critical Reader on Race and Empire*. New York: State University of New York Press, 119–135.

Stolp, Mareli. 2016. "Van opera tot 'politopera'? Nuwe strominge in Suid-Afrikaanse operakomposisie en –resepsie." *LitNet Akademies* 13(1), 138–160.

Stowe, David W. 2016. *Song of Exile: The Enduring Mystery of Psalm 137*. Oxford: Oxford University Press.

Subotnik, Rose Rosengard. 1991. "Whose *Magic Flute*? Intimations of Reality at the Gates of the Enlightenment." *19th-Century Music* 15(2), 132–150.

Svevo, Italo. 2018 [1923]. *Confessions of Zeno*, trans. Beryl de Zoete. London: riverrun.

Swed, Mark. 2017. "Music Review, 'Refuse the Hour' Tinkers with Time; William Kentridge's Transformation of His Installation into Opera Is a Fresh Revelation." *Los Angeles Times*, November 20. https://www-proquest-com.libproxy.ucl.ac.uk/docview/1965998828?pq-origsite=primo.

Symonds, Dominic and Pamela Karantonis, eds. 2013. *The Legacy of Opera: Reading Music Theatre as Experience and Performance*. Boston: Brill.

Taylor, Chloë, 2009. *The Culture of Confession from Augustine to Foucault: A Genealogy of the "Confessing Animal."* New York: Routledge.

Taylor, Diana. 2003. *The Archive and the Repertoire: Performing Cultural Memory in the Americas*. Durham, NC: Duke University Press.

Taylor, Jane, ed. 2009. *Handspring Puppet Company*. Johannesburg: David Krut.

Taylor, Jane and William Kentridge. 2009. "In Dialogue: William Kentridge with Jane Taylor." In *Handspring Puppet Company*, 176–209.

Taylor, Jane. 2003. "Taking Stock: The Making of a Bourgeois Life—*The Confessions of Zeno*." *South African Theatre Journal* 17(1), 233–244.

Taylor, Jane. 2001. *Confessions of Zeno* [libretto]. Frankfurt am Main: schauspielfrankfurt.

Taylor, Timothy D. 1995. "When We Think about Music and Politics: The Case of Kevin Volans." *Perspectives of New Music* 33(1/2), 504–536.

Tettlebaum, Marianne. 2008. "Whose Magic Flute?" *Representations* 102(1), 76–93.

Thieme, John. 2001. *Postcolonial Con-Texts: Writing Back to the Canon*. London: Continuum.

Till, Nicholas. 2011. "Orpheus Conquistador." In *Opera Indigene: Re/Presenting First Nations and Indigenous Cultures*, 14–29.

Tome, Lillian, ed. 2013. *William Kentridge: Fortuna*. London: Thames and Hudson.

Tommasini, Anthony. 2015. "Review: Finding Beauty in a Wrenching 'Lulu' at the Met." *New York Times*, November 5. https://www.nytimes.com/2015/11/07/arts/music/metropolitan-opera-lulu-review.html.

TRC. n.d. "Welcome to the Official Truth and Reconciliation Commission Website." https://www.justice.gov.za/trc/.

TRC. n.d. "The Committees of the TRC." https://www.justice.gov.za/trc/trccom.html.

TRC. 2003. *Truth and Reconciliation Commission of South Africa Volume Six*. Cape Town: Truth and Reconciliation Commission.

TRC. 2002. *Truth and Reconciliation Commission of South Africa Report Volume Seven*. Cape Town: Truth and Reconciliation Commission.

Tuck, Eve K. and K. Wayne Yang. 2012. "Decolonization Is not a Metaphor." *Decolonization: Indigeneity, Education & Society* 1(1), 1–40.

Tyldesley, Joy. 2017. *Stories from Ancient Greece & Rome*. Oxford: Oxbow Books.

Van den Berg, Klaus. 2019. "The Opera House as Urban Exhibition Space." In *Operatic Geographies*, 213–233.

Van der Hoven, Lena. 2020. "'We Can't Let Politics Define the Arts': Interviews with South African Opera Singers." In *African Theatre 19: Opera & Music Theatre*, 77–89.

268 Bibliography

Van der Hoven, Lena and Liani Maasdorp. 2020. "'Opera Is an Art Form for Everyone': Black Empowerment in the South African Opera Adaptations *Unogumbe* (2013) and *Breathe—Umphefumlo* (2015). In *African Theatre 19: Opera & Music Theatre*, 52–76.

Verdoolaege, Annelies. 2005. "Media Representations of the South African Truth and Reconciliation Commission and their Commitment to Reconciliation." *Journal of African Cultural Studies* 17(2), 181–199.

Verstraete, Pieter. 2013. "Turkish Post-Migrant 'Opera' in Europe: A Socio-Historical Perspective on Aurality." In *The Legacy of Opera: Reading Music Theatre as Experience and Performance*, ed. Dominic Symonds and Pamela Karantonis, Boston: Brill, 185–207.

Vogeley, Nancy. 1996. "Italian Opera in Early National Mexico." *Modern Language Quarterly* 57(2), 279–288.

Vokwana, Thembela. 2006/2007. "Opera in Africa: Music of the People, for the People, by the People." *New Music SA Bulletin* 5–6, 12–16.

Volans, Kevin. 2020. "Response to 'Between the Musical Anti- and Post-Apartheid: Structures of Crisis in Kevin Volans's String Quartet No.5, Dancers on a Plane.'" *SAMUS: South African Music Studies* 40, 17–22.

Volans, Kevin. 2002. *Confessions of Zeno*. London: Chester Music.

Volans, Kevin. 2002. "Anmerkungen zur Musik von *Confessions of Zeno*." In *Confessions of Zeno* [production program]. Programmheft Nr. 21, Frankfurt am Main: Schauspielfrankfurt, 22.

Walton, Benjamin. 2012. "Italian Operatic Fantasies in Latin America." *Journal of Modern Italian Studies* 17(4), 460–471.

Wandor, Michelene. 2002. "Salamone Rossi, Judaism and the Musical Canon." *European Judaism: A Journal for the New Europe* 35(2), 26–35.

Wickman, Dorothy. n.d. "Opera on the Goldfields." https://ballaratheritage.com.au/article/opera-on-the-goldfields/.

Wilmer, Stephen E. 2018. *Performing Statelessness in Europe*. Cham: Springer.

Withers, Charles W. K. 2017. *Zero Degrees: Geographies of the Prime Meridian*. Cambridge, MA: Harvard University Press.

Woodward, Kathleen. 1993. "Late Theory, Late Style: Loss and Renewal in Freud and Barthes." In *Aging & Gender in Literature: Studies in Creativity*, ed. Anne Wyatt-Brown and Janice Rossin. Charlottesville: University of Virginia Press, 82–101.

York, Geoffrey. 2011. "*Winnie: The Opera*—On Home Turf and Ready for Her Close-Up." *Globe and Mail*, April 22. https://www.theglobeandmail.com/arts/music/winnie-the-opera---on-home-turf-and-ready-for-her-close-up/article597725/.

Zenenga, Praise. 2015. "The Total Theater Aesthetic Paradigm in African Theater." In *The Oxford Handbook of Dance and Theater*, ed. Nadine George-Graves. New York: Oxford University Press, 236–251.

Žižek, Slavoj and Mladen Dolar. 2002. *Opera's Second Death*. London: Routledge.

Index

For the benefit of digital users, indexed terms that span two pages (e.g., 52–53) may, on occasion, appear on only one of those pages.

Abbate, Carolyn 113
Abibigro 215. *See also* African total theater
abstraction 58, 85, 101
accountability 54, 58, 71–73
accounting 71–73
Acrisius, death of 132–33, 252
adaptation 37–38, 40–41, 59–60, 123–24, 125
Africa(n)
    continent 16, 77, 84, 95, 168, 192, 205–6, 229–30
    First World War in 205–6, 225
    freedom fighters 232
    music 58, 83–85, 87, 88–89, 140–41
    opera and 17, 30, 216
    partitioning of 130, 223, 226–27
    performance traditions 43, 215–17, 220, 238–39
    proverb(s) 155–56
    puppetry 42–43
    as representation of nature 113
    ritual processions 173–74
    scramble for 130
    societies 147, 216
    sound 210, 212
    time 147–48
Africanization 37–38, 123
African National Congress 77
African total theater 31, 203, 215–17, 219–20, 222, 237–38. *See also* total work of art
Agamben, Giorgio. *See* bare life
agency 76–77, 79, 90, 193
allegory 101, 117, 119, 126–27
Al Naharot Bavel 168–71, 183, 184–85, 195–96, 197. *See also* Rossi, Salamone
ambiguity
    formal 54
    generic 105, 122–23, 242

    of opera in the postcolony 33, 51, 52, 151, 246, 248
    of postcolonizing subject 21–22, 52, 57
    towards Europe 5, 22, 41–42
anatomy 34, 49–50
ANC. *See* African National Congress
André, Naomi 14
animation 14, 35–36, 100–1, 132, 172–73
apartheid 55, 82, 88, 90
    collaborator 77
    crimes 35–36, 49–50, 67
    era 56, 57, 70, 245
    Kentridge and 4–5
    opera and 14–15, 28, 179–80, 181
    regime 49–50, 179–80, 181
    and whiteness 4, 36
appropriation 25–26, 29, 58, 63, 96–98
archive
    colonialism and 223–24
    document or source 99–103, 104–5, 121–22, 125–26, 205, 207–8
    performative 12
    research 108–9, 163–64
    time and 131–32
    and trace 14
    universal 133, 134–35
    voice as 127
aria 131, 149–50
army 100, 205–6
    See also military
arrival 25, 33, 41–42, 162
    as climax or closure 182–83, 197
    colonial 131–32
    and departure 17, 194, 196
    and dwelling 194
    of opera in the colony 5–6, 25–26, 27, 29, 52
    site of 180, 192

270 Index

artifice 41, 42, 52
    of Europe in the colonial sphere 32
    musical 81–82, 112, 140–41
    of opera 32, 48, 103–4, 124
    of puppet performance 46–47, 48, 50
Aspden, Suzanne 178–79, 180–81
audience
    bewilderment 228, 242–43
    as co–creator 48–49, 217–18
    deception of the 48, 252
    expectation 9, 243
    ideal or intended 21–22, 37–38, 92, 125–
        26, 180–81, 199
    opera 1–2, 8, 9–10, 176–77
    position 182–83
    relationship between performer
        and 78, 201
Austro-Hungarian Empire 56, 59–60, 245
automation 113, 244–45
automaton 98, 99, 114–15, 138–40, 141, 208
avant-garde 8, 21–22, 124, 125, 141–42,
    210–12, 214

Babylon 168, 170, 183
bare life 49–50, 51
Barthes, Roland 102–3. *See also*
    camera lucida
bell(s) 145, 155–56, 234
belonging 162, 187, 191–92, 197, 199, 200–
    1, 244
    politics of 189, 200, 201
Benjamin, Walter 106–7, 108–9, 174
Berg, Alban 150
Berger, Karol 142, 144, 149–50
Bergson, Henri 147
Berlin Conference 130, 206, 226–27
Berlioz, Hector 140, 153–54. *See also* Le
    spectre de la rose
Bhabha, Homi 128–29, 174–76, 201, 205–6,
    224–26, 231, 233. *See also* foot power
bifurcation. *See* splitting
bird 116, 229
    song 117
Black
    body 49–50, 111, 121–22, 126–27
    history 13–14, 121–22, 223
    opera 14–15, 29
    reason 229–30
    sonic selfhood 231
    subject 5, 29, 35–36, 236
    suffering 36
    victims 113–15

blackboard 96–98
black box
    airplane 93, 185
    theater 93, 109, 124, 125
Black Box/Chambre Noire 6–7, 17, 20–21, 41,
    93, 139–40, 185, 244–45
    as adaptation 123–24
    background projections 98–99, 113–15,
        117–19, 120, 121–22, 125–26
    cast 98, 99
    description 96–99
    historical content 245
    international circulation 127–28
    music 98–99, 104–5, 111–13, 121–
        23, 125–26
    reception 104
    scene
        "Ach, ich fühl's" 120–21, 128–29
        "Die Wahrheit" 115–16
        "Fairground" 111–15
        "In diesen heil'gen Hallen" 117–19
        "Lament from the March of the
          Priests" 121–24, 126–27
        "March of the Priests" 98–99
        "Rhino" 120
black hole 136–37
Blackness
    fetishization of 114–15, 126–27
    and modernism 5
    and personhood 221–22
    and rationality 229–30
    See also race
Bloechl, Olivia 53, 78–79, 80
bonunu 215. *See also* African total theater
Bourdin, Martial 138–39
bourgeois 57, 66, 70, 77, 81–82, 110, 111
    European subject 54, 56–57, 76, 84–85
    opera 110
    postcolonizing subject 55, 87–90, 245
Brecht, Bertold 103
Bunraku 42–43
Butler, Judith 71–72, 73–74, 106–7, 108–9,
    119, 198

Cairo 179–80
calendar 144–45
call and response 111–12, 155–56, 168–69,
    190, 197
camera 93, 96–99
Camera Lucida 102–3
camera obscura 96–98
CAPAB. *See* Cape Performing Arts Board

Index 271

Cape Performing Arts Board 37–38
Cape Town 179–80
Cape Town Opera 37–38
capitalism 147, 174, 218–19
carrier. *See* porter
cave 96–98. *See also* Plato
Cavell, Stanley 79
Charon 112–13
Chilembwe, John 207, 208–10, 225
choir 29, 89, 145, 241. *See also* chorus
chorus 61, 85–86, 155–56, 171, 190
Christianity 144–45
Christov–Bakargiev, Carolyn 5
chrononormativity 131, 132, 141, 144, 146–
    47, 150, 158
  resistance to 146–47, 148, 150–51, 155–
    56, 157–58
cinema 23, 137–38. *See also* film
citizenship 197–98, 199–201
civility
  opera and 29, 93, 150–51, 158, 179
  singing and 29, 122–23, 126–27, 145
  white 92
civilization 3–4, 28, 101, 179. *See also*
    civility/civilizing mission
civilizing mission 12–13, 28–29, 96–98,
    114–15, 119, 121, 222, 231
  music and 231
  time and 130, 144–45, 150–51
  See also civility/missionary
classroom 96–98. *See also* blackboard
clock 135–36, 137–38, 140, 156–57
  time 130, 131, 141, 143, 144, 145–46,
    150, 157–58
Coetzee, J. M. 73, 77, 79, 86–87
co-evalness, denial of 145–47
collaboration 18–19, 251
collaborator(s)
  apartheid 77
  Kentridge 18, 58, 132, 138–39, 163–64,
    167, 205
collage 121–22, 207–8, 212, 236, 237
  form 224–25, 244
  history as 223, 224–25
  musical 104, 120, 210–12
collectivism 43–44, 112–13, 175
colonialism
  contradictory nature of 225, 238
  critique of 1–2
  cultural 43, 222, 230–31
  damages of 49–50, 95, 147–48, 156–
    57, 205–6

experience of 100–1, 156–57, 220,
    224, 236
extraction and 27–28, 41, 244–45
forms of 15–16
fragmentation and 202, 223–24, 227–
    28, 237
histories of 13–14, 21–22, 100–1, 126–
    27, 128–29
labor and 221
legacy of 2–3, 4–5, 25–26, 36
opera and 1, 5–6, 12–13, 23–24, 27–29,
    33, 90, 179–80
race and 221–22
relationship with Enlightenment 22–23
song and 145–46
sound and 145, 152, 155–56, 230–31, 233
South African puppetry and 43
struggles against 15–16, 76–77, 136, 137,
    138, 146–47, 155–56, 174, 207, 222
time and 130, 131–32, 137, 142–43, 144–
    48, 150–51
totalitarianism and 202–3, 221–22
victims of 50, 94, 107–8, 128, 222,
    244–45
violence of 76, 90, 93–94, 114–15, 116–17
whiteness and 3–4
coloniality
  pervasiveness of 100–1
  relationship with modernity 12–13, 16,
    22–23, 27–28, 143–44, 218–19, 236,
    244, 250
  as thing 221–22, 230–31, 233
  and truth 74–76
colonial metropole. *See* metropole
colonial project, the
  First World War as culmination
    of 206, 226–28
colonial subject 53, 59–60, 76, 77, 145–
    46, 155–56
  as agent 148, 222, 233
  construction of the 3
commandement 202–3. *See also* Mbembe,
    Achille
commemoration 17, 94, 106–7, 204
Common Festival 31, 215. *See also* African
    total theatre
communal performance 31, 42–43, 50–51,
    203, 220
community 44, 76–77, 112–13, 126, 194–95,
    202, 216
complicity 36, 53, 87–88, 90, 94, 121, 124,
    245–46. *See also* guilt

272 Index

confession
closure afforded by 87–88
ethics of 73–74, 245–46
Fanon on 53, 74–76, 77, 89–90
Foucault on 17, 53, 71–72, 74, 79–80, 81–82
opera and 53, 55, 77–81, 90, 151
performance of 17, 53, 54–55, 58, 71–72, 77, 79, 83
as political engagement 63, 74, 89–90
post–apartheid 55, 69, 70–71, 77, 88
postcolonial 17, 53–54, 55, 74–77, 245
as self–creation 72–73, 74–75
theories of 17, 55, 70–77
truth and 72–74, 75–76, 79, 80, 81, 116
confessional novel 58
Confessions of Zeno (novel) 37, 54, 56, 59–60, 65, 81–82, 245
Confessions of Zeno (opera) 6–7, 17, 37, 54, 61–67, 116, 245
background projections 70, 71–73, 80–81, 82
libretto 58
music for 61–63, 80–81, 82–90, 245
"Carla's Song" 84
"Chorus of Trees" 85
"Death of the Father" 82, 85–86
"Four Sisters" 82–84
"Mayhem" 87–88
"Pseudo–Scientific Chorus" 85–87
as opera 54
performance history 55–56
stage setting 63–65, 87–88
and TRC 67, 69
confessor 77
Conrad, Joseph 138
Cooppan, Vilashini 137–38, 144, 146–47, 157–58
Cox, Emma 172–73, 175–76, 201
CTO. *See* Cape Town Opera
culture
colonial 29, 90, 110
vs nature 92, 110–11, 112–13, 122–23, 126–27

Dada(ism) 11, 207, 226–27
dance 98, 119–21, 132–33, 141, 152, 154, 187–88, 195
death 49–50, 132–33, 135, 136–37, 154
decay. *See* entropy
decolonization 76, 146–47, 249, 250–51

dehumanization 112, 175–76, 204
Derrida, Jacques 106–7, 108–9
Deutsche Bank 93, 127–28
De Wit, Luc 132, 208–10, 226–27
diaspora 175
directionality 196
discipline 29, 130–31
disembodiment. *See* embodiment
displacement 161–62, 187, 188–89, 201
forced 159, 160, 174
imagery of 164–65, 174–75
Jewish 4–5, 184
opera and 180
and perpetual motion 192
territorial expansion and 190–91
dispossession 126–27, 151, 175, 186–87
Dlamini, Hamilton 208–10, 221–22, 225, 226–27, 230
Dlamini, Jacob 77, 89–90
Dolar, Mladen 92
doubling 67, 245
and splitting 63, 67, 72–73, 90
Dudley, Joanna 153–54, 167, 208–10, 229–31, 236
durée 147
Dürer, Albrecht 119–20
Durrant, Sam 101, 106–7, 108
dwelling 160, 193–95, 197, 201. *See also* home

Eberty, Felix 133
Eckstein, Soho. *See Drawings for Projection*
Edensor, Tim 193–95
Einstein, Albert 112–13, 138–39. *See also* relativity
emancipation 173–74
embankment 160, 161, 163–64, 165–67, 182–83, 201. *See also* Tiber
embodiment 42, 46, 49–50, 67, 76, 126, 162, 195, 243–44. *See also* singing body
empire
Austro–Hungarian 56, 59–60, 245
German 99–101, 104–5, 229–30
Roman 165
encounter
colonial 12, 15–16, 100–1, 111–12, 114–15, 229–30
cultural 43, 51
sonic 113, 121–22
Enlightenment 94–95, 126, 128–29, 142, 243–45

Index 273

dark underside of 22–23, 119, 124, 128–29, 244–45 (*see also* modernity/coloniality bind)
ideals and preoccupations of the 22, 78, 96–98, 117
individualism 43–44, 46, 50
man 121
Plato and 23, 96
project 96, 111
rationality 100, 110–11
entanglement 147, 157–58. *See also* Mbembe, Achille
entropy 133–35, 136–37, 165–67
envoicement 125–26, 244–45
Eoan Group 181
ephemerality
of Black and colonized history 14, 126
of Kentridge's visual practice 14, 126, 165–67
of opera 14, 125–26
of performance 167, 200–1
equality 110–11, 115
estrangement 40–41, 42, 49–51, 67, 189, 190
ethics
of confession 73–74, 245–46
of form 109
of melancholy 108, 128–29
of observation 175–76
eugenics 100–1
Eurocentrism 57, 77, 84
Eurochronology 144, 145–46, 148, 150–51, 155–56, 157. *See also* chrononormativity
Europe
intertextual references to 5, 37, 40, 41–42, 58
as origin and aspiration 3–4, 5, 28–29, 179
shadow of 87–88, 90
writing back to 16, 26, 39, 51–52, 210–12 (*see also* postcolonial con-text)
See also metropole
European
canonical works 37–38, 40–41, 51
culture 27–28, 41, 50, 54, 113, 179
heritage 4–6, 21–22, 36, 40–41, 243–44
music 82, 87, 88–89, 212
subject 57, 74–75, 76
temporality 131–32, 142–43, 144–46, 149, 158, 245–46
excess 9–10, 101
exoticism 84–85, 145–46

experimental theatre 6, 93, 109, 125, 238–39
extra-colonial
cultural traditions 32, 46, 203
definition of 25n.2
performance 25–26, 31–32, 50–51, 52, 216
extraction
colonial 27–28, 41, 244–45
operatic innovation and 12–13, 27–28, 218–19, 220

Fabian, Johannes 145–47. *See also* coevalness, denial of
falsehood 73–74, 93. *See also* truth
Fanon, Frantz
Black Skin White Masks 221–22
on confession 17, 53, 74–76, 77, 89–90
"On Violence" 233
The Wretched of the Earth 207, 208–10
See also confession
fate 46, 85–86, 132–33, 240
fellow travelers 20–21, 56, 94, 132, 201
film 63, 89–90, 99–100, 119–20, 135, 138, 148–49
Drawings for Projection 70, 172–73, 247
History of the Main Complaint 63
Johannesburg, 2nd Greatest City after Paris 172–73
Oh, to Believe in Another World 247
Stereoscope 63
Zeno Drawing 56
Florentine Camerata 92, 159
folk song 84–85, 168–69, 171, 187–88
foot power 174–75
footstep 175, 193
form
collage 224–25
compositional or musical 58, 123–24, 149–50
confessional 70–71
distinction between genre and 8
durational 197
ethics of 109
opera as 8–9, 10, 250 (*see also* genre)
and unboundedness 11–12, 77, 128–29
formlessness 12, 226. *See also* unboundedness
fortuna 22, 109
Foucault, Michel 17, 53, 74, 79–80, 81–82, 83n.116, *See also* confession

274   Index

fracture. *See* fragmentation
fragmentation 40, 151, 204, 244
　colonialism and 202, 223–24, 227–28,
　　230, 237
　form and 224–25, 226
　historical 223–24
　linguistic 227–28
freedom 157, 173–74, 193, 195, 198, 199.
　　See also liberation
Freud, Sigmund 105–7, 109, 128
future 108–9, 153–55, 157–58, 242, 252
futurism 153–55

Galison, Peter 130, 131–32, 138–39,
　　143–44
Gandhi, Leela 3, 15–16
gender 113, 121–22
genocide 93–94, 100–1, 104
genre
　ambiguity 105
　distinction between form and 8
　and history 153
　indeterminacy of 6, 105
　Kentridge on 7
　of Kentridge's performance pieces 6–
　　7, 8, 243
　mixing 123, 129, 140–41
　opera as 6, 8–9, 10, 250
German South-West Africa. *See* Namibia
Germany 93, 100–1, 124, 127–28, 229
Gesamtkunstwerk 11, 205
　correspondences with African total
　　theater 216, 217–18
　Kentridge and 11–12, 204
　return of the 214–15
　twentieth century 203, 212, 219, 237
　Wagner and 11, 203, 217–19, 236
Ghanaian proverb, the head and the load are
　　the troubles of the neck 205–6
ghosts 14, 36, 125–26, 157–58
Gilroy, Paul 124–25
globalization 147, 162, 216–17
global South 16, 173–74, 189–90, 203
Goiris, Greta 132, 205, 208
gramophone 40–41, 233, 234, 235–36, 247
Greenwich
　observatory 130, 138
grief 93, 105–6, 108, 120–21, 128–29
Guarracino, Serena 94, 96–98, 100, 119
guilt 53–54, 58, 72, 83n.116, 87–88, 107, 121,
　　124. *See also* complicity

Handspring Puppet Company 20, 26–27,
　　34–35, 37–38, 42–43, 53, 58, 243–44.
　　See also puppet
Hashirim Asher Lish'lomo 184–85. *See also*
　　Rossi, Salamone
The Head & The Load 7, 243, 244
　background to 205, 206–7
　cast 208–10
　fragmentation and collage 224–26, 236,
　　237, 244
　historical content 205–6, 224, 226–27, 245
　libretto and language 207, 228, 229
　music 210, 233–35
　quotations and intertexts 210, 225,
　　229, 234–36
　scene
　　"Advanced arithmetic" 230–31, 236
　　"Je te veux" 225–26
　　"Kaiser Waltz" 229–30
　　"Kwanukimpi" 230
　　"Procession to war" 206–7, 232–36
　　"Recruiting" 232
　　"Ursonate" 226–28
　structure 206–7
　as total work of art 204–5, 212–14,
　　220, 237–38
　visuals 207–8, 234
the head and the load are the troubles of the
　　neck (proverb) 205–6
Heidegger, Martin 194–95. *See also* dwelling
Herero 98, 100–1, 112–15, 120–21, 125–27
　case for reparations 127–28
　massacre 93, 100, 101–2, 104, 119, 121–22
　music 104–5, 111–12, 125–26, 128–29
　revolt 136
　voices 127
heritage
　European 4–6, 21–22, 36, 40–41, 243–44
　morbidity of 124–25
Hindemith, Paul 212
historiography 100–1, 106–7, 108–9, 137–38
history 253
　Black 13–14, 121–22, 223–24
　as burden 175, 205–6
　as collage 223, 224–25
　colonial 96–98, 100–1, 212–14, 220, 223
　constructed nature of 100–1, 103,
　　185, 224
　flow of 173–74
　and genre 153
　incommensurate 174

Index   275

Indigenous 13–14, 223–24
and memory 186–87
multifaceted nature of 161–62, 165
of opera 12, 17, 25–26, 27–28, 124–25
and permanence 200–1
as performance 126
recovery of 13–14, 107–9, 126–27, 224, 238, 244–45
Holocaust 93–94, 100–1, 124, 185
home 160, 168, 194–95
hunt 119–20
Huyssen, Andreas 196

ideology 102–3
illusion 46–48, 65–66, 96–98, 103
Il Ritorno d'Ulisse in Patria 26–27, 54
as postcolonial con-text 38–40, 51–52
Prologue 44–46
staging 33–37, 38, 67, 244
video backdrop 35–36, 38, 51
improvisation 122–23, 131–32
India 84
indigenous
culture 31–32, 33
epistemology 30–31, 43–44, 114–15, 249
forms of narration 32, 33, 42–43
history 13–14, 223–24
operatic portrayal of 145–46
performance 42–43, 52, 236–37, 243–44, 253
recovery 15–16, 33
social and spiritual integration 216–17, 244
temporality 136, 144–46, 147–48, 156–58
inhabitation 193–95, 197
physical 178
politics of 197–98
sonic 178, 201 (*see also* presencing)
See also dwelling
institution
definition of 9
opera as 9, 250
integration 31, 122–23, 126–27, 203, 215, 216, 226, 236–37
interculturalism 30–31, 84, 126–27, 183–85, 190
intermediality 6, 154–55, 158, 242, 247–48, 251
International Meridian Conference 130
intertextuality
artistic 134–35

in Kentridge's work 18, 21–22, 37, 40, 206–7
literary 152, 207
musical 63, 83–85, 99, 104–5, 140, 153, 169, 190
irrationality 113. *See also* rationality
Isango Ensemble 30–31, 37–38
Italy
southern 162, 168–69, 171, 187, 188–90, 192
Ives, Charles 167
Ives, George 167

Jerusalem 162, 170, 183–84, 185
Jew, also Jewish, also Jewishness 5–6, 60, 184–85, 187
Johannesburg 19, 56, 74, 140–41
Joyce, James 59–60
Junction Avenue Theatre Company 4–5, 20

Kaiser Wilhelm II 93–94, 116, 207, 208–10, 229–30
Kanter, Jodi 108
Keats, John 152
Kentourage. *See* Kentridge, collaborators
Kentridge, William
Almost Don't Tremble 247
animations 14, 35–36, 63, 172–73
anti–apartheid activities 4–5, 20
Arc/Procession: Develop, Catch Up, Even Surpass 172–73
as auteur figure 18–19
on being an artist 11
birthplace 1
Black Box/Chambre Noire (*see Black Box/ Chambre Noire*)
collaborative process 18–19
collaborators 18, 58, 132, 138–39, 163–64, 167, 205
commentary on his own work 18
Confessions of Zeno (*see Confessions of Zeno*)
on Dada 11, 226–27
Die Winterreise 247–48
drawings 14, 22, 35–36, 56, 70, 101–2, 163–64, 165, 172–73
Drawings for Projection 35–36, 70, 172–73, 247
European heritage 4–5, 21–22
on genre 7
on Gesamtkunstwerk 11

276 Index

Kentridge, William (*cont.*)
  *A Guided Tour of the Exhibition: for
    Soprano with Handbag* 246–47
  The Head & the Load (*see The Head &
    the Load*)
  History of the Main Complaint 35–36
  *I Am not Me, the Horse Is not
    Mine* 243, 246–47
  Il Ritorno d'Ulisse in Patria (*see Il Ritorno
    d'Ulisse in Patria*)
  interdisciplinary performance pieces 6,
    10, 54, 243–44, 246–47
  international standing 1–2
  and intertextuality 18, 21–22, 37, 40, 41–
    42, 206–7
  Jewish identity 4–5
  *Johannesburg, 2nd Greatest City after
    Paris* 172–73
  lecture performances 247–48
  More Sweetly Play the Dance 172–73, 174–
    75, 206–7
  Notes towards a Model Opera 172–73,
    206–7, 246–47
  Oh, to Believe in Another World 247–48
  on opera 7, 9–10, 11–12
  as opera director 6, 20, 26–27, 54
  Paper Music 246–47
  Phenakistoscope 247
  processional practice 172–75, 196, 206–7
  Receiver 247
  The Refusal of Time 132, 247
  Refuse the Hour (*see Refuse the Hour*)
  Return 241–42
  on shadows 65–66
  Singer Trio 247
  sound technologies in his work 247
  South African identity 2–3, 4–5, 19
  Stereoscope 63
  subject position 4–5, 22
  Telegrams from the Nose 246–47
  theatre work 20, 37, 54, 247–48
  Triumphs and Laments (*see Triumphs and
    Laments*)
  Ubu and the Truth Commission 58, 68–69
  visual practice 14
  Waiting for the Sibyl (*see Waiting for
    the Sibyl*)
  Zeno at 4am 55
  Zeno Drawing 56
kora 212, 233–35
Kouyaté, N'faly 233–34

Kreisler, Fritz
  Liebesleid 229

labor 64, 142–43, 154, 217, 218–19, 221,
  236, 237
lament 161–62, 165–67, 168–69, 175, 190–
  91, 195–96
Lampedusa 162, 168
land 179–80, 183, 187, 221–22, 223
language 112, 113, 207, 227–30, 238
lecture 132, 151–52, 245–46
Le Spectre de la Rose 140, 153–55
Levine, Caroline
  on institutions 9 (*see also* form)
liberation 157, 173–74
lie. *See* falsehood
Ligeti, György 141–42
liveness 9–10, 46, 182–83, 243–44
Lloyd, David 107–8
localization 37–38, 42. *See also* adaptation/
  Africanization
loss
  adaptation and 123–24, 125
  colonial 93–94, 116, 121, 128–29
  of history 13, 185
  of innocence 110, 124–25
  mobility and 191–92, 195–96
  opera and 92, 93–94, 107
  response to 105–6

machine 138–40, 154
  body as 135, 140, 175
  migrant as 175
  relationship between human and 139–
    40, 175
magic 47–48, 110–11, 119–20, 144
Magic Flute, The (opera)
  and Enlightenment 95, 96–98, 115–16, 124
  Kentridge production of 99–100, 119–
    20, 125–26
  as melancholy opera 110–11
  music of 104–5, 115–16
  recording 104, 117, 120
  relationship to *Black Box/Chambre
    Noire* 94–95
  tonality in 99n.26
  visual and musical references to 98–100
Mahlangu, Nhlanhla 18, 208–10, 226–27,
  233, 235–36, 241
Makgalemele, Alfred 104–5, 121–23, 126–
  27, 128–29

Index **277**

Maltz-Leca, Leora 21–22, 65, 71–73, 173–74, 196
Mann, Heinrich 113–14
map 99–100, 143–44, 202, 226–27
Maqoma, Gregory 205
maquette 95. *See also* miniature theatre
marching band 104–5, 117, 167, 232, 233–34, 235
Masilo, Dada 132, 133, 152, 154
Masina, Ann 167, 190, 212, 233–34
Mbembe, Achille
    on the colonized subject 221–22
    Critique of Black Reason 229–30
    on history 13, 223, 224
    nocturnal face of capitalism 218–19
    on the postcolony 33, 202
    on temporality 147–49, 157–58
Mda, Zakes. *See* Common Festival
mechanics/mechanism
    exposure of 23–24, 46–47, 48, 103, 124, 138–40
    operatic 218–19
megaphone 41, 93, 98–99, 120–21, 138–39, 141–42, 247
melancholy 137–38, 154
    ethical 128–29
    history 126
    mourning and 106–7, 108–9, 128–29
    object 92–93, 111, 112–13, 219
    opera and 92–93, 94, 107, 110–11, 129
    postcolonial 124–25
    and race 92
    truth and 116
memorialization 17, 94, 100–1, 108, 185, 244–45. *See also* commemoration
memory 93, 102–3, 126, 137–38, 157–58, 185
metronome 141–42, 157–58
metropole
    impact of colonialism on 202
    melancholy of the former 125
    relationship between colony and 28, 36–37, 143–44, 151, 179
    as theory's norm 16
Meyburgh, Catherine 132
Mignolo, Walter 12–13, 22–23, 27–28, 218–19, 236, 244, 250
migrant 168–69, 181–82, 194, 197–98
    depiction of 164–65, 175, 195–96
    theater 198, 199

migration 168–69, 188–89, 191–92, 195
    ambiguity of 191–92, 195–96, 197
    nationalist responses to 200
military 174, 190–91
    music 104–5 (*see also* marching band)
Miller, Philip 18–19, 140–41
    Black Box/Chambre Noire 99, 104–5, 111–12, 121–23
    The Head & the Load 210–12
    Refuse the Hour 140, 155
    Triumphs and Laments 167–69
miniature theatre 95–96, 244–45
minimalism 61–62
missionary 28–29, 144–45
    education 29
    music 29, 145
    See also civilizing mission
mobile sculpture 241
mobility 159, 160, 174–75, 195
    affordances of 195–96
    and inhabitation 192, 194–95, 197
    and performance 171–76
    postcolonial 160
    regimes of 192–93, 195–96, 197, 201
    and stasis 177–78, 233–34
modernism 21–22, 207
    and race 5
modernity
    colonial subject's experience of 236
    dark underside of 74, 218–19, 244
    destruction caused by 174, 236
    European (*see* Western modernity)
    labor and 107–8, 142, 218–19
    opera and 12–13, 23–24, 27–28, 179–80, 218–19, 245–46, 249–50
    and spirituality 46
    and technology 135, 236
    time and 130–31, 142, 147–48, 157–58
    Western 130, 131, 158, 174, 179–80, 216–17
modernity/coloniality bind 12–13, 16, 22–23, 27–28, 143–44, 218–19, 236, 244, 250. *See also* Mignolo, Walter
Monostatos 92, 111, 117. *See also* Magic Flute
Monteverdi, Claudio. *See* Il Ritorno d'Ulisse in Patria
monumentality 159, 161–62, 165, 176–77, 200–1, 244
motet 167, 184–85
motion. *See* mobility

278 Index

mourning 17, 104–5, 119, 120–21, 244–45
  forms of 125
  incomplete 93, 106–8, 128
  opera and 107, 109, 120–21, 124, 128–
    29, 151
  as performance 126
  postcolonial 107–10, 116, 120–21, 128,
    129, 244–45
  as repair 106–9, 128
  successful 106–7, 109
  the work of 93, 94–95, 105–7, 109, 126
movement. *See* mobility
Mozart, Wolfgang Amadeus .
  Turkish music 104–5
  See also Magic Flute
muyanga, neo 252

Nama 93, 101
Namibia 93–94, 99–100, 101, 104–5, 127–
    28, 244–45
Nanni, Giordano 144–46, 155–56
narrative 101, 131, 137–38, 151–52, 182–
    83, 243
narrator 98
nation 137–38, 201
  postcolonial 124
nationalism 168, 174, 189, 200–1
native 147–48, 158. *See also* Indigenous
nature 111
  vs culture 92, 110–11, 112–13, 122–
    23, 126–27
Nazism 100–1, 104, 219
Ndebele
  people 189–90, 191
  song 171, 189–90, 191, 197
Ndebele, Njabulo 73
nostalgia 153
Novak, Jelena. *See* postopera
Ntabeni, Bham 167, 190, 191–92

oceanic spacetime 137–38
Ode to a Grecian Urn 152
opera
  as African form 30–31
  audiences 1–2, 8–9, 10, 180–81, 199,
    228, 243
  Black 14–15, 29 (*see also* André, Naomi)
  circulation 1–2, 25–26, 27–29, 52,
    249–106
  and colonial extraction 12–13, 27–28,
    218–19, 220

as colonial form 27–29, 31–32
and colonialism 1, 5–6, 12–13, 25–29, 33,
    90, 179–80
contemporary 249, 250–51, 252
depiction of colonized persons 131, 145–
    46, 158
episodic 151–52
and gender 100, 113
as genre 6, 8–10, 24, 243–44, 250, 251
and historical recovery 13–14,
    15–16, 204
history of 12, 17, 25–26, 27–28, 124–25
as Indigenous form 14–15, 25–26, 30–33,
    52, 243–44
as institution 9, 159–60, 181–82, 249–
    50, 251
institutions of 1–2, 10, 159–60 (*see also*
    opera house)
Italian 181
Kentridge performance pieces as 6–7, 8,
    10, 54, 243–44
and language 228–29
as melancholy form 92–93, 107,
    109, 128–29
and narration 14, 32, 150, 151–52
origins of 92, 93, 107 (*see also* Greek
    theater)
performers 8–9, 180–81, 199
and place 177–82, 192, 199, 201 (*see also*
    opera house)
as postcolonial con–text 26, 52
as postcolonizing subject 5–6
processional 17, 169, 177–78, 192,
    199, 201
procession in 176–78
and race 14–16, 90, 112–13, 131,
    181, 245–46
and recovery of Greek theater
    tradition 26–27, 92, 159, 241–42, 250
in South Africa 14–15, 29, 33, 37–38,
    181, 250–51
as storytelling through music 30–33,
    42–43, 52
technologies of 12–13, 218–19
theater (*see* opera house)
and time 17, 131, 149–51, 155–56,
    158, 245–46
and totality (*see* total work of art)
and unboundedness 12, 243
and visual art 214–15
Western 100, 131, 192, 197

opera house 9–10, 27, 96, 159–60, 176–77,
    178–80, 199
  Khedivial 179–80
  Metropolitan Opera 180
  Nico Malan 179–80
organ 140
organicism 216–17, 222, 238
orientalism 104–5, 119–20, 131
Other
  colonial 94, 125–26, 131, 145–46
  of Enlightenment 110–11
  migrant as 175, 189, 201
  of opera 121–22, 123, 128–29, 145–46,
    199, 219
  racialized 92–93, 94, 110–11, 112–
    13, 229–30
  south as 192

palimpsest 169
Pamina 115–17, 119–21, 128–29
pangolin 113–15
Papageno 110–11, 115–16
paradox 65–66, 73, 117, 128–29, 165
  of colonial subjectivity 225
  Zeno's 65–66, 90
performance
  communal 31, 42–43, 50–51, 203, 220
  embodied 126
  Indigenous 42–43, 52, 236–37, 243–
    44, 253
  processional 172–73, 201
permanence 133, 134–35, 159, 161–62,
    163, 200–1
  historical 200–1
  operatic 159–60, 162, 176–77, 181–
    82, 244
Perseus 132–33, 252
perspective 89–90, 182–83, 196, 241–42
photograph 93, 102–3, 135
pizzica 171, 187–89, 195–96, 197
place
  ambiguity of 192
  contested nature of 162, 186–87
  making 160, 181–82, 192, 201
  opera and 177–82, 192, 199
  and performance 192–93
  sonic evocation of 162, 169, 199
  See also displacement/dwelling/home
Plato 65–66
  cave parable 22–23, 65, 96
pleasure spiral 83n.116

porter(s) 205–6, 231–33, 236
post–apartheid
  confession 55, 77
  opera 14–15
  reconciliation 43–44, 53
  subject 4, 36, 49–50
  See also apartheid
postcolonial con-text 26, 39–40, 41–42, 52
postcolonial subject 2–4, 15–16, 49–50
  historicity of the 147–48
postcolonized subject. See postcolonial
    subject
postcolonizing subject 15–16, 36, 41, 87–
    88, 245
  ambiguous position of the 21–22, 52
  author as 2–3
  definition of 2–4
  Kentridge as 2–3, 5
  opera as 5–6
  whiteness and 3, 4
postopera 7–8
power
  confession and 71, 74–75, 76–77
  opera as symbol of 179–80
  relation between colonizer and
    colonizer 58, 111–12, 113, 115
praying mantis 98–99, 113–15
presence
  embodied 126, 162, 197–98, 201
  operatic 181, 199
  and personhood 197–98
  sonic 121–22, 127–28, 197–98
  vocal 162
  See also presencing
presencing 121–22, 126, 197–99
prime meridian 130, 138, 143
primitivism
  colonial imaginaries of 12, 32, 145–46
  formlessness and 12
  music and 131
  timelessness and 130, 145–46
privilege 88, 90, 197–98, 199
process 23–24, 46–47, 121–22, 172–73
procession
  funeral 171, 193
  The Head & The Load 232, 244
  and inhabitation 194–95, 197, 199
  in Kentridge's work 172–75, 196, 206–7
  military 174
  operatic 176–78, 244
  and representation 175, 201

280 Index

procession (*cont.*)
  sacramental 193
  Triumphs and Laments 163, 167, 168–
    69, 172
  See also triumphus
processional
  aesthetics 175–77, 201
  ethics 201
  opera 17, 169, 177–78, 192, 199, 201
  performance 172–73, 177–78, 201
  structure 161–62, 172–73
progress 92, 120–21, 130, 131, 142–43, 144–
  45, 174, 236–37. *See also* teleology
psalm 137, By the rivers of Babylon 170. *See*
  also Al naharot Bavel
psychoanalysis 60–61, 69, 70–72, 74, 76
puppet 67
  African 42–43
  and agency 44, 46, 47, 48
  artifice of 46–47, 48, 50
  in *Confessions of Zeno* 63, 245
  in *Il Ritorno d'Ulisse in Patria* 34–35, 44,
    49–50, 243–44
  Japanese 42–43
  in ritual theater 42–43
  shadow 63–65, 67, 245
  in South Africa 43
  subjectivity 43–44, 47, 48–51, 67, 243–44
  theater 96
  and voice 48–49, 50
  in Western opera 17, 42–43, 46
puppeteer 43–44, 46–47, 64–65
puppetry. *See* puppet

Queen of the Night 111–15, 116,
  117, 126–27
quotation 58, 63, 83–84, 88–89, 104, 192,
  207. *See also* intertextuality

race
  and colonialism 221–22
  Irish 3–4
  Italian 3–4
  and melancholy 92
  and modernism 5
  and music 58
  and opera 14–16, 112–13, 181, 246
  and rationality 229–30
  in South Africa 58, 181
  and violence 101, 185
  See also Black/Blackness/whiteness

rationality 22, 28–29, 86–87, 124, 144
  race and 229–30
  See also Enlightenment
reason. *See* rationality
recitative 131, 149–50
reconciliation 43–44, 51, 58, 68–69, 88, 124–
  25, 238–39
recovery
  cultural 51
  of Greek theater 26–27, 92, 159, 241–42, 250
  historical 13–14, 107–9, 126–27, 224,
    238, 244–45
  indigenous 15–16, 33
  postcolonial 146–47, 248
refugee 160, 170, 175, 181–82, 188–89, 194
refusal 40, 106, 137–38, 146–47, 155–56
Refuse the Hour 6–7, 17, 20–21, 37, 200–1,
  226, 245–46, 247
  background to 131–32
  background projection 152, 154
  lecture 132–37, 151–52
  music for 131–32, 140–42
  scene
    "Berlioz breakdown" 153–54
    "Colonial invasions" 155–57
    "Prologue metronome" 141–42
    "Slow quick quick slow" 152
relativity 132, 136, 138–39, 157–58
remembrance. *See* memorialization
repair 128–29, 158, 245–46
reparation 127–28
repetition 116, 128, 157, 197, 234
representation 23–24
  in Kentridge's works 1–2
  in Kevin Volans's music 58
  opera and 246
  politics of 126–28, 175, 245–46
return
  definition of 25
  operatic 26–27, 51–52, 237–38, 241–42,
    243–44, 253
  to pre-coloniality 33, 52, 146–47
  as rediscovery 26
reverse graffiti 163–64, 165
rhinoceros 100, 119–21, 126–27
Rifkin, Mark 33, 131, 147–49
Rilke, Rainer Maria 169
ritual 215, 216–17
Rome 161, 183–84, 185
  eternal city 165–67, 192
  history of 161–63, 165

Rossi, Salamone 167, 168–69, 183–85
Rousseau, Jean–Jacques 79–80

Said, Edward 1, 27
Sarastro 96–98, 113, 117–20. *See also*
Magic Flute
Sayiwela 189–90, 191–92, 195–96
scale 88–90, 165–67, 176, 177, 193
of the political 57, 88, 90
Scherzinger, Martin 58, 63
Schmitz, Aron Ettore. *See* Svevo, Italo
Schoenberg, Arnold 212
Schumann, Robert (big game hunter) 119–20
Schwitters, Kurt 207, 226–27, 247–48. *See*
also Ursonate
science 42, 61, 86–87, 138–39
segregation 58. *See also* apartheid
Shabangu, Mncedisi 208–10, 225, 227–28,
230, 232–33
shadow 23, 96, 233
of Europe 87–88, 90
as individual and type 65–66, 89–90
play 65, 72–73
projection 61, 63–65, 89–90, 116, 163, 176
puppetry 63–65
shadow culture 14–15. *See also*
André, Naomi
Sheller, Mimi 194
new mobilities paradigm 159
Shepherd, Kyle 18, 241
Sibisi, Thuthuka 18, 163, 168–69, 183, 186–
87, 195–96, 205
Sibyl, Cumaean 240, 241–42
singing body 46, 48–49, 121–22, 238
discipline of 145
and presence 198
spectacle of 7, 126–27
See also embodiment/voice
site-specific performance 177–78, 182–83,
192–93, 199, 244
song
communal 145, 198
and confession 79–81
as enactment of freedom 198
and evocation of place 199
folk 84–85, 171, 187–88
protest 155–56, 157
versus speech 61–62, 78, 89
sound
and colonialism 230–31, 233
effect 141, 153–54, 171–72

historical affordance of 153
mechanical 153–54
as medium 247
and place 169, 199
and selfhood 231
technologies 247
and time 145, 146, 149, 152
world 140–41
South
of Africa 28, 189–90, 191, 192
of Italy 162, 168–69, 171, 187, 188–90, 192
South Africa 56–57, 190–91, 245. *See also*
apartheid/post-apartheid
colonialism in 15–16, 29
opera in 14–15, 28, 29, 37–38,
181, 250–51
and postcolony 14–15, 21–22
Soyinka, Wole 30–31, 32, 216–17
speech 80–81, 84–85, 89
splitting 65, 80–81, 82, 84–85, 87–
89, 128–29
of belonging 199
and doubling 63, 66, 72–73, 90
spoken word. *See* speech
stasis 142, 149–50, 152, 175, 194
string quartet 54, 58, 63, 82, 83–84
Stroh violin 153–54
subaltern 100–1, 126–27
subject
coherent 63, 65, 66
colonial (*see* colonial subject)
confessing 66, 71, 72, 74, 79–82
displaced 160, 181–82, 190, 194, 197–
98, 199
fractured 230, 233
as individual and as type 66, 176, 193
political 67
postcolonial (*see* postcolonial subject)
postcolonizing (*see* postcolonizing
subject)
racialized 74–75, 121–22
split 65, 84–85, 88–89, 90
and truth 73, 74–75
subjection 3
subjectivity 3, 36, 74, 90
of migrant 198
of puppets 43–44, 47, 48–51, 67,
243–44
of voice 14
Subotnik, Rose 110–11, 112
suspension of disbelief 46, 47–48, 103

282 Index

Svevo, Italo 54, 56, 59–60, 245. *See also*
    Confessions of Zeno
Swakopmund 104

talking cure. *See* psychoanalysis
Tamino 115–16, 119–21
tammurriata 171, 187–89, 195–96, 197
Taylor, Chloë 74, 76
Taylor, Jane 54, 56–58, 71–72, 80–81, 88–89
Taylor, Timothy D. 58, 63
technology 120–21, 154–55, 219–20, 236–
    37, 244–45
    nineteenth century 138–40, 153
    opera and 12–13, 218–19
    sound 247
Teitelbaum, Felix. *See Drawings for
    Projection*
teleology 87–88, 109, 131, 147, 149–50, 151–
    52, 157–58, 196
    disruption of 234
tempo 141–42
temporality 14, 17
    colonial 17–132, 142–43, 144–46, 150–
        51, 155–56
    Indigenous 136, 144–45, 147–48, 157–58
    musical 131, 141, 149
    normative 131 (*see also*
        chrononormativity)
    operatic 17, 131–32, 149–51, 157–58
    postcolonial 137–38, 147–49, 150–
        51, 155–56, 157, 158 (*see also*
        entanglement/ temporal multiplicity)
    pre–modern 142–43, 144, 145–47, 148,
        149–50, 156
    Western 131–32, 142–43, 144–46, 149,
        158, 245–46
        resistance to 146–47, 148, 150–51, 155–
            56, 157–58
    temporal multiplicity 147–48, 149, 154–55,
        156–58. *See also* Rifkin, Mark
Tevereterno 161
theater 199
    African 30–31, 43, 148(*see also* African
        total theater)
    black box 93, 109, 124, 125
    European 37
    Greek 26–27, 92, 93, 107
    Indigenous 52
    migrant 198–99
    miniature 95–96, 103, 244–45
    operating 34, 42, 49–50

South African 68–69
    See also opera house
Theunissen, Sabine 132, 205, 208
Tiber 160, 161, 163–64, 168–69, 182,
    183, 201
time
    as breath 135, 151
    clock 130, 131, 141, 143, 144, 145–46
    and coloniality 131–32, 143–46, 150–51
    as commodity 142–43
    different ways of being in 131, 150–
        51, 156–58
    heterogeneous 147–48, 156, 157–58
    industrial 142–43, 144–45
    irregular 144, 148–49
    linear 131, 147–48, 149–50
    and nature 144–45, 151
    and order 137, 141, 144–45, 149
    and the other 131, 144, 145–46 (*see also*
        Fabian, Johannes)
    passing of 200–1
    perception of 152, 154–55
    playing or singing in 131, 145
    politics of 131, 137, 146–47, 150–51
    reversal of 132–33, 134–35, 146–
        47, 148–49
    and sound 145–46
    standardization of 130–32, 136,
        137, 143–47
    stopping of 135, 149–50
    technologies of 136, 145
    zone 136, 137
totalitarianism 203, 236–37, 244
    colonialism as 202
    and knowledge 224
    and language 228
    legacies of 204, 205, 237–38
    total work of art and 219, 236–37
totality 151, 220, 244
    colonial 202, 203–4, 221–23, 233, 236–37
    dark underside of 228–29
    operatic (*see* total work of art)
    political 203, 205, 236–37
total theater. *See* African total theater
total work of art 11–12, 17, 203–5, 212–20,
    237, 244
    Indigenous (*see* African total theater)
    postcolonial affordance of 204, 205, 212–
        14, 236–39
    See also Gesamtkunstwerk
Totenliste 121–22, 126–27

Index 283

trace 13–14, 100–1, 106–7
Tracey, Andrew 62
train 132–33, 143–44
Trajan's Column 161–62
transculturalism 40–41. *See also*
    interculturalism
translation 37–38, 123, 207, 228
transportation 143–44, 206, 232, 233
Trauerarbeit 93, 98–99, 104–6, 120, 125,
    128–29. *See also* mourning
TRC. *See* Truth and Reconciliation
    Commission
Trieste 59–60, 74
triumph 165–67, 168–69, 172, 195–96, 197
  underside of 161–62, 174, 190–91
Triumphs and Laments 160, 244
  background to 161–64, 174
  frieze 161–62, 163–67, 182, 185, 196
  medium 182
  music 167–72, 183, 186–87, 188, 189–91,
    195–96, 197
  musical intertexts 168–69, 195–96, 197
    African 189–92
    Italian 188–89
    Quello che non ricordo 185–87
    religious 170–71, 183, 187
  performance 163, 167, 171–72, 192–
    93, 197
  place in 162, 182–83, 187, 189–90, 192
  source material 160, 163–64
triumphus 161–62, 174, 177
truth 69, 101–3, 115–16
  colonial subject and 74–76
  and confession 71, 72–74, 75–76
  is beauty, beauty truth 152
  and shadow 65
  voice and 78–80
Truth and Reconciliation Commission 43–
    44, 53, 57–58, 67–69, 74, 77, 88
Tutu, Archbishop Desmond 67, 68
Tzara, Tristan 207

ubuntu 43–44
Ulisse, also Ulysses 36, 39, 42, 49–50, 51–
    52, 136, 243–44. *See also Il Ritorno
    d'Ulisse in Patria*
unboundedness 11–12, 77, 122–24, 128–29,
    243, 245–46, 252
unbounded work of art 11–12, 226
uncertainty 22–23, 224
unconscious 64–65. *See also* consciousness

Urry, John 194
  new mobilities paradigm 159
Ursonate 207, 226–28, 247–48

ventriloquism 49
victim 77, 88, 94, 107–8, 121, 128–29,
    222, 244–45
violence
  abstraction of 101
  colonial 76, 90, 116–17
  and displacement 168
voice
  Black 121–22
  and body 46, 48–49, 121–22, 126–27, 140
  and confession 79–81, 90
  and gender 121–22, 128–29
  inhuman 153–54
  and interiority 79–81
  in Kentridge's works 10
  as medium 10
  operatic 8–9, 48–49, 80, 121–22, 180–
    81, 228
  and presence 125–26, 127, 162
  and scale 89
  and subjectivity 14, 49–50
  unamplified 9–10
Volans, Kevin 54, 58, 61–63, 83–84, 245
  Hunting: Gathering 58, 84
  Surface Tension 84n.117
  White Man Sleeps 58, 84
  See also Confessions of Zeno/string quartet

Wagner, Richard 150, 203, 217–19
  Parsifal 234–36
  See also Gesamtkunstwerk
Waiting for the Sibyl 7
  background to 240–41
  collapsing chairs 252
  libretto 240–41
  music for 241
  staging 241–42
walking 193, 194–95, 244
waltz 120–21, 140
war
  First World, 17, 56–57, 60–61, 70, 204,
    205–6, 244, 245
  in German South–West Africa 93–94, 100–1
  horror of 225
  irrationality of 229
  Jewish–Roman 184
  Second World 185

284　Index

WeiWei, Ai 134–35
Wena ukhuluma kanjani 189–91,
　　192, 195–96
West Africa Conference. *See* Berlin Conference
whiteness
　and colonial power 3–4, 221–22
　diasporic 4
　Kentridge and 4–5
　modernism and 5
　opera and 14–15, 112–13
　and personhood 221–22
　postcolonial 3
　postcolonizing subject and 3
　in South Africa 4
　subordinate forms of 3–4

Windhoek 101

Young, LaMonte 134–35

Zauberflöte, Die. See Magic Flute
Zenenga, Praise 31, 215, 220
Zeno
　character 56–57, 69, 72–74, 77, 80–82,
　　116, 245
　paradox of motion 65–66, 90
Zimbabwe 162, 171, 189–90, 191
Žižek, Slavoj 92
Zulu
　kingdom 190–91
　music 171, 189–91, 197